FRENCH FOGLE is Professor of English Literature in Claremont Graduate School, Claremont, California. He is on the advisory boards of the *Huntington Library Quarterly* and the *Journal of the History of Ideas* and has published articles and reviews in such journals as the *American Scholar,* the *Huntington Library Quarterly, Seventeenth-Century News,* and *The Personalist.* He is a past president of the Milton Society of America.

He received the A.B. degree from Marietta College and the M.A. and Ph.D. degrees from Columbia University. He has taught at Columbia University, Barnard College, The City College of the City University of New York, New York University, Scripps College, and Pomona College; and has lectured at Northwestern University. He was the compiler, with F. A. Patterson, of the two-volume *Index* to the Columbia edition of *The Works of John Milton,* and the author of *A Critical Study of William Drummond of Hawthornden.* He is the editor of Milton's *History of Britain,* forthcoming in Volume V of the Yale edition of *The Complete Prose Works of John Milton.*

THE NORTON LIBRARY
SEVENTEENTH-CENTURY SERIES

J. MAX PATRICK, *General Editor*

The Complete Poetry
of
HENRY VAUGHAN

EDITED WITH AN INTRODUCTION,
NOTES, AND VARIANTS BY
FRENCH FOGLE

The Norton Library
W · W · NORTON & COMPANY · INC ·
NEW YORK

W. W. Norton & Company, Inc. is also the publisher of *The Norton Anthology of English Literature,* edited by M. H. Abrams, Robert M. Adams, David Daiches, E. Talbot Donaldson, George H. Ford, Samuel Holt Monk, and Hallett Smith; *The American Tradition in Literature,* edited by Sculley Bradley, Richmond Croom Beatty, and E. Hudson Long; *World Masterpieces,* edited by Maynard Mack, Kenneth Douglas, Howard E. Hugo, Bernard M. W. Knox, John C. McGalliard, P. M. Pasinetti, and René Wellek; *The Norton Reader,* edited by Arthur M. Eastman, Caesar R. Blake, Hubert M. English, Jr., Alan B. Howes, Robert T. Lenaghan, Leo F. McNamara, and James Rosier; and the NORTON CRITICAL EDITIONS, in hardcover and paperbound: authoritative texts, together with the leading critical interpretations, of major works of British, American, and Continental literature.

CONTENTS

ILLUSTRATIONS

INTRODUCTION

The critical attention directed to the poetry of Henry Vaughan over the past twenty-five years far exceeds that of the preceding three hundred. He now seems to be firmly established as one of the finest of the pure lyric voices of the seventeenth century. But in his own lifetime there is little evidence that his poetic gifts were acknowledged beyond a very limited circle. The closest he came to a second edition was when the unsold sheets of *Silex Scintillans,* Part I (1650), were reissued with only minor revision five years later with the new poems of Part II. The most notable of his public admirers was the little known poetess Mrs. Katherine Philips, the "matchless Orinda" of a coterie of dabblers in verse. His cousin John Aubrey was interested enough to ask him for biographical details of his life and work (along with those relating to his twin brother Thomas and his friend Thomas Powell), but little use was made of them. He was noticed briefly in Anthony Wood's *Historia et Antiquitates Universitatis Oxoniensis* in 1674 and in Edward Phillips' *Theatrum Poetarum* in 1675. There is a short account of him and his brother Thomas in the 1721 edition of Wood's *Athenae Oxoniensis,* but thereafter he received no major attention until H. F. Lyte edited his religious verse in 1847.

The relative neglect Vaughan suffered in his own century is not difficult to understand. The civil commotions of the 1640s and the conflicting loyalties that continued into the Commonwealth period did not provide the tranquillity and calm necessary for the appreciation of his best poetry. After his withdrawal from London around 1642, he lived obscurely in Wales, an ardent sympathizer with the losing Royalist cause, unknown to the larger world of English letters. His earliest verse, the *Poems* of 1646, is mainly conventional and derivative, although some recent critics have found it deserving of higher praise than it formerly received from those preoccupied with his religious poetry. Whatever its merits, it contained little to whet the literary appetites that had feasted on Donne, Jonson, and some of the lesser wits of the time. The poetry written as a result of his now much-discussed "conversion" around 1648, the poetry on which his present reputation mainly depends, was even less designed to appeal to a wide audience involved in the political and religious upheavals of the time. The poems of *Silex Scintillans* are deeply meditative in manner and mood; the most frequent note is one of rejection of the contemporary world and withdrawal into an inner realm of peace and light and unity. Vaughan's deepest impulse is toward a retirement from the confusions of the temporal to a point from which all things can be seen in the light of eternity. It is not surprising that the bright stillness of his visionary, ideal world should have had little appeal for those with a taste for the new realism and the spirit of satire that were to mark the coming decades. Vaughan's last volume of poetry, *Thalia Rediviva* (1678), with its remains of earlier secular verse and some additional religious pieces, could only evoke faint echoes of a world which had gone past recall.

The later nineteenth century saw a considerable growth of interest in Vaughan. Grosart's edition of the prose and verse in 1871 and E. K. Chambers' of the poems in 1896 made his work widely available. Their inadequacies were largely overcome by the scholarly edition of L. C. Martin in 1914, further revised and supplemented by the second edition of 1957. The past quarter-century has seen intensive study of the major influences on Vaughan's poetry and of the qualities of mind, temperament, and poetic technique that set him off from other luminaries of the seventeenth-century galaxy. The "influences"—Herbert, the Bible, the Hermetic philosophy, Nature—have been carefully and exhaustively examined, but they tell us little about his essential style or quality as a poet; in fact, they have too often been allowed to obscure his true poetic merits. His verbal gifts, his complex imagery, and his essential simplicity of statement have also been closely studied in an attempt to sort out the ingredients of his poetic formula. We have been helped to a fuller understanding of the man and his work, but the mystery remains and the source of his appeal continues to elude the critics. The sensitive reader is still able to make his own discoveries in Vaughan's world of light and ultimate simpilicity.

The Latin poems of Vaughan's composition have been newly translated by Dr. John Carey, Dean of Keble College, Oxford. Grosart's translations and Blunden's selections are very loose verse paraphrases, which omit or mistranslate a considerable part of the text. Marilla's prose translations are only of the secular poems, of course, but even they are open to question on matters of style and interpretation. Professor Carey's new translations make available the most faithful reflection of the sense and tone of Vaughan's Latin poems.

It is a pleasure to acknowledge my deep indebtedness to the Librarian and staff of the Huntington Library for making so readily available the materials on which this edition is based. I am also indebted to the British Museum and to the librarians of Harvard University, the University of Illinois, and Yale University for providing microfilms of their first editions, for purposes of collation. It will be evident too that although I have differed at many points in the text from the superb edition of L. C. Martin, I have also profited greatly from his deep learning and scholarship. All references to his edition of the *Works* are to the second edition of 1957.

BIOGRAPHICAL OUTLINE

1621/22 Henry (the elder) and Thomas, twin sons born to Thomas and Denise Vaughan of Trenewydd, or Newton, in the Parish of Llansantffraed, Breconshire.

1632–38 Henry and Thomas under tutelage of Matthew Herbert, clergyman and noted schoolmaster of Llangattock.

1638–40 Probably at Jesus College, Oxford. No records of Henry, but Thomas admitted 4 May 1638 and matriculated 14 December 1638.

1640 To London for study of law. Not known in which Inn, if any, he resided. Felt literary influence of Sons of Ben—Randolph, Cartwright, Cleveland, Davenant, Habington, Carew. May have known James Howell.

1642 Recalled to Wales on outbreak of Civil War. At some time before 1645 clerk to Sir Marmaduke Lloyd, chief justice of Great Sessions of Brecon. By 1646 had probably seen some service as Royalist in Civil War.

1646 *Poems, with The tenth Satyre of Juvenal Englished* published. Entered Stationers' Hall 15 September. About this time married Catherine Wise.

1647 Dedication of *Olor Iscanus* dated from Newton this year, although the volume was not published until 1651. May have been for another volume of verse, partly suppressed, partly in *Olor,* intended for publication in 1647.

1648 Death of William, a younger brother (age unknown), in July. May have influenced Henry's "conversion."

1650   *Silex Scintillans,* Part I, published.

1651   *Olor Iscanus* published, with four short prose trans-
        lations—*Of the Benefit Wee may get by our Enemies;
        Of the Diseases of the Mind and the Body. A Dis-
        course; Of the Diseases of the Mind, and the Body,
        and which of them is most pernicious;* and *The
        Praise and Happinesse of the Countrie-Life.*

1652   *The Mount of Olives: Or, Solitary Devotions.*

1654   *Flores Solitudinis* (three prose translations—*Of
        Temperance and Patience, Of Life and Death,* and
        The World Contemned—and a life of St. Paulinus
        of Nola).

1655   *Silex Scintillans,* the "second edition" (the original
        Part I with the new Part II). Translation of *Her-
        metical Physick,* by Henry Nollius. Evidence—
        though not conclusive—suggests that by this year
        Vaughan's first wife had died and he had married
        her younger sister Elizabeth.

1657   Translation of *The Chymists Key,* by Henry Nol-
        lius, published by Eugenius Philalethes (Thomas
        Vaughan).

1666   Death of his brother Thomas.

1673   Letter to John Aubrey (15 June) says he had "prac-
        tised [physic] now for many years with good suc-
        cess." May have begun practice as early as 1640s.
        No record of his medical degree.

1678   *Thalia Rediviva,* with some poems by his brother
        Thomas.

1695   Died 23 April; buried in Llansantffraed churchyard.

POEMS

(1646)

A note on the title page opposite

The "Gent." is a purely honorary title. The quotation is from Persius, *Satires,* I, 122–23: "I will not sell [my book] for all your Iliads."

POEMS,

WITH

The tenth SATYRE of

IVUENAL

ENGLISHED.

By *Henry Vaughan*, Gent.

——— Tam nil, nullâ tibi vendo
Illiade ———

LONDON,

Printed for G. *Badger*, and are to be sold at his
shop under Saint *Dunstans* Church in
Fleet-street. 1 6 4 6.

To all Ingenious Lovers

OF

POESIE.

Gentlemen,

   To you alone, whose more refined Spirits *out-wing
these dull Times, and soare above the drudgerie of durty*
Intelligence, *have I made sacred these* Fancies: *I know*
5 *the yeares, and what course entertainment they affoord*
Poetry. *If any shall question that* Courage *that durst
send me abroad so late, and revell it thus in the* Dregs
of an Age, they have my silence: only,

Languescente seculo, liceat ægrotari;[1]

10 *My more calme* Ambition, *amidst the common noise,
hath thus exposed me to the World: You have here a*
Flame, *bright only in its owne* Innocence, *that kindles
nothing but a generous* Thought; *which though it may
warme the* Bloud, *the fire at highest is but* Platonick,
15 *and the* Commotion, *within these limits, excludes* Danger: *For the* Satyre, *it was of purpose borrowed, to
feather some slower Houres; And what you see here, is
but the* Interest: *It is one of his, whose* Roman *Pen had
as much true* Passion, *for the infirmities of that state, as*
20 *we should have* Pitty, *to the distractions of our owne:
Honest (I am sure) it is, and offensive cannot be, except
it meet with such* Spirits *that will quarrell with* Antiqui-
tie, *or purposely* Arraigne *themselves; These indeed may
thinke, that they have slept out so many* Centuries *in*
25 *this* Satyre, *and are now awaked; which, had it been
still* Latine, *perhaps their Nap had been Everlasting:*

[1] When the whole world is languishing, one may be permitted
to be sick.

But enough of these,—It is for you only that I have ad-
ventured thus far, and invaded the Presse with Verse;
to whose more noble Indulgence, I shall now leave it;
30 *and so am gone.——*

H. V.

To my Ingenuous
Friend, *R. W.*[1]

When we are dead, and now, no more
Our harmless mirth, our wit, and score[2]
Distracts the Towne; when all is spent
That the base niggard world hath lent
5   Thy purse, or mine; when the loath'd noise
Of Drawers, Prentises, and boyes
Hath left us, and the clam'rous barre
Items no pints i'th' Moone, or Starre;[3]
When no calme whisp'rers wait the doores,
10   To fright us with forgotten scores;
And such aged, long bils[4] carry,
As might start an Antiquary;
When the sad tumults of the Maze,
Arrests, suites, and the dreadfull face
15   Of Seargeants are not seene, and wee
No Lawyers Ruffes, or Gownes must fee:
When all these Mulcts are paid, and I
From thee, deare wit, must part, and dye;
Wee'le beg the world would be so kinde,
20   To give's one grave, as wee'de one minde;
There (as the wiser few suspect,
That spirits after death affect)
Our soules shall meet, and thence will they
(Freed from the tyranny of clay)
25   With equall wings, and ancient love
Into the Elysian fields remove,

TO MY INGENUOUS FRIEND, R.W.

[1] Never positively identified. Perhaps the same as the R.W. killed at Rowton Heath. See O–8.

[2] Tally of debts.

[3] Probably names of rooms in a tavern.

[4] Possibly in the double sense of (1) halberds, weapons carried by officers of the law, and (2) lists of debts.

Where in those blessed walkes they'le find,
More of thy Genius, and my mind:
  First, in the shade of his owne bayes,
30   Great *B E N*[5] they'le see, whose sacred Layes,
The learned Ghosts admire, and throng,
To catch the subject of his Song.
Then *Randolph*[6] in those holy Meades,
His Lovers, and *Amyntas* reads,
35   Whilst his Nightingall close by,
Sings his, and her owne Elegie;
From thence dismiss'd by subtill roades,
Through airie paths, and sad aboads;
They'le come into the drowsie fields
40   Of Lethe, which such vertue yeelds,
That (if what Poets sing be true)
The streames all sorrow can subdue.
Here on a silent, shady greene,
The soules of Lovers oft are seene,
45   Who in their lifes unhappy space,
Were murther'd by some perjur'd face.
All these th' inchanted streames frequent,
To drowne their Cares, and discontent,
That th' inconstant, cruell sex
50   Might not in death their spirits vex:
  And here our soules bigge with delight
Of their new state will cease their flight:
And now the last thoughts will appeare,
They'le have of us, or any here;
55   But on those flowry banks will stay,
And drinke all sense, and cares away.
  So they that did of these discusse,
  Shall find their fables true in us.

[5] Ben Jonson.

[6] Thomas Randolph (1605–35), with allusions to his comedy *The Jealous Lovers,* to his pastoral *Amyntas,* and to his poem "On the Death of a Nightingale."

[P–2]   Les Amours.

    Tyrant farewell: This heart, the prize
    And triumph of thy scornfull eyes,
    I sacrifice to Heaven, and give
    To quit my sinnes, that durst believe
5   A Womans easie faith, and place
    True joyes in a changing face.
      Yet e're I goe; by all those teares,
    And sighs I spent 'twixt hopes, and feares;
    By thy owne glories, and that houre
10   Which first inslav'd me to thy power;
    I beg, faire One, by this last breath,
    This tribute from thee after death.
    If when I'm gone, you chance to see
    That cold bed where I lodged bee:
15   Let not your hate in death appeare,
    But blesse my ashes with a teare:
    This influxe from that quickning eye,
    By secret pow'r, which none can spie,
    The cold dust shall informe, and make
20   Those flames (though dead) new life partake.
    Whose warmth help'd by your tears shall bring,
    O're all the tombe a sudden spring
    Of Crimson flowers, whose drooping heads
    Shall curtaine o're their mournfull beds:
25   And on each leafe by Heavens command,
    These Emblemes to the life shall stand:
      Two Hearts, the first a shaft withstood;
    The second, shot, and washt in bloud;
    And on this heart a dew shall stay,
30   Which no heate can court away;
    But fixt for ever witnesse beares,
    That hearty sorrow feeds on teares.
      Thus Heaven can make it knowne, and true,
    That you kill'd me, 'cause I lov'd you.

[P–3]   To Amoret.[1]

                        The Sigh.

        Nimble Sigh on thy warme wings,
            Take this Message, and depart,
        Tell *Amoret*, that smiles, and sings,
        At what thy airie voyage brings,
5   That thou cam'st lately from my heart.

        Tell my lovely foe, that I
        Have no more such spies to send,
            But one or two that I intend
        Some few minutes ere I dye,
10   To her white bosome to commend.

        Then whisper by that holy Spring
            Whei ɔ for her sake I would have dyed,
        Whilst tho e water Nymphs did bring
            Flowe rs to cure what she had tryed;
15   And of my faith, and love did sing.

        That if my *Amoret*, if she
            In after-times would have it read,
        How her beauty murther'd mee,
        With all my heart I will agree,
20   If shee'le but love me, being dead.

TO AMORET. THE SIGH.

[1] F. E. Hutchinson (*Henry Vaughan: A Life and Interpretation*
[Oxford, 1947], pp. 51–52) thinks it probable that the Amoret of
these poems can be identified with Catherine Wise, Vaughan's first
wife. He also thinks that Amoret and the Etesia of *Thalia Rediviva*
(below, T–15–21) may be the same, but see James D. Simmonds,
"Henry Vaughan's Amoret and Etesia," *PQ*, XLII, 1 (January
1963), 137–42, for a different view.

[P–4]   To his Friend

                        Being in Love.

Aske Lover, ere thou dyest; let one poor breath
Steale from thy lips, to tell her of thy Death;
Doating Idolater! can silence bring
Thy Saint propitious? or will *Cupid* fling
5   One arrow for thy palenes? leave to trye
This silent Courtship of a sickly eye;
Witty to tyranny, She too well knowes
This but the incense of thy private vowes,
That breaks forth at thine eyes, and doth betray
10   The sacrifice thy wounded heart would pay;
Aske her, foole, aske her, if words cannot move,
The language of thy teares may make her love:
    Flow nimbly from me then; and when you fall
On her breasts warmer snow, O may you all,
15   By some strange Fate fixt there, distinctly lye
The much lov'd Volume of my Tragedy.
    Where if you win her not, may this be read,
The cold that freez'd you so, did strike me dead.

[P–5]   Song.

Amyntas goe, thou art undone,
    Thy faithfull heart is crost by fate;
That Love is better not begunne,
    Where Love is come to love too late;
5   *Had she professed hidden fires,*
        Or shew'd one knot that tyed her heart:
I could have quench'd my first desires,
    And we had only met to part;

But *Tyrant, thus to murther men,*
10   *And shed a Lovers harmles bloud,*
And burne him in those flames agen,
    Which he at first might have withstood;
Yet, who that saw faire Chloris *weep*
    Such sacred dew, with such pure grace;
15 *Durst thinke them fained teares, or seeke*
    For Treason in an Angels face:
This is her Art, though this be true,
    Mens joyes are kil'd with griefes and feares;
Yet she like flowers opprest with dew,
20   *Doth thrive and flourish in her teares:*
This Cruell thou hast done, and thus,
    That Face hath many servants slaine.
Though th' end be not to ruine us,
    But to seeke glory by our paine.

[P–6]   To Amoret,

                    Walking in a Starry
                    Evening.

If *Amoret,* that glorious Eye,
    In the first birth of light,
    And death of Night,
Had with those elder fires you spye
5   Scatter'd so high
        Received forme, and sight;

We might suspect in the vast Ring,
    Amidst these golden glories,
    And fierie stories;
10 Whether the Sunne had been the King,
        And guide of Day,
        Or your brighter eye should sway;

But, *Amoret,* such is my fate,
That if thy face a Starre
15   Had shin'd from farre,
I am perswaded in that state
'Twixt thee, and me,
Of some predestin'd sympathie.

For sure such two conspiring minds,
20   Which no accident, or sight,
Did thus unite;
Whom no distance can confine,
Start, or decline,[1]
One, for another, were design'd.

[P–7]   To Amoret gone from him.

Fancy, and I, last Evening walkt,
And, *Amoret,* of thee we talkt;
The West just then had stolne the Sun,
And his last blushes were begun:
5   We sate, and markt how every thing
Did mourne his absence; How the Spring
That smil'd, and curl'd about his beames,
Whilst he was here, now check'd her streames;
The wanton Eddies of her face
10   Were taught lesse noise, and smoother grace;
And in a slow, sad channell went,
Whisp'ring the banks their discontent:
The carelesse ranks of flowers that spread
Their perfum'd bosomes to his head,
15   And with an open, free Embrace,
Did entertaine his beamy face;
Like absent friends point to the West,
And on that weake reflection feast.

TO AMORET, WALKING IN A STARRY EVENING.
[1] Disturb, or cause to deviate.

If Creatures then that have no sence,
20   But the loose tye of influence,
(Though fate, and time each day remove
Those things that element their love)
At such vast distance can agree,
    Why, *Amoret,* why should not wee.

[P–8]   A Song to *Amoret.*

If I were dead, and in my place,
    Some fresher youth design'd,
To warme thee with new fires, and grace
    Those Armes I left behind;

5   Were he as faithfull as the Sunne,
        That's wedded to the Sphere;
His bloud as chaste, and temp'rate runne,
    As Aprils mildest teare;

Or were he rich, and with his heapes,
10   And spacious share of Earth,
Could make divine affection cheape,
    And court his golden birth:

For all these Arts I'de not believe,
    (No though he should be thine)
15   The mighty Amorist could give
        So rich a heart as mine.

Fortune and beauty thou mightst finde,
    And greater men then I:
But my true resolved minde,
20   They never shall come nigh.

For I not for an houre did love,
    Or for a day desire,
But with my soule had from above,
    This endles holy fire.

[P–9]   An Elegy.

'Tis true, I am undone; Yet e're I dye,
I'le leave these sighes, and teares a legacye
To after-Lovers; that remembring me,
Those sickly flames which now benighted be,
5 Fann'd by their warmer sighs may love;[1] and prove
In them the Metamorphosis[2] of Love.
'Twas I (when others scorn'd) vow'd you were fair,
And sware that breath enrich'd the courser aire,
Lent Roses to your cheekes, made *Flora* bring
10 Her Nymphs with all the glories of the Spring
To waite upon thy face, and gave my heart
A pledge to *Cupid* for a quicker dart,
To arme those eyes against my selfe; to me
Thou owest that tongues bewitching harmonye:
15 I courted Angels from those upper joyes,
And made them leave their spheres to heare thy voice:
I made the Indian curse the houres he spent
To seeke his pearles, and wisely to repent
His former folly, and confesse a sinne
20 Charm'd by the brighter lustre of thy skinne.
I borrow'd from the winds, the gentler wing
Of *Zephirus*, and soft soules of the Spring:
And made (to ayre those cheeks wth fresher grace)
The warme Inspirers dwell upon thy face.
               Oh! jam satis———[3]

AN ELEGY.

[1] Perhaps a misprint for "live"?

[2] The reading of the Huntington and Illinois copies of the 1646 edition of the *Poems*. Other copies, e.g., the British Museum (C.56.b.16.) and Harvard copies, read "Metempsuchosis."

[3] Martial, *Epigrams*, IV, 89: "Ohe, jam satis est, ohe, libelle." Tr. Walter C. A. Ker, Loeb Library: "Ho, there! Ho, there! 'tis now enough, my little book."

[P–10]   A Rhapsodie.[1]

Occasionally written upon a meeting with some of his friends
  at the Globe Taverne,[2] in a Chamber painted over head
  with a Cloudy Skie, and some few dispersed Starres, and
  on the sides with Land-scapes, Hills, Shepheards, and
  Sheep.

      Darknes, & Stars i' th' mid day! they invite
      Our active fancies to beleeve it night:
      For Tavernes need no Sunne, but for a Signe,
      Where rich Tobacco, and quick tapers shine;
5   And royall, witty Sacke, the Poets soule,
      With brighter Suns then he doth guild the bowl;
      As though the Pot, and Poet did agree,
      Sack should to both Illuminator be.
      That artificiall Cloud with it's curl'd brow,
10   Tels us 'tis late; and that blew space below
      Is fir'd with many Stars; Marke, how they breake
      In silent glaunces o're the hills, and speake
      The Evening to the Plaines; where shot from far,
      They meet in dumbe salutes, as one great Star.
15   The roome (me thinks) growes darker; & the aire
      Contracts a sadder colour, and lesse faire:
      Or is't the Drawers skill, hath he no Arts
      To blind us so, we cann't know pints from quarts?
      No, no, 'tis night; looke where the jolly Clowne
20   Musters his bleating heard, and quits the Downe.

A RHAPSODIE.

[1] The 1646 reading of the title as "A Rhapsodis," as Martin (*The Works of Henry Vaughan* [Oxford, 1957], p. 701) points out, has no etymological basis. It seems probable that the final *s* is a misprint for an *e*.

[2] Now thought to be the Globe Tavern in Fleet Street, rather than the one in Southwark.

Harke! how his rude pipe frets the quiet aire,
Whilst ev'ry Hill proclaimes *Lycoris*[3] faire.
Rich, happy man! that canst thus watch, and sleep,
Free from all cares; but thy wench, pipe & sheep.
25 But see the Moone is up; view where she stands
Centinell o're the doore, drawn by the hands
Of some base Painter, that for gaine hath made
Her face the Landmarke to the tipling trade.
This Cup to her, that to *Endymion* give;[4]
30 'Twas wit at first, and wine that made them live:
Choake may the Painter! and his Boxe disclose
No other Colours then his fiery Nose;
And may we no more of his pencill see,
Then two Churchwardens, and Mortalitie.
35 Should we goe now a wandring, we should meet
With Catchpoles,[5] whores, & Carts in 'ev'ry street:
Now when each narrow lane, each nooke & Cave,
Signe-posts, & shop-doors, pimp for ev'ry knave,
When riotous sinfull plush, and tell tale spurs
40 Walk Fleet street, & the Strand, when the soft stirs
Of bawdy, ruffled Silks, turne night to day;
And the lowd whip, and Coach scolds all the way;
When lust of all sorts, and each itchie bloud
From the Tower-wharfe to Cymbelyne, and Lud,[6]
45 Hunts for a Mate, and the tyr'd footman reeles
'Twixt chaire-men, torches, & the hackny wheels:
   Come, take the other dish; it is to him
   That made his horse a Senatour:[7] Each brim

[3] Conventional name for a pastoral mistress.

[4] An allusion to the classical myth of Diana, goddess of the moon, and Endymion.

[5] Petty officers of justice, especially a warrant officer who arrests for debt (OED). Since the sixteenth century a word of contempt.

[6] Tower wharf was at the southeast corner of walled London. Lud and Cymbeline were legendary kings of Britain, whose statues were set up at Ludgate in the west wall. Vaughan obviously means across all London.

[7] Caligula, according to Suetonius.

Looke big as mine; The gallant, jolly Beast
50   Of all the Herd (you'le say) was not the least.
        Now crown the second bowle, rich as his worth,
I'le drinke it to; he! that like fire broke forth
Into the Senates face, crost Rubicon,[8]
And the States pillars, with their Lawes thereon:
55   And made the dull gray beards, & furr'd gowns fly
Into *Brundusium*[9] to consult, and lye:
        This to brave *Sylla!*[10] why should it be sed,
We drinke more to the living, then the dead?
Flatt'rers, and fooles doe use it: Let us laugh
60   At our owne honest mirth; for they that quaffe
To honour others, doe like those that sent
Their gold and plate to strangers to be spent:
        Drink deep; this Cup be pregnant; & the wine
Spirit of wit, to make us all divine,
65   That big with Sack, and mirth we may retyre
Possessours of more soules, and nobler fire;
And by the influxe of this painted Skie,
And labour'd formes, to higher matters flye;
So, if a Nap shall take us, we shall all,
70   After full Cups have dreames Poeticall.

Lets laugh now, and the prest grape drinke,
Till the drowsie Day-Starre winke;
And in our merry, mad mirth run
Faster, and further then the Sun;
75   *And let none his Cup forsake,*
Till that Starre againe doth wake;
So we men below shall move
        Equally with the gods above.

[8] Julius Caesar.
[9] Brundisium (modern Brindisi) in southeast Italy, to which Pompey and his friends of the Roman Senate fled when Caesar advanced on Rome.
[10] Probably Lucius Cornelius Sulla (138–78 B.C.), whose dictatorship of Rome set the pattern for that of Julius Caesar.

[P–11] To Amoret, *of the difference 'twixt him, and other Lovers, and what true Love is.*

Marke, when the Evenings cooler wings
　　Fanne the afflicted ayre, how the faint Sunne,
　　　　Leaving undone,
　　　　What he begunne,
5 Those spurious flames suckt up from slime, and earth[1]
　　　　To their first, low birth,
　　　　Resignes, and brings.

They shoot their tinsill beames, and vanities,
　　Thredding with those false fires their way;
10　　　　But as you stay
　　　　And see them stray,
You loose the flaming track, and subt'ly they
　　　　Languish away,
　　　　And cheate your Eyes.

15 Just so base, Sublunarie Lovers hearts
　　Fed on loose prophane desires,
　　　　May for an Eye,
　　　　Or face comply:
But those removed, they will as soone depart,
20　　　　And shew their Art,
　　　　And painted fires.

Whil'st I by pow'rfull Love, so much refin'd,
　　That my absent soule the same is,
　　　　Carelesse to misse,
25　　　　A glaunce, or kisse,
Can with those Elements of lust and sence,
　　　　Freely dispence,
　　　　And court the mind.

TO AMORET, OF THE DIFFERENCE. . . .
　　[1] Martin (*Works*, 1957, p. 701) suggests the *ignis fatuus*.

Thus to the North the Loadstones move,
30   And thus to them th' enamour'd steel aspires:
Thus, *Amoret,*
I doe affect;
And thus by winged beames, and mutuall fire,
Spirits and Stars conspire,
35   And this is L O V E.

[P–12]   To Amoret
WEEPING.

Leave, *Amoret,* melt not away so fast
Thy Eyes faire treasure, Fortunes wealthiest Cast
Deserves not one such pearle; for these well spent,
Can purchase Starres, and buy a Tenement
5 For us in Heaven; though here the pious streames
Availe us not; who from that Clue[1] of Sun-beams
Could ever steale one thread? or with a kinde
Perswasive Accent charme the wild, lowd winde?
Fate cuts us all in Marble, and the Booke
10 Forestalls our glasse of minutes; we may looke,
But seldome meet a change; thinke you a teare
Can blot the flinty Volume? shall our feare,
Or griefe adde to their triumphes? and must wee
Give an advantage to adversitie?
15 Deare, idle Prodigall! is it not just
We beare our Stars? What though I had not dust
Enough to cabinett a worme? nor stand
Enslav'd unto a little durt, or sand?
I boast a better purchase, and can shew
20 The glories of a soule that's simply true.
But grant some richer Planet at my birth
Had spyed me out, and measur'd so much earth
Or gold unto my share; I should have been
Slave to these lower Elements, and seen

TO AMORET WEEPING.
1 (Or clew) a ball of thread or yarn.

25 My high borne soul flagge with their drosse, & lye
　　 A pris'ner to base mud, and Alchymie;
　　 I should perhaps eate Orphans, and sucke up
　　 A dozen distrest widowes in one Cup;
　　 Nay further, I should by that lawfull stealth,
30 (Damn'd Usurie) undoe the Common-wealth;
　　 Or Patent it in Soape, and Coales, and so
　　 Have the Smiths curse me, and my Laundres too;
　　 Geld[2] wine, or his friend Tobacco; and so bring
　　 The incens'd subject Rebell to his King;
35 And after all (as those first sinners fell)
　　 Sinke lower then my gold; and lye in Hell.
　　　　 Thanks then for this deliv'rance! blessed pow'rs,
　　 You that dispence mans fortune, and his houres,
　　 How am I to you all engag'd! that thus
40 By such strange meanes, almost miraculous,
　　 You should preserve me; you have gone the way
　　 To make me rich by taking all away.
　　 For I (had I been rich) as sure as fate,
　　 Would have bin medling with the King, or State,
45 Or something to undoe me; and 'tis fit
　　 (We know) that who hath wealth, should have no wit.
　　 But above all, thanks to that providence,
　　 That arm'd me with a gallant soule, and sence
　　 'Gainst all misfortunes; that hath breath'd so much
50 Of Heav'n into me, that I scorne the touch
　　 Of these low things; and can with courage dare
　　 What ever fate, or malice can prepare:
　　 I envy no mans purse, or mines; I know,
　　 That loosing them, I've lost their curses too;
55 And, *Amoret,* (although our share in these
　　 Is not contemptible, nor doth much please)
　　 Yet whilst Content, and Love we joyntly vye,[3]
　　　　 We have a blessing which no gold can buye.

[2] Probably in the sense of tax, as Grosart (*Works*, II, 27) specu-
lates, analogous to the tax paid to the crown before and after the
Conquest (OED).
[3] Match one with another.

[P–13]   UPON THE
                    PRIORIE GROVE,[1]

                    His usuall Retyrement.

         Haile sacred shades! coole, leavie House!
         Chaste Treasurer of all my vowes,
         And wealth! on whose soft bosome layd
         My loves faire steps I first betrayd:
5   Henceforth no melancholy flight,
         No sad wing, or hoarse bird of Night,
         Disturbe this Aire, no fatall throate
         Of Raven, or Owle, awake the Note
         Of our laid Eccho, no voice dwell
10   Within these leaves, but *Philomel.*
         The poisonous Ivie here no more
         His false twists on the Oke shall score,
         Only the Woodbine here may twine,
         As th' Embleme of her Love, and mine;
15   The Amorous Sunne shall here convey
         His best beames, in thy shades to play;
         The active ayre, the gentlest show'rs,
         Shall from his wings raine on thy flowers;
         And the Moone from her dewie lockes
20   Shall decke thee with her brightest drops:
         What ever can a fancie move,
             Or feed the eye; Be on this Grove;
                 And when at last the Winds, and Teares
         Of Heaven, with the consuming yeares,
25   Shall these greene curles bring to decay,
         And cloathe thee in an aged Gray:

UPON THE PRIORIE GROVE.
    [1] The wooded grounds of Brecon Priory, the home of Col. Her-
bert Price, probably a friend of the family of Catherine Wise,
who became Vaughan's first wife. See Hutchinson, *Life*, pp. 52–53.
The poem apparently celebrates their first meeting and courtship.

(If ought a Lover can foresee;
Or if we Poets, Prophets be)
From hence transplanted, thou shalt stand
30   A fresh Grove in th' Elysian Land;
Where (most blest paire!) as here on Earth
Thou first didst eye our growth, and birth;
So there againe, thou 'lt see us move
In our first Innocence, and Love:
35   And in thy shades, as now, so then,
Wee'le kisse, and smile, and walke agen.

FINIS.

IVVENALS
TENTH
SATYRE
TRANSLATED.

Nèc verbum verbo curabit reddere fidus
Interpres ——————

LONDON,
Printed for *G. B.* and are to be sold at his Shop
under Saint *Dunstans* Church. 1646.

JUVENALS tenth Satyre
                 TRANSLATED.[1]

   In all the parts of Earth, from farthest West,
   And the Atlanticke Isles, unto the East
   And famous Ganges; Few there be that know
   What's truly good, and what is good in show
5 Without mistake: For what is't we desire,
   Or feare discreetly? to what e're aspire,
   So throughly blest; but ever as we speed,
   Repentance seales the very Act, and deed.
   The easie gods mov'd by no other Fate,
10 Then our owne pray'rs whole Kingdomes ruinate,
   And undoe Families, thus strife, and warre
   Are the swords prize, and a litigious barre
   The Gownes prime wish; vain confidence to share
   In empty honours, and a bloudy care,
15 To be the first in mischiefe, makes him dye
   Fool'd 'twixt ambition, and credulitie;
   An oilie tongue with fatall, cunning sence,
   And that sad vertue ever, Eloquence,
   Are th' others ruine; but the common curse,
20 And each dayes ill waits on the rich mans purse:
   He, whose large acres, and imprison'd gold
   So far exceeds his Fathers store of old,
   As Brittish Whales the Dolphins doe surpasse.
     In sadder times therefore, and when the Lawes

JUVENALS TENTH SATYRE TRANSLATED.

  [1] For a modern text and translation see *Juvenal and Persius*, tr.
G. G. Ramsay, Loeb Library (1918), pp. 192–221. The Latin
quotation on the title page is from Horace, *Ars Poetica*, 133–34:
"nec verbo verbum curabis reddere fidus / interpres" ("if you do
not seek to render word for word as a slavish translator"); see the
Satires, Epistles, Ars Poetica, tr. H. Rushton Fairclough, Loeb Library (1926), pp. 460–61.

25 Of *Nero's fiat* raign'd; an armed band
Ceas'd[2] on *Longinus*,[3] and the spacious Land
Of wealthy *Seneca*,[4] besieg'd the gates
Of *Lateranus*,[5] and his faire estate
Divided as a spoile; In such sad Feasts,
30 Souldiers (though not invited) are the guests.
Though thou small peeces of the blessed Mine
Hast lodg'd about thee; travelling in the shine
Of a pale Moone, if but a Reed doth shake,
Mov'd by the wind, the shadow makes thee quake.
35 Wealth hath its cares, and want hath this reliefe,
It neither feares the Souldier, nor the Thiefe;
Thy first choyce vowes, and to the Gods best knowne,
Are for thy stores encrease, that in all towne
Thy stocke be greatest, but no poyson lyes
40 I'th' poore mans dish, he tasts of no such spice:
Be that thy care, when with a Kingly gust,
Thou suck'st whole Bowles clad in the guilded dust
Of some rich minerall; whilst the false Wine
Sparkles aloft, and makes the draught Divine.
45   Blam'st thou the Sages then? because the one[6]
Would still be laughing, when he would be gone
From his owne doore, the other[7] cryed to see
His times addicted to such vanity?
Smiles are an easie purchase, but to weep
50 Is a hard act, for teares are fetch'd more deep;
Democritus his nimble Lungs would tyre
With constant laughter, and yet keep entire
His stocke of mirth, for ev'ry object was
Addition to his store; though then (Alas!)
55 Sedans, and Litters, and our Senat Gownes,

2 Seized.
3 A lawyer whom Nero had banished.
4 The philosopher, whose offer of his personal wealth to placate Nero was finally and partially accepted.
5 Plautius Laternus, a Roman senator, later executed for his part in the Pisonian conspiracy.
6 Democritus of Abdera.
7 Heraclitus of Ephesus.

With Robes of honour, fasces, and the frownes
Of unbrib'd Tribunes were not seene; but had
He lived to see our *Roman Prætor* clad
In *Joves* owne mantle, seated on his high
60 Embroyder'd Chariot 'midst the dust and Crie
Of the large Theatre, loaden with a Crowne
Which scarse he could support, (for it would downe,
But that his servant props it) and close by
His page a witnes to his vanitie:
65 To these his Scepter, and his Eagle adde
His Trumpets, Officers, and servants clad
In white, and purple; with the rest that day,
He hir'd to triumph for his bread, and pay;
Had he these studied, sumptuous follies seene,
70 'Tis thought his wanton, and effusive spleene
Had kill'd the Abderite, though in that age
(When pride & greatnes had not swell'd the stage
So high as ours) his harmles, and just mirth
From ev'ry object had a suddaine birth;
75 Nor wast alone their avarice, or pride,
Their triumphs, or their cares he did deride;
Their vaine contentions, or ridiculous feares;
But even their very poverty, and teares.
He would at fortunes threats as freely smile
80 As others mourne; nor was it to beguile
His crafty passions; but this habit he
By nature had, and grave Philosophie.
He knew their idle and superfluous vowes,
And sacrifice, which such wrong zeale bestowes,
85 Were meere Incendiaries;[8] and that the gods
Not pleas'd therewith, would ever be at ods;
Yet to no other aire, nor better place
Ow'd he his birth, then the cold, homely *Thrace*;
Which shewes a man may be both wise, & good,
90 Without the brags of fortune, or his bloud.
　　　But envy ruines all: What mighty names
Of fortune, spirit, action, bloud, and fame,

[8] Things that inflame passions or strife (OED).

Hath this destroy'd? yea, for no other cause
Then being such; their honour, worth, and place,
95 Was crime enough; their statues, arms & crowns;
Their ornaments of Triumph, Chariots, Gowns,
And what the Herauld with a learned care,
Had long preserv'd, this madnes will not spare.
So once *Sejanus*[9] Statue Rome allow'd
100 Her Demi-god, and ev'ry Roman bow'd
To pay his safeties vowes; but when that face
Had lost *Tyberius* once, it's former grace
Was soone eclips'd; no diff'rence made (Alas!)
Betwixt his Statue then, and common Brasse;
105 They melt alike, and in the Workmans hand
For equall, servile use, like others stand.
Goe now fetch home fresh Bayes, and pay new vowes
To thy dumbe Capitoll gods! thy life, thy house,
And state are now secur'd; *Sejanus* lyes
110 I'th' Lictors hands; ye gods! what hearts, & eyes
Can one dayes fortune change? the solemne crye
Of all the world is, Let *Sejanus* dye:
They never lov'd the man they sweare, they know
Nothing of all the matter; when, or how,
115 By what accuser, for what cause, or why,
By whose command, or sentence he must dye.
But what needs this? the least pretence will hit,
When Princes feare, or hate a Favourite.
A large Epistle stuff'd with idle feare,
120 Vaine dreames, and jealousies, directed here
From *Caprea* does it;[10] And thus ever dye
Subjects, when once they grow prodigious high.
'Tis well, I seeke no more; but tell me how
This tooke his friends? no private murmurs now?
125 No teares? no solemne mourner seene? must all
His Glory perish in one funerall?
O still true Romans! State-wit bids them praise
The Moone by night; but court the warmer rayes

[9] Once the favorite of Tiberius, destroyed by the Romans when
he lost the favor of the emperor.
[10] A famous letter from Tiberius on Capri sealed Sejanus' doom.

O' th' Sun by day; they follow fortune still,
130 And hate, or love discreetly, as their will
And the time leades them; This tumultuous fate
Puts all their painted favours out of date:
　　And yet this people that now spurne, & tread
This mighty Favourites once honour'd head,
135 Had but the Tuscaine goddesse,[11] or his Stars
Destin'd him for an Empire, or had wars,
Treason, or policie, or some higher pow'r
Opprest secure *Tyberius*; that same houre
That he receiv'd the sad Gemonian doome,[12]
140 Had crown'd him Emp'ror of the world, & Rome.
　　But Rome is now growne wise, & since that she
Her Suffrages, and ancient Libertie,
Lost in a Monarchs name; she takes no care
For Favourite, or Prince; nor will she share
145 Their fickle glories, though in *Cato's* dayes
She rul'd whole States, & Armies with her voice,
Of all the honours now within her walls,
She only doats on Playes, and Festivalls:
Nor is it strange; for when these Meteors fall,
150 They draw an ample ruine with them; All
Share in the storm; each beame sets with the Sun,
And equall hazard friends, and flatt'rers run.
This makes, that circled with distractive feare
The livelesse, pale Sejanus limbes they teare,
155 And least the action might a witnesse need,
They bring their servants to confirme the deed,
Nor is it done for any other end,
Then to avoid the title of his friend.
　　So fals ambitious man, and such are still
160 All floating States built on the peoples will:

[11] Nortia, the Etruscan goddess of Fortune. Sejanus was from Etruria.
[12] Derived from the *scalae Gemoniae*, steps on the Aventine Hill leading to the Tiber, to which the bodies of executed criminals were dragged to be thrown into the river (OED). The term is not in Juvenal.

Hearken all you! whom this bewitching lust
Of an houres glory, and a little dust
Swels to such deare repentance! you that can
Measure whole kingdoms with a thought or span
165 Would you be as *Sejanus?* would you have
So you might sway as he did, such a grave?
Would you be rich as he? command, dispose,
All Acts, and Offices? All friends, and foes?
Be Generalls of Armies, and Colleague
170 Unto an Emperour? breake, or make a league?
No doubt you would; for both the good, and bad,
An equall itch of honour ever had:
But O what State can be so great, or good,
As to be bought with so much shame, and bloud!
175 Alas! *Sejanus* will too late confesse
'Twas only pride, and greatnes made him lesse:
For he that moveth with the lofty wind
Of Fortune, and ambition, unconfin'd
In act, or thought; doth but increase his height,
180 That he may loose it with more force, & weight;
Scorning a base, low ruine, as if he
Would of misfortune, make a Prodigie.
      Tell mighty *Pompey, Crassus,* and O thou[13]
That mad'st Rome kneele to thy victorious brow,
185 What but the weight of honours, and large fame
After your worthy Acts, and height of name,
Destroy'd you in the end? the envious Fates
Easie to further your aspiring States,
Us'd them to quell you too; pride, and excesse
190 In ev'ry Act did make you thrive the lesse:
Few Kings are guiltie of gray haires, or dye
Without a stab, a draught, or trecherie:
And yet to see him, that but yesterday
Saw letters first, how he will scrape, and pray;
195 And all her Feast-time tyre *Minervaes* eares
For Fame, for Eloquence, and store of yeares
To thrive and live in; and then lest he doates,
His boy assists him with his boxe, and notes;

13 Julius Caesar.

Foole that thou art! not to discerne the ill
200 These vows include; what, did Rom's Consull kill
Her *Cicero*? what, him whose very dust
Greece celebrates as yet;[14] whose cause though just,
Scarse banishment could end; nor poyson save
His free borne person from a forraigne grave:
205 All this from Eloquence! both head, and hand,
The tongue doth forfeit; pettie wits may stand
Secure from danger, but the nobler veine,
With losse of bloud the barre doth often staine.

    ❋   ❋   ❋   ❋   ❋   } *Carmen*
O fortunatam natam me Consule Romam. } *Ciceroni-*
    ❋   ❋   ❋   ❋   ❋   } *anum.*[15]

210 Had all been thus, thou might'st have scorn'd the sword
Of fierce *Antonius*, here is not one word
Doth pinch, I like such stuffe; 'tis safer far
Then thy Philippicks, or Pharsalia's war:
What sadder end then his, whom Athens saw
215 At once her Patriot, Oracle, and Law?[16]
Unhappy then is he, and curs'd in Stars,
Whom his poore Father, blind with soot, & scars
Sends from the Anviles harmles chime, to weare
The factious gowne, and tyre his Clients eare,
220 And purse with endles noise; Trophies of war
Old rusty armour, with an honour'd scar;
And wheeles of captiv'd Chariots, with a peece
Of some torne Brittish Galley, and to these
The Ensigne too, and last of all the traine
225 The pensive pris'ner loaden with his Chaine,
Are thought true Roman honors; these the Greek
And rude Barbarians equally doe seeke.

[14] Demosthenes.

[15] From *De suo Consulatu*, the poem by Cicero written in praise
of his consulship translated by Ramsay, "O happy Fate for the
Roman State / Was the date of my great Consulate!" See *Juvenal
and Persius*, Loeb Library, p. 202, n. 1.

[16] Demosthenes took poison when pursued by political enemies.
His father appears to have been a blacksmith who became wealthy
by the manufacture of swords.

Thus aire, and empty fame, are held a prize
Beyond faire vertue; for all vertue dyes
230 Without reward; And yet by this fierce lust
Of Fame, and titles to ovtlive our dust,
And Monuments; (though all these things must dye
And perish like our selves) whole Kingdomes lye
Ruin'd, and spoil'd: Put *Hannibal* i'th' scale,
235 What weight affords the mighty Generall?
This is the man, whom Africks spacious Land
Bounded by th' Indian Sea, and Niles hot sand,
Could not containe; (Ye gods! that give to men
Such boundles appetites, why state you them
240 So short a time? either the one deny,
Or give their acts, and them Eternitie)
All Æthiopia, to the utmost bound
Of *Titans* course, (then which no Land is found
Lesse distant from the Sun) with him that ploughs
245 That fertile soile where fam'd Iberus flowes,
Are not enough to conquer; past now o're
The Pyrene hills, The Alps with all its store
Of Ice, and Rocks clad in eternall snow
(As if that Nature meant to give the blow)
250 Denyes him passage; straight on ev'ry side
He wounds the Hill, and by strong hand divides
The monstrous pile, nought can ambition stay,
The world, and nature yeeld to give him way:
And now past o're the Alps, that mighty bar
255 'Twixt France, and Rome, feare of the future war
Strikes Italy; successe, and hope doth fire
His lofty spirits with a fresh desire.
All is undone as yet (saith he) unlesse
Our Pænish[17] forces we advance, and presse
260 Upon Rome's selfe; break downe her gates, & wall,
And plant our Colours in *Suburra's* Vale.[18]

---

[17] Punic, Carthaginian.
[18] The valley between the Viminal and Esquiline Hills of Rome.

O the rare sight! if this great souldier wee
Arm'd on his Getick[19] Elephant might see!
But what's the event? O glory! how the itch
265 Of thy short wonders doth mankinde bewitch!
He that but now all Italy, and Spaine,
Had conquer'd o're, is beaten out againe;
And in the heart of Africk, and the sight
Of his owne Carthage, forc'd to open flight.
270 Banish'd from thence, a fugitive he posts
To Syria first, then to Bythinia's Coasts;
Both places by his sword secur'd; though he
In this distresse must not acknowledg'd be;
Where once a Generall he triumphed, now
275 To shew what Fortune can, he begs as low.
     And thus that soule, which through all nations hurl'd
Conquest, and warre, and did amaze the world;
Of all those glories rob'd at his last breath,
Fortune would not vouchsafe a souldiers death,
280 For all that bloud the field of Cannæ boasts,
And sad Apulia fill'd with Roman ghoasts:
No other end (freed from the pile, and sword)
Then a poore Ring would Fortune him afford.[20]
     Goe now ambitious man! new plots designe,
285 March o're the snowie Alps, and Apennine;
That after all, at best thou mayst but be
A pleasing story to posteritie!
     The *Macedon*[21] one world could not containe,
We heare him of the narrow Earth complaine,
290 And sweat for roome, as if Seryphus Ile,
Or Gyara had held him in Exile:
But Babylon this madnes can allay,
And give the great man but his length of clay;
The highest thoughts, and actions under Heaven,
295 Death only with the lowest dust layes even.

19 Not connected with the Getae of Thrace, of course, but with
the Gaetuli of North Africa.
20 To avoid extradition by the Romans, Hannibal destroyed himself by poison concealed in a ring.
21 Alexander the Great.

It is believed (if what Greece writes be true)
That *Xerxes* with his Persian Fleet did hewe
Their waies throgh mountains, that their sails full blowne,
Like clouds hung over Athos, and did drowne
300 The spacious Continent, and by plaine force
Betwixt the Mount, and it made a divorce;
That Seas exhausted were, and made firme land,
And Sestos joyned unto Abidos Strand;
That on their march, his Meades but passing by,
305 Dranke thee Scamander, and Melenus dry;
With what soe're incredible designe
Sostratus[22] sings inspired with pregnant Wine:
But what's the end? He that the other day
Divided Hellespont, and forc'd his way
310 Through all her angry billowes; that assigned
New punishments unto the waves, and wind:
No sooner saw the Salaminian Seas,
But he was driven out by *Themistocles*,
And of that Fleet (suppos'd to be so great,
315 That all mankinde shar'd in the sad defeate)
Not one Sayle sav'd, in a poore Fishers boat,
Chas'd o're the working surge, was glad to float,
Cutting his desp'rate course through the tyr'd floud,
And fought againe with Carkasses, and bloud.
320 O foolish mad ambition! these are still
The famous dangers that attend thy will.
    Give store of dayes, good *Jove*, give length of yeares,
Are the next vowes; these with religious feares,
And Constancie we pay; but what's so bad,
325 As a long, sinfull age? what crosse more sad
Then misery of yeares? how great an Ill
Is that, which doth but nurse more sorrow still?
It blacks the face, corrupts, and duls the bloud,
Benights the quickest eye, distasts the food,
330 And such deep furrowes cuts i'th' Checker'd skin
As in th'old Okes of Tabraca[23] are seene.

[22] An unknown poet.
[23] A town in Numidia. See *Juvenal and Persius*, Loeb Library, p. 209, n. 1.

Youth varies in most things; strength, beauty, **wit**,
Are severall graces; but where age doth hit,
It makes no diff'rence; the same weake voice,
335 And trembling ague in each member lyes:
A generall, hatefull baldnes, with a curst
Perpetuall pettishnes; and which is worst,
A foule, strong fluxe of humors, and more paine
To feed, then if he were to nurse again.
340 So tedious to himselfe, his wife, and friends,
That his owne sonnes, and servants, wish his end,
His tast, and feeling dyes; and of that fire
The am'rous Lover burnes in, no desire:
Or if there were, what pleasure could it be,
345 Where lust doth raigne without abilitie?
Nor is this all, what matters it, where he
Sits in the spacious Stage? who can nor see,
Nor heare what's acted, whom the stiller voice
Of spirited, wanton ayres, or the loud noise
350 Of Trumpets cannot pierce; whom thunder can
But scarse informe who enters, or what man
He personates, what 'tis they act, or say?
How many Scænes are done? what time of day?
Besides that little bloud, his carkasse holds,
355 Hath lost its native warmth, & fraught wth colds,
Catarrhs, and rheumes, to thick, black jelly turns,
And never but in fits, and feavers burnes;
Such vast infirmities, so huge a stock
Of sicknes, and diseases to him flock,
360 That *Hyppia* ne're so many Lovers knew,
Nor wanton *Maura*; Phisick never slew
So many Patients, nor rich Lawyers spoile
More Wards, and Widowes; it were lesser toile
To number out what Mannors, and Demaines,
365 *Licinius*[24] razer purchas'd: One complaines
Of weaknes in the back, another pants
For lack of breath, the third his eyesight wants;

[24] Vaughan supplies this name for an unnamed barber who apparently had become rich in lands.

Nay some so feeble are, and full of paine,
That Infant like they must be fed againe.
370 These faint too at their meales; their wine they spill,
And like young birds, that wait the Mothers Bill
They gape for meat; but sadder far then this
Their senslesse ignorance, and dotage is;
For neither they, their friends, nor servants know,
375 Nay those themselves begot, and bred up too
No longer now they'le owne; for madly they
Proscribe them all, and what on the last day,
The Misers cannot carry to the Grave
For their past sinnes, their prostitutes must have.
380   But grant age lack'd these plagues; yet must they see
As great, as many: Fraile Mortalitie
In such a length of yeares, hath many falls,
And deads a life with frequent funerals.
The nimblest houre in all the span, can steale
385 A friend, or brother from's; there's no Repeale
In death, or time; this day a wife we mourne,
To morrowes teares a sonne, and the next Urne
A Sister fills; Long-livers have assign'd
These curses still: That with a restles mind,
390 An age of fresh renewing cares they buye,
And in a tide of teares grow old and dye.
    Nestor, (if we great *Homer* may believe)
In his full strength three hundred yeares did live:[25]
Happy (thou'lt say) that for so long a time
395 Enjoy'd free nature, with the grape, and Wine
Of many Autumnes; but I prethee, heare
What *Nestor* sayes himselfe, when he his deare
Antilochus[26] had lost, how he complaines
Of life's too large Extent, and copious paines?
400 Of all he meets, he askes what is the cause
He lived thus long; for what breach of their Laws
The gods thus punish'd him? what sinne had he
Done worthy of a long lifes miserie?

[25] Juvenal does not give Nestor's exact age.
[26] Nestor's son.

Thus *Peleus* his *Achilles* mourned, and he[27]
405 Thus wept that his *Ulysses* lost at Sea.
Had *Priam* dyed, before *Phereclus* Fleet
Was built, or *Paris* stole the fatall Greeke,
Troy had yet stood, and he perhaps had gone
In peace unto the lower shades; His sonne
410 Saved with his plenteous offspring, and the rest
In solemne pompe bearing his fun'rall Chest;
But long life hinder'd this: Unhappy he,
Kept for a publick ruine, lived to see
All Asia lost, and e're he could expire,
415 In his owne house saw both the sword, and fire;
All white with age, and cares, his feeble arme
Had now forgot the warre; but this Allarme
Gathers his dying spirits; and as wee
An aged Oxe worne out with labour, see,
420 By his ungratefull Master, after all
His yeares of toyle, a thankles victime fall:
So he by *Joves* owne Altar; which shewes, wee
Are no where safe from Heaven, and destinie:
Yet dyed a man; but his surviving Queene,[28]
425 Freed from the Greekish sword was barking seen.
    I haste to Rome, and Pontus King[29] let passe,
With Lydian *Cræsus*, whom in vaine (Alas!)
Just *Solons* grave advice bad to attend,
That happines came not before the end.
430   What man more blest in any age to come
Or past, could Nature shew the world, or Rome,
Then *Marius*[30] was? if 'midst the pompe of war,
And triumphs fetch'd with Roman bloud from far
His soule had fled; Exile, and fetters then,
435 He ne're had seen, nor known *Mynturna's* fenne;
Nor had it, after Carthage got, been sed,
A Roman Generall had beg'd his bread.

[27] Laertes, who mourned the loss of his son Ulysses.
[28] Hecuba, supposed to have been metamorphosed into a dog.
[29] Mithridates.
[30] Gaius Marius (157–86 B.C.), noted Roman general.

Thus *Pompey* th' envious gods, & Romes ill stars
(Freed from *Campania's* feavers, and the Wars)
440 Doom'd to *Achilles* sword: Our publick vowes
Made *Cæsar* guiltles; but sent him to loose
His head at Nile; This curse *Cethegus* mist;
This *Lentulus*,[31] and this made him resist
That mangled by no Lictors axe, fell dead
445 Entirely *Catiline,* and saved his head.
  The anxious Matrons, with their foolish zeale,
Are the last Votaries, and their Appeale
Is all for beauty; with soft speech, and slow,
They pray for sons, but with a louder vow
450 Commend a female feature: All that can
Make woman pleasing now they shift, and scan:
And why reprov'd they say, *Latona's* paire[32]
The Mother never thinks can be too faire.
  But sad *Lucretia* warnes to wish no face
455 Like hers; *Virginia* would bequeath her grace
To Crooke-backe *Rutila* in exchange; for still
The fairest children do their Parents fill
With greatest cares; so seldome Chastitie
Is found with beauty; though some few there be
460 That with a strict, religious care contend
Th' old, modest, Sabine Customes to defend:
Besides, wise nature to some faces grants
An easie blush, and where shee freely plants,
A lesse Instruction serves; but both these joyn'd,
465 At *Rome* would both be forc'd or else purloyn'd.
  So steel'd a forehead vice hath, that dares win,
And bribe the Father to the Childrens sin;
But whom have gifts defiled not? what good face
Did ever want these tempters? pleasing grace
470 Betraies it selfe; what time did *Nero* mind
A course, maim'd shape? what blemish'd youth confin'd
His goatish Pathick?[33] whence then flow these joies
Of a faire issue? whom these sad annoies

[31] Figures in Catiline's conspiracy.
[32] Apollo and Artemis.
[33] Catamite.

Waite, and grow up with; whom perhaps thou'lt see
475 Publick Adulterers, and must be
Subject to all the Curses, Plagues, and awe
Of jealous mad men, and the *Julian* Law;[34]
Nor canst thou hope they'le find a milder Starre,
Or more escapes then did the God of Warre;
480 But worse then all, a jealous braine confines
His furie to no Law; what rage assignes,
Is present justice: Thus the rash Sword spils
This Lechers bloud, the scourge another kils.
But thy spruce boy must touch no other face
485 Then a *Patrician*? Is of any race
So they be rich; *Servilia* is as good
With wealth, as shee that boasts *Iulus*[35] blood:
To please a servant all is cheape; what thing
In all their stocke to the last suite, and Ring
490 But lust exacts? the poorest whore in this,
As generous as the *Patrician* is.
    But thou wilt say what hurt's a beauteous skin
With a chaste soule? aske *Theseus* sonne,[36] and him
That *Stenobæa* murther'd;[37] for both these
495 Can tell how fatall 'twas in them to please;
A woman spleene then carries most of fate,
When shame and sorrow aggravate her hate:
Resolve me now, had *Silius*[38] been thy sonne,
In such a hazzard what should he have done?
500 Of all *Romes* youth, this was the only best,
In whom alone beauty, and worth did rest:
This *Messalina* saw, and needs he must
Be ruin'd by the Emp'rour, or her lust,

[34] The body of law governing marriage and adultery, passed by Augustus.

[35] Better known as Ascanius, son of Aeneas, from whom some of the noblest Roman families claimed descent.

[36] Hippolytus, who rejected the advances of his stepmother Phaedra.

[37] Bellerophon.

[38] Gaius Silius, with whom Messalina, wife of Claudius, was infatuated. Both were put to death.

All in the face of *Rome*, and the worlds eye,
505 Though *Cesars* wife, a publicke Bigamie
Shee dares attempt; and that the act might beare
More prodigie, the notaries appeare,
And Augures to't; and to compleat the sin
In solemne forme, a dowrie is brought in;
510 All this (thou'lt say) in private might have past,
But shee'le not have it so; what course at last?
What should he doe? If *Messaline* be crost
Without redresse thy *Silius* will be lost;
If not, some two daies length is all he can
515 Keep from the grave; just so much as will span
This newes to *Hostia*, to whose fate he owes
That *Claudius* last his owne dishonour knowes.
    But he obeyes, and for a few houres lust,
Forfeits that glory should outlive his dust,
520 Nor was it much a fault; for, whether he
Obey'd, or not; 'twas equall destinie:
So fatall beauty is, and full of wast,
That neither wanton can be safe, nor chast.
What then should man pray for? what is't that he
525 Can beg of Heaven, without Impiety?
Take my advice: first to the Gods commit
All cares; for they things competent, and fit
For us foresee; besides man is more deare
To them, then to himselfe: we blindly here
530 Led by the world, and lust, in vaine assay
To get us portions, wives, and sonnes; but they
Already know all that we can intend,
And of our Childrens Children see the end.
    Yet that thou may'st have something to commend
535 With thankes unto the Gods for what they send;
Pray for a wise, and knowing soule; a sad
Discreet, true valour, that will scorne to adde
A needlesse horrour to thy death; that knowes
'Tis but a debt which man to nature owes;
540 That starts not at misfortunes, that can sway,
And keep all passions under locke and key;

That covets nothing, wrongs none, and preferres
An honest want before rich injurers;
All this thou hast within thy selfe, and may
545 Be made thy owne, if thou wilt take the way;
What boots the worlds wild, loose applause? what can
Fraile, perillous honours adde unto a man?
What length of years, wealth, or a rich faire wife?
Vertue alone can make a happy life.
550 To a wise man nought comes amisse: but we
Fortune adore, and make our Deity.

FINIS.

OLOR ISCANUS

(1651)

Ad Posteros.[1]

Diminuat ne sera *dies* præsentis *honorem,*
  Quis, qualisq;[2] *fui, percipe* Posteritas.
CAMBRIA *me genuit,* patulis *ubi* vallibus *errans*
  Subjacet aeriis montibus ISCA pater.
5 *Inde* sinu placido *suscepit maximus arte*
  HERBERTUS,[3] Latiæ *gloria prima* Scholæ,
Bis ternos, *illo me Conducente, per* annos
  Profeci, & geminam Contulit unus opem,
Ars *&* amor, mens *atq;*[3] manus *certare solebant,*
10 *Nec lassata Illi* mensve, manusve *fuit.*
Hinc qualem cernis crevisse: Sed *ut mea Certus*
  Tempora Cognoscas, dura *fuere, scias.*
Vixi, divisos cum fregerat *hæresis Anglos*
  Intèr Tysiphonas *presbyteri & populi.*
15 His *primùm* miseris *per* amæna *furentibus* arva
  Prostravit sanctam *vilis avena* rosam,[4]

[1] Vaughan's guarded statements in this poem bearing on his connection with the civil wars have produced conflicting opinions as to whether or not he was an active participant, but the strong probability is that he *was* directly involved. The main question concerns the extent and nature of his involvement. See Hutchinson, *Life,* pp. 55–58, and E. L. Marilla, "Henry Vaughan and the Civil War," *JEGP,* XLI (1942), 514–26.

[2] Terminal "q," or "q;" (whether in roman or italic, with or without the acute ['] accent mark) in Vaughan's Latin texts abbreviates *que.*

[3] Matthew Herbert, rector of Llangattock, who was schoolmaster to Henry and Thomas Vaughan from 1632 to 1638. See the Latin epigram to him below, O–45. Hutchinson (*Life,* pp. 27–29, 109–10, 201–2) gives a good account of Matthew Herbert.

[4] King Charles I was frequently referred to as "The Rose" by the Royalists. Vaughan's antipathy to Parliamentarians and Puri-

Turbârunt fontes, *& fusis* pax *perit undis,*
  Mæstaq; Cœlestes obruit umbra dies.
Duret ut Integritas *tamen, &* pia gloria, *partem*
20   *Me nullam in tantâ* strage *fuisse, scias;*
Credidimus nempè insonti vocem *esse Cruori,*
  Et vires *quæ post funera* flere *docent.*
Hinc Castæ, fidæq; *pati me more* parentis
  Commonui, & Lachrymis fata *levare meis;*
25 *Hinc nusquàm horrendis violavi* Sacra *procellis,*
  Nec mihi mens *unquàm, nec* manus *atra fuit.*
Si pius *es, ne plura petas;* Satur *Ille recedat*
  Qui sapit, *& nos non Scripsimus* Insipidis.

[To Posterity

In case a later age should belittle the honor of this present
time, read here, Posterity, who and what I was. I was born in
Wales, where father Usk meanders through wide valleys beneath cloud-capped mountains. Then that very great scholar
Mr. Herbert, the pride of Latin scholarship, took me into his
gentle care. With him as my master I made good progress for
six years. Though one man, he gave me a double treasure:
learning and love. His mind and his hand competed in my
education, and neither was weak! You see what sort of a
man I have grown into as a result, but in order that you may
be well informed about the times in which I lived, let me
tell you that they were cruel. I lived when religious con-
troversy had split the English people into factions: I lived
among the furious conflicts of Church and State. At the out-
set, while the wretched inhabitants raged through their pleas-

---

tans, evident in the following lines, never seems to have slack-
ened. It colors nearly all of his statements on the political and
religious issues and events of his day.

ant fields, the base weed laid low the holy rose. They disturbed the fountains, and peace perished beneath the flood, and a gloomy shadow overspread the light of heaven. But in order that my integrity and my reputation for piety may survive, let me tell you that I took no part in that great slaughter. I firmly believed that innocent blood has a voice, and a strength which wins tears after death. Thus I schooled myself to endure suffering like a chaste and faithful mother, and to make my fate easier to bear by watering it with my tears. So you see, I have never done violence to sacred things by stirring up fearful tumults, and neither my mind nor my hand has ever been malevolent. If you fear God, seek to know no more. Let the wise man go from here having heard enough: as for fools, I do not write for them.]

OLOR ISCANUS.

A COLLECTION

OF SOME SELECT

POEMS,

AND

TRANSLATIONS,

Formerly written by

Mr. Henry Vaughan *Silurist*.

Publiſhed by a Friend.

Virg. Georg.
Flumina amo, Sylvaſq. Inglorius————

LONDON,
Printed by *T.W.* for *Humphrey Moſeley,*
and are to be ſold at his ſhop, at the
Signe of the Prince's Arms in St. *Pauls*
Church-yard, 1651.

——O quis me gelidis in vallibus ISCÆ
Sistat, & Ingenti ramorum protegat umbrâ![1]

[1] "O who will set me in the cool valleys of the Usk and shield me with the generous shade of the branches!"—adapted from Virgil, *Georgics*, II, 488–89.

TO
The truly Noble, and most
Excellently accomplish'd, the
Lord KILDARE DIGBY.[1]

MY LORD,

It is a Position *anciently* known, and *modern Experience* hath allowed it for a *sad truth,* that *Absence* and
time, (like *Cold weather,* and an *unnaturall dormition*)
5 will *blast* and *wear* out of memorie the most *Endearing
obligations*; And hence it was that some *Politicians* in
Love have lookt upon the *former* of these *two* as a main
remedy against the *fondness* of that *Passion.* But for my
own part (my Lord) I shall deny this *Aphorisme* of the
10 *people,* and beg leave to assure your *Lordship,* that,
though these *reputed obstacles* have lain long in my way,
yet neither of them could *work* upon me: for I am now
(without adulation) as *warm* and *sensible* of those *numerous* favours, and *kind Influences* receiv'd sometimes
15 from your Lordship, as I really was at the *Instant* of
fruition. I have no *plott* by *preambling* thus, to set any
rate upon this present *addresse,* as if I should presume
to value a *Return* of this nature equall with your Lordships *Deserts,* but the *designe* is, to let you see that this
20 *habit* I have got of being *troublesome* flowes from two
excusable principles, Gratitude, and Love. These inward
Counsellours (I know not how discreetly) perswaded
me to this *Attempt* and *Intrusion* upon your *name,* which
if your Lordship will vouchsafe to own as the *Genius* to
25 these *papers,* you will *perfect* my *hopes,* and place me

DEDICATION.
1 Son of Robert, first Lord Digby, and Sara, daughter of Richard,
Earl of Cork. He succeeded to the title in 1642.

at my full *height*. This was the *Ayme,* my Lord, and is
the *End* of this work, which though but a *Pazzarello* to
the *voluminosè Insani,*[2] yet as *Jezamin* and the *Violet*
find room in the *bank* as well as *Roses* and *Lillies,* so
30 happily may this, and (if *shin'd* upon by your *Lordship*)
please as much. To whose *Protection,* Sacred as your
Name, and those eminent *Honours* which have alwayes
attended upon't through so many *generations,* I humbly
offer it, and remain in all *numbers* of *gratitude,*

My honour'd Lord,

Newton by *Usk*
this 17. of *De-*
cemb. 1647.[3]

Your most affectionate,
humblest Servant
VAUGHAN.

The Publisher[1] to the Reader.

It was the glorious Maro,[2] *that referr'd his* Legacies
to the Fire, *and though* Princes *are seldome* Executors,
yet there came a Cæsar *to his* Testament, *as if the* Act
of a Poet *could not be* repeal'd *but by a* King. *I am not*
5 *Reader* Augustus vindex: *Here is no* Royall Rescue, *but*
here is a Muse *that* deserves *it. The* Author *had long*
agoe condemn'd these Poems *to* Obscuritie, *and the*
Consumption *of that* Further Fate, *which* attends *it.*

[2] The Italian is faulty, but the general meaning would appear
to be: though but a little madcap (work) compared with the copious (works of the) mad ones, or inspired geniuses.

[3] Some three to four years before the actual publication of the
volume.

THE PUBLISHER TO THE READER.

[1] Probably Humphrey Moseley, possibly Thomas Powell.

[2] Virgil, whose literary remains were reportedly saved from destruction by Augustus.

This Censure *gave them a* Gust *of* Death, *and they have*
10 partly *known that* Oblivion, *which our* Best Labours
must come to *at* Last. *I present thee then not onely with*
a Book, *but with a* Prey, *and in this* kind *the first* Re-
coveries *from* Corruption. *Here is a* Flame *hath been*
sometimes extinguished: *Thoughts that have been* lost
15 *and* forgot, *but now they* break out *again like the* Pla-
tonic Reminiscencie. *I have not the Author's* Approbation *to the* Fact, *but I have* Law *on my* Side, *though*
never a Sword: *I hold it no man's* Præogative *to* fire
his own House. *Thou seest how* Saucie *I am* grown, *and*
20 *if thou doest expect I should* Commend *what is* published, *I must tell thee,* I crie no Sivill[3] Oranges. *I will*
not say, Here is Fine *or* Cheap: *that were an* Injurie *to*
the Verse *it selfe, and to the* Effects *it can* produce.
Read on, and thou wilt find thy Spirit ingag'd: *not by*
25 *the* Deserts *of what wee call* Tolerable, *but by the*
Commands *of a* Pen, *that is* Above it.

Upon the most Ingenious
pair of Twins, *Eugenius Philalethes,*[1]
and the *Authour* of these
Poems.

What *Planet* rul'd your *birth?* what *wittie star?*
That you so like in *Souls* as *Bodies* are!
So like in *both,* that you seem *born* to free
The *starrie art* from *vulgar* Calumnie.
5 My *doubts* are solv'd, from hence my *faith* begins,
Not only your *faces,* but your *wits* are *Twins.*

[3] I.e., Seville.
UPON THE MOST INGENIOUS PAIR OF TWINS. . . .
[1] Thomas Vaughan, twin brother of Henry.

When this bright *Gemini* shall from earth ascend,
They will *new light* to dull-ey'd mankind lend,
Teach the *Star-gazers*, and delight their *Eyes*,
10   Being fixt a *Constellation* in the Skyes.

T. Powell Oxoniensis.[2]

To my friend the Authour
upon these his *Poems*.

I Call'd it once my *sloth:* In such an age
So many *Volumes deep*, I not a *page?*
But I recant, and vow 'twas thriftie Care
That kept my *Pen* from spending on *slight ware*,
5   And breath'd it for a *Prize*, whose pow'rfull *shine*
Doth both *reward* the striver, and *refine*;
Such are thy *Poems*, friend: for since th'hast writ,
I cann't reply to any *name*, but *wit*;
And lest amidst the *throng* that make us *grone*,
10   Mine prove a groundless *Heresie* alone,
Thus I dispute, Hath there not rev'rence bin
Pay'd to the *Beard* at doore, for *Lord* within?
Who notes the *spindle-leg*, or *hollow eye*
Of the *thinne Usher*, the *faire Lady* by?
15   Thus I *sinne* freely, *neighbour* to a *hand*
Which while I aime to *strengthen*, gives *Command*
For my *protection*, and thou art to me
At once my *Subject* and *Securitie*.

I. Rowlandson Oxoniensis.[1]

---

[2] Thomas Powell (1608–60), fellow of Jesus College, Oxford, the friend who prepared this volume for the press. See title page. See also Hutchinson, *Life*, pp. 75 *et passim*.

TO MY FRIEND THE AUTHOUR. . . .

[1] Either James or John Rowlandson. Both names appear on the records of Queen's College, Oxford, between 1630 and 1640. See Chambers, *Poems*, II, 335.

Upon the following
Poems.

I Write not here, as if thy *last* in store
Of learned *friends*, 'tis known that thou hast *more*;
Who, were they told of this, would find a way
To rise a guard of *Poets* without *pay*,
5   And bring as many *hands* to thy *Edition*,
As th'*City* should unto their *May'rs* Petition,
But thou wouldst none of this, lest it should be
Thy *Muster* rather, than our *Courtesie*,
Thou wouldst not beg as *Knights* do, and appeare
10 Poet by *Voice*, and *suffrage* of the *Shire*,
That were enough to make thy *Muse* advance
Amongst the *Crutches*, nay it might enhance
Our *Charity*, and we should think it fit
The *State* should build an *Hospital* for wit.
15   But here needs no *reliefe:* Thy richer *Verse*
Creates all *Poets*, that can but *reherse*,
And they, like *Tenants* better'd by their *land*,
Should pay thee *Rent* for what they understand,
Thou art not of that *lamentable Nation*,
20 Who make a blessed *Alms* of *approbation*,
Whose *fardel-notes* are *Briefes* in ev'ry thing,
But, that they are not licens'd *By the King*.
Without such *scrape-requests* thou dost come forth
Arm'd (though I speak it) with thy *proper worth*,
25 And needest not this *noise* of friends, for wee
Write out of *love*, not thy *necessitie*;
And though this *sullen age* possessed be
With some strange *Desamour* to Poetrie,
Yet I suspect (thy fancy so delights)

30   The *Puritans* will turn thy *Proselytes,*
      And that thy *flame* when once abroad it *shines,*
      Will bring thee as many *friends,* as thou hast *lines.*

EUGENIUS PHILALETHES[1]
Oxoniensis.

Olor Iscanus.

[O–2]   To the River *Isca.*[1]

When *Daphne's* Lover[2] here first wore the *Bayes,*
Eurotas[3] secret streams heard all his *Layes.*
And holy *Orpheus,* Natures *busie* Child
By headlong *Hebrus* his deep *Hymns* Compil'd.
5 Soft *Petrarch* (thaw'd by *Laura's* flames) did weep
On *Tybers*[4] banks, when she (*proud fair!*) cou'd sleep;
Mosella boasts *Ausonius,*[5] and the *Thames*
Doth murmure *SIDNEYS Stella*[6] to her *streams,*
While *Severn* swoln with *Joy* and *sorrow,* wears
10 *Castara's*[7] smiles mixt with fair *Sabrin's*[8] tears.

UPON THE FOLLOWING POEMS.
  [1] Thomas Vaughan, Henry's twin brother.
TO THE RIVER ISCA.
  [1] The Usk in Brecon (Brecknock) on or near which Vaughan
spent the major part of his life and from which he took his title
Olor Iscanus. See O–44, below.
  [2] Apollo.
  [3] A river in Laconia, in the southern Peloponnesus.
  [4] Actually the Arno's, not the Tiber's.
  [5] A fourth-century Latin poet who celebrated the Moselle River.
  [6] The lady of Sir Philip Sidney's sonnet sequence *Astrophil and
Stella.*
  [7] Lucy, daughter of William Herbert, Lord Powys, and celebrated as Castara in the poetry of William Habington, who eventually married her.
  [8] *Sabrina* was the Roman name for the Severn. The name was
given by Geoffrey of Monmouth to an early British maiden who

Thus *Poets* (like the *Nymphs,* their *pleasing themes*)
Haunted the *bubling Springs* and *gliding streams,*
And *happy banks!* whence such *fair flowres* have sprung,
But happier those where they have *sate* and *sung!*

15 *Poets* (like *Angels*) where they once appear
Hallow the *place,* and each succeeding year
Adds *rev'rence* to't, such as at length doth give
This aged faith, *That there their Genii live.*
Hence th'*Auncients* say, That, from this *sickly aire*

20 They passe to *Regions* more *refin'd* and *faire,*
To *Meadows* strow'd with *Lillies* and the *Rose,*
And *shades* whose *youthfull green* no *old age* knowes,
Where all in *white* they walk, discourse, and Sing
Like Bees *soft murmurs,* or a *Chiding Spring.*

25 But *Isca,* whensoe'r those *shades* I see,
And thy *lov'd Arbours* must no more *know* me,
When I am layd to *rest* hard by thy *streams,*
And my *Sun sets,* where first it *sprang* in beams,
I'le leave behind me such a *large, kind light,*

30 As shall *redeem* thee from *oblivious night,*
And in these *vowes* which (living yet) I pay
Shed such a *Previous* and *Enduring Ray,*
As shall from age to age thy *fair name* lead
'Till *Rivers* leave to *run,* and *men* to *read.*

35 First, may all *Bards* born after me
(When I am *ashes*) sing of thee!
May thy *green banks* and *streams* (or none)
Be both their *Hill* and *Helicon;*
May *Vocall Groves* grow there, and all

40 The *shades* in them *Propheticall,*
Where (laid) men shall more *faire truths* see
Than *fictions* were of *Thessalie.*
May thy gentle *Swains* (like *flowres*)
Sweetly spend their *Youthfull houres,*

45 And thy *beauteous Nymphs* (like *Doves*)
Be *kind* and *faithfull* to their *Loves;*

---

by her death in the Severn became the guardian spirit of the river.
Cf. Milton, *Comus,* lines 824 ff., and Spenser, *Faerie Queene,* II, x,
17–19.

Garlands, and *Songs*, and *Roundelayes*,
Mild, dewie *nights*, and Sun-shine *dayes*,
The *Turtles voyce, Joy* without *fear*,
50   *Dwell* on thy *bosome* all the year!
May the *Evet*[9] and the *Tode*
Within thy Banks have no abode,
Nor the *wilie, winding Snake*
Her *voyage* through thy *waters* make.
55   In all thy *Journey* to the *Main*
No *nitrous Clay*, nor *Brimstone-vein*
Mixe with thy *streams*, but may they passe
Fresh as the *aire*, and cleer as *Glasse*,
And where the *wandring Chrystal* treads
60   *Roses* shall *kisse*, and *Couple* heads.
The *factour-wind*[10] from far shall bring
The *Odours* of the *Scatter'd* Spring,
And *loaden* with the rich *Arreare*,
Spend it in *Spicie whispers* there.
65   No *sullen heats*, nor *flames* that are
Offensive, and *Canicular*,[11]
Shine on thy *Sands*, nor *pry* to see
Thy *Scalie, shading familie*,
But *Noones* as mild as *Hesper's* rayes,
70   Or the first *blushes* of fair *dayes*.
What *gifts* more *Heav'n* or *Earth* can adde
With all those *blessings* be thou *Clad!*
    Honour, Beautie,
    Faith and *Dutie,*
75   *Delight* and *Truth,*
        With *Love,* and *Youth*
Crown all about thee! And what ever *Fate*
Impose else-where, whether the graver state,
Or some toy else, may those *lowd, anxious Cares*
80 For *dead* and *dying things* (the Common *Wares*
And *showes* of time) ne'r break thy *Peace*, nor make
Thy *repos'd Armes* to a new warre *awake!*

[9] A salamander. See OED under "Newt."
[10] Factor in the sense of mercantile agent.
[11] Related to the rising of the Dog Star, Sirius, or the dog days.

But *Freedome, safety, Joy* and *blisse*
United in one loving *kisse*
85   *Surround* thee quite, and *stile* thy borders
The Land redeem'd from all disorders!

[O–3]   The Charnel-house.

Blesse me! what damps are here? how stiffe an aire?
Kelder[1] of mists, a second *Fiats*[2] care,
Frontspeece o'th' grave and darkness, a Display
Of ruin'd man, and the disease of day;
5 Leane, bloudless shamble, where I can descrie
Fragments of men, Rags of Anatomie;
Corruptions ward-robe, the transplantive bed
Of mankind, and th'Exchequer of the dead.
How thou arrests my sense? how with the sight
10 My *Winter'd* bloud growes stiffe to all delight?
Torpedo[3] to the Eye! whose least glance can
Freeze our wild lusts, and rescue head-long man;
Eloquent silence! able to Immure
An *Atheists* thoughts, and blast an *Epicure.*
15 Were I a *Lucian,* Nature in this dresse
Would make me wish a Saviour, and Confesse.
Where are you shoreless thoughts, vast tenter'd hope,
Ambitious dreams, *Aymes* of an Endless scope,
Whose stretch'd Excesse runs on a string too high
20 And on the rack of self-extension dye?
Chameleons[4] of state, Aire-monging band,
Whose breath (like Gun-powder) blowes up a land,

THE CHARNEL-HOUSE.

[1] Womb, from the Dutch (OED).

[2] A reference to the *Fiat lux* (Let there be light) of Gen. 1.3.

[3] A flat fish, or ray, that stuns or numbs by means of electrical charges.

[4] Noted not only for changing color but also for living on air, hence visionary or irrationally aspiring.

Come see your dissolution, and weigh
What a loath'd nothing you shall be one day,
25 As th' Elements by Circulation passe
From one to th'other, and that which first was
Is so again, so 'tis with you; The grave
And Nature but Complott, what the one gave,
The other takes; Think then, that in this bed
30 There sleep the Reliques of as proud a head
As stern and subtill as your own, that hath
Perform'd, or forc'd as much, whose tempest-wrath
Hath levell'd Kings with slaves, and wisely then
Calme these high furies, and descend to men;
35 Thus *Cyrus* tam'd the *Macedon*,[5] a tombe
Checkt him, who thought the world too straight a Room.[6]
    Have I obey'd the *Powers* of a face,
A beauty able to undoe the Race
Of easie man? I look but here, and strait
40 I am Inform'd, the lovely Counterfeit
Was but a smoother Clay. That famish'd slave
Begger'd by wealth, who starves that he may save,
Brings hither but his sheet; Nay, th'*Ostrich-man*[7]
That feeds on *steele* and *bullet*, he that can
45 Outswear his *Lordship*, and reply as tough
To a kind word, as if his tongue were *Buffe*,[8]
Is *Chap*-faln here, wormes without wit, or fear
Defie him now, death hath disarm'd the *Bear*.
Thus could I run o'r all the pitteous score
50 Of erring men, and having done meet more,
Their shuffled *Wills*, abortive, vain *Intents*,
Phantastick *humours*, perillous *Ascents*,
False, empty *honours*, traiterous *delights*,
And whatsoe'r a blind Conceit Invites;

[5] Alexander, who was depressed by thoughts of mortality on see-ing the epitaph on the tomb of Cyrus. See Plutarch, *Lives* (*Alexander*, lxix), Loeb Library, VII, 417.

[6] Cf. Vaughan's translation of Juvenal's Tenth Satire, lines 288–90 (P–14).

[7] The soldier, whose diet, like the ostrich's, included metals.

[8] A rough leather of which soldiers' jackets were made.

55 But these and more which the weak vermins swell,
   Are Couch'd in this Accumulative Cell
   Which I could scatter; But the grudging Sun
   Calls home his beams, and warns me to be gone,
   Day leaves me in a double night, and I
60 Must bid farewell to my sad library.
   Yet with these notes. Henceforth with thought of thee
   I'le season all succeeding Jollitie,
   Yet damn not mirth, nor think too much is fit,
   Excesse hath no *Religion*, nor *Wit*,
65 But should wild bloud swell to a lawless strain
   One Check from thee shall *Channel* it again.

[O–4]   *In Amicum fœneratorem.*[1]

   Thanks mighty *Silver*! I rejoyce to see
   How I have spoyl'd his thrift, by spending thee.
   Now thou art gone, he courts my wants with more,
   His *Decoy* gold, and bribes me to restore.
5   As lesser lode-stones with the *North* consent
   Naturally moving to their Element,
   As bodyes swarm to th' Center, and that fire
   Man stole from heaven, to heav'n doth still aspire,
   So this vast crying summe drawes in a lesse,
10 And hence this bag more Northward layd I guesse,
   For 'tis of *Pole-star* force, and in this sphere
   Though th'least of many rules the master-bear.
   Prerogative of debts! how he doth dresse
   His messages in *Chink*? not an Expresse
15 Without a fee for reading, and 'tis fit,
   For gold's the best restorative of wit,
   O how he gilds them o'r! with what delight
   I read those lines, where Angels[2] doe Indite?

IN AMICUM FŒNERATOREM.
   [1] "On a friend, a moneylender."
   [2] An angel was a coin as well as a spiritual being.

But wilt have money *Og*[3]? must I dispurse?
20   Will nothing serve thee but a *Poets* curse?
Wilt rob an Altar thus? and sweep at once
What *Orpheus*-like I forc'd from stocks and stones?
'Twill never swell thy *Bag*, nor ring one peale
In thy dark *Chest*. Talk not of *Shreeves*,[4] or gaole,
25   I fear them not. I have no land to glutt
Thy durty appetite, and make thee strutt
Nimrod[5] of acres; I'le no Speech prepare
To court the *Hopefull Cormorant*, thine heire.
Yet there's a Kingdome, at thy beck, if thou
30   But kick this drosse, *Parnassus* flowrie brow
I'le give thee with my *Tempe*, and to boot
That horse which struck a fountain with his foot.[6]
A Bed of Roses I'le provide for thee,
And Chrystal Springs shall drop thee melodie;
35   The breathing shades wee'l haunt, where ev'ry leafe
Shall *Whisper* us asleep, though thou art deafe;
Those waggish *Nymphs* too which none ever yet
Durst make love to, wee'l teach the Loving fit,
Wee'l suck the *Corall* of their lips, and feed
40   Upon their spicie breath, a meale at need,
Rove in their *Amber-tresses*, and unfold
That glist'ring grove, the Curled wood of gold,
Then peep for babies,[7] a new Puppet-play,
And riddle what their *pratling Eyes* would say.
45   But here thou must remember to dispurse,
For without money all this is a Curse,
Thou must for more bags call, and so restore
This Iron-age to gold, as once before;

[3] A name of reproach, deriving from Og, king of Bashan and the last of the remnant of giants, who was delivered into the hands of the Israelites. See Deut. 3.1–11, and Ps. 136.20.

[4] Obsolete form of sheriff (OED).

[5] The mighty hunter of Gen. 10.8–9, who became a symbol of tyranny and proud ambition.

[6] The winged horse Pegasus of Greek mythology who created the fountain Hippocrene by striking Mount Helicon with his hoof.

[7] To engage in amorous eye-play.

This thou must doe, and yet this is not all,
50   For thus the Poet would be still in thrall,
Thou must then (if live thus) my neast of honey,
Cancell old bonds, and beg to lend more money.

[O–5]   To his friend——.[1]

I Wonder, *James*, through the whole Historie
Of ages, such *Entailes* of povertie
Are layd on Poets; Lawyers (they say) have found
A trick to cut them, would they were but bound
5   To practise on us, though for this thing wee
Should pay (if possible) their bribes and fee.
Search (as thou canst) the old and moderne store
Of *Rome* and ours, in all the wittie score
Thou shalt not find a rich one; Take each Clime
10   And run o'r all the pilgrimage of time
Thou'lt meet them poor, and ev'ry where descrie
A thredbare, goldless genealogie.
Nature (it seems) when she meant us for Earth
Spent so much of her treasure in the birth
15   As ever after niggards her, and Shee,
Thus stor'd within, beggers us outwardly.
Wofull profusion! at how dear a rate
Are wee made up? all hope of thrift and state
Lost for a verse: When I by thoughts look back
20   Into the wombe of time, and see the Rack
Stand useless there, untill we are produc'd
Unto the torture, and our soules infus'd
To learn afflictions, I begin to doubt
That as some tyrants use from their chain'd rout
25   Of slaves to pick out one whom for their sport
They keep afflicted by some lingring art,

TO HIS FRIEND——.
    [1] The "friend" has not been identified positively, but the
"*James*" of the first line has led some critics to conjecture James
Howell.

So wee are meerly thrown upon the stage
The mirth of fooles, and Legend of the age.
When I see in the ruines of a sute
30 Some nobler brest, and his tongue sadly mute
Feed on the *Vocall silence* of his Eye,
And knowing cannot reach the remedie,
When soules of baser stamp shine in their store,
And he of all the throng is only poore,
35 When *French* apes for forraign fashions pay,
And *English* legs are drest th'outlandish way,
So fine too, that they their own shadows wooe,
While he walks in the *sad* and *Pilgrim-shooe*,
I'm mad at Fate, and angry ev'n to sinne,
40 To see deserts and learning clad so thinne:
To think how th'earthly Usurer can brood
Upon his bags, and weigh the pretious food
With palsied hands, as if his soul did feare
The Scales could rob him of what he layd there;
45 Like Divels that on hid Treasures sit, or those
Whose jealous Eyes trust not beyond their nose
They guard the durt, and the bright Idol hold
Close, and Commit adultery with gold.
A Curse upon their drosse! how have we sued
50 For a few scatter'd *Chips?* how oft pursu'd
Petitions with a blush, in hope to squeeze
For their souls health, more than our wants a peece?
Their steel-rib'd Chests and Purse (rust eat them both!)
Have cost us with much paper many an oath,
55 And Protestations of such solemn sense,
As if our soules were sureties for the Pence.
Should we a full nights learned cares present,
They'l scarce return us one short houres Content,
'Las! they're but quibbles, things we Poets feign,
60 The short-liv'd Squibs and Crackers of the brain.
    But wee'l be wiser, knowing 'tis not they
That must redeem the hardship of our way,
Whether a Higher Power, or that starre
Which neerest heav'n, is from the earth most far[2]

2 Saturn.

65 Oppresse us thus, or angel'd from that Sphere
   By our strict Guardians are kept luckless here,
   It matters not, wee shall one day obtain
   Our native and Celestiall scope again.

[O–6]   To his retired friend,[1] an Invitation
                    to *Brecknock.*

   Since last wee met, thou and thy horse (my dear,)
   Have not so much as drunk, or litter'd here,
   I wonder, though thy self be thus deceast,
   Thou hast the spite to Coffin up thy beast;
 5 Or is the *Palfrey* sick, and his rough hide
   With the penance of *One Spur* mortifide?
   Or taught by thee (like *Pythagoras's Oxe*)[2]
   Is then his master grown more *Orthodox?*
   What ever 'tis, a sober cause't must be
10 That thus long bars us of thy Companie.
   The Town believes thee lost, and didst thou see
   But half her suffrings, now distrest for thee,
   Thou'ldst swear (like *Rome*) her foule, polluted walls
   Were sackt by *Brennus*, and the salvage *Gaules*.[3]
15 Abominable face of things! here's noise
   Of bang'd Mortars, blew Aprons,[4] and Boyes,
   Pigs, Dogs, and Drums, with the hoarse hellish notes
   Of politickly-deafe Usurers throats,
   With new fine *Worships*, and the old cast *teame*
20 Of Justices vext with the *Cough*, and *flegme.*

TO HIS RETIRED FRIEND, . . .

   [1] Unidentified. Brecknock, or Brecon, was not far from Newton,
where Vaughan presumably was living at this time.
   [2] Martin (*Works*, 1957, p. 706) cites Iamblichus' *De Vita
Pythagorae*, 13. 61, where Pythagoras is said to have persuaded an
ox to stop eating beans in a field.
   [3] During the civil wars the inhabitants had pulled down the
town walls in order to make Brecon an open city.
   [4] The marks of tradesmen (Martin, *Works*, 1957, p. 706).

Midst these the *Crosse* looks sad, and in the *Shire-*
-Hall furs of an old *Saxon Fox* appear,[5]
With brotherly Ruffs and Beards, and a strange sight
Of high Monumentall Hats ta'ne at the fight
25 Of *Eighty eight*;[6] while ev'ry *Burgesse* foots
The mortall *Pavement* in eternall boots.
    Hadst thou been batc'lour, I had soon divin'd
Thy Close retirements, and Monastick mind,
Perhaps some Nymph had been to visit, or
30 The beauteous Churle was to be waited for,
And like the *Greek*,[7] e'r you the sport would misse
You stai'd, and stroak'd the *Distaffe* for a kisse.
But in this age, when thy coole, settled bloud
Is ty'd t'one flesh, and thou almost grown good,
35 I know not how to reach the strange device,
Except (*Domitian* like)[8] thou murther'st flyes;
Or is't thy pietie? for who can tell
But thou may'st prove devout, and love a Cell,
And (like a Badger) with attentive looks
40 In the dark hole sit rooting up of books.
Quick Hermit! what a peacefull Change hadst thou
Without the noise of *haire-cloth*, *Whip*, or *Vow*?
But is there no redemption? must there be
No other penance but of liberty?
45 Why two months hence, if thou continue thus
Thy memory will scarce remain with us,
The Drawers have forgot thee, and exclaim
They have not seen thee here since *Charles* his raign,[9]

[5] Hutchinson (*Life*, p. 83) suggests Walter Rumsey as the justice "vext with the *Cough*, and *flegme*," and one Eltonhead as the "old *Saxon Fox*."

[6] Presumably the defeat of the Spanish Armada in 1588, but the connection with the tall hats is unclear.

[7] Hercules, during his subserviency to Omphale.

[8] Suetonius (*Domitian*, 3) notes that Domitian spent part of his day catching flies and piercing them with pins.

[9] This line is cited by Hutchinson (*Life*, p. 83) who dates the poem after the execution—in January 1649—of Charles I, probably in March (see below, lines 73–75) at the time of the Great Sessions.

Or if they mention thee, like some old man
50 That at each word inserts—Sir, *as I can*
Remember—So the *Cyph'rers* puzzle mee
With a dark, cloudie character of thee.
That (certs!) I fear thou wilt be lost, and wee
Must ask the *Fathers* e'r 't be long for thee.
55 Come! leave this sullen state, and let not Wine
And precious Witt lye dead for want of thine,
Shall the dull *Market-land-lord* with his *Rout*
Of sneaking Tenants durtily swill out
This harmlesse liquor? shall they knock and beat
60 For Sack, only to talk of *Rye*, and *Wheat?*
O let not such prepost'rous tipling be
In our *Metropolis*, may I ne'r see
Such *Tavern-sacrilege*, nor lend a line
To weep the *Rapes* and *Tragedy* of wine!
65 Here lives that *Chimick*, quick fire which betrayes
Fresh Spirits to the bloud, and warms our layes,
I have reserv'd 'gainst thy approach a Cup
That were thy Muse stark dead, shall raise her up,
And teach her yet more Charming words and skill
70 Than ever *Cœlia, Chloris, Astrophil,*
Or any of the Thredbare names Inspir'd
Poore riming lovers with a *Mistris* fir'd.
Come then! and while the slow Isicle hangs
At the stiffe thatch, and Winters frosty pangs
75 Benumme the year, blith (as of old) let us
'Midst noise and War, of Peace, and mirth discusse.
This portion thou wert born for: why should wee
Vex at the times ridiculous miserie?
An age that thus hath fool'd it selfe, and will
80 (Spite of thy teeth and mine) persist so still.
Let's sit then at this *fire*, and while wee steal
A Revell in the Town, let others seal,
Purchase or Cheat, and who can, let them pay,
Till those black deeds bring on the darksome day;

For reservations about this dating, see Marilla, *Secular Poems*,
pp. 189–90.

85 Innocent spenders wee! a better use
   Shall wear out our short Lease, and leave th'obtuse
   Rout to their *husks*; They and their bags at best
   Have cares in *earnest*, wee care for a *Jest*.

[O–7]   *Monsieur Gombauld.*[1]

I 'ave read thy Souls fair night-peece, and have seen
Th'*Amours* and Courtship of the *silent Queen*,
Her stoln descents to Earth, and what did move her
To Juggle first with *Heav'n*, then with a *Lover*,
5 With *Latmos* lowder rescue, and (alas!)
To find her out a *Hue and Crie* in Brasse,[2]
Thy Journall of deep Mysteries, and sad
Nocturnall Pilgrimage, with thy dreams clad
In fancies darker than thy *Cave*, Thy *Glasse*
10 Of sleepie draughts, and as thy soul did passe
In her calm voyage what discourse she heard
Of Spirits, what dark Groves and ill-shap'd guard
Ismena[3] lead thee through, with thy proud flight
O'r *Periardes*,[4] and deep, musing night
15 Neere fair *Eurotas* banks, what solemn *green*
The neighbour shades weare, and what forms are seen

MONSIEUR GOMBAULD.

[1] Jean Ogier de Gombauld (1570?–1666), French poet, who
wrote a prose romance, *L'Endimion* (Paris, 1624), translated into
English by Richard Hurst and published by Samuel Browne (London, 1639).

[2] A reference to the action of the inhabitants about Mount
Latmos, who awoke Endymion and frightened Diana back to her
proper orbit by making noises on instruments of copper and brass.

[3] In the Gombauld story, the protectress of Endymion in his
quest for Diana.

[4] A mountain in Greater Armenia, the source of the Euphrates,
over which Endymion passes.

In their large Bowers, with that sad path and seat
Which none but light-heel'd *Nymphs* and *Fairies* beat;
Their solitary life, and how exempt
20 From Common frailtie, the severe contempt
They have of Man, their priviledge to live
A *Tree*, or *Fountain*, and in that *Reprieve*
What ages they consume, with the sad *Vale*
Of *Diophania*, and the mournfull tale,
25 Of th' bleeding vocall *Myrtle*;[5] These and more
Thy richer thoughts we are upon the score
To thy rare fancy for, nor doest thou fall
From thy first Majesty, or ought at all
Betray Consumption, thy full vig'rous *Bayes*
30 Wear the same *green*, and scorn the lene decayes
Of *stile*, or *matter*; Just so have I known
Some *Chrystal* spring, that from the neighbour down
Deriv'd her birth, in gentle murmurs steal
To their next Vale, and proudly there reveal
35 Her streams in lowder accents, adding still
More noise and waters to her Channell, till
At last swoln with Increase she glides along
The Lawnes and Meadows in a wanton throng
Of frothy billows, and in one great name
40 Swallows the tributary brooks drown'd fame.
    Nor are they meere Inventions, for we
In th' same peece find scatter'd *Philosophie*
And hidden, disperst truths that folded lye
In the dark shades of deep *Allegorie*,
45 So neatly weav'd, like *Arras*, they descrie
Fables with *Truth*, *Fancy* with *Historie*.
So that thou hast in this thy curious mould
Cast that commended mixture wish'd of old,[6]

[5] Endymion cuts a sprig from a myrtle, which then bleeds and moans, finally revealing the presence of one Diophania, a beautiful girl unhappy in love, who had taken refuge in the myrtle to avoid marrying a loathsome suitor chosen for her by her father.

[6] Martin (*Works*, 1957, p. 707) suggests the Horatian formula, "*utile dulci*," as the "commended mixture."

Which shall these Contemplations render far
50 Lesse mutable, and lasting as their star,
And while there is a *People*, or a *Sunne*,
Endymions storie with the *Moon* shall runne.

[O–8] An Elegie on the death of Mr. *R. W.*[1] slain in the late unfortunate differences at *Routon* Heath, neer *Chester*, 1645.

I Am Confirm'd, and so much wing is given
To my wild thoughts, that they dare strike at heav'n.
A full years griefe I struggled with, and stood
Still on my sandy hopes uncertain good,
5 So loth was I to yeeld, to all those fears
I still oppos'd thee, and denyed my tears.
But thou art gone! and the untimely losse
Like that one day, hath made all others Crosse.
Have you seen on some Rivers flowrie brow
10 A well-built *Elme*, or stately *Cedar* grow,
Whose Curled tops gilt with the Morning-ray
Becken'd the Sun, and whisperd to the day,
When unexpected from the angry *North*
A fatall sullen whirle-wind sallies forth,
15 And with a full-mouth'd blast rends from the ground
The *Shady twins*, which rushing scatter round
Their sighing leafes, whilst overborn with strength,
Their trembling heads bow to a prostrate length;
So forc'd fell he; So Immaturely Death
20 Stifled his able heart and active breath.
The world scarce knew him yet, his early Soule
Had but new-broke her day, and rather stole

AN ELEGIE ON THE DEATH OF MR. R.W. . . .
  [1] Perhaps, but not positively, the same as the subject of "To my Ingenuous Friend, *R.W.*," (P–1). The battle of Rowton Heath, a Royalist defeat, was fought on 24 September 1645. See S. R. Gardiner, *The History of the Great Civil War* (London, 1894), II, 344–45.

A sight, than gave one; as if subt'ly she
Would learn our stock, but hide his treasurie.
25 His years (should time lay both his *Wings* and *glasse*
Unto his charge) could not be summ'd (alas!)
To a full *score*; Though in so short a span
His riper thoughts had purchas'd more of man
Than all those worthless livers, which yet quick,
30 Have quite outgone their own *Arithmetick*.
He seiz'd perfections, and without a dull
And mossie *gray* possess'd a solid skull,
No Crooked knowledge neither, nor did he
Wear the friends name for Ends and policie,
35 And then lay't by; As those *lost Youths* of th'stage
Who only flourish'd for the *Play's* short age
And then retir'd, like *Jewels* in each part
He wore his friends, but chiefly at his heart.
   Nor was it only in this he did excell,
40 His equall valour could as much, as well.
He knew no *fear* but of his *God*; yet durst
No injurie, nor (as some have) e'r purs't
The sweat and tears of others, yet would be
More forward in a royall gallantrie
45 Than all those vast pretenders, which of late
Swell'd in the ruines of their King and State.
He weav'd not *Self-ends*, and the *Publick* good
Into one piece, nor with the peoples bloud
Fill'd his own veins; In all the doubtfull way
50 *Conscience* and *Honour* rul'd him. O that day
When like the *Fathers* in the *Fire* and *Cloud*
I mist thy face! I might in ev'ry *Crowd*
See Armes like thine, and men advance, but none
So neer to lightning mov'd, nor so fell on.[2]
55 Have you observ'd how soon the nimble *Eye*
Brings th' *Object* to *Conceit*, and doth so vie
Performance with the *Soul*, that you would swear
The *Act* and *apprehension* both lodg'd there,

[2] These and some lines which follow have been taken to indicate Vaughan's active participation in the battle or his presence in the vicinity.

Just so mov'd he: like *shott* his active hand
60 Drew bloud, e'r well the foe could understand.
But here I lost him. Whether the last turn
Of thy few sands call'd on thy hastie urn,
Or some fierce rapid fate (hid from the Eye)
Hath hurl'd thee Pris'ner to some distant skye
65 I cannot tell, but that I doe believe
Thy Courage such as scorn'd a base Reprieve.
What ever 'twas, whether that day thy breath
Suffer'd a *Civill* or the *Common* death,
Which I doe most suspect, and that I have
70 Fail'd in the *glories* of so known a grave,
Though thy lov'd ashes misse me, and mine Eyes
Had no acquaintance with thy Exequies,
Nor at the last farewell, torn from thy sight
On the *Cold sheet* have fix'd a *sad delight*,
75 Yet what e'r pious hand (in stead of mine)
Hath done this office to that dust of thine,
And till thou rise again from thy low bed
Lent a Cheap pillow to thy quiet head,
Though but a private *turffe*, it can do more
80 To keep thy name and memory in store
Than all those *Lordly fooles* which lock their bones
In the dumb piles of Chested brasse, and stones.
Th'art rich in thy own fame, and needest not
These *Marble-frailties*, nor the *gilded blot*
85 Of posthume honours; There is not one sand
Sleeps o'r thy grave, but can outbid that hand
And pencill too, so that of force wee must
Confesse their *heaps* shew lesser than thy *dust*.
       And (blessed soule!) though this my sorrow can
90 Adde nought to thy perfections, yet as man
Subject to Envy, and the common fate
It may redeem thee to a fairer date;
As some blind Dial, when the day is done,
Can tell us at mid-night, *There was a Sun*,
95 So these perhaps, though much beneath thy fame,
May keep some weak remembrance of thy name,

And to the faith of better times Commend
Thy loyall upright life, and gallant End.

100   *Nomen & arma locum servant, te, amice, nequivi*
        Conspicere,——[3]

[O–9]   Upon a Cloke lent him by
                  Mr. *J. Ridsley*.[1]

Here, take again thy *Sack-cloth*! and thank heav'n
Thy Courtship[2] hath not kill'd me; Is't not Even
Whether wee dye by peecemeale, or at once
Since both but ruine, why then for the nonce
5 Didst husband my afflictions, and cast o're
Me this forc'd *Hurdle*[3] to inflame the score?
Had I neer *London* in this *Rug* been seen
Without doubt I had executed been
For some bold *Irish* spy, and crosse a sledge
10 Had layn mess'd up for their *foure gates* and *bridge*.[4]
When first I bore it, my oppressed feet
Would needs perswade me, 'twas some *Leaden sheet*;
Such deep Impressions, and such dangerous holes
Were made, that I began to doubt my soals,
15 And ev'ry step (so neer necessity)
Devoutly wish'd some honest Cobler by,
Besides it was so short, the *Jewish* rag
Seem'd Circumcis'd, but had a *Gentile* shag.[5]

[3] From Virgil, *Aeneid*, VI, 507–8: "Your name and arms watch
over the place; you, my friend, I could not descry. . . ."
UPON A CLOKE LENT HIM BY MR. J. RIDSLEY.
   [1] Unidentified.
   [2] Courteous behavior; courtesy (OED).
   [3] A frame of wicker work and/or wire, but also meaning a sledge
on which traitors were drawn to execution (see line 9, below).
   [4] Cut into portions for distribution to the traditional four gates
of the city walls and London Bridge.
   [5] The long, uncut or untrimmed nap of the coarse cloth.

Hadst thou been with me on that day, when wee
20 Left craggie *Biston*,[6] and the fatall *Dee*,
When beaten with fresh storms, and late mishap
It shar'd the office of a *Cloke*, and *Cap*,
To see how 'bout my clouded head it stood
Like a thick *Turband*, or some Lawyers *Hood*,
25 While the stiffe, hollow pletes on ev'ry side
Like *Conduit-pipes* rain'd from the *Bearded hide*,
I know thou wouldst in spite of that day's fate
Let loose thy mirth at my new shape and state,
And with a shallow smile or two professe
30 Some *Sarazin* had lost the *Clowted Dresse*.
Didst ever see the *good wife* (as they say)
March in her short cloke on the *Christning* day,
With what soft motions she salutes the Church,
And leaves the Bedrid Mother in the lurch;
35 Just so Jogg'd I, while my dull horse did trudge
Like a Circuit-beast plagu'd with a goutie Judge.
  But this was Civill. I have since known more
And worser pranks: One night (as heretofore
Th' hast known) for want of change (a thing which I
40 And *Bias*[7] us'd before me) I did lye
Pure *Adamite*,[8] and simply for that end
Resolv'd, and made this for my bosome-*friend*.
O that thou hadst been there next morn, that I
Might teach thee new *Micro-cosmo-graphie*![9]
45 Thou wouldst have ta'ne me, as I naked stood,
For one of th' *seven pillars* before the floud,[10]

[6] Beeston Castle, one of the outposts of Chester, which the Royalists surrendered and evacuated on 16 November 1645. See Hutchinson, *Life*, p. 65.

[7] One of the Seven Wise Men of Greece, born about 570 B.C. at Priene in Ionia. When the town was under attack and all citizens were preparing to flee with their possessions, he was urged to do the same, but he is said to have replied that he carried all his possessions with him. See Cicero, *Paradoxa*, i.

[8] Naked.

[9] Referring to the maplike lines in miniature over his body.

[10] As Martin (*Works*, 1957, p. 708) suggests, this line may represent a fusion of the seven pillars of wisdom mentioned in Prov.

Such *Characters* and *Hierogliphicks* were
In one night worn, that thou mightst justly swear
I'd slept in *Cere-cloth*,[11] or at *Bedlam* where
50 The mad men lodge in straw, I'le not forbear
To tell thee all, his wild *Impress* and *tricks*
Like *Speeds* old *Britans* made me look, or *Picts*;[12]
His villanous, biting, *Wire-embraces*
Had seal'd in me more strange formes and faces
55 Than *Children* see in dreams, or thou hast read
In *Arras*, *Puppet-playes*, and *Ginger-bread*,
With *angled Schemes*, and *Crosses* that bred fear
Of being handled by some *Conjurer*,
And neerer thou wouldst think (such *strokes* were drawn)
60 I'd been some rough statue of *Fetter-lane*,[13]
Nay, I believe, had I that instant been
By *Surgeons* or *Apothecaries* seen,
They had Condemned my raz'd skin to be
Some walking *Herball*, or *Anatomie*.
65   But (thanks to th'day!) 'tis off. I'd now advise

9.1 and the two pillars, one of stone and one of brick, set up by the descendants of Seth to preserve their astronomical discoveries from the flood prophesied by Adam. See Josephus, *Jewish Antiquities*, I, ii, 3, Loeb Library, IV, 33.

[11] Cloth smeared or impregnated with wax or some glutinous matter, used as a winding sheet (OED).

[12] John Speed's *History of Great Britaine*, in the editions of 1611 and later, contained portraits of the early Britons nude, covered entirely with tattoo work and paintings. Speed also notes (p. 181) that the Picts were so called because they painted their bodies.

[13] According to Stow (*Survey of London*, 1603, p. 375) Fetter Lane ran off Fleet Street by the east end of St. Dunstan's in the West. Martin (*Works*, 1957, p. 708) notes that an Edward Marshall (1578–1675), master mason and stonecutter, resided in Fetter Lane, and the DNB reports him a noted maker of tombs. The figures which usually adorned such monuments may explain the "rough statue" of this line. It is also interesting, in the light of line 64, below, that John Gerard (1545–1612), the famous herbalist, also seems to have lived in Fetter Lane. See Norman G. Brett-James, *The Growth of Stuart London* (London, 1935), p. 445.

Thee friend to put this peece to Merchandize;
The *Pedlars* of our age have business yet,
And gladly would against the *Fayr-day* fit
Themselves with such a *Roofe*, that can secure
70 Their *Wares* from *Dogs and Cats* rain'd in showre,
It shall performe; or if this will not doe
'Twill take the *Ale-wives* sure; 'Twill make them *two*
Fine Roomes of *One*, and spread upon a stick
Is a partition without Lime or Brick.
75 *Horn'd* obstinacie! how my heart doth fret
To think what *Mouthes* and *Elbowes* it would set
In a wet day? have you for two pence e're
Seen King *Harryes*[14] Chappell at *Westminster*,
Where in their dustie gowns of *Brasse* and *Stone*
80 The Judges lye, and markt you how each one
In sturdie Marble-plets about the knee
Bears up to shew his legs and symmetrie?
Just so would this; That I think't weav'd upon
Some stiffneckt *Brownists*[15] exercising loome.
85 O that thou hadst it when this Jugling fate
Of Souldierie first seiz'd me! at what rate
Would I have bought it then, what was there but
I would have gi'n for the *Compendious hutt*?
I doe not doubt but (if the weight could please,)
90 'Twould guard me better than a *Lapland-lease*,
Or a *German* shirt with Inchanted lint
Stuff'd through, and th'devils *beard* and *face* weav'd
in't.[16]
But I have done. And think not, friend, that I
This freedome took to Jeere thy Courtesie,
95 I thank thee for't, and I believe my Muse
So known to thee, thou'lt not suspect abuse;
She did this, 'cause (perhaps) thy *love* paid thus
Might with my *thanks* out-live thy *Cloke*, and *Us*.

[14] Henry VII.
[15] Followers of Robert Browne (1550?–1633?), a radical Puritan.
[16] The specific meanings of terms in these lines are uncertain,
but they carry the general implication of magical protective powers.

[O–10]   Upon Mr. *Fletchers* Playes,
                    published, 1647.[1]

I Knew thee not, nor durst *attendance* strive
Labell to *wit*, *Verser remonstrative*,
And in some *Suburb-page* (scandal to thine)
Like *Lent* before a *Christmasse* scatter mine.
5 This speaks thee not, since at the utmost rate
Such *remnants* from thy *peece* Intreat their date;
Nor can I *dub* the *Coppy*, or afford
Titles to *swell* the *reare* of *Verse* with Lord,
Nor politickly big to *Inch* low fame
10 Stretch in the *glories* of a strangers name,
And Clip those *Bayes* I Court, weak *striver* I,
But a faint *Echo* unto *Poetrie*.
I have not *Clothes* t'adopt me, nor must sit
For *Plush* and *Velvets* sake *Esquire* of wit,
15 Yet *Modestie* these *Crosses* would improve,
And *Rags* neer thee, some *Reverence* may move.
    I did believe (great *Beaumont* being dead,)
Thy *Widow'd Muse* slept on his *flowrie bed*;
But I am *richly* Cosen'd, and can see
20 Wit *transmigrates*, his *Spirit* stayd with thee,
Which *doubly* advantag'd by thy *single* pen
In *life* and *death* now treads the *Stage* agen;
And thus are wee freed from that *dearth* of wit
Which *starv'd* the Land since into *Schismes* split,
25 Wherein th'hast done so much, wee must needs guesse
Wits last *Edition* is now i'th' *Presse*,
For thou hast *drain'd* Invention, and he
That writes hereafter, doth but *pillage* thee.

UPON MR. FLETCHERS PLAYES, PUBLISHED, 1647.
    [1] The first folio edition of *Comedies and Tragedies written by
Francis Beaumont and John Fletcher Gentlemen. Never printed
before, and now published by the Authours Originall Copies*
(London, 1647). Fletcher had died in 1625.

But thou hast *plotts*; and will not the *Kirk* strain
30 At the *Designes* of such a *Tragick brain?*
Will they themselves think safe, when they shall see
Thy most *abominable policie?*
Will not the *Eares*[2] assemble, and think't fit
Their *Synod fast*, and *pray*, against thy wit?
35 But they'le not *tyre* in such an *idle Quest*,
Thou doest but *kill*, and *Circumvent* in *Jest*,
And when thy anger'd Muse *swells* to a blow
'Tis but for *Field*'s, or *Swansteed*'s overthrow.[3]
Yet shall these *Conquests* of thy *Bayes* outlive
40 Their *Scotish zeale*, and *Compacts* made to grieve
The *Peace* of *Spirits*, and when such deeds fayle
Of their foule Ends, a *faire name* is thy *Bayle*.
    But (happy thou!) ne'r saw'st these *stormes*, our *aire*
Teem'd with even in thy time, though *seeming faire*;
45 Thy gentle *Soule* meant for the *shade*, and *ease*
Withdrew betimes into the *Land* of *Peace*;
So *neasted* in some Hospitable shore
The *Hermit-angler*, when the *mid-Seas* roare
Packs up his *lines*, and (ere the tempest *raves*,)
50 Retyres, and leaves his *station* to the *waves*.
Thus thou diedst almost with our *peace*, and wee
This *breathing time* thy last fair *Issue* see,
Which I think such (if *needless Ink* not soyle
So *Choice a Muse*,) others are but thy *foile*;
55 This, or that *age* may write, but never see
A *Wit* that dares run *Paralell* with thee.
True, *B E N*[4] must live! but bate *him*, and thou hast
Undone all *future wits*, and match'd the *past*.

[2] The Puritans.
[3] Usually identified with Nathan Field and Eliard (or Eyllaerdt)
Swanston, two prominent actors of the early seventeenth century.
Marilla (*Secular Poems*, p. 219) suggests a confusion of Swanston
with another actor's name, William Barsted (Barstead), to form
the "*Swansteed*."
[4] Ben Jonson.

[O–11] Upon the *Poems* and *Playes* of the ever memorable Mr. *William Cartwright*.[1]

I Did but *see* thee! and how *vain* it is
To *vex* thee for it with *Remonstrances*,[2]
Though *things* in fashion, let those *Judge*, who sit
Their *twelve-pence* out, to *clap* their *hands* at *wit*;
5 I fear to *Sinne* thus *neer* thee; for (*great Saint*!)
'Tis known, *true beauty* hath no need of *paint*.
    Yet, since a *Labell* fixt to thy fair *Hearse*
Is all the *Mode*, and *tears* put into *Verse*
Can teach *Posterity* our present *griefe*
10 And their own *losse*, but never give *reliefe*;
I'le tell them (and a *truth* which needs no *passe*,)
That *wit* in *Cartwright* at her *Zenith* was,
Arts, Fancy, Language, all *Conven'd* in thee,
With those *grand Miracles* which *deifie*
15 The old worlds *Writings*, kept yet from the *fire*,
Because they *force* these worst times to *admire*.
Thy matchless *Genius*, in all thou didst write,
Like the *Sun*, wrought with such *stayd heat*, and *light*,
That not a *line* (to the most *Critick* he)
20 Offends with *flashes*, or *obscuritie*.
    When thou the *wild* of *humours* trackst, thy *pen*
So Imitates that *Motley stock* in men,
As if thou hadst in all their *bosomes* been,
And seen those *Leopards* that lurk within.

UPON THE POEMS AND PLAYES OF THE EVER MEMORABLE MR.
WILLIAM CARTWRIGHT.

[1] William Cartwright (1611–43), whose *Comedies, Tragi-Comedies, with other Poems* was published in 1651 with the following poem included among the commendatory tributes. Cartwright's extraordinary reputation among his contemporaries as classicist, poet, playwright, and preacher is difficult for a modern reader, limited to his surviving printed works, to understand. He was at Oxford during Vaughan's stay there.

[2] Demonstrations, or proofs.

25 The am'rous *Youth* steals from thy *Courtly page*
His *vow'd Addresse*, the *Souldier* his *brave rage*;
And those *soft beauteous Readers* whose *looks* can
Make some men *Poets*, and make any man
A *Lover*, when thy *Slave* but *seems* to dye,[3]
30 Turn all his *Mourners*, and melt at the *Eye*.
Thus, thou thy *thoughts* hast *drest* in such a *strain*
As doth not only *speak*, but *rule* and *raign*,
Nor are those *bodyes* they assum'd, *dark Clouds*,
Or a *thick bark*, but *clear, transparent shrouds*,
35 Which who *lookes* on, the *Rayes* so strongly beat
They'l *brushe* and *warm* him with a *quickning heat*,
So *Souls* shine at the *Eyes*, and *Pearls* display
Through the *loose-Chrystal-streams* a *glaunce of day*.
But what's all this unto a *Royall Test?*
40 Thou art the *Man*, whom great *Charles* so exprest![4]
Then let the *Crowd* refrain their *needless humme*,
When *Thunder* speaks, then *Squibs* and *Winds* are
    dumb.

[3] A reference to Cartwright's tragi-comedy, *The Royal Slave*, performed before the king and queen at Oxford in 1636 and twice (1639 and 1640) printed there while Vaughan was in residence.
[4] Charles I publicly mourned Cartwright on the day of his funeral in Oxford.

[O–12] To the best, and most accomplish'd Couple——[1]

Blessings as rich and fragrant crown your heads
    As the mild heav'n on *Roses* sheds,
    When at their Cheeks (like Pearls) they weare
    The Clouds that court them in a teare,
5   And may they be fed from above
    By him which first ordain'd your love!

Fresh as the *houres* may all your pleasures be,
    And healthfull as *Eternitie*!
    Sweet as the flowres *first breath*, and Close
10   As th'*unseen spreadings* of the Rose,
    When he unfolds his Curtain'd head,
    And makes his bosome the *Suns bed*.

Soft as *your selves* run your whole lifes, and cleare
    As your own *glasse*, or *what shines* there;
15   Smooth as heav'ns *face*, and bright as he
    When without *Mask*, or *Tiffanie*,
    In all your time not one *Jarre* meet
    But peace as silent as his *feet*.

Like the dayes *Warmth* may all your Comforts be,
20   *Untoil'd* for, and *Serene* as he,
    Yet free and full as is that *sheafe*
    Of Sun-beams gilding ev'ry leafe,
    When now the *tyrant-heat* expires
    And his Cool'd locks breath milder fires.

TO THE BEST, AND MOST ACCOMPLISH'D COUPLE——

[1] Hutchinson (*Life*, p. 81) thinks it not improbable that the couple was Katherine Fowler (the "matchless Orinda") and James Philips, married in August 1648. See O–16, below, and her tribute to Vaughan, signed "*Orinda*," before *Thalia Rediviva*.

25   And as those *parcell'd glories* he doth shed
        Are the *faire Issues* of his head,
        Which ne'r so distant are soon known
        By th' *heat* and *lustre* for his own,
        So may each branch of yours wee see
30   Your *Coppyes*, and our *Wonders* be!

      And when no more on Earth you must remain
        Invited hence to heav'n again,
        Then may your vertuous, virgin-flames
        Shine in those *Heires* of your fair names,
35   And teach the world that mysterie
        Your selves in your Posteritie!

      So you to both worlds shall *rich presents* bring,
      And *gather'd* up to heav'n, leave here a *Spring*.

[O–13]   An Elegie on the death of Mr. *R. Hall*, slain at *Pontefract*, 1648.[1]

      I Knew it would be thus! and my Just fears
      Of thy great spirit are Improv'd to tears.
      Yet flow these not from any base distrust
      Of a fair name, or that thy honour must
5   Confin'd to those cold reliques sadly sit
      In the same Cell an obscure Anchorite.
      Such low distempers *Murther*, they that must
      Abuse thee so, *weep* not, but *wound* thy dust.
        But I past such dimme Mourners can descrie
10   Thy fame above all Clouds of obloquie,

AN ELEGIE ON THE DEATH OF MR. R. HALL, SLAIN AT PONTEFRACT, 1648.

[1] Hutchinson (*Life*, p. 61) gives good reasons for identifying the subject with a Dr. Hall, a clergyman, killed during a Royalist sally from Pontefract against the Parliamentary besiegers in the fall of 1648. Pontefract finally surrendered on 22 March 1649.

And like the Sun with his victorious rayes
Charge through that darkness to the last of dayes.
'Tis true, fair *Manhood* hath a *female* Eye,
And tears are beauteous in a Victorie,
15   Nor are wee so high-proofe, but griefe will find
Through all our guards a way to wound the mind;
But in thy fall what addes the brackish summe
More than a blott unto thy *Martyrdome*,
Which scorns such wretched suffrages, and stands
20   More by thy single worth, than our whole bands.
Yet could the puling tribute rescue ought
In this sad losse, or wert thou to be brought
Back here by tears, I would in any wise
Pay down the summe, or quite Consume my Eyes.
25   Thou fell'st our double ruine, and this rent
Forc'd in thy life shak'd both the *Church and tent,*
Learning in others steales them from the *Van,*
And basely wise *Emasculates* the man,
But lodged in thy brave soul the *bookish feat*
30   Serve'd only as the light unto thy *heat;*
Thus when some quitted action, to their shame,
And only got a *discreet Cowards* name,
Thou with thy bloud mad'st purchase of renown,
And diedst the glory of the *Sword* and *Gown,*
35   Thy bloud hath hallow'd *Pomfret,* and this blow
(Prophan'd before) hath Church'd the Castle now.
        Nor is't a Common valour we deplore,
But such as with *fifteen* a *hundred* bore,
And lightning like (not coopt within a wall)
40   In stormes of *fire* and *steele* fell on them all.
Thou wert no *Wool-sack* souldier,[2] nor of those
Whose Courage lies in *winking* at their foes,
That live at *loop-holes,* and consume their breath
On *Match* or *Pipes,* and sometimes *peepe* at death;
45   No, it were sinne to number these with thee,
But that (thus poiz'd) our losse wee better see.

[2] A soldier who sits safely behind defensive works, often constructed of woolsacks.

The fair and open valour was thy *shield*,
And thy known station, the *defying field*.
   Yet these in thee I would not *Vertues* call,
50 But that this age must know, that thou hadst all.
Those richer graces that adorn'd thy mind
Like stars of the *first magnitude*, so shin'd,
That if oppos'd unto these lesser lights
All we can say, is this, *They were fair nights*.
55 Thy *Piety* and *Learning* did unite,
And though with *Sev'rall beames* made up *one light*,
And such thy Judgement was, that I dare swear
Whole *Counsels* might as soon, and *Synods* erre.
   But all these now are out! and as some *Star*
60 Hurl'd in Diurnall motions from far,
And seen to droop at night, is vainly sed
To fall, and find an *Occidentall bed*,
Though in that other world what wee Judge *West*
Proves *Elevation*, and a new, fresh *East*.
65 So though our weaker sense denies us sight
And bodies cannot trace the *Spirits* flight,
Wee know those graces to be still in thee,
But wing'd above us to eternitie.
Since then (thus flown) thou art so much refin'd,
70 That we can only reach thee with the mind,
I will not in this *dark* and *narrow glasse*
Let thy scant *shadow* for *Perfections* passe,
But leave thee to be read more high, more queint,
In thy own bloud a *Souldier* and a *Saint*.

75   —— *Salve æternum mihi maxime Palla*!
      Æternumq; vale!——[3]

[3] Virgil, *Aeneid*, XI, 97–98: "Forever hail, O great Pallas, and farewell forever."

[O–14]   To my learned friend, Mr. *T. Powell*,
upon His Translation of *Malvezzi's*
Christian Politician.[1]

Wee thank you, worthy Sir, that now we see
Malvezzi languag'd like our Infancie,
And can without suspition entertain
This forraign States-man to our brest or brain,
5 You have enlarg'd his praise, and from your store
By this Edition made his worth the more.
Thus by your learned hand (amidst the *Coile*)
Outlandish plants thrive in our thankless soile,
And wise men after death, by a strange fate,
10 Lye *Leiguer*[2] here, and beg to serve our *State.*
Italy now, though *Mistris* of the *Bayes,*
Waits on this *Wreath,* proud of a forraign praise,
For, wise *Malvezzi,* thou didst lye before
Confin'd within the language of one shore,
15 And like those *Stars* which neer the *Poles* doe steer
Wer't but in one part of the *Globe* seen cleer,
Provence and *Naples* were the best and most
Thou couldst shine in, fixt to that single Coast,
Perhaps some *Cardinal* to be thought wise
20 And honest too, would ask, *what was thy price?*

TO MY LEARNED FRIEND, MR. T. POWELL. . . .
[1] Thomas Powell's translation of Virgilio Malvezzi's *Il Ritratto
del Privato Politico Christiano* (Bologna, 1635) apparently was
never printed. In a letter to John Aubrey, 7 July 1673, Vaughan
says that he has the manuscript of the translation in his custody
and "not yet printed." See Martin, *Works* (1957), p. 690. The
anonymous translation of 1647, *The Pourtract of the Politicke
Christian-Favourite,* formerly thought to have been Powell's, is
scornfully referred to in the letter as "traduced" rather than faith-
fully translated. See T–1, T–9.
[2] A variant form of *leager,* or *ledger,* in the sense of a representa-
tive, agent, or ambassador. OED, s.v. Ledger, A, 6, 7. Malvezzi had
been ambassador to England.

Then thou must pack to *Rome*, where thou mightst lye
E'r thou shouldst have new cloathes eternally,
For though so neer the *seav'n hills*, ne'rthelesse
Thou cam'st to *Antwerp* for thy *Roman* dresse;[3]
25 But now thou art come hither, thou mayst run
Through any Clime as well known as the *Sun*,
And in thy *sev'rall dresses* like the *year*
Challenge acquaintance with each peopled Sphere.
  Come then rare Politicians of the time,
30 Brains of some standing, Elders in our Clime,
See here the method: A wise, solid state
Is quick in acting, friendly in debate,
Joynt in advice, in resolutions just,
Mild in successe, true to the Common trust.
35 It cements ruptures, and by gentle hand
Allayès the heat and burnings of a land,
Religion guides it, and in all the Tract
Designes so twist, that heav'n confirms the act;
If from these lists you wander as you steere,
40 Look back, and *Catechise* your actions here,
These are the *Marks* to which true States-men tend,
And *greatness* here with *goodness* hath one End.

[O–15] To my worthy friend Master *T. Lewes*.[1]

Sees not my friend, what a deep snow
Candies our Countries wooddy brow?
The yeelding branch his load scarse bears
Opprest with snow, and *frozen tears*,
5   While the *dumb* rivers slowly float,
All bound up in an *Icie Coat*.

[3] A Latin translation of Malvezzi's *Il Ritratto del Privato Politico Christiano* was published in Amsterdam, 1641.
TO MY WORTHY FRIEND MASTER T. LEWES.
[1] Thomas Lewis, rector of Llanfigan, across the Usk from Newton. See Hutchinson, *Life*, pp. 81, 110–11.

Let us meet then! and while this world
In wild *Excentricks* now is hurld,
Keep wee, like nature, the same *Key*,
10   And walk in our forefathers way;
Why any more cast wee an Eye
On what *may come*, not what is *nigh?*
Why vex our selves with *feare*, or *hope*
And cares beyond our *Horoscope?*
15   Who into future times would peere
Looks oft beyond his terme set here,
And cannot goe into those grounds
But through a *Church-yard* which them bounds;
Sorrows and sighes and searches spend
20   And draw our bottome[2] to an end,
But discreet Joyes lengthen the lease
Without which life were a disease,
And who this age a Mourner goes,
Doth with his tears but feed his foes.

2 Fundamental being, or essence (OED).

[O–16] To the most Excellently accomplish'd, Mrs *K. Philips*.[1]

Say wittie fair one, from what Sphere
Flow these rich numbers you shed here?
For sure such *Incantations* come
From thence, which strike your Readers dumbe.

5   A strain, whose measures gently meet
Like *Virgin-lovers*, or times *feet*,
Where language *Smiles*, and accents rise
As quick, and pleasing as your *Eyes*,
The *Poem* smooth, and in each line

10   Soft as *your selfe*, yet *Masculine*;
Where no Coorse trifles blot the page
With matter borrow'd from the age,
But thoughts as Innocent, and high
As *Angels* have, or *Saints* that dye.

15   These Raptures when I first did see
New miracles in Poetrie,
And by a hand, their God would misse
His *Bayes* and *Fountaines* but to kisse,
My weaker *Genius* (crosse to fashion)

20   Slept in a silent admiration,
A Rescue, by whose grave disguise
Pretenders oft have past for wise,

TO THE MOST EXCELLENT ACCOMPLISH'D, MRS K. PHILIPS.

[1] Mrs. Katherine Philips (1631–64), the "matchless Orinda" of brief literary fame. Vaughan must have seen her poems in manuscript, since they were not published until 1664, and that surreptitiously. The authorized edition appeared three years later. There is no evidence that Vaughan and Mrs. Philips ever met, although they did exchange poetic tributes. See her poem, signed *"Orinda,"* before *Thalia Rediviva*, below, and see O–12, above. For a discussion of the relationship between the two, see Philip W. Souers, *The Matchless Orinda* (Cambridge, Massachusetts, 1931), pp. 71–73.

And yet as *Pilgrims* humbly touch
Those *Shrines* to which they bow so much,
25   And Clouds in Courtship flock, and run
To be the Mask unto the Sun,
·So I concluded, It was true
I might at distance worship you
A *Persian* Votarie, and say
30   *It was your light shew'd me the way.*
So *Lodestones* guide the duller *Steele*,
And high perfections are the *Wheele*
Which moves the lesse, for gifts divine
Are strung upon a *Vital line*
35   Which touch'd by you, Excites in all
Affections *Epidemicall.*
And this made me (a truth most fit)
Adde my weak *Eccho* to your wit,
Which pardon, Lady, for Assayes
40   Obscure as these might blast your Bayes,
As Common hands soyle *Flowres*, and make
That dew they wear, *weepe* the mistake.
But I'le wash off the *staine*, and vow
No *Lawrel* growes, but for your *Brow.*

[O–17]   An Epitaph upon the Lady *Elizabeth,*
Second Daughter to his late
Majestie.[1]

Youth, Beauty, Vertue, Innocence
Heav'ns royall, and select Expence,
With Virgin-tears, and sighs divine,
Sit here the *Genii* of this shrine,
5   Where now (thy fair soule wing'd away,)
They guard the *Casket* where she lay.

AN EPITAPH UPON THE LADY ELIZABETH. . . .
   [1] The second daughter of Charles I, Elizabeth, born in 1635
and died at Carisbrooke, Isle of Wight, 8 September 1650.

Thou hadst, e'r thou the light couldst see,
Sorrowes layd up, and stor'd for thee,
Thou suck'dst in woes, and the *brests* lent
10   Their *Milk* to thee, but to lament;
Thy portion here was *griefe*, thy years
Distilld no other rain, but tears,
Tears without noise, but (understood)
As lowd, and shrill as any bloud;[2]
15   Thou seem'st a *Rose-bud* born in *Snow*,
A flowre of purpose sprung to bow
To headless tempests, and the rage
Of an Incensed, stormie Age.
Others, e're their afflictions grow,
20   Are tim'd, and season'd for the blow,
But thine, as *Rhumes* the tend'rest part,
Fell on a *young* and *harmless* heart.
And yet as *Balm-trees* gently spend
Their tears for those, that doe them rend,
25   So mild and pious thou wert seen,
Though full of *Suffrings*, free from *spleen*,
Thou didst not murmure, nor revile,
But drank'st thy *Wormwood* with a *smile*.
As envious Eyes blast, and Infect
30   And cause misfortunes by aspect,
So thy sad stars dispens'd to thee
No Influxe, but Calamitie,
They view'd thee with *Ecclypsed* rayes,
And but the *back-side* of bright dayes.[3]

*   *   *

35   These were the Comforts she had here,
As by an unseen hand 'tis cleer,
Which now she reads, and smiling wears
A Crown with him, who wipes off tears.[4]

[2] In Gen. 4.10 Abel's blood is said to cry from the ground.

[3] The reverse, or dark, side of bright days. Some following lines were apparently omitted here. Cf. *"Back-side"* in T–31, line 15, below.

[4] Cf. Rev. 7.17, "and God shall wipe away all tears from their eyes."

[O–18]   To Sir *William D'avenant,* upon his *Gondibert.*[1]

Well, wee are rescued! and by thy rare Pen
Poets shall live, when *Princes* dye like men.
Th'hast cleer'd the prospect to our harmless *Hill,*
Of late years clouded with imputed Ill,
5 And the *Soft, youthfull Couples* there may move
As chast as *Stars* converse and smile above.
Th'hast taught their *Language,* and their *love* to flow
Calme as *Rose-leafes,* and coole as *Virgin-snow,*
Which doubly feasts us, being so refin'd
10 They both *delight,* and *dignifie* the mind,
Like to the watrie Musick of some Spring,
Whose pleasant flowings at once *wash* and *sing.*
    And where before *Heroick Poems* were
Made up of *Spirits, Prodigies,* and *fear,*
15 And shew'd (through all the *Melancholy flight,*)
Like some dark Region overcast with night,
As if the Poet had been quite dismay'd,
While only *Giants* and *Inchantments* sway'd,
Thou like the *Sun,* whose *Eye* brooks no disguise
20 Hast Chas'd them hence, and with Discoveries
So rare and learned fill'd the place, that wee
Those fam'd *Grandeza's*[2] find out-done by thee,
And under-foot see all those *Vizards* hurl'd,
Which bred the wonder of the former world.
25 'Twas dull to sit, as our fore-fathers did,
At *Crums* and *Voyders,*[3] and because unbid

TO SIR WILLIAM D'AVENANT, UPON HIS GONDIBERT.

[1] Davenant (1606–68) brought his heroic poem *Gondibert* to a close in the middle of the third book while he was a prisoner in Cowes Castle, in October 1650, awaiting execution, as he thought, for crimes against Parliament. The poem was published in 1651.

[2] Magnificent displays.

[3] Trays or vessels used to clear dining tables of dishes and food.

Refrain wise appetite. This made thy *fire*
Break through the *ashes* of thy aged *Sire*[4]
To lend the world such a Convincing light
30 As shewes his *fancy* darker than his sight.
Nor was't alone the *bars* and *length* of dayes
(Though those gave *strength* and *stature* to his *bayes*,)
Encounter'd thee, but what's an old Complaint
And kills the fancy, a *forlorn Restraint*;
35 How couldst thou mur'd in solitarie stones
Dresse *BIRTHA'S smiles*,[5] though well thou might'st her
      grones?
And, strangely Eloquent, thy self divide
'Twixt *Sad misfortunes*, and a *Bloomie Bride?*
Through all the tenour of thy ample Song
40 Spun from thy own rich store, and shar'd among
Those fair *Adventurers*, we plainly see
Th' *Imputed* gifts, *Inherent* are in thee.
Then live for ever (and by high desert)
In thy own *mirrour*, matchless *Gondibert*,
45 And in *bright Birtha* leave thy *love* Inshrin'd
Fresh as her *Emrauld*,[6] and *fair* as her *mind*,
While all Confesse thee (as they ought to doe)
The Prince of *Poets*, and of *Lovers* too.

[4] Probably Homer, although Jonson and Shakespeare have been suggested as candidates.

[5] The heroine of *Gondibert*, who at one point is called a "bloomy Bride."

[6] Duke Gondibert gave Birtha an emerald for a bridal stone.

[O–19]   *Tristium Lib.* 5⁰. *Eleg.* 3ᵃ.[1]
To his fellow-Poets at *Rome*, upon the birth-day of *Bacchus*.

This is the day (blith god of *Sack*) which wee
If I mistake not, Consecrate to thee,
When the soft *Rose* wee marry to the *Bayes*,
And warm'd with thy own wine reherse thy praise,
5   'Mongst whom (while to thy *Poet* fate gave way)
I have been held no small part of the day,
But now, dull'd with the Cold *Bears* frozen seat,
Sarmatia holds me, and the warlike *Gete*.
My former life, unlike to this my last,
10   With *Romes* best wits of thy full Cup did tast,
Who since have seen the savage *Pontick* band,
And all the *Choler* of the Sea and Land:
Whether sad Chance, or heav'n hath this design'd,
And at my birth some fatall Planet shin'd,
15   Of right thou shouldst the *Sisters* knots undoe,
And free thy *Votarie* and *Poet* too.
Or are you Gods (like us) in such a state
As cannot alter the decrees of fate?
I know with much adoe thou didst obtain
20   Thy *Jovial godhead*, and on earth thy pain
Was no whit lesse, for wandring thou didst run
To the *Getes* too, and Snow-weeping *Strymon*,
With *Persia*, *Ganges*, and what ever streams
The thirsty *Moore* drinks in the mid-day beames.
25   But thou wert twice-born, and the Fates to thee
(To make all sure) doubled thy miserie,

TRISTIUM LIB. 5⁰. ELEG. 3ᵃ.

[1] For the Latin text see Ovid, *Tristia, Ex Ponto,* tr. Arthur Leslie Wheeler, Loeb Library (1924), pp. 220–22, where the English title of the elegy is "An Appeal to Bacchus." Vaughan's descriptive title is his addition.

My suffrings too are many: if it be
Held safe for me to boast adversitie,
Nor was't a Common blow, but from above
30   Like his, that died for Imitating *Jove*,
Which when thou heardst, a ruine so divine
And *Mother*-like, should make thee pitty mine.
And on this day, which *Poets* unto thee
Crown with full bowles, ask, *What's become of me?*
35   *Help* bucksome God then! so may thy lov'd *Vine*
Swarm with the num'rous grape, and *big* with Wine
Load the kind *Elm*, and so thy *Orgyes* be
With priests lowd showtes, and *Satyrs* kept to thee*!*
So may in death *Lycurgus* ne'r be blest,
40   Nor *Pentheus* wandring ghost find any rest!
And so for ever bright (thy Chiefe desires,)
May thy *Wifes Crown* outshine the lesser fires!
If but now, mindfull of my love to thee,
Thou wilt, in what thou canst, my helper be.
45   You *Gods* have Commerce with your selves, try then
If *Cæsar* will restore me *Rome* agen.
        And you my trusty friends (the Jollie Crew
Of careless *Poets*!) when, without me, you
Perform this dayes glad Myst'ries, let it be
50   Your first Appeal unto his Deitie,
And let one of you (touch'd with my sad name)
Mixing his wine with tears, lay down the same,
And (sighing) to the rest this thought Commend,
O! Where is Ovid *now our banish'd friend?*
55   This doe, if in your brests I e'r deserv'd
So large a share, nor spitefully reserv'd,
Nor basely sold applause, or with a brow
Condemning others, did my selfe allow.
And may your happier wits grow lowd with fame
60   As you (my best of friends!) preserve my name.

[O–20] *De Ponto, Lib.* 3⁰.[1]
To his friends (after his many sollicitations)
refusing to petition *Cæsar*
for his releasement.

You have Consum'd my language, and my pen
Incens'd with begging scorns to write agen.
You grant, you knew my sute: My Muse, and I
Had taught it you in frequent Elegie,
5 That I believe (yet seal'd) you have divin'd
Our *Repetitions,* and *forestal'd* my mind,
So that my thronging Elegies, and I
Have made you (more then *Poets*) prophesie.
But I am now awak'd; forgive my dream
10 Which made me Crosse the *Proverb* and the *Stream,*
And pardon, friends, that I so long have had
Such good thoughts of you, I am not so mad
As to continue them. You shall no more
Complain of troublesome *Verse,* or write o're
15 How I endanger you, and vex my *Wife*
With the sad legends of a banish'd life.
I'le bear these plagues my selfe: for I have past
Through greater ones, and can as well at last
These pettie Crosses. 'Tis for some young beast
20 To kick his bands, or wish his neck releast
From the sad Yoke. Know then, That as for me
Whom Fate hath us'd to such calamitie,
I scorn her spite and yours, and freely dare
The highest ills your malice can prepare.
25 'Twas Fortune threw me hither, where I now
Rude *Getes* and *Thrace* see, with the snowie brow

DE PONTO, LIB. 3⁰.
[1] See Ovid, *Ex Ponto*, III, vii (*Ad amicos*), Loeb Library, pp.
414–16. Vaughan adds the descriptive phrase following "To his
friends."

Of Cloudie *Æmus*, and if she decree
Her sportive pilgrims *last bed* here must be
I am content; nay more, she cannot doe
30 That Act which I would not consent unto.
I can delight in vain hopes, and desire
That state more then her *Change* and *Smiles*, then high'r
I hugge a strong *despaire*, and think it brave
To *baffle* faith, and give those hopes a *grave*.
35 Have you not seen cur'd wounds enlarg'd, and he
That with the first wave sinks, yielding to th'free
Waters, without th'Expence of armes or breath
Hath still the easiest, and the quickest death.
Why nurse I sorrows then? why these desires
40 Of Changing *Scythia* for the *Sun* and *fires*
Of some calm kinder aire? what did bewitch
My frantick hopes to flye so vain a pitch,
And thus out-run my self? Mad-man! could I
Suspect fate had for me a Courtesie?
45 These errours grieve: And now I must forget
Those pleas'd *Idœa's* I did frame and set
Unto my selfe, with many fancyed *Springs*
And *Groves*, whose only losse new sorrow brings.
And yet I would the worst of fate endure,
50 E're you should be repuls'd, or lesse secure,
But (base, low soules!) you left me not for this,
But 'cause you durst not. *Cæsar* could not misse
Of such a trifle, for I know that he
Scorns the *Cheap triumphs* of my miserie.
55   Then since (degen'rate friends) not he, but you
Cancell my hopes, and make afflictions new,
You shall Confesse, and fame shall tell you, I
At *Ister* dare as well as *Tyber* dye.

[O–21]   *De Ponto, lib. 4°. Eleg.* 3ᵃ.[1]
          To his Inconstant friend, translated for
          the use of all the *Judases* of this
          touch-stone-Age.

Shall I complain, or not? Or shall I mask
Thy hatefull name, and in this bitter task
Master my just Impatience, and write down
Thy crime alone, and leave the rest unknown?
5 Or wilt thou the succeeding years should see
And teach thy person to posteritie?
No, hope it not; for know, most wretched man,
'Tis not thy base and weak detraction can
Buy thee a *Poem*, nor move me to give
10 Thy name the honour in my Verse to live.
     Whilst yet my *Ship* did with no stormes dispute
And temp'rate winds *fed* with a calme salute
My prosp'rous sailes, thou wert the only man
That with me then an equall fortune ran,
15 But now since angry heav'n with Clouds and night
Stifled those *Sun*-beams, thou hast ta'ne thy flight,
Thou know'st I want thee, and art meerly gone
To shun that rescue, I rely'd upon;
Nay, thou dissemblest too, and doest disclame
20 Not only my *Acquaintance*, but my name;
Yet know (though deafe to this) that I am he
Whose *years* and *love* had the same *Infancie*
With thine, Thy *deep familiar*, that did share
Soules with thee, and partake thy *Joyes* or *Care*,

DE PONTO, LIB. 4⁰. ELEG. 3ᵃ.
    [1] See Ovid, *Ex Ponto*, IV, iii (*Ad amicum instabilem*), Loeb Library, pp. 430–34. The phrase "translated . . . Age" is added by Vaughan. He uses "touch-stone" apparently in the sense simply of black or dark-colored.

25 Whom the same *Roofe* lodg'd, and my *Muse* those nights
So solemnly endear'd to her delights;
But now, perfidious traitour, I am grown
The *Abject* of thy brest, not to be known
In that *false Closet* more; Nay, thou wilt not
30 So much as let me know, I am forgot.
If thou wilt say, thou didst not love me, then
Thou didst dissemble: or, if love agen,
Why now Inconstant? came the Crime from me
That wrought this Change? Sure, if no Justice be
35 Of my side, thine must have it. Why dost hide
Thy reasons then? for me, I did so guide
My selfe and actions, that I cannot see
What could offend thee, but my miserie.
'Las! if thou wouldst not from thy store allow
40 Some rescue to my wants, at least I know
Thou couldst have writ, and with a line or two
Reliev'd my *famish'd Eye*, and eas'd me so.
I know not what to think! and yet I hear,
Not pleas'd with this, th'art *Witty*, and dost Jeare;
45 Bad man! thou hast in this those tears kept back
I could have shed for thee, shouldst thou but lack.
Know'st not that *Fortune* on a *Globe* doth stand,
Whose *upper* slipprie part without command
Turns *lowest* still? the sportive leafes and wind
50 Are but dull *Emblems* of her fickle mind,
In the whole world there's nothing I can see
Will throughly parallel her wayes, but thee.
All that we hold, hangs on a slender twine
And our best states by sudden chance decline;
55 Who hath not heard of *Crœsus* proverb'd gold
Yet knowes his foe did him a pris'ner hold?
He that once aw'd *Sicilia's* proud Extent
By a poor art could famine scarse prevent;
And mighty *Pompey* e'r he made an end
60 Was glad to beg his slave to be his friend;
Nay, he that had so oft *Romes* Consull bin,
And forc'd *Jugurtha*, and the *Cimbrians* in,

Great *Marius*! with much want, and more disgrace
In a foul Marsh was glad to hide his face.
65 A divine hand swayes all mankind, and wee
Of one short houre have not the certaintie;
Hadst thou one day told me, the time should be
When the *Getes* bowes, and th'*Euxine* I should see,
I should have check'd thy madness, and have thought
70 Th' hadst need of all *Anticira* in a draught;
And yet 'tis come to passe! nor though I might
Some things foresee, could I procure a sight
Of my whole destinie, and free my state
From those eternall, higher *tyes* of fate.
75 Leave then thy pride, and though now *brave* and *high*,
Think thou mayst be as *poore* and *low* as I.

[O–22]   *Tristium Lib. 3⁰. Eleg. 3ª.*[1]
          To his Wife at *Rome*, when he was sick.

Dearest! if you those fair Eyes (wondring) stick
On this strange Character, know, *I am sick*.
Sick in the *skirts* of the lost world, where I
Breath hopeless of all Comforts, but to dye.
5   What heart (think'st thou?) have I in this sad seat
Tormented 'twixt the *Sauromate* and *Gete*?
Nor *aire* nor *water* please: their very *skie*
Looks strange and unaccustom'd to my Eye,
I scarse dare breath it, and I know not how
10   The Earth that bears me shewes unpleasant now.
Nor *Diet* here's, nor *lodging* for my Ease,
Nor any one that *studies* a disease;
No friend to comfort me, none to defray
With smooth discourse the Charges of the day.

TRISTIUM LIB. 3⁰. ELEG. 3ª.
[1] See Ovid, *Tristia*, III, iii, Loeb Library, pp. 108–14. Vaughan
provides the descriptive title.

15   All tir'd alone I lye, and (thus) what e're
      Is absent, and at *Rome* I fancy here,
      But when thou com'st, I blot the *Airie Scrowle*,
      And give thee full possession of my soule,
      Thee (absent) I embrace, thee only *voice*,
20   And night and day *bely* a Husbands Joyes;
      Nay, of thy name so oft I mention make
      That I am thought distracted for thy sake;
      When my tir'd Spirits faile, and my sick heart
      Drawes in that *fire* which actuates each part,
25   If any say, th'art come! I force my pain,
      And hope to see thee, gives me life again.
      Thus I for thee, whilst thou (perhaps) more blest
      Careless of me doest breath all peace and rest,
      Which yet I think not, for (*Deare Soule!*) too well
30   Know I thy griefe, since my first woes befell.
      But if strict heav'n my stock of dayes hath spun
      And with my life my errour wilbe gone,
      How easie then (*O Cæsar!*) wer't for thee
      To pardon one, that now doth cease to be?
35   That I might yeeld my native aire this breath,
      And banish not my ashes after death;
      Would thou hadst either spar'd me untill dead,
      Or with my bloud redeem'd my absent head,
      Thou shouldst have had both freely, but O! thou
40   Wouldst have me live to dye an *Exile* now.
      And must I then from *Rome* so far meet death,
      And double by the place my losse of breath?
      Nor in my last of houres on my own bed
      (In the sad Conflict) rest my dying head?
45   Nor my soules *Whispers* (the last pledge of life,)
      Mix with the tears and kisses of a wife?
      My last words none must treasure, none will rise
      And (with a teare) seal up my vanquish'd Eyes,
      Without these *Rites* I dye, distrest in all
50   The *splendid sorrowes* of a Funerall,
      Unpittied, and unmourn'd for, my sad head
      In a strange Land goes friendless to the dead.

When thou hear'st this, O how thy faithfull soule
Will sink, whilst griefe doth ev'ry part controule!
55   How often wilt thou look this way, and Crie,
O where is't yonder that my love doth lye!
Yet spare these tears, and mourn not now for me,
Long since (*dear heart!*) have I been dead to thee,
Think then I dyed, when *Thee* and *Rome* I lost
60   That death to me more griefe then this hath Cost;
Now, if thou canst (but thou canst not) *best wife*
Rejoyce, my Cares are ended with my life,
At least, yeeld not to sorrowes, frequent use
Should make these miseries to thee no newes.
65   And here I wish my Soul died with my breath
And that no part of me were free from death,
For, if it be Immortall, and outlives
The body, as *Pythagoras* believes,
Betwixt these *Sarmates ghosts*, a *Roman I*
70   Shall wander, vext to all Eternitie.
     But thou (for after death I shall be free,)
Fetch home these bones, and what is left of me,
A few *Flowres* give them, with some *Balme*, and lay
Them in some *Suburb-grave* hard by the way,
75   And to Informe posterity, who's there,
This sad Inscription let my marble weare,
  „ *Here lyes the soft-soul'd Lecturer of Love,*
  „ *Whose envy'd wit did his own ruine prove.*
But thou, (who e'r thou beest, that passing by
80   Lendst to this *sudden stone* a *hastie* Eye,)
If e'r thou knew'st of *Love* the sweet disease,
Grudge not to say, *May* Ovid *rest in peace!*
This for my tombe: but in my books they'l see
More strong and lasting Monuments of mee,
85   Which I believe (though fatall) will afford
An Endless name unto their ruin'd Lord.
     And now thus gone, It rests for love of me
Thou shewst some sorrow to my memory;
Thy Funerall offrings to my ashes beare
90   With Wreathes of *Cypresse* bath'd in many a teare,

Though nothing there but dust of me remain,
Yet shall that *Dust* perceive thy pious pain.
But I have done, and my tyr'd sickly head
Though I would fain write more, desires the bed;
95   Take then this word (perhaps my last to tell)
Which though I want, I wish it thee, *Fare-well.*

[O–23]   *Ausonii Cupido, Edyl.* 6.[1]

In those blest fields of *Everlasting aire*
(Where to a *Myrtle*-grove the soules repaire
Of deceas'd *Lovers*,) the sad, thoughtfull ghosts
Of *Injur'd Ladyes* meet, where each accoasts
5 The other with a sigh, whose very breath
Would break a heart, and (*kind Soules!*) love in death.
A thick wood clouds their *walks*, where day scarse peeps,
And on each hand Cypresse and Poppey *sleepes*,
The drowsie Rivers *slumber*, and *Springs* there
10 *Blab* not, but softly melt into a teare,
A sickly dull aire *fans* them, which can have
When most in force scarce breath to *build* a wave.
On either bank through the still shades appear
A *Scene* of pensive flowres, whose bosomes wear
15 Drops of a *Lover's* bloud, the *Emblem'd* truths
Of deep despair, and Love-slain *Kings* and *Youths.*
The *Hyacinth*, and self-enamour'd Boy
Narcissus flourish there, with *Venus* Joy
The spruce *Adonis*, and that *Prince* whose flowre
20 Hath sorrow languag'd on him to this houre;

AUSONII CUPIDO, EDYL. 6.
   [1] See the "Cupido Cruciatur," in *Ausonius,* tr. Hugh G. Evelyn-White, Loeb Library (1919), I, 206–14. Humphrey Moseley, publisher of *Olor Iscanus,* had published another translation of this poem, of inferior poetic quality, just two years before in *Europa. Cupid Crucified. Venus Vigils,* with annotations by Thomas Stanley (London, 1649).

All sad with love they hang their heads, and grieve
As if their passions in each leafe did *live*;
And here (*alas!*) these soft-soul'd Ladies stray,
And (oh! too late!) treason in love betray.

25   Her blasted birth sad *Semele* repeats,
And with her *tears* would quench the thund'rers *heats*,
Then shakes her bosome, as if fir'd again,
And fears another lightnings *flaming train*.
The lovely *Procris* (here) bleeds, sighes, and swounds,

30 Then wakes, and kisses him that gave her wounds.
Sad *Hero* holds a torch forth, and doth light
Her lost *Leander* through the waves and night.
Her *Boateman* desp'rate *Sapho* still admires,
And nothing but the *Sea* can quench her *fires*.

35 Distracted *Phœdra* with a restless Eye
Her disdain'd Letters reads, then casts them by.
Rare, faithfull *Thysbe* (sequestred from these)
A silent, unseen sorrow doth best please,
For her *Loves* sake, and last *good-night*, poor she

40 Walks in the shadow of a *Mulberrie*.
Neer her young *Canace* with *Dido* sits
A lovely Couple, but of desp'rate wits,
Both dy'd alike, both pierc'd their tender brests,
This with her *Fathers* Sword, that with her *Guests*.

45 Within the thickest *textures* of the Grove
Diana in her *Silver-beams* doth rove,
Her Crown of stars the *pitchie aire* Invades,
And with a faint light *gilds* the silent shades,
Whilst her sad thoughts fixt on her *sleepie Lover*

50 To *Latmos*-hill, and his retirements move her.
A thousand more through the wide, darksome wood
Feast on their cares, the *Maudlin-Lovers* food,
For *griefe* and *absence* doe but *Edge* desire,
And Death is *fuell* to a Lovers *fire*.

55   To see these *Trophies* of his wanton bow
Cupid comes in, and all in triumph now
(Rash, unadvised Boy!) disperseth round
The sleepie Mists, his *Wings* and *quiver* wound

With noise the quiet aire. This sudden stirre
60 Betrayes his *godship*, and as we from far
A clouded, sickly *Moon* observe, so they
Through the *false Mists* his *Ecclyps'd torch* betray.
A hot pursute they make, and though with care,
And a slow wing he softly *stems* the aire,
65 Yet they (as subtill now as he) surround
His silenc'd course, and with the thick night bound
Surprize the *Wag*. As in a dream we strive
To voyce our thoughts, & vainly would revive
Our Entraunc'd tongues, but can not speech enlarge
70 'Till the Soule wakes and reassumes her Charge,
So joyous of their *Prize*, they flock about
And vainly *Swell* with an *Imagin'd* shout.
   Far in these shades, and melancholy Coasts
A *Myrtle* growes, well known to all the ghosts,
75 Whose stretch'd top (like a *great man* rais'd by Fate)
Looks big, and scorns his neighbours low estate;
His *leavy arms* into a *green Cloud* twist,
And on each Branch doth *sit* a lazie mist.
A fatall tree, and luckless to the gods,
80 Where for *disdain* in life (loves *worst* of *Ods*,)
The *Queen* of shades, fair *Proserpine* did rack
The sad *Adonis*, hither now they pack
This little *God*, where, first disarm'd, they *bind*
His skittish wings, then both his hands behind
85 His back they tye, and thus secur'd at last
The *peevish wanton* to the tree make fast.
Here at adventure without *Judge* or Jurie
He is condemn'd, while with united furie
They all assaile him; As a thiefe at Bar
90 Left to the Law, and mercy of his Star,
Hath *Bills* heap'd on him, and is question'd there
By all the men that have been rob'd that year,
So now what ever *Fate*, or their own *Will*
Scor'd up in life, *Cupid* must pay the bill.
95 Their *Servants* falshood, Jealousie, disdain,
And all the plagues that *abus'd Maids* can feign,
Are layd on him, and then to heighten spleen

Their own deaths crown the summe. Prest thus between
His faire accusers, 'tis at last decreed,
100 He by those weapons, that they died, should bleed.
One grasps an *airie Sword*, a second holds
Illusive *fire*, and in *vain*, wanton folds
Belyes a flame; Others lesse kind appear
To let him bloud, and from the purple tear
105 Create a *Rose*. But *Sapho* all this while
Harvests the aire, and from a thicken'd pile
Of Clouds like *Leucas-top*, spreads underneath
A *Sea* of *Mists*, the peaceful billowes breath
Without all noise, yet so exactly move
110 They seem to *Chide*, but distant from above
Reach not the eare, and (thus prepar'd) at once
She doth o'rwhelm him with the *airie Sconce*.
Amidst these tumults, and as fierce as they
Venus steps in, and without thought, or stay
115 Invades her *Son*; her old disgrace is cast
Into the *Bill*, when *Mars* and *Shee* made *fast*
In their Embraces were expos'd to all
The *Scene* of gods stark naked in their *fall*.
Nor serves a *verball* penance, but with hast
120 From her fair brow (O happy flowres so plac'd!)
She tears a *Rosie garland*, and with this
Whips the *untoward Boy*, they gently kisse
His *snowie skin*, but she with angry hast
Doubles her strength, untill bedew'd at last
125 With a thin bloudie sweat, their *Innate Red*,
(As if griev'd with the Act) grew pale and dead.
This *layd* their spleen: And now (*kind soules!*) no more
They'l punish him, the torture that he bore,
Seems greater then his crime; with joynt Consent
130 *Fate* is made guilty, and *he* Innocent.
As in a dream with dangers we contest,
And *fictious pains* seem to afflict our rest,
So frighted only in these shades of night
Cupid (got loose) stole to the upper light,

135 Where ever since (for malice unto these)
  The *spitefull Ape* doth either *Sex* displease.
  But O that had these *Ladyes* been so wise
  To keep his *Arms,* and give him but his *Eyes!*

[O–24]   *Boet. Lib.* 1. *Metrum* 1.[1]

  I Whose first year flourish'd with youthfull verse,
  In slow, sad numbers now my griefe reherse;
  A broken stile my sickly lines afford,
  And only tears give weight unto my words;
5 Yet neither fate nor force my Muse cou'd fright
  The only faithfull Consort of my flight;
  Thus what was once my green years greatest glorie,
  Is now my Comfort, grown decay'd and hoarie,
  For killing Cares th'Effects of age spurr'd on
10 That griefe might find a fitting Mansion;
  O'r my young head runs an untimely gray,
  And my loose skin shrinks at my blouds decay.
  Happy the man! whose death in prosp'rous years
  Strikes not, nor shuns him in his age and tears.
15 But O how deafe is she to hear the Crie
  Of th' opprest Soule, or shut the weeping Eye!
  While treacherous Fortune with slight honours fed
  My first estate, she almost drown'd my head,
  But now since (clouded thus) she hides those rayes,
20 Life adds unwelcom'd length unto my dayes;
  Why then, my friends, Judg'd you my state so good?
  He that may fall once, never firmly stood.

BOET. LIB. 1. METRUM 1.
 [1] See Boethius, *Tractates, De Consolatione Philosophiae,* I,
Met. i, with the English translation of The Consolation by "I. T."
(1609), rev. by H. F. Stewart, Loeb Library (1918), pp. 128–30.

[O–25]   *Metrum 2.*[1]

O In what haste with Clouds and Night
Ecclyps'd, and having lost her light,
The dull Soule whom distraction rends
Into outward Darkness tends!
5   How often (by these mists made blind,)
Have earthly cares opprest the mind!
     This Soule sometimes wont to survey
The spangled *Zodiacks firie way*
Saw th'early Sun in Roses drest
10 With the Coole Moons unstable Crest,
And whatsoever wanton Star
In various Courses neer or far
Pierc'd through the orbs, he cou'd full well
Track all her Journey, and would tell
15 Her Mansions, turnings, Rise and fall,
By Curious Calculation all.
Of sudden winds the hidden Cause,
And why the Calm Seas quiet face
With Impetuous waves is Curld,
20 What spirit wheeles th'harmonious world,
Or why a Star dropt in the *West*
Is seen to rise again by *East*,
Who gives the warm Spring temp'rate houres
Decking the Earth with spicie flowres,
25 Or how it Comes (for mans recruit)
That Autumne yeelds both Grape and fruit,
With many other Secrets, he
Could shew the Cause and Mysterie.
     But now that light is almost out,
30 And the brave Soule lyes Chain'd about

METRUM 2.
[1] See Boethius, *De Consolatione*, I, Met. ii, Loeb Library, p. 134.

With outward Cares, whose pensive weight
Sinks down her Eyes from their first height,
And clean Contrary to her birth
Poares on this vile and foolish Earth.

[O–26]   *Metrum 4.*[1]

Whose calme soule in a settled state
Kicks under foot the frowns of Fate,
And in his fortunes bad or good
Keeps the same temper in his bloud,
5   Not him the flaming Clouds above,
Nor *Ætna's* fierie tempests move,
No fretting seas from shore to shore
Boyling with Indignation o're
Nor burning thunderbolt that can
10   A mountain shake, can stirre this man.
Dull Cowards then! why should we start
To see these tyrants act their part?
Nor hope nor fear what may befall
And you disarm their malice all.
15   But who doth faintly fear, or wish
And sets no law to what is his,
Hath lost the buckler, and (poor Elfe!)
Makes up a Chain to bind himselfe.

METRUM 4.
   [1] See Boethius, *De Consolatione*, I, Met. iv, Loeb Library,
pp. 140–42.

[O–27]   *Metrum* 5.[1]

> O Thou great builder of this starrie frame,
> Who fixt in thy eternall throne dost tame
> The rapid Spheres, and lest they jarre
> Hast giv'n a law to ev'ry starre!
5 > Thou art the Cause that now the Moon
> With full orbe dulls the starres, and soon
> Again growes dark, her light being done,
> The neerer still she's to the Sun.
> Thou in the early hours of night
10 > Mak'st the coole Evening-star shine bright,
> And at Sun-rising ('cause the least)
> Look pale and sleepie in the East.
> Thou, when the leafes in Winter stray,
> Appointst the Sun a shorter way,
15 > And in the pleasant Summer-light
> With nimble houres doest wing the night.
> Thy hand the various year quite through
> Discreetly tempers, that what now
> The North-wind tears from ev'ry tree
20 > In Spring again restor'd we see.
> Then what the *winter-starrs* between
> The furrowes in meer seed have seen
> The Dog-star since (grown up and born)
> Hath burnt in Stately, full-ear'd Corn.
25 >   Thus by Creations law controll'd
> All things their proper stations hold
> Observing (as thou didst intend)
> Why they were made, and for what end.
> Only humane actions thou
30 > Hast no Care of, but to the flow

METRUM 5.

[1] See Boethius, *De Consolatione,* I, Met. v, Loeb Library,
pp. 154–58.

And Ebbe of Fortune leav'st them all,
Hence th' Innocent endures that thrall
Due to the wicked, whilst alone
They sit possessours of his throne,
35   The Just are kill'd, and Vertue lyes
Buried in obscurities,
And (which of all things is most sad)
The good man suffers by the bad.
No perjuries, nor damn'd pretence
40   Colour'd with holy, lying sense
Can them annoy, but when they mind
To try their force, which most men find,
They from the highest sway of things
Can pull down great, and pious Kings.
45   O then at length, thus loosely hurl'd
Look on this miserable world
Who e'r thou art, that from above
Doest in such order all things move!
And let not man (of divine art
50   Not the least, nor vilest part)
By Casuall evills thus bandied, be
The sport of fates obliquitie.
But with that faith thou guid'st the heaven,
Settle this Earth, and make them even.

[O–28]   *Metrum 6.*[1]

When the Crabs fierce Constellation
Burns with the beams of the bright Sun,
Then he that will goe out to sowe,
Shall never reap where he did plough,
5   But in stead of Corn may rather
The old worlds diet, Accorns gather.

METRUM 6.
    [1] See Boethius, *De Consolatione,* I, Met. vi, Loeb Library,
p. 162.

Who the Violet doth love
Must seek her in the flowrie grove,
But never when the *Norths* cold wind
10   The *Russet* fields with frost doth bind.
If in the Spring-time (to no end)
The tender Vine for Grapes we bend,
Wee shall find none, for only (still)
Autumne doth the Wine-presse fill.
15   Thus for all things (in the worlds prime)
The wise God seal'd their proper time,
Nor will permit those seasons he
Ordain'd by turns, should mingled be;
Then whose wild actions out of season
20   Crosse to nature, and her reason,
Would by new wayes old orders rend,
Shall never find a happy End.

[O–29]   *Metrum 7.*[1]

Curtain'd with Clouds in a dark night
The Stars cannot send forth their light.
And if a sudden Southern blast
The Sea in rolling waves doth cast,
5   That angrie Element doth boile,
And from the deep with stormy Coile
Spues up the Sands, which in short space
Scatter, and puddle his Curl'd face;
Then those Calme waters, which but now
10   Stood clear as heavens unclouded brow,
And like transparent glasse did lye
Open to ev'ry searchers Eye,
Look foulely stirr'd, and (though desir'd)
Resist the sight, because bemir'd,

METRUM 7.
   [1] See Boethius, *De Consolatione,* I, Met. vii, Loeb Library, pp. 168–70.

15   So often from a high hills brow
          Some Pilgrim-spring is seen to flow,
          And in a straight line keep her Course
          'Till from a Rock with headlong force
          Some broken peece blocks up her way
20   And forceth all her streams astray.
              Then thou that with inlightned Rayes,
          Wouldst see the truth, and in her wayes
          Keep without *Errour*; neither fear
          The future, nor too much give ear
25   To present Joyes; And give no scope
          To griefe, nor much to flatt'ring hope.
          For when these Rebels raign, the mind
          Is both a Pris'ner, and stark blind.

[O–30]   *Lib. 2. Metrum 1.*[1]

          Fortune (when with rash hands she quite turmoiles
          The state of things, and in tempestuous foiles
          Comes whirling like *Euripus*,) beats quite down
          With headlong force the highest Monarchs crown,
5   And in his place unto the throne doth fetch
          The despis'd looks of some mechanick wretch.
          So Jests at tears and miseries, is proud,
          And laughs to hear her vassals grone aloud.
          These are her sports, thus she her wheele doth drive
10   And plagues man with her blind prerogative;
          Nor is't a favour of Inferiour strain,
          If once kickt down, she lets him rise again.

LIB. 2. METRUM 1.
[1] See Boethius, *De Consolatione*, II, Met. i, Loeb Library,
pp. 176–78.

[O–31]   *Metrum 2.*[1]

                If with an open, bounteous hand
                (Wholly left at Mans Command)
                Fortune should in one rich flow
                As many heaps on him bestow
5   Of massie gold, as there be sands
                Tost by the waves and winds rude bands,
                Or bright stars in a Winter-night
                Decking their silent Orbs with light,
                Yet would his lust know no restraints,
10   Nor cease to weep in sad Complaints.
                Though heaven should his vowes reguard,[2]
                And in a prodigall reward
                Return him all he could implore,
                Adding new honours to his store,
15   Yet all were nothing. Goods in sight
                Are scorn'd, and lust in greedy flight
                Layes out for more; What measure then
                Can tame these wild desires of men?
                Since all wee give both last and first
20   Doth but inflame, and feed their thirst;
          For how can he be rich, who 'midst his store
          Sits sadly pining, and believes he's poore.

METRUM 2.
    [1] See Boethius, *De Consolatione*, II, Met. ii, Locb Library,
p. 182.
    [2] Variant form for *regard*.

[O–32]   *Metrum* 3.[1]

    When the Sun from his Rosie bed
    The dawning light begins to shed,
    The drowsie sky uncurtains round,
    And the (but now bright) stars all drown'd
5   In one great light, look dull and tame,
    And homage his victorious flame.
    Thus, when the warm *Etesian* wind
    The Earth's seald bosome doth unbind,
    Straight she her various store discloses,
10   And purples every Grove with Roses;
    But if the Souths tempestuous breath
    Breaks forth, those blushes pine to death.
    Oft in a quiet sky the deep
    With unmov'd waves seems fast asleep,
15   And oft again the blustring North
    In angrie heaps provokes them forth.
      If then this world, which holds all Nations,
    Suffers it selfe such alterations,
    That not this mighty, massie frame,
20   Nor any part of it can Claime
    One certain course, why should man prate,
    Or Censure the designs of Fate?
    Why from fraile honours, and goods lent
    Should he expect things permanent?
25 Since 'tis enacted by divine decree
    That nothing mortall shall eternall be.

METRUM 3.
  [1] See Boethius, *De Consolatione,* II, Met. iii, Loeb Library,
pp. 186–88.

[O–33]   *Metrum 4.*[1]

    Who wisely would for his retreat
    Build a secure and lasting seat,
    Where stov'd in silence he may sleep
    Beneath the *Wind*, above the *Deep*;
5   Let him th' high hils leave on one hand,
    And on the other the false sand;
    The first to winds lyes plain and even
    From all the blustring points of heaven;
    The other hollow and unsure,
10   No weight of building will endure.
    Avoyding then the envied state
    Of buildings bravely situate,
    Remember thou thy selfe to lock
    Within some low neglected Rock;
15   There when fierce heaven in thunder Chides,
    And winds and waves rage on all sides,
    Thou happy in the quiet fense
    Of thy poor Cell with small Expence
    Shall lead a life serene and faire,
20   And scorn the anger of the aire.

METRUM 4.
[1] See Boethius, *De Consolatione*, II, Met. iv, Loeb Library, pp. 194–96.

[O–34]   *Metrum 5.*[1]

Happy that first white age! when wee
Lived by the Earths meere Charitie,
No soft luxurious Diet then
Had Effeminated men,
5   No other meat, nor wine had any
Then the Course Mast, or simple honey,
And by the Parents care layd up
Cheap *Berries* did the Children sup.
No pompous weare was in those dayes
10   Of gummie Silks, or Skarlet bayes,
Their beds were on some flowrie brink
And clear Spring-water was their drink.
The shadie Pine in the Suns heat
Was their Coole and known Retreat,
15   For then 'twas not cut down, but stood
The youth and glory of the wood.
The daring Sailer with his slaves
Then had not cut the swelling waves,
Nor for desire of forraign store
20   Seen any but his native shore.
No stirring Drum had scarr'd that age,
Nor the shrill Trumpets active rage,
No wounds by bitter hatred made
With warm bloud soil'd the shining blade;
25   For how could hostile madness arm
An age of love to publick harm?
When Common Justice none withstood,
Nor sought rewards for spilling bloud.

METRUM 5.
   [1] See Boethius, *De Consolatione,* II, Met. v, Loeb Library, pp.
204–6. With the opening here (translating *Felix nimium prior
aetas*) compare the opening of S–21.

O that at length our age would raise
30 Into the temper of those dayes!
But (worse then *Ætna*'s fires!) debate
And Avarice inflame our state.
Alas! who was it that first found
Gold hid of purpose under ground,
35 That sought out Pearles, and div'd to find
Such pretious perils for mankind*!*

[O–35]   *Metrum 6.*[1]

He that thirsts for glories prize,
Thinking that the top of all,
Let him view th'Expansed skies,
And the Earths Contracted ball,
5 'Twill shame him then, the name he wan
Fils not the short *walk* of one man.

2.

O why vainly strive you then
To shake off the bands of Fate,
Though fame through the world of men
10 Should in all tongues your names relate,
And with proud titles swell that storie
The Darke grave scorns your brightest glorie.

3.

There with Nobles beggers sway,
And Kings with Commons share one dust,
15 What newes of *Brutus* at this day,
Or *Fabricius* the Just?
Some rude *Verse* Cut in stone, or led
Keeps up the names, but they are dead.

METRUM 6.
  [1] An error for *Metrum 7*. See Boethius, *De Consolatione*, II, Met.
vii, Loeb Library, p. 218.

4.

So shall you, one day (past reprieve)
20   Lye (perhaps) without a name,
But if dead you think to live
       By this aire of humane fame,
Know, when time stops that posthume breath,
You must endure a second death.

[O–36]   *Metrum 7.*[1]

That the world in constant *force*
Varies her *Concordant course*;
That *seeds* jarring *hot* and *cold*
Doe the *breed* perpetuall hold;
5   That in his golden Coach the *Sun*
Brings the *Rosie day* still on;
That the *Moon* swayes all those *lights*
Which *Hesper* ushers to *dark nights*;
That *alternate tydes* be found
10   The Seas *ambitious* waves to bound,
Lest o'r the wide Earth without End
Their *fluid Empire* should extend;
All this frame of *things* that *be*,   ⎫
Love which rules *Heaven*, *Land*, and *Sea*, ⎬
15   Chains, keeps, orders as we see.   ⎭
This, if the raines he once cast by,
All things that now by turns comply,
Would fall to discord, and this frame
Which now by sociall faith they tame,
20   And comely orders in that fight
And jarre of things would perish quite.

METRUM 7.
    [1] An error for *Metrum* 8. See Boethius, *De Consolatione*, II,
Met. viii, Loeb Library, p. 222. Not only does Vaughan draw
heavily on Felltham (see Martin, *Works*, 1957, p. 712), but he
also expands the last three lines of Boethius into six in order to
make the application to England.

This in a holy league of peace
    Keeps King and People with Increase;
And in the sacred nuptiall bands
25   Tyes up chast hearts with willing hands,
And this keeps firm without all doubt
Friends by his bright Instinct found out.
    O happy Nation then were you
If love which doth all things subdue,
30   That rules the spacious heav'n, and brings
Plenty and Peace upon his wings,
Might rule you too! and without guile
Settle once more this floting Ile!

[O–37]   *Casimirus, Lib. 4. Ode 28.*[1]

All-mighty *Spirit*! thou that by
Set *turns* and *changes* from thy high
And glorious *throne*, dost here below
Rule all, and all things dost *foreknow*;
5   Can those *blind plots* wee here discusse
Please thee, as thy *wise Counsels* us?
When thou thy *blessings* here dost strow,
And poure on *Earth*, we flock and flow
With *Joyous strife*, and *eager care*
10   Strugling which shall have the best share
In thy *rich gifts*, just as we see
Children about *Nuts* disagree.

CASIMIRUS, LIB. 4. ODE 28.
[1] Maciej Kazimierz Sarbiewski (Mathias Casimirus Sarbievius) (1595–1640) was a Polish Jesuit poet who gained wide fame for his Neo-Latin odes and epigrams, first published at Cologne in 1625 and later in three editions at Amsterdam (1630, 1632, and 1634). Selections from these were translated by G. Hills as *The Odes of Casimire* (London, 1646), reprinted by The Augustan Reprint Society, No. 44, with an Introduction by Maren-Sofie Røstvig (Los Angeles, 1953). This ode appears in the Amsterdam, 1632 edition, p. 188, as "Ad Divinam Sapientiam." It was not included in Hills' translations.

Some that a *Crown* have got and foyl'd
Break it; Another sees it *spoil*'d
15   E're it is *gotten:* Thus the *world*
Is all to *peece-meals* cut, and hurl'd
By *factious hands,* It is a *ball*
Which *Fate* and *force* divide 'twixt all
The *Sons* of *men.* But ô good *God!*
20   While these for *dust* fight, and a *Clod,*
Grant that poore I may *smile,* and be
At rest, and *perfect peace* with thee.

[O–38]   *Casimirus, Lib. 2. Ode 8.*[1]

It would lesse vex *distressed man*
If *Fortune* in the same *pace* ran
To *ruine* him, as he did *rise;*
But highest *states* fall in a trice.
5   No *great Successe* held ever *long:*
A restless *fate* afflicts the throng
Of *Kings* and *Commons,* and lesse dayes
Serve to *destroy* them, then to *raise.*
Good luck *smiles* once an age, but *bad*
10   Makes *Kingdomes* in a *minute* sad,
And ev'ry *houre* of *life* wee drive,
Hath o're us a *Prerogative.*
    Then leave (by *wild Impatience* driv'n,
And *rash resents,*) to rayle at *heav'n,*
15   Leave an *unmanly, weak complaint*
That *Death* and *Fate* have no restraint.
In the same houre that gave thee *breath,*
Thou hadst ordain'd thy houre of *death,*
But *he* lives *most,* who here will *buy*
20   With a few tears, *Eternitie.*

CASIMIRUS, LIB. 2. ODE 8.
    [1] Ode 7, "Ad Publium Memmium," in the Amsterdam, 1632
edition, pp. 57–58, and in Hills' translation of 1646.

[O–39]   *Casimirus, Lib. 3. Ode 22.*[1]

Let not thy *youth* and *false delights*
Cheat thee of *life*; Those *headdy flights*
But wast thy *time*, which posts away
Like *winds* unseen, and swift as they.
5   *Beauty* is but meer *paint*, whose *die*
With times *breath* will *dissolve* and *flye*,
'Tis *wax*, 'tis *water*, 'tis a *glasse*
It *melts*, *breaks*, and *away* doth *passe*.
'Tis like a *Rose* which in the *dawne*
10   The *aire* with gentle breath doth *fawne*
And *whisper* too, but in the houres
Of *night* is sullied with smart showres.
Life spent, is wish'd for but in vain,
Nor can past *years* come back again.
15   Happy the *Man*! who in this *vale*
Redeems his time, shutting out all
Thoughts of the *world*, whose *longing Eyes*
Are ever *Pilgrims* in the *skyes*,
That views his *bright home*, and desires
20   To *shine* amongst those *glorious fires*.

[O–40]   *Casimirus Lyric. Lib. 3. Ode 23.*[1]

'Tis not *rich furniture* and *gems*
With *Cedar-roofes*, and ancient *stems*,
Nor yet a *plenteous, lasting floud*
Of *gold*, that makes man *truly good*.

CASIMIRUS, LIB. 3. ODE 22.
[1] See Casimire (Sarbiewski), *Lyricorum* (Amsterdam, 1632),
p. 120, "Ad Caesarem Pausilipium." Not in the Hills translations.
CASIMIRUS LYRIC. LIB. 3. ODE 23.
[1] See Casimire (Sarbiewski), *Lyricorum* (Amsterdam, 1632),
pp. 120–22, "Ad Julium Ariminum." Not in the Hills translations.

5 Leave to Inquire in what *faire fields*
 A *River* runs which *much gold* yeelds,
 Vertue alone is the *rich prize*
 Can purchase *stars*, and buy the *skies*.
 Let others build with *Adamant*,
10 Or pillars of *carv'd Marble* plant,
 Which *rude* and *rough* sometimes did dwell
 Far under *earth*, and neer to *hell*.
 But *richer* much (from *death* releast)
 Shines in the *fresh groves* of the *East*
15 The *Phœnix*, or those *fish* that dwell
 With *silver'd scales* in *Hiddekel*.[2]
 Let others with rare, various *Pearls*
 Their *garments* dresse, and in *forc'd Curls*
 Bind up their *locks*, look *big* and *high*,
20 And shine in *robes* of *Scarlet-die*.
 But in my thoughts more *glorious* far
 Those *native stars*, and *speckles* are
 Which *birds* wear, or the *spots* which wee
 In *Leopards* dispersed see.
25 The harmless *sheep* with her warm *fleece*
 Cloathes *man*, but who his *dark heart* sees
 Shall find a *Wolfe* or *Fox* within
 That kills the *Castor*[3] for his *skin*.
 Vertue alone, and nought else can
30 A diffrence make 'twixt *beasts* and *man*,
 And on her *wings* above the *Spheres*
 To the *true light* his *spirit* bears.

[2] Biblical name for the Tigris River (Gen. 2.14), Vaughan's substitution for Casimire's Hydaspes, modern Jhelum River, in India.
[3] The beaver.

[O–41]   *Casimirus, Lib. 4. Ode 15.*[1]

Nothing on *Earth,* nothing at all
Can be exempted from the *thrall*
Of peevish *weariness!* The *Sun*
Which our *fore-fathers* Judg'd to run
5   *Clear* and *unspotted,* in our dayes
Is tax'd with *sullen, Ecclips'd rayes.*
What ever in the *glorious skie*
Man sees, his rash, *audacious Eye*
Dares Censure it, and in meer *spite*
10   At *distance* will condemn the *light.*
The *wholsome mornings,* whose *beams* cleer
Those *hills* our *fathers* walkt on here
Wee fancy not, nor the *Moons* light
Which through their *windows* shin'd at *night,*
15   Wee change the *Aire* each year, and scorn
Those *Seates,* in which we first were *borne.*
Some nice, affected *wand'rers* love
Belgia's mild winters, others remove
For want of *health* and *honestie*
20   To *Summer* it in *Italie;*
But to no end: The *disease* still
Sticks to his *Lord,* and kindly will
To *Venice* in a *Barge* repaire,
Or *Coach* it to *Vienna's* aire,
25   And then (too late with *home* Content,)
They leave this *wilfull banishment.*
But he, whose *Constancie* makes sure
His *mind* and *mansion,* lives secure
From such *vain tasks,* can *dine* and *sup*
30   Where his *old parents* bred him up.

CASIMIRUS, LIB. 4. ODE 15.
[1] See Casimire (Sarbiewski), *Lyricorum* (Amsterdam, 1632), pp. 166–67, "Ad Munatium." In the Hills translations, pp. 75–79.

Content (no doubt!) most times doth dwell
In Countrey-shades, or to some Cell
Confines it selfe, and can alone
Make simple straw, a Royall Throne.

[O–42]   Casimirus, Lib. 4. Ode 13.[1]

If weeping Eyes could wash away
Those Evills they mourn for night and day,
Then gladly I to cure my fears
With my best Jewells would buy tears.
5   But as dew feeds the growing Corn,
So Crosses that are grown forlorn
Increase with griefe, teares make teares way,
And cares kept up, keep cares in pay.[2]
That wretch whom Fortune finds to feare,
10   And melting still into a teare,
She strikes more boldly, but a face
Silent and drie doth her amaze.
Then leave thy teares, and tedious tale
Of what thou doest misfortunes call,
15   What thou by weeping think'st to ease,
Doth by that Passion but Increase;
Hard things to Soft will never yield,
'Tis the drie Eye that wins the field;
A noble patience quells the spite
20   Of Fortune, and disarms her quite.

CASIMIRUS, LIB. 4. ODE 13.
  [1] See Casimire (Sarbiewski), Lyricorum (Amsterdam, 1632), pp.
164–65, "Ad Caesarem Pausilippium." This ode is translated by
Hills, pp. 71–73.
  [2] In receipt of wages (OED).

[O–43]   The Praise of a Religious life by
Mathias Casimirus.
In Answer to that Ode of *Horace,*
Beatus Ille qui procul negotiis, &c.[1]

Flaccus not so: That worldly *He*
Whom in the Countreys *shade* we see
Ploughing his own *fields*, seldome can
Be justly stil'd, *The Blessed man.*
5   That title only fits a *Saint*,
Whose free thoughts far above restraint
And weighty Cares, can gladly part
With *house* and *lands*, and leave the smart
Litigious troubles, and lowd strife
10   Of this world for a better life.
He fears no *Cold*, nor *heat* to blast
His *Corn*, for his *Accounts* are cast,
He *sues* no man, nor stands in Awe
Of the *devouring Courts* of Law;
15   But all his time he spends in *tears*
For the *Sins* of his youthfull years,
Or having tasted those *rich Joyes*
Of a Conscience without *noyse*
Sits in some fair *shade*, and doth give
20   To his *wild thoughts* rules how to live.

THE PRAISE OF A RELIGIOUS LIFE. . . .
[1] This appears in Casimire (Sarbiewski), *Lyricorum* (Amsterdam, 1632), p. 212, as "Palinodia ad secundam libri Epodon Odam
Q. Horatii Flacci, *Beatus ille qui procul negotiis.* Laus Otii Re-
ligiosi." It appears in the Hills translations, pp. 125–35. On the
prevalence of the *Beatus ille* theme in seventeenth-century poetry,
see Maren-Sofie Røstvig, *The Happy Man: Studies in the Meta-
morphoses of a Classical Ideal, 1600–1700* (Oxford, 1954). Miss
Røstvig has a second volume with the same title (Oxford, 1958)
dealing with the period 1700–1760.

He in the *Evening*, when on high
The *Stars* shine in the *silent skye*
Beholds th'*eternall flames* with mirth,
And *globes* of *light* more large then *Earth*,
25   Then weeps for *Joy*, and through his tears
Looks on the *fire-enamel'd* Spheres,
Where with his *Saviour* he would be
Lifted above mortalitie.
Mean while the *golden stars* doe set,
30   And the *slow-Pilgrim* leave all wet
With his own tears, which flow so fast
They make his *sleeps* light, and soon past.
By this, the *Sun* o're night *deceast*
Breaks in *fresh Blushes* from the *East*,
35   When mindfull of his former *falls*
With *strong Cries* to his *God* he calls,
And with such *deep-drawn sighes* doth move
That he turns *anger* into *love*.
    In the Calme *Spring*, when the Earth *bears*,
40   And feeds on *Aprils breath*, and *tears*,
His Eyes accustom'd to the *skyes*
Find here *fresh objects*, and like *spyes*
Or busie *Bees* search the soft *flowres*
Contemplate the *green fields*, and *Bowres*,
45   Where he in *Veyles*, and *shades* doth see
The *back Parts* of the *Deitye*.²
Then sadly sighing sayes, „ *O how*
„ *These flowres With hasty, stretch'd heads grow*
„ *And strive for heav'n, but rooted here*
50   „ *Lament the distance with a teare!*
„ *The Honey-suckles Clad in white,*
„ *The Rose in Red point to the light,*
„ *And the Lillies hollow and bleak*
„ *Look, as if they would something speak,*
55   „ *They sigh at night to each soft gale,*
„ *And at the day-spring weep it all.*

---

² God told Moses (Exod. 33.23), "thou shalt see my back parts:
but my face shall not be seen."

„ *Shall I then only* (*wretched I!*)
„ *Opprest with Earth, on Earth still lye?*
Thus speaks he to the neighbour trees
60   And many sad *Soliloquies*
To *Springs*, and *Fountaines* doth impart,
Seeking God with a longing heart.
    But if to ease his busie breast
He thinks of *home*, and taking rest,
65   A *Rurall Cott*, and *Common fare*
Are all his *Cordials* against *Care*.
There at the *doore* of his low *Cell*
Under some *shade*, or neer some *Well*
Where the *Coole Poplar* growes, his *Plate*
70   Of Common *Earth*, without more *state*
Expect their *Lord. Salt* in a *shell*,
Green *Cheese*, thin *beere, Draughts* that will *tell*
No *Tales*, a *hospitable Cup*,
With some *fresh berries* doe make up
75   His healthfull feast, nor doth he wish
For the fatt *Carp*, or a rare dish
Of *Lucrine Oysters*; The swift *Quist*[3]
Or *Pigeon* sometimes (if he list)
With the *slow Goose* that loves the *stream*,
80   Fresh, various *Sallads*, and the *Bean*
By Curious *Pallats* never sought,
And to Close with, some Cheap unbought
Dish for *digestion*, are the most
And Choicest *dainties* he can *boast*.
85   Thus feasted, to the *flowrie Groves*,
Or pleasant *Rivers* he removes,
Where neer some *fair Oke* hung with Mast
He shuns the *Souths* Infectious blast.
On shadie *banks* sometimes he lyes,
90   Sometimes the open *Current tryes*,
Where with his *line* and *feather'd flye*
He sports, and takes the *Scaly frie*.
Mean-while each *hollow wood* and *hill*
Doth ring with *lowings* long and shrill,

[3] A ringdove (Martin, *Works* [1957], p. 713).

95 And shadie *Lakes* with *Rivers* deep,
  Eccho the *bleating* of the *Sheep.*
  The *Black-bird* with the pleasant *Thrush*
  And *Nightingale* in ev'ry Bush
  Choice *Musick* give, and *Shepherds* play
100 Unto their *flocks* some loving *Lay;*
  The thirsty *Reapers* in thick throngs
  Return home from the *field* with Songs,
  And the *Carts* loden with ripe *Corn*
  Come groning to the well-stor'd *Barn.*
105 Nor passe wee by as the least good,
  A *peacefull, loving neighbourhood,*
  Whose *honest Wit,* and *Chast discourse*
  Make none (by hearing it) the *worse,*
  But *Innocent* and *merry* may
110 Help (without *Sin*) to spend the day.
  Could now the *Tyrant-usurer*
  Who *plots* to be a *Purchaser*
  Of his poor neighbours *seat,* but taste
  These *true delights,* ô with what haste
115 And hatred of his wayes would he
  Renounce his *Jewish Crueltie,*
  And those *Curs'd summes* which poor men borrow
  On *use*[4] to day, *remit* to morrow!

[4] Interest, usury (OED).

[O–44]   *Ad fluvium Iscam.*[1]

    Isca parens florum, placido qui spumeus ore
        Lambis lapillos aureos,
    Qui mœstos hyacinthos, & picti ἄνθεα *tophi*
        Mulces susurris humidis,
5   *Dumq; novas* pergunt *menses* Consumere *Lunas*
        Cœlumq; mortales *terit,*
    Accumulas cum Sole *dies, œvumq; per omne*
        Fidelis Induras *latex,*
    O quis[2] *Inaccessos & quali murmure lucos*
10   *Mutumq;* Solaris *nemus!*
    Per te discerpti credo Thracis *ire querelas*
        Plectrumq; divini senis.

[To the River Usk

Usk, father of flowers, foaming from your peaceful source you bathe the golden pebbles and comfort with dewy whispers the sad hyacinths and the little flowers that grow in the many-colored rock. While the passing months continue to devour new moon after new moon, and while heaven wears away the generations of men, you heap up days like the sun and endure through all eternity, a never-failing stream. O how and with what murmuring you console the unvisited woods and the voiceless grove! I believe that the plaintive songs of poor torn Orpheus drift along your waters and the sound of strings touched by that old and godlike man.]

AD FLUVIUM ISCAM.

   1 With this compare his English poem on the Usk, O–2, above.
   2 Marilla (*Secular Poems*, p. 55) prints *quis* but regards this as a misprint for *quos*. *Quis* is the original—and the better—reading.

[O–45]   *Venerabili viro, præceptori suo olim*
& semper Colendissimo M^{ro.}
Mathæo Herbert.[1]

Quod vixi, Mathæe, *dedit* Pater, *hæc tamen olim*
    Vita fluet, nec erit fas meminisse datam.
Ultrà Curâsti Solers, perituraq; mecum
    Nomina post Cineres *das resonare* meos.
5   *Divide discipulum: brevis hæc & lubrica nostri*
    Pars vertat Patri, *Posthuma vita* tibi.

VENERABILI VIRO . . . MATHÆO HERBERT.
  [1] On Matthew Herbert see O–1, n. 2.

[To that Venerable Man Mr. Matthew Herbert,
Once His Tutor, and Always the Object
of His Especial Regard

It was my father, Matthew, who gave me life, but one day
that life will pass, and it will be impossible for anyone to
remember his gift any more. With shrewd judgment, you have
been more provident than he. My name, which would have
perished with me, will now, through your gift, resound beyond my grave. Divide your pupil in two: this brief and
transient part of me may be ascribed to my father; my life
after death, to you.]

[O–46]   *Præstantissimo viro,* Thomæ Poëllo *in
suum de Elementis opticæ libellum.*[1]

    Vivaces *oculorum* Ignes *&* lumina dia
      Fixit in angusto *maximus* orbe *Deus,*
    Ille Explorantes radios *dedit, &* vaga lustra
      In quibus Intuitûs *lexq; modusq; latent.*
5   *Hos* tacitos Jactus, lususq; volubilis orbis
      Pingis in Exiguo, *magne Poëlle,* libro,
    Excursusq; situsq;, *ut* Lynceus opticus, *edis*
      Quotq; modis fallunt, *quotq; adhibenda* fides.
    Æmula naturæ manus! *&* mens *Conscia cœli!*
10   *Illa videre* dedit, *vestra videre* docet.

PRÆSTANTISSIMO VIRO, THOMÆ POËLLO. . . .

   [1] On Thomas Powell see "Upon the most Ingenious *pair* of Twins . . ." following "The Publisher to the Reader" of *Olor Iscanus.* Powell published his *Elementa Opticae* in 1651, with these verses prefixed.

[To that Outstanding Man Thomas Powell, On His Treatise Concerning the Elements of Optics

Almighty God has placed the lively fires of His divine gift of sight in a tiny ball. He has given us perceptive rays, and mysterious cells in which the law and means of vision are concealed. It is these silent beams, these playful movements of the rolling eyeball which you depict, great Powell, in your little book. Sharp-sighted as Lynceus, you describe the projections and positions of the eyes, and tell of the various ways in which they may deceive, and how much faith is to be placed in them. Hand rivaling nature! Mind in tune with heaven! Nature gave sight: you teach it!]

[O–47]   *Ad Echum.*

   O Quæ frondosæ per amœna Cubilia *sylvæ*
   Nympha volas, lucoq; loquax *spatiaris in alto,*
   Annosi numen *nemoris, saltusq; verendi*
   Effatum, *cui sola placent* postrema *relatu*!
5   *Te per* Narcissi *morientis verba, precesq;*
   Per pueri Lassatam animam, *&* Conamina *vitæ*
   Ultima, *palantisq; precor* suspiria *linguæ.*
   Da quo secretæ hæc Incædua devia *sylvæ,*
   Anfractusq; *loci dubios, &* lustra *repandam.*
10 *Sic tibi* perpetuâ *(meritoq;) hæc regna* Juventâ
   Luxurient, dabiturq; tuis, sinè fine, viretis
   Intactas *Lunæ* lachrymas, *& lambere* rorem
   Virgineum, *Cæliq;* animas *haurire tepentis.*
   Nec cedant ævo stellis, *sed* lucida *sempèr*
15 *Et* satiata sacro *æterni* medicamine *veris*
   Ostendant longè vegetos, *ut Sydera,* vultus!
   Sic spiret Muscata Comas, *& Cynnama passim*!
   Diffundat levis umbra, in funere qualia spargit
   Phœnicis rogus *aut Pancheæ* nubila *flammæ*!

[To Echo

O nymph flitting through the pleasant recesses of the leafy woodland and sauntering, talkative, in the depths of the grove, goddess of the primeval forest, voice of the haunted glade, caring to answer only the last snatches of what we say; I beg you by the words of prayer which dying Narcissus uttered, by his failing breath, by his life's last struggles, by the sighs of his faltering tongue, grant me the key to these pathless tracts of remote woodland, where no ax has sounded, to the perplexed windings of this place, and to the forest lairs. Then may these realms of yours flourish (as they deserve) with perpetual youth: then may your grassy clearings never cease to drink the moon's chaste tears and the virgin dew, or to inhale the warm breezes of heaven. May they equal the stars in age. Always shining, and saturated with the sacred elixir of eternal spring, may they show their bright faces far and wide, like stars. Then may the musk and cinnamon breathe forth foliage all around, and may the soft shade diffuse scents like those which spread from the funeral pyre of the Phoenix or from the smoke of flaming incense.]

SILEX SCINTILLANS

Part One

(1650)

Authoris (de se) Emblema.

Tentâsti, fateor, sine vulnere sæpius, & me
   Consultum voluit Vox, *sine voce, frequens;*
Ambivit placido divinior aura meatu,
   Et frustrà sancto murmure præmonuit.
5 *Surdus eram, mutusq;* Silex: *Tu, (quanta tuorum*
   Cura tibi est!) aliâ das renovare viâ,
Permutas Curam: Jamq; irritatus Amorem
   Posse negas, & vim, Vi, *superare paras,*
Accedis propior, molemq;, & Saxea *rumpis*
10 *Pectora, fitq;* Caro, *quod fuit ante* Lapis.
En lacerum! Cœlosq; tuos ardentia tandem
   Fragmenta, *& liquidas ex* Adamante *genas.*
Sic olim undantes Petras, Scopulosq; *vomentes*
   Curâsti, O populi providus usq; tui![1]
15 *Quam miranda tibi manus est!* Moriendo, *revixi;*
   Et fractas *jam sum* ditior *inter* opes.[2]

AUTHORIS (DE SE) EMBLEMA.

[1] See Exod. 17.6 for the story of Moses striking the rock to provide water for the children of Israel.

[2] The exact nature of the personal misfortunes Vaughan refers to is not known. Probably the death of his younger brother William in 1648, possibly ill health and the tragedy of the civil wars are all in his mind.

[The Author's Emblem (of Himself)

Often enough have you attempted, I confess, to capture me
without wounding me. Your speechless voice has tried un-
ceasingly to bring me to my senses. Your divine breath has
striven to win me over by its gentle motion, warning me in
vain with sacred murmuring. I was deaf and dumb: a flint.
So you consent (how great is your care for your dear ones!)
to reform me in another way: you change your method com-
pletely and now, provoked, you declare that love cannot suc-
ceed: you plan to conquer force by force. You launch your
attack and shatter that boulder, my stony heart. What was
stone, becomes flesh. Look at it, broken in pieces! Look, its
fragments are flashing at last to heaven and to you, and my
cheeks are wet with tears wrung from flint. In the same way,
ever provident for your people, you once commanded dry
rocks to overflow and crags to gush with water. How mar-
velous your hand is! By dying I have gained new life: amidst
the wreckage of my worldly fortunes, I am now richer than
ever.]

A *note on the engraved title page* (*1650*) (to be found opposite p. 384)

The emblem appears only in the edition of 1650, not in
the "second edition" of 1655. The subtitle is an acknowledg-
ment of Vaughan's indebtedness to George Herbert, who
had used the same subtitle for *The Temple* (1633). The en-
graver of the title page is unknown.

[S–2]   The Dedication.[1]

> My God, thou that didst dye for me,
> These thy leaths fruits I offer thee.
> Death that to me was life, and light
> But darke, and deep pangs to thy sight.
> 5   Some drops of thy all-quickning bloud
> Fell on my heart, these made it bud
> And put forth thus, though, Lord, before
> The ground was curs'd, and void of store.
>   Indeed, I had some here to hire
> 10 Which long resisted thy desire,
> That ston'd thy Servants, and did move
> To have thee murther'd for thy Love,
> But, Lord, I have expell'd them, and so bent
> Begge thou wouldst take thy Tenants Rent.

THE DEDICATION.
[1] A more extended form of dedication, including this poem, appears before the second part of *Silex Scintillans* (1655).

Silex Scintillans, &c.

[S-3]   Regeneration.

A Ward, and still in bonds, one day
         I stole abroad,
It was high-spring, and all the way
       Primros'd, and hung with shade;
5   Yet, was it frost within,
           And surly winds
Blasted my infant buds, and sinne
      Like Clouds ecclips'd my mind.

2.

Storm'd thus; I straight perceiv'd my spring
10   Meere stage, and show,
My walke a monstrous, mountain'd thing
        Rough-cast with Rocks, and snow;
        And as a Pilgrims Eye
          Far from reliefe,
15 Measures the melancholy skye
        Then drops, and rains for griefe,

3.

So sigh'd I upwards still, at last
        'Twixt steps, and falls
I reach'd the pinacle, where plac'd
20   I found a paire of scales,
        I tooke them up and layd
          In th'one late paines,
The other smoake, and pleasures weigh'd
      But prov'd the heavier graines;

4.

25   With that, some cryed, *Away*; straight I
                    Obey'd, and led
    Full East, a faire, fresh field could spy
                Some call'd it, *Jacobs Bed*;[1]
        A Virgin-soile, which no
30   Rude feet ere trod,
    Where (since he stept there,) only go
            Prophets, and friends of God.[2]

5.

    Here, I repos'd; but scarse well set,
                A grove descryed
35   Of stately height, whose branches met
                And mixt on every side;
        I entred, and once in
                    (Amaz'd to see't,)
    Found all was chang'd, and a new spring
40   Did all my senses greet;

6.

    The unthrift Sunne shot vitall gold
                A thousand peeces,
    And heaven its azure did unfold
                Checqur'd with snowie fleeces,
45   The aire was all in spice
                And every bush
    A garland wore; Thus fed my Eyes
            But all the Eare lay hush.

REGENERATION.
    [1] See Gen. 28.11, 19. Jacob called the place Bethel (house of God).
    [2] Wisd. of Sol. 7.27 (Genevan version) says that Wisdom "passing into holy souls" from age to age, produces "friends of God and prophets." And in James 2.23 it is said that Abraham "was called the friend of God."

7.

Only a little Fountain lent
           Some use for Eares,
50
And on the dumbe shades language spent
        The Musick of her teares;
    I drew her neere, and found
        The Cisterne full
55   Of divers stones, some bright, and round
    Others ill-shap'd, and dull.

8.

The first (pray marke,) as quick as light
        Danc'd through the floud,
But, th'last more heavy then the night
60   Nail'd to the Center stood;
    I wonder'd much, but tyr'd
        At last with thought,
My restless Eye that still desir'd
    As strange an object brought;

9.

65   It was a banke of flowers, where I descried
        (Though 'twas mid-day,)
Some fast asleepe, others broad-eyed
    And taking in the Ray,
    Here musing long, I heard
70   A rushing wind
Which still increas'd, but whence it stirr'd
    No where I could not find;

10.

I turn'd me round, and to each shade
        Dispatch'd an Eye,
75   To see, if any leafe had made
    Least motion, or Reply,

> But while I listning sought
> My mind to ease
> By knowing, where 'twas, or where not,
> 80   It whisper'd; *Where I please.*[3]

> Lord, then said I, *On me one breath,*
> *And let me dye before my death!*

> Cant. Cap. 5. ver. 17.[4]
> *Arise O North, and come thou South-wind, and blow upon*
> *my garden, that the spices thereof may flow out.*

[S–4]   Death.

A Dialogue.

Soule.

> 'Tis a sad Land, that in one day
> Hath dull'd thee thus, when death shall freeze
> Thy bloud to Ice, and thou must stay
> Tenant for Yeares, and Centuries,
> 5   How wilt thou brook't?——

Body.

> I cannot tell,——
> But if all sence wings not with thee,
> And something still be left the dead,
> I'le wish my Curtaines off to free
> 10   Me from so darke, and sad a bed;

[3] John 3.8, "The wind bloweth where it listeth, and thou hearest the sound thereof, but canst not tell whence it cometh, and whither it goeth: so is every one that is born of the Spirit."

[4] The reference should be to Song of Sol. 4.16. Vaughan blends the Genevan "Arise, O North, and come O South, and blow on my garden . . ." with the King James "Awake, O north wind; and come, thou south; blow upon my garden. . . ."

A neast of nights, a gloomie sphere,
Where shadowes thicken, and the Cloud
Sits on the Suns brow all the yeare,
And nothing moves without a shrowd;

Soule.

15   'Tis so: But as thou sawest that night
        Wee travell'd in, our first attempts
        Were dull, and blind, but Custome straight
        Our feares, and falls brought to contempt,

        Then, when the gastly *twelve* was past
20   We breath'd still for a blushing *East*,
        And bad the lazie Sunne make hast,
        And on sure hopes, though long, did feast;

        But when we saw the Clouds to crack
        And in those Cranies light appear'd,
25   We thought the day then was not slack,
        And pleas'd our selves with what wee feard;

        Just so it is in death. But thou
        Shalt in thy mothers bosome sleepe
        Whilst I each minute grone to know
30   How neere Redemption creepes.

Then shall wee meet to mix again, and met,
'Tis last good-night, our Sunne shall never set.

Job. Cap: 10. *ver.* 21. 22.[1]
*Before I goe whence I shall not returne, even to the land
of darknesse, and the shadow of death;*

*A Land of darknesse, as darkenesse it selfe, and of the
shadow of death, without any order, and where the light is
as darknesse.*

DEATH. A DIALOGUE.
[1] The King James version of Job 10.21–22.

[S–5]   Resurrection and
                     Immortality:

Heb. cap. 10. ve: 20.[1]
By that new, and living way, which he hath prepared for us, through the veile, which is his flesh.

Body.

1.

Oft have I seen, when that renewing breath
            That binds, and loosens death
Inspir'd a quickning power through the dead
            Creatures a bed,
5   Some drowsie silk-worme creepe
            From that long sleepe
And in weake, infant hummings chime, and knell
            About her silent Cell
Untill at last full with the vitall Ray
10   She wing'd away,
            And proud with life, and sence,
            Heav'ns rich Expence,
Esteem'd (vaine things!) of two whole Elements
            As meane, and span-extents.
15 Shall I then thinke such providence will be
            Lesse friend to me?
            Or that he can endure to be unjust
            Who keeps his Covenant even with our dust.

Soule.

2.

Poore, querulous handfull! was't for this
20   I taught thee all that is?
Unbowel'd nature, shew'd thee her recruits,[2]
         And Change of suits
       And how of death we make
         A meere mistake,
25 For no thing can to *Nothing* fall, but still
        Incorporates by skill,
And then returns, and from the wombe of things
         Such treasure brings
      As *Phenix*-like renew'th
30   Both life, and youth;
For a preserving spirit doth still passe
        Untainted through this Masse,
Which doth resolve, produce, and ripen all
        That to it fall;
35   Nor are those births which we
       Thus suffering see
Destroy'd at all; But when times restles wave
        Their substance doth deprave
And the more noble *Essence* finds his house
40   Sickly, and loose,
      He, ever young, doth wing
        Unto that spring,
And *source* of spirits, where he takes his lot
       Till time no more shall rot
45 His passive Cottage; which (though laid aside,)
        Like some spruce Bride,
Shall one day rise, and cloath'd with shining light
        All pure, and bright
     Re-marry to the soule, for 'tis most plaine
50   Thou only fal'st to be refin'd againe.

---

[2] The OED cites this use of the word as meaning "A means of
recruital."

3.

Then I that here saw darkly in a glasse[3]
                But mists, and shadows passe,
And, by their owne weake *Shine*, did search the springs
                And Course of things
55   Shall with Inlightned Rayes
                Peirce all their wayes;
And as thou saw'st, I in a thought could goe
                To heav'n, or Earth below
To reade some *Starre*, or *Min'rall*, and in State
60   There often sate,
                So shalt thou then with me
                (Both wing'd, and free,)
Rove in that mighty, and eternall light
                Where no rude shade, or night
65 Shall dare approach us; we shall there no more
                Watch stars, or pore
                Through melancholly clouds, and say
                Would it were Day!
        One everlasting *Saboth* there shall runne
70   Without *Succession*, and without a *Sunne*.

Dan: Cap: 12. ver: 13.[4]
But goe thou thy way untill the end be, for thou shalt rest,
and stand up in thy lot, at the end of the dayes.

[S–6]   Day of Judgement.

When through the North a fire shall rush
                And rowle into the East,
And like a firie torrent brush
                And sweepe up *South*, and *West*,

---

[3] I Cor. 13.12, "For now we see through a glass, darkly; . . ."
[4] The Genevan version of the verse.

5   When all shall streame, and lighten round
               And with surprizing flames
     Both stars, and Elements confound
               And quite blot out their names,

     When thou shalt spend thy sacred store
10   Of thunders in that heate
     And low as ere they lay before
               Thy six-dayes-buildings beate,

     When like a scrowle the heavens shal passe
               And vanish cleane away,
15   And nought must stand of that vast space
               Which held up night, and day,

     When one lowd blast shall rend the deepe,
               And from the wombe of earth
     Summon up all that are asleepe
20   Unto a second birth,

     When thou shalt make the Clouds thy seate,
               And in the open aire
     The Quick, and dead, both small and great
               Must to thy barre repaire;

25   O then it wilbe all too late
               To say, *What shall I doe?*
     Repentance there is out of date
               And so is *mercy* too;

     Prepare, prepare me then, O God!
30   And let me now begin
     To feele my loving fathers *Rod*
               Killing the man of sinne!

     Give me, O give me Crosses here,
               Still more afflictions lend,
35   That pill, though bitter, is most deare
               That brings health in the end;

Lord, God! I beg nor friends, nor wealth
                    But pray against them both;
        Three things I'de have, my soules chief health!
40   And one of these seme loath,

A living *F A I T H*, a *H E A R T* of flesh,
                The *W O R L D* an Enemie,
This last will keepe the first two fresh,
                    And bring me, where I'de be.

1 Pet. 4. 7.[1]
Now the end of all things is at hand, be you therefore
sober, and watching in prayer.

DAY OF JUDGEMENT.
    [1] The Genevan version of the verse.

[S–7]   Religion.

My God, when I walke in those groves,
And leaves thy spirit doth still fan,
I see in each shade that there growes
An Angell talking with a man.

5   Under a *Juniper*,[1] some house,
           Or the coole *Mirtles* canopie,[2]
           Others beneath an *Oakes* greene boughs,[3]
           Or at some *fountaines* bubling Eye;[4]

RELIGION.
    [1] I Kings 19.5. The angel of the Lord touched and spoke to
Elijah when he was sleeping under a juniper.
    [2] Zech. 1.11, "the angel of the Lord that stood among the
myrtle trees. . . ."
    [3] Judg. 6.11, "there came an angel of the Lord, and sat under
an oak. . . ."
    [4] Gen. 16.7. The angel of the Lord found Hagar by a fountain.

Here *Jacob* dreames, and wrestles;[5] there
10   *Elias* by a Raven is fed,
Another time by th' Angell, where
He brings him water with his bread;[6]

In *Abr'hams* Tent the winged guests[7]
(O how familiar then was heaven!)
15   Eate, drinke, discourse, sit downe, and rest
Untill the Coole, and shady *Even*;

Nay thou thy selfe, my God, in *fire*,
Whirle-winds, and *Clouds*, and the *soft voice*[8]
Speak'st there so much, that I admire
20   We have no Conf'rence in these daies;

Is the truce broke? or 'cause we have
A mediatour now with thee,
Doest thou therefore old Treaties wave
And by appeales from him decree?

25   Or is't so, as some green heads say
That now all miracles must cease?
Though thou hast promis'd they should stay
The tokens of the Church, and peace;

[5] Gen. 28.11–12; 32.24–30, tell, respectively, of Jacob's vision of the ladder with angels ascending and descending, and of his wrestling with God.

[6] I Kings 17.6, tells of the ravens feeding Elijah; in I Kings 19.5–8, an angel provides him with "a cake baken on the coals, and a cruse of water. . . ."

[7] Gen. 18.1–8. The Lord appeared in the form of three men to Abraham, sitting in the tent door, and they ate and drank with him. The two angels who came to Lot in Sodom "at even" (Gen. 19.1) had presumably been with Abraham earlier in the day.

[8] Vaughan compresses a number of passages which tell of God's speaking from fire (Exod. 3.2–6; Lev. 9.24; Deut. 4.12; 5.4), from cloud (Exod. 24.16; Num. 11.25), from fire and cloud (Deut. 5.22), in a still small voice (I Kings 19.12), and out of the whirl-wind (Job 38.1; 40.6).

No, no; Religion is a Spring
30   That from some secret, golden Mine
Derives her birth, and thence doth bring
Cordials in every drop, and Wine;

But in her long, and hidden Course
Passing through the Earths darke veines,
35   Growes still from better unto worse,
And both her taste, and colour staines,

Then drilling on, learnes to encrease
False *Ecchoes*, and Confused sounds,
And unawares doth often seize
40   On veines of *Sulphur* under ground;

So poison'd, breaks forth in some Clime,
And at first sight doth many please,
But drunk, is puddle, or meere slime
And 'stead of Phisick, a disease;

45   Just such a tainted sink we have
Like that *Samaritans* dead *Well*,[9]
Nor must we for the Kernell crave
Because most voices like the *shell*.

Heale then these waters, Lord; or bring thy flock,
50   Since these are troubled, to the springing rock,
Looke downe great Master of the feast; O shine,
And turn once more our *Water* into *Wine!*

Cant. cap. 4. ver. 12.[10]
*My sister, my spouse is as a garden Inclosed, as a Spring
shut up, and a fountain sealed up.*

[9] John 4.6–14. The water of Jacob's well was dead in contrast
with the water of life offered by Jesus to the woman of Samaria.
[10] The Genevan version of Song of Sol. 4.12.

[S–8]   The Search.

       'Tis now cleare day: I see a Rose
       Bud in the bright East, and disclose
       The Pilgrim-Sunne; all night have I
       Spent in a roving Extasie
5   To find my Saviour; I have been
       As far as *Bethlem*, and have seen
       His Inne, and Cradle; Being there
       I met the *Wise-men*, askt them where
       He might be found, or what starre can
10   Now point him out, grown up a Man?
       To *Egypt* hence I fled, ran o're
       All her parcht bosome to *Nile's* shore
       Her yearly nurse; came back, enquir'd
       Amongst the *Doctors*, and desir'd
15   To see the *Temple*, but was shown
       A little dust, and for the Town
       A heap of ashes, where some sed
       A small bright sparkle was a bed,
       Which would one day (beneath the pole,)
20   Awake, and then refine the whole.
         Tyr'd here, I come to *Sychar*;[1] thence
       To *Jacobs wel*, bequeathed since
       Unto his sonnes, (where often they
       In those calme, golden Evenings lay
25   Watring their flocks, and having spent
       Those white dayes, drove home to the Tent
       Their *well-fleec'd* traine;) And here (O fate!)
       I sit, where once my Saviour sate;
       The angry Spring in bubbles swell'd
30   Which broke in sighes still, as they fill'd,
       And whisper'd, *Jesus had been there*
       But *Jacobs children would not heare*.

THE SEARCH.
  [1] John 4.5–6.

Loath hence to part, at last I rise
But with the fountain in my Eyes,
35 And here a fresh search is decreed
He must be found, where he did bleed;
I walke the garden, and there see
Idæa's of his Agonie,
And moving anguishments that set
40 His blest face in a bloudy sweat;
I climb'd the Hill, perus'd the Crosse
Hung with my gaine, and his great losse,
Never did tree beare fruit like this,
Balsam of Soules, the bodyes blisse;
45 But, O his grave! where I saw lent
(For he had none,) a Monument,
An undefil'd, and new-heaw'd one,
But there was not the *Corner-stone*;[2]
Sure (then said I,) my Quest is vaine,
50 Hee'le not be found, where he was slaine,
So mild a Lamb can never be
'Midst so much bloud, and Crueltie;
I'le to the Wilderness, and can
Find beasts more mercifull then man,
55 He liv'd there safe, 'twas his retreat
From the fierce *Jew*, and *Herods* heat,
And forty dayes withstood the fell,
And high temptations of hell;
With Seraphins there talked he
60 His fathers flaming ministrie,
He heav'nd their *walks*, and with his eyes
Made those wild shades a Paradise,
Thus was the desert sanctified
To be the refuge of his bride;[3]
65 I'le thither then; see, It is day,
The Sun's broke through to guide my way.
     But as I urg'd thus, and writ down
What pleasures should my Journey crown,

[2] Christ. See Acts 4.10–11; I Pet. 2.5–6.
[3] The woman of Rev. 12.1–6, commonly interpreted to mean the
Church, the Bride of Christ.

What silent paths, what shades, and Cells,
70 Faire, virgin-flowers, and hallow'd *Wells*
I should rove in, and rest my head
Where my deare Lord did often tread,
Sugring all dangers with successe,
Me thought I heard one singing thus;

1.

75 Leave, leave, thy gadding thoughts;
Who Pores
and spies
Still out of Doores
descries
80 Within them nought.

2.

The skinne, and shell of things
Though faire,
are not
Thy wish, nor pray'r
85 but got
My meer Despair
of wings.

3.

To rack old Elements,
or Dust
90 and say
Sure here he must
needs stay
Is not the way,
nor just.

95 Search well another world; who studies this,
Travels in Clouds, seeks *Manna*, where none is.

Acts Cap. 17. ver. 27, 28.[4]
That they should seek the Lord, if happily they might feel
after him, and finde him, though he be not far off from every
one of us, for in him we live, and move, and have our being.

[4] The King James version.

[S–9]   *Isaacs* Marriage.

Gen. cap. 24. ver. 63.[1]

And Isaac *went out to pray in the field at the Even-tide, and he lift up his eyes, and saw, and behold, the Camels were coming.*

> Praying! and to be married? It was rare,
> But now 'tis monstrous; and that pious care
> Though of our selves, is so much out of date,
> That to renew't were to degenerate.
> 5 But thou a Chosen sacrifice wert given,
> And offer'd up so early unto heaven
> Thy flames could not be out; Religion was
> Ray'd into thee, like beams into a glasse,
> Where, as thou grewst, it multipli'd and shin'd
> 10 The sacred Constellation of thy mind.
> But being for a bride, prayer was such
> A decryed course, sure it prevail'd not much.
> Had'st ne'r an oath, nor Complement? thou wert
> An odde dull sutor; Hadst thou but the art
> 15 Of these our dayes, thou couldst have coyn'd thee twenty
> New sev'ral oathes, and Complements (too) plenty;
> O sad, and wilde excesse! and happy those
> White dayes, that durst no impious mirth expose!
> When Conscience by lew'd use had not lost sense,
> 20 Nor bold-fac'd custome banish'd Innocence;
> Thou hadst no pompous train, nor *Antick* crowd
> Of young, gay swearers, with their needlesse, lowd
> Retinue; All was here smooth as thy bride
> And calm like her, or that mild Evening-tide;

ISAACS MARRIAGE.
   [1] The King James version, using the alternative "pray" offered in the margins of early editions (e.g., 1612) for "meditate," and retaining "lift" of the early editions as a past tense.

25 Yet, hadst thou nobler guests: Angels did wind
     And rove about thee, guardians of thy minde,
     These fetch'd thee home thy bride, and all the way
     Advis'd thy servant what to do, and say;
     These taught him at the *well*, and thither brought
30 The Chast, and lovely object of thy thought;
     But here was ne'r a Complement, not one
     Spruce, supple cringe, or study'd look put on,
     All was plain, modest truth: Nor did she come
     In *rowles* and *Curles*, mincing and stately dumb,
35 But in a Virgins native blush and fears
     Fresh as those roses, which the day-spring wears.
     O sweet, divine simplicity! O grace
     Beyond a Curled lock, or painted face!
     A *Pitcher* too she had, nor thought it much
40 To carry that, which some would scorn to touch;
     With which in mild, chast language she did wooe
     To draw him drink, and for his Camels too.
        And now thou knewest her coming, It was time
     To get thee wings on, and devoutly climbe
45 Unto thy God, for Marriage of all states
     Makes most unhappy, or most fortunates;
     This brought thee forth, where now thou didst undress
     Thy soul, and with new pinions refresh
     Her wearied wings, which so restor'd did flye
50 Above the stars, a track unknown, and high,
     And in her piercing flight perfum'd the ayer
     Scatt'ring the *Myrrhe*, and incense of thy pray'r.
     So from[2] *Lahai-roi's* Well some spicie cloud
     Woo'd by the Sun swels up to be his shrowd,
55 And from his moist wombe weeps a fragrant showre,
     Which, scatter'd in a thousand pearls, each flowre
     And herb partakes, where having stood awhile

[2] An asterisk appeared here in the 1650 edition with a note in the right margin from line 53 to 61, which read: *"A wel in the South Country where* Jacob *dwelt, between* Cadesh, & Bered; Heb. *the well of him that liveth, and seeth me."*

And something coold the parch'd, and thirstie Isle,
The thankful Earth unlocks her self, and blends,
60 A thousand odours, which (all mixt,) she sends
Up in one cloud, and so returns the skies
That dew they lent, a breathing sacrifice.
    Thus soar'd thy soul, who (though young,) didst inherit
Together with his bloud, thy fathers spirit,
65 Whose active zeal, and tried faith were to thee
Familiar ever since thy Infancie.
Others were tym'd, and train'd up to't but thou
Diddst thy swift yeers in piety out-grow,
Age made them rev'rend, and a snowie head,
70 But thou wert so, e're time his snow could shed;
Then, who would truly limne thee out, must paint
First, a *young Patriarch,* then a *marri'd Saint.*

[S–10]   The
                    Brittish Church.

        Ah! he is fled!
And while these here their *mists,* and *shadows* hatch,
        My glorious head
Doth on those hills of Mirrhe, and Incense watch.[1]
5   Haste, hast my dear,
        The Souldiers here
      Cast in their lots again,
        That seamlesse coat
        The Jews touch'd not,
10   These dare divide, and stain.[2]

THE BRITTISH CHURCH.
  [1] Song of Sol. 4.6, "I will get me to the mountain of myrrh, and to the hill of frankincense."
  [2] Matt. 27.35 and John 19.23–24, describing the actions of the Roman soldiers at the Crucifixion, refer back to Ps. 22.18, "They part my garments among them, and cast lots upon my vesture."

2.

O get thee wings!
Or if as yet (until these clouds depart,
        And the day springs,)
Thou think'st it good to tarry where thou art,
15   Write in thy bookes
                My ravish'd looks,
            Slain flock, and pillag'd fleeces,
                And hast thee so
                As a young Roe
20   Upon the mounts of spices.[3]
    *O Rosa Campi! O lilium Convallium! quomodò nunc
    facta es pabulum Aprorum!*[4]

[S–11]   The Lampe.

'Tis dead night round about: Horrour doth creepe
And move on with the shades; stars nod, and sleepe,
And through the dark aire spin a firie thread
Such as doth gild the lazie glow-worms bed.
5   Yet, burn'st thou here, a full day; while I spend
My rest in Cares, and to the dark world lend
These flames, as thou dost thine to me; I watch
That houre, which must thy life, and mine dispatch;

[3] Song of Sol. 8.14, "Make haste, my beloved, and be thou like
to a roe or to a young hart upon the mountains of spices."

[4] "O rose of the field! O lily of the valleys! how art thou now
become the food of wild boars!" Apparently a fusion of Song of
Sol. 2.1 and Ps. 80.13. Hutchinson (*Life*, p. 122, n. 4) points out
that Vaughan takes *Rosa* from Tremellius' Latin Bible, whereas the
Vulgate has *flos.* But the Vulgate reads *flos campi,* whereas the
Tremellius version reads *rosa Sharonis,* Vaughan's Latin thus cross-
ing the two readings and providing the Latin equivalent of the
Genevan "rose of the field." The marginal notation for "wilde
bore" of the Genevan version of Ps. 80.13 reads, "That is, aswell
they that hate our religion, as they that hate our persons." Vaughan
apparently has in mind the anti-Laudians.

But still thou doest out-goe me, I can see
10 Met in thy flames, all acts of piety;
Thy light, is *Charity*; Thy heat, is *Zeale*;
And thy aspiring, active fires reveale
Devotion still on wing; Then, thou dost weepe
Still as thou burn'st, and the warme droppings creepe
15 To measure out thy length, as if thou'dst know
What stock, and how much time were left thee now;
Nor dost thou spend one teare in vain, for still
As thou dissolv'st to them, and they distill,
They're stor'd up in the socket, where they lye,
20 When all is spent, thy last, and sure supply,
And such is true repentance, ev'ry breath
Wee spend in sighes, is treasure after death;
Only, one point escapes thee; That thy Oile
Is still out with thy flame, and so both faile;
25 But whensoe're I'm out, both shalbe in,
And where thou mad'st an end, there I'le begin.

Mark Cap. 13. ver. 35.[1]
*Watch you therefore, for you know not when the master of
the house commeth, at Even, or at mid-night, or at the Cock-
crowing, or in the morning.*

[S–12]   Mans fall, and Recovery.

Farewell you Everlasting hills! I'm Cast
Here under Clouds, where stormes, and tempests blast
This sully'd flowre
Rob'd of your Calme, nor can I ever make
5 Transplanted thus, one leafe of his t'awake,
But ev'ry houre
He sleepes, and droops, and in this drowsie state
Leaves me a slave to passions, and my fate;

THE LAMPE.
[1] The King James version, with "you" for "ye" in two places.

Besides I've lost
10 A traine of lights, which in those Sun-shine dayes
Were my sure guides, and only with me stayes
(Unto my cost,)
One sullen beame, whose charge is to dispense
More punishment, than knowledge to my sense;
15 Two thousand yeares
I sojourn'd thus; at last *Jeshuruns*[1] king
Those famous tables did from *Sinai* bring;
These swell'd my feares,
Guilts, trespasses, and all this Inward Awe,
20 For sinne tooke strength, and vigour from the Law.
Yet have I found
A plenteous way, (thanks to that holy one!)
To cancell all that e're was writ in stone,
His saving wound
25 Wept bloud, that broke this Adamant, and gave
To sinners Confidence, life to the grave;
This makes me span
My fathers journeys, and in one faire step
O're all their pilgrimage, and labours leap,
30 For God (made man,)
Reduc'd th'Extent of works of faith; so made
Of their *Red Sea,* a *Spring*; I wash, they wade.

Rom. Cap. 18. ver. 19.[2]

*As by the offence of one, the fault came on all men to con-
demnation*; *So by the Righteousness of one, the benefit
abounded towards all men to the Justification of life.*

MANS FALL, AND RECOVERY.
[1] Poetical name for the people of Israel.
[2] The Genevan version of Rom. 5.18 (not 18.19, as in the text),
except that Vaughan prefers the *"Righteousness"* of the King James
version to the "justifying" of the Genevan.

[S–13]   The Showre.

'Twas so, I saw thy birth: That drowsie Lake
From her faint bosome breath'd thee, the disease
Of her sick waters, and Infectious Ease.
                    But, now at Even
5   Too grosse for heaven,
Thou fall'st in teares, and weep'st for thy mistake.

                    2.

Ah! it is so with me; oft have I prest
Heaven with a lazie breath, but fruitles this
Peirc'd not; Love only can with quick accesse
10   Unlock the way,
                    When all else stray
The smoke, and Exhalations of the brest.

                    3.

Yet, if as thou doest melt, and with thy traine
Of drops make soft the Earth, my eyes could weep
15   O're my hard heart, that's bound up, and asleep,
                    Perhaps at last
                    (Some such showres past,)
My God would give a Sun-shine after raine.

[S–14]   Distraction.

        O Knit me, that am crumbled dust! the heape
                Is all dispers'd, and cheape;
            Give for a handfull, but a thought
                And it is bought;
5   Hadst thou

Made me a starre, a pearle, or a rain-bow,
    The beames I then had shot
    My light had lessend not,
        But now
10 I find my selfe the lesse, the more I grow;
        The world
Is full of voices; Man is call'd, and hurl'd
    By each, he answers all,
    Knows ev'ry note, and call,
15   Hence, still
Fresh dotage tempts, or old usurps his will.
Yet, hadst thou clipt my wings, when Coffin'd in
    This quicken'd masse of sinne,
    And saved that light, which freely thou
20   Didst then bestow,
        I feare
I should have spurn'd, and said thou didst forbeare;
    Or that thy store was lesse,
    But now since thou didst blesse
25   So much,
I grieve, my God! that thou hast made me such.
        I grieve?
O, yes! thou know'st I doe; Come, and releive
    And tame, and keepe downe with thy light
30   Dust that would rise, and dimme my sight,
    Lest left alone too long
    Amidst the noise, and throng,
        Oppressed I
Striving to save the whole, by parcells dye.

[S–15]   **The Pursuite.**

    Lord! what a busie, restles thing
        Hast thou made man?
    Each day, and houre he is on wing,
        Rests not a span;

5   Then having lost the Sunne, and light
                By clouds surpriz'd
        He keepes a Commerce in the night
                With aire disguis'd;
        Hadst thou given to this active dust
10   A state untir'd,
        The lost Sonne had not left the huske
                Nor home desir'd;[1]
        That was thy secret, and it is
                Thy mercy too,
15   For when all failes to bring to blisse,
                Then, this must doe.
        Ah! Lord! and what a Purchase will that be
        To take us sick, that sound would not take thee?

[S–16]   Mount of Olives.

        Sweete, sacred hill! on whose fair brow
        My Saviour sate, shall I allow
                Language to love
        And Idolize some shade, or grove,
5   Neglecting thee? such ill-plac'd wit,
        Conceit, or call it what you please
                Is the braines fit,
                And meere disease;

                        2.

        Cotswold, and Coopers both have met
10   With learned swaines, and Eccho yet
                Their pipes, and wit;[1]

THE PURSUITE.
    [1] See in the story of the Prodigal Son, Luke 15.16–19.
MOUNT OF OLIVES.
    [1] The Cotswolds had been celebrated in poems by Drayton, Jonson, and others appearing in *Annalia Dubrensia. Upon the yeerely celebration of Mr. Robert Dovers Olimpick Games upon Cotswold-Hills* (London, 1636), and Cooper's Hill had been cele-

But thou sleep'st in a deepe neglect
Untouch'd by any; And what need
The sheep bleat thee a silly Lay
15   That heard'st both reed
     And sheepward play?

3.

Yet, if Poets mind thee well
They shall find thou art their hill,
   And fountaine too,
20 Their Lord with thee had most to doe;
He wept once, walkt whole nights on thee,
And from thence (his suff'rings ended,)
    Unto glorie
    Was attended;

4.

25 Being there, this spacious ball
Is but his narrow footstoole all,
   And what we thinke
Unsearchable, now with one winke
He doth comprise; But in this aire
30 When he did stay to beare our Ill
    And sinne, this Hill
    Was then his Chaire.

[S–17]   The Incarnation, and
       Passion.

Lord! when thou didst thy selfe undresse
Laying by thy robes of glory,
To make us more, thou wouldst be lesse,
And becam'st a wofull story.

---

brated in a poem of that name (1642) by Sir John Denham. As
Martin (*Works*, 1957, p. 731) points out, Vaughan may have had
in mind Thomas Randolph's poem, "An Eglogue on the noble As-
semblies revived on Cotswold Hills, by M. Robert Dover."

5   To put on Clouds instead of light,
And cloath the morning-starre with dust,
Was a translation of such height
As, but in thee, was ne'r exprest;

Brave wormes, and Earth! that thus could have
10   A God Enclos'd within your Cell,
Your maker pent up in a grave,
Life lockt in death, heav'n in a shell;

Ah, my deare Lord! what couldst thou spye
In this impure, rebellious clay,
15   That made thee thus resolve to dye
For those that kill thee every day?

O what strange wonders could thee move
To slight thy precious bloud, and breath!
Sure it was *Love*, my Lord; for *Love*
20   Is only stronger far than death.

[S–18]   The Call.

Come my heart! come my head
In sighes, and teares!
'Tis now, since you have laine thus dead
Some twenty years;
5   Awake, awake,
Some pitty take
Upon your selves——
Who never wake to grone, nor weepe,
Shall be sentenc'd for their sleepe.

2.

10   Doe but see your sad estate,
How many sands
Have left us, while we careles sate
With folded hands;

What stock of nights,
15   Of dayes, and yeares
In silent flights
Stole by our eares,
How ill have we our selves bestow'd
Whose suns are all set in a Cloud?

3.

20   Yet, come, and let's peruse them all;
And as we passe,
What sins on every minute fall
Score on the glasse;
Then weigh, and rate
25   Their heavy State
Untill
The glasse with teares you fill;
That done, we shalbe safe, and good,
Those beasts were cleane, that chew'd the Cud.[1]

[S–19]   ¶

Thou that know'st for whom I mourne,[1]
And why these teares appeare,
That keep'st account, till he returne
Of all his dust left here;
5   As easily thou mightst prevent
As now produce these teares,
And adde unto that day he went
A faire supply of yeares.

THE CALL.
   [1] Lev. 11.3, "Whatsoever parteth the hoof, and is clovenfooted, and cheweth the cud, among the beasts, that shall ye eat." And see Deut. 14.6.
"THOU THAT KNOW'ST FOR WHOM I MOURNE"
   [1] Thought to be his brother William, who died in 1648.

But 'twas my sinne that forc'd thy hand
10   To cull this *Prim-rose* out,
That by thy early choice forewarn'd
        My soule might looke about.
O what a vanity is man!
        How like the Eyes quick winke
15 His Cottage[2] failes; whose narrow span
        Begins even at the brink!
Nine months thy hands are fashioning us,
        And many yeares (alas!)
E're we can lisp, or ought discusse
20   Concerning thee, must passe;
Yet have I knowne thy slightest things
        A *feather*, or a *shell*,
A *stick*, or *Rod* which some Chance brings
        The best of us excell,
25 Yea, I have knowne these shreds out last
        A faire-compacted frame
And for one *Twenty* we have past
        Almost outlive our name.
Thus hast thou plac'd in mans outside
30   Death to the Common Eye,
That heaven within him might abide,
        And close eternitie;
Hence, youth, and folly (mans first shame,)
        Are put unto the slaughter,
35 And serious thoughts begin to tame
        The wise-mans-madnes *Laughter*;[3]
Dull, wretched wormes! that would not keepe
        Within our first faire bed,
But out of *Paradise* must creepe
40   For ev'ry foote to tread;
Yet, had our Pilgrimage bin free,
        And smooth without a thorne,
Pleasures had foil'd Eternitie,
        And *tares* had choakt the *Corne*.

[2] His body.
[3] Eccles. 2.2, "I said of laughter, It is mad."

45   Thus by the Crosse Salvation runnes,
          Affliction is a mother,
      Whose painefull throws yield many sons,
          Each fairer than the other;
      A silent teare can peirce thy throne,
50   When lowd Joyes want a wing,
      And sweeter aires streame from a grone,
          Than any arted string;
      Thus, Lord, I see my gaine is great,
          My losse but little to it,
55   Yet something more I must intreate
          And only thou canst doe it.
      O let me (like him,) know my End!
          And be as glad to find it,
      And whatsoe'r thou shalt Commend,
60   Still let thy Servant mind it!
      Then make my soule white as his owne,
          My faith as pure, and steddy,
      And deck me, Lord, with the same Crowne
          Thou hast crownd him already!

[S–20]   Vanity of Spirit.

      Quite spent with thoughts I left my Cell, and lay
      Where a shrill spring tun'd to the early day.
          I beg'd here long, and gron'd to know
          Who gave the Clouds so brave a bow,
5   Who bent the spheres, and circled in
          Corruption with this glorious Ring,[1]
          What is his name, and how I might
          Descry some part of his great light.
      I summon'd nature: peirc'd through all her store,
10 Broke up some seales, which none had touch'd before,

VANITY OF SPIRIT.
    [1] Cf. the "great *Ring*" of S–67, line 2.

Her wombe, her bosome, and her head
Where all her secrets lay a bed
I rifled quite, and having past
Through all the Creatures, came at last
15   To search my selfe, where I did find
Traces, and sounds of a strange kind.
Here of this mighty spring, I found some drills,[2]
With Ecchoes beaten from th' eternall hills;
Weake beames, and fires flash'd to my sight,
20   Like a young East, or Moone-shine night,
Which shew'd me in a nook cast by
A peece of much antiquity,
With Hyerogliphicks quite dismembred,
And broken letters scarce remembred.
25 I tooke them up, and (much Joy'd,) went about
T' unite those peeces, hoping to find out
The mystery; but this neer done,
That little light I had was gone:
It griev'd me much. At last, said I,
30   *Since in these veyls my Ecclips'd Eye*
May not approach thee, (for at night
Who can have commerce with the light?)
I'le disapparell, and to buy
But one half glaunce, most gladly dye.

[2] Small streams, rills.

[S–21]   The Retreate.[1]

Happy those early dayes! when I
Shin'd in my Angell-infancy.
Before I understood this place
Appointed for my second race,
5   Or taught my soul to fancy ought
But a white, Celestiall thought,
When yet I had not walkt above
A mile, or two, from my first love,
And looking back (at that short space,)
10   Could see a glimpse of his bright-face;
When on some *gilded Cloud,* or *flowre*
My gazing soul would dwell an houre,
And in those weaker glories spy
Some shadows of eternity;
15   Before I taught my tongue to wound
My Conscience with a sinfull sound,
Or had the black art to dispence
A sev'rall sinne to ev'ry sence,

THE RETREATE.

[1] Although this poem bears superficial similarities to the *Intimations* ode, there is no reliable evidence that Wordsworth ever knew it. The purpose of "The Retreate" is not so much that of presenting a "philosophy" of childhood as that of recapturing that pure vision of life and the world which might be attained through the innocence associated with infancy, before the soul had become stained by worldly experience. Cf. S–51, lines 5–6, and S–114, lines 19–20. Merritt Y. Hughes ("The Theme of Pre-existence and Infancy in *The Retreate,*" *PQ,* XX [1941], 484–500) makes the point that the retreat is not so much *to* childhood as *from* the evil of the world (cf. "from those follies a resolv'd Retreat," S–63, line 33). See also L. C. Martin, "Henry Vaughan and the Theme of Infancy," in *Seventeenth Century Studies, Presented to Sir Herbert Grierson* (Oxford, 1938), pp. 243–55.

But felt through all this fleshly dresse
20   Bright *shootes* of everlastingnesse.[2]
O how I long to travell back
And tread again that ancient track!
That I might once more reach that plaine,
Where first I left my glorious traine,
25   From whence th' Inlightned spirit sees
That shady City of Palme trees;[3]
But (ah!) my soul with too much stay
Is drunk, and staggers in the way.
Some men a forward motion love,
30   But I by backward steps would move,
And when this dust falls to the urn
In that state I came return.

[S–22]   ¶

Come come, what doe I here?
        Since he is gone[1]
Each day is grown a dozen year,
        And each houre, one;
5   Come, come!
Cut off the sum,
By these soil'd teares!
(Which only thou
Know'st to be true,)
10   Dayes are my feares.

[2] Owen Felltham, *Resolves*, I, 64 (ed. Cumming, 1820, p. 129) speaks of the soul as "a shoot of everlastingness."

[3] From the top of Pisgah, Moses viewed the valley of Jericho, "the city of Palm trees," part of the land promised by God to the seed of Abraham (Deut. 34.1–4).

"COME, COME, WHAT DOE I HERE?"

[1] Probably his younger brother William, who died in 1648.

2.

Ther's not a wind can stir,
  Or beam passe by,
But strait I think (though far,)
  Thy hand is nigh;
15   Come, come!
  Strike these lips dumb:
  This restles breath
  That soiles thy name,
  Will ne'r be tame
20   Untill in death.

3.

Perhaps some think a tombe
  No house of store,
But a dark, and seal'd up wombe,
  Which ne'r breeds more.
25   Come, come!
  Such thoughts benum;
  But I would be
  With him I weep
  A bed, and sleep
30   To wake in thee.

[S–23]   ¶ Midnight.

When to my Eyes
(Whilst deep sleep others catches,)
  Thine hoast of spyes
The starres shine in their watches,
5   I doe survey
    Each busie Ray,
And how they work, and wind,
    And wish each beame
    My soul doth streame,

10   With the like ardour shin'd;
            What Emanations,
            Quick vibrations
    And bright stirs are there?
            What thin Ejections,
15   Cold Affections,
    And slow motions here?

                    2.

            Thy heav'ns (some say,)
    Are a firie-liquid light,
            Which mingling aye
20 Streames, and flames thus to the sight.
            Come then, my god!
            Shine on this bloud,
    And water in one beame,
            And thou shalt see
25   Kindled by thee
    Both liquors burne, and streame.
            O what bright quicknes,
            Active brightnes,
    And celestiall flowes
30   Will follow after
            On that water,
    Which thy spirit blowes!

            Math. Cap. 3. ver. xi.[1]
*I indeed baptize you with water unto repentance, but he
that commeth after me, is mightier than I, whose shooes I am
not worthy to beare, he shall baptize you with the holy
Ghost, and with fire.*

MIDNIGHT.
    [1] The King James version.

[S–24]   ¶ Content.

Peace, peace! I know 'twas brave,
     But this corse fleece
I shelter in, is slave
          To no such peece.[1]
5   When I am gone,
I shall no ward-robes leave
          To friend, or sonne
But what their own homes weave,

2.

Such, though not proud, nor full,
10   May make them weep,
And mourn to see the wooll
          Outlast the sheep;
          Poore, Pious weare!
Hadst thou bin rich, or fine
15   Perhaps that teare
Had mourn'd thy losse, not mine.

3.

Why then these curl'd, puff'd points,[2]
          Or a laced story?[3]
Death sets all out of Joint
20   And scornes their glory;

CONTENT.
[1] Piece [of apparel], with punning allusion to the "peace" of line 1.
[2] Tagged laces or cords of various materials used for attaching hose to doublet, lacing a bodice, etc., often objects of great finery in the dress of the period.
[3] Fabrication or falsehood?

Some Love a *Rose*
In hand, some in the skin;
But crosse to those,
I would have mine *within.*

[S–25]   ¶

Joy of my life![1] while left me here,
    And still my Love!
How in thy absence thou dost steere
    Me from above!
5   A life well lead
    This truth commends,
    With quick, or dead
    It never ends.

2.

Stars are of mighty use: The night
10   Is dark, and long;
The Rode foul, and where one goes right,
    Six may go wrong.
    One twinkling ray
    Shot o'r some cloud,
15   May clear much way
    And guide a croud.

3.

Gods Saints are shining lights: who stays
    Here long must passe
O're dark hills, swift streames, and steep ways
20   As smooth as glasse;

"JOY OF MY LIFE!"
    [1] Thought to be either his brother William or his first wife Catherine. See Hutchinson, *Life,* pp. 195–96.

But these all night
Like Candles, shed
Their beams, and light
Us into Bed.

4.

25   They are (indeed,) our Pillar-fires[2]
Seen as we go,
They are that Cities shining spires
We travell too;
A swordlike gleame
30   Kept man for sin
First *Out*;[3] This beame
Will guide him *In*.

[S–26]   The Storm.

I See the use:[1] and know my bloud
Is not a Sea,
But a shallow, bounded floud
Though red as he;
5   Yet have I flows, as strong as his,
And boyling stremes that rave
With the same curling force, and hisse,
As doth the mountain'd wave.

2.

But when his waters billow thus,
10   Dark storms, and wind
Incite them to that fierce discusse,[2]
Else not Inclin'd,

[2] Cf. the pillar of fire which guided the Israelites, Exod. 13.21.
[3] The flaming sword which guarded Eden, Gen. 3.24.
THE STORM.
[1] Moral or application (OED).
[2] Debate (OED). Vaughan's use here is cited as an example of this meaning.

>Thus the Enlarg'd, inraged air
>>Uncalmes these to a floud,
15>But still the weather that's most fair
>>Breeds tempests in my bloud;

3.

>Lord, then round me with weeping Clouds,
>>And let my mind
>In quick blasts sigh beneath those shrouds
20>>A spirit-wind,
>So shall that storme purge this *Recluse*
>>Which sinfull ease made foul,
>And *wind,* and *water* to thy use
>>Both *wash,* and *wing* my soul.

[S–27]   The
                 Morning-watch.

>O Joyes! Infinite sweetnes! with what flowres,
>And shoots of glory, my soul breakes, and buds!
>>All the long houres
>>Of night, and Rest
5>>Through the still shrouds
>>Of sleep, and Clouds,
>This Dew fell on my Breast;
>>O how it *Blouds,*
>And *Spirits* all my Earth! heark! In what Rings,
10>And *Hymning Circulations* the quick world
>>Awakes, and sings;
>>The rising winds,
>>And falling springs,
>>Birds, beasts, all things
15>>Adore him in their kinds.
>>Thus all is hurl'd

In sacred *Hymnes,* and *Order,* The great *Chime*
And *Symphony* of nature. Prayer is
20   The world in tune,
                                A spirit-voyce,
                                And vocall joyes
                        Whose *Eccho is* heav'ns blisse.
                                O let me climbe[1]
When I lye down! The Pious soul by night
25   Is like a clouded starre, whose beames though sed
                                To shed their light
                                Under some Cloud
                                Yet are above,
                                And shine, and move
30   Beyond that mistie shrowd.
                                So in my Bed
That Curtain'd grave, though sleep, like ashes, hide
My lamp, and life, both shall in thee abide.

[S–28]   The Evening-watch.

A Dialogue.

Body.
Farewell! I goe to sleep; but when
The day-star springs, I'le wake agen.

Soul.
Goe, sleep in peace; and when thou lyest
Unnumber'd in thy dust, when all this frame
5   Is but one dramme, and what thou now descriest
In sev'rall parts shall want a name,
Then may his peace be with thee, and each dust
Writ in his book, who ne'r betray'd mans trust!

THE MORNING-WATCH.
  [1] E. C. Pettet (*Of Paradise and Light* [Cambridge, 1960], p. 123) suggests that here and in S–9, line 44, "climbe" carries the meaning of "pray."

Body.

Amen! but hark, e'r we two stray,
10   How many hours do'st think 'till day?

Soul.

Ah! go; th'art weak, and sleepie. Heav'n
Is a plain watch, and without figures winds
All ages up; who drew this Circle, even
          He fils it; Dayes, and hours are *Blinds.*
15   Yet, this take with thee; The last gasp of time
Is thy first breath, and mans *eternall Prime.*

[S–29]   ¶

Silence, and stealth of dayes! 'tis now
          Since thou art gone,[1]
Twelve hundred houres, and not a brow
          But Clouds hang on.
5   As he that in some Caves thick damp
          Lockt from the light,
Fixeth a solitary lamp,
          To brave the night,
And walking from his Sun, when past
10   That glim'ring Ray
Cuts through the heavy mists in haste
          Back to his day,
So o'r fled minutes I retreat
          Unto that hour
15   Which shew'd thee last, but did defeat
          Thy light, and pow'r,
I search, and rack my soul to see
          Those beams again,
But nothing but the snuff to me
20   Appeareth plain;

"SILENCE, AND STEALTH OF DAYES!"
    [1] Thought to be on the death of his brother William in 1648.

That dark, and dead sleeps in its known,
   And common urn,
 But those fled to their Makers throne,
   There shine, and burn;
25 O could I track them! but souls must
   Track one the other,
And now the spirit, not the dust
   Must be thy brother.
Yet I have one *Pearle*[2] by whose light
30   All things I see,
And in the heart of Earth, and night
   Find Heaven, and thee.

[S–30]   Church-Service.

Blest be the God of Harmony, and Love!
   The God above!
   And holy dove!
Whose Interceding, spirituall grones
5   Make restless mones
   For dust, and stones,
 For dust in every part,
 But a hard, stonie heart.

     2

O how in this thy Quire of Souls I stand
10   (Propt by thy hand)
   A heap of sand!
Which busie thoughts (like winds) would scatter quite
   And put to flight,
   But for thy might;
15 Thy hand alone doth tame
  Those blasts, and knit my frame,

[2] Variously interpreted as his wife or the Bible.

3.

So that both stones, and dust, and all of me
Joyntly agree
To cry to thee,
20 And in this Musick by thy Martyrs bloud
Seal'd, and made good
Present, O God!
The Eccho of these stones
—My sighes, and grones.

[S–31]   Buriall.

O Thou! the first fruits of the dead,
And their dark bed,
When I am cast into that deep
And senseless sleep
5   The wages of my sinne,
O then,
Thou great Preserver of all men!
Watch o're that loose
And empty house,
10   Which I sometimes liv'd in.

2.

It is (in truth!) a ruin'd peece
Not worth thy Eyes,
And scarce a room but wind, and rain
Beat through, and stain
15   The seats, and Cells within;
Yet thou
Led by thy Love wouldst stoop thus low,
And in this Cott
All filth, and spott,
20   Didst with thy servant Inne.

3.

And nothing can, I hourely see,
   Drive thee from me,
Thou art the same, faithfull, and just
   In life, or Dust;
25   Though then (thus crumm'd[1]) I stray
    In blasts,
Or Exhalations, and wasts
    Beyond all Eyes
    Yet thy love spies
30   That Change, and knows thy Clay.

4.

The world's thy boxe: how then (there tost,)
   Can I be lost?
But the delay is all; Tyme now
   Is old, and slow,
35   His wings are dull, and sickly;
    Yet he
Thy servant is, and waits on thee,
    Cutt then the summe,
    Lord haste, Lord come,
40   O come Lord *Jesus* quickly!

Rom. Cap. 8. ver. 23.[2]
*And not only they, but our selves also, which have the first
fruits of the spirit, even wee our selves grone within our selves,
waiting for the adoption,* to wit, *the redemption of our body.*

BURIALL.
 [1] Crumbled, reduced to particles, or dust.
 [2] The King James version.

[S–32]   Chearfulness.

Lord, with what courage, and delight
            I doe each thing
When thy least breath sustaines my wing!
            I shine, and move
5   Like those above,
            And (with much gladnesse
            Quitting sadnesse,)
Make me faire dayes of every night.

                    2.

Affliction thus, meere pleasure is,
10   And hap what will,
If thou be in't, 'tis welcome still;
            But since thy rayes
            In Sunnie dayes
            Thou dost thus lend
15   And freely spend,
Ah! what shall I return for this?

                    3.

O that I were all Soul! that thou
            Wouldst make each part
Of this poor, sinfull frame pure heart!
20   Then would I drown
            My single one,
            And to thy praise
            A Consort raise
Of *Hallelujahs* here below.

[S–33] ¶

Sure, there's a tye of Bodyes! and as they
        Dissolve (with it,) to Clay,
Love languisheth, and memory doth rust
        O'r-cast with that cold dust;
5 For things thus *Center'd*,[1] without *Beames*, or *Action*
        Nor give, nor take *Contaction*,[2]
And man is such a Marygold, these fled,
        That shuts, and hangs the head.

2.

Absents within the Line[3] Conspire, and *Sense*
10   Things distant doth unite,
Herbs sleep unto the *East*, and some fowles thence
        Watch the Returns of light;
But hearts are not so kind: false, short delights
        Tell us the world is brave,
15 And wrap us in Imaginary flights
        Wide of a faithfull grave;
Thus *Lazarus* was carried out of town;[4]
        For 'tis our foes chief art
By distance all good objects first to drown,
20   And then besiege the heart.
But I will be my own *Deaths-head*; and though
        The flatt'rer say, *I live*,
Because Incertainties we cannot know
        Be sure, not to believe.

"SURE, THERE'S A TYE OF BODYES!"
  [1] In repose, at rest.
  [2] The action of touching, contact.
  [3] The line of life. The phrase means, those who are absent from each other while still alive.
  [4] Apparently inferred from John 11.38, where the grave is described as a cave, presumably outside Bethany.

[S–34]   Peace.

        My Soul, there is a Countrie
            Far beyond the stars,
        Where stands a winged Centrie
            All skilfull in the wars,
5   There above noise, and danger
                Sweet peace sits crown'd with smiles,
        And one born in a Manger
                Commands the Beauteous files,
        He is thy gracious friend,
10   And (O my Soul awake!)
        Did in pure love descend
                To die here for thy sake,
        If thou canst get but thither,
                There growes the flowre of peace,
15   The Rose that cannot wither,
                Thy fortresse, and thy ease;
        Leave then thy foolish ranges;
                For none can thee secure,
        But one, who never changes,
20   Thy God, thy life, thy Cure.

[S–35]   The Passion.

            O My chief good!
            My dear, dear God!
            When thy blest bloud
        Did Issue forth forc'd by the Rod,
5   What pain didst thou
            Feel in each blow!
            How didst thou weep,
            And thy self steep
        In thy own precious, saving teares!

10   What cruell smart
            Did teare thy heart!
            How didst thou grone it
            In the spirit,
O thou, whom my soul Loves, and feares!

2.

15   Most blessed Vine!
            Whose juice so good
            I feel as Wine,
But thy faire branches felt as bloud,
            How wert thou prest
20   To be my feast!
            In what deep anguish
            Didst thou languish,
What springs of Sweat, and bloud did drown thee!
            How in one path
25   Did the full wrath
            Of thy great Father
            Crowd, and gather,
Doubling thy griefs, when none would own thee!

3.

            How did the weight
30   Of all our sinnes,
            And death unite
To wrench, and Rack thy blessed limbes!
            How pale, and bloudie
            Lookt thy Body!
35   How bruis'd, and broke
            With every stroke!
How meek, and patient was thy spirit!
            How didst thou cry,
            And grone on high
40   *Father forgive,*
            And let them live,
I dye to make my foes inherit!

4.

O blessed Lamb!
That took'st my sinne,
45   That took'st my shame
How shall thy dust thy praises sing!
I would I were
One hearty tear!
One constant spring!
50   Then would I bring
Thee two small mites, and be at strife
Which should most vie,
My heart, or eye,
Teaching my years
55   In smiles, and tears
To weep, to sing, thy *Death*, my *Life*.

[S–36]

Rom. Cap. 8. ver. 19.
Etenim res Creatæ exerto Capite observantes expectant re-
velationem Filiorum Dei.[1]

And do they so? have they a Sense
Of ought but Influence?
Can they their heads lift, and expect,
And grone too?[2] why th'Elect

"AND DO THEY SO?"

[1] "For the things of creation watching with lifted head look for the revelation of the Sons of God." This Latin version of Beza's translation of the passage does not appear in all editions of the translation, but it does occur in two of Thomas Vautrollier's print-ings (London, 1576 and 1582), with the addition of *quasi* before *exerto*. Some of the Continental editions of Beza's translation of this passage vary considerably from this reading.

[2] Rom. 8.22, "For we know that the whole creation groaneth."

5   Can do no more: my volumes sed
           They were all dull, and dead,
       They judg'd them senslesse, and their state
           Wholly Inanimate.
           Go, go; Seal up thy looks,
10   And burn thy books.

2.

       I would I were a stone, or tree,
           Or flowre by pedigree,
       Or some poor high-way herb, or Spring
           To flow, or bird to sing!
15   Then should I (tyed to one sure state,)
           All day expect my date;
       But I am sadly loose, and stray
           A giddy blast each way;
           O let me not thus range!
20   Thou canst not change.

3.

       Sometimes I sit with thee, and tarry
           An hour, or so, then vary.
       Thy other Creatures in this Scene
           Thee only aym, and mean;
25   Some rise to seek thee, and with heads
           Erect peep from their beds;
       Others, whose birth is in the tomb,
           And cannot quit the womb,
           Sigh there, and grone for thee,
30   Their liberty.

4.

       O let not me do lesse! shall they
           Watch, while I sleep, or play?
       Shall I thy mercies still abuse
           With fancies, friends, or newes?
35   O brook it not! thy bloud is mine,
           And my soul should be thine;

O brook it not! why wilt thou stop
After whole showres one drop?
Sure, thou wilt joy to see
40   Thy sheep with thee.

[S–37]   The Relapse.

My God, how gracious art thou! I had slipt
Almost to hell,
And on the verge of that dark, dreadful pit
Did hear them yell,
5 But O thy love! thy rich, almighty love
That sav'd my soul,
And checkt their furie, when I saw them move,
And heard them howl;
O my sole Comfort, take no more these wayes,
10   This hideous path,
And I wil mend my own without delayes,
Cease thou thy wrath!
I have deserv'd a thick, Egyptian damp,
Dark as my deeds,
15 Should *mist* within me, and put out that lamp
Thy spirit feeds;
A darting Conscience full of stabs, and fears;
No shade but *Yewgh*,
Sullen, and sad Ecclipses, Cloudie spheres,
20   These are my due.
But he that with his bloud, (a price too deere,)
My scores did pay,
Bid me, by vertue from him, chalenge here
The brightest day;
25 Sweet, downie thoughts; soft *Lilly*-shades; Calm streams;
Joyes full, and true;
Fresh, spicie mornings; and eternal beams
These are his due.

[S–38]   The Resolve.

I have consider'd it; and find
       A longer stay
Is but excus'd neglect. To mind
       One path, and stray
5   Into another, or to none,
       Cannot be love;
When shal that traveller come home,
       That will not move?
If thou wouldst thither, linger not,
10   Catch at the place,
Tell youth, and beauty they must rot,
       They'r but a *Case*;[1]
Loose, parcell'd hearts wil freeze: The Sun
       With scatter'd locks
15   Scarce warms, but by contraction
       Can heat rocks;
Call in thy *Powers*; run, and reach
       Home with the light,
Be there, before the shadows stretch,
20   And *Span* up night;[2]
Follow the *Cry* no more: there is
       An ancient way
All strewed with flowres, and happiness
       And fresh as *May*;
25   There turn, and turn no more; Let wits,
       Smile at fair eies,
Or lips; But who there weeping sits,
       Hath got the *Prize*.[3]

THE RESOLVE.

   [1] Chance, or accident.

   [2] The OED cites this example to illustrate the use of "span up" to mean figuratively to extend, to make taut or tight.

   [3] Martin (*Works*, 1957, p. 735) notes that lines 9–28 of this poem appeared in an anthology of verse, *Witt's Recreations*, in the editions of 1650, 1654, 1663, and 1667, with the introductory note

[S–39]   The Match.

Dear friend![1] whose holy, ever-living lines
                    Have done much good
            To many, and have checkt my blood,
My fierce, wild blood that still heaves, and inclines,
5   But is still tam'd
            By those bright fires which thee inflam'd;
Here I joyn hands, and thrust my stubborn heart
                    Into thy *Deed*,[2]
            There from no *Duties* to be freed,
10 And if hereafter *youth*, or *folly* thwart
                    And claim their share,
            Here I renounce the pois'nous ware.

                        ii

Accept, dread Lord, the poor Oblation,
                    It is but poore,
15   Yet through thy Mercies may be more.
O thou! that canst not wish my souls damnation,
                    Afford me life,
            And save me from all inward strife!

---

by the editor: "I would commend to thy sharpest view and serious
consideration; The Sweet Cælestiall sacred Poems by Mr. *Henry
Vaughan*, intituled *Silex Scintillans*.

> There plumes from Angels wings, he'l lend thee,
> Which every day to heaven will send thee.
> (*Heare him thus invite thee home.*)"

                                    (sig. Bb 8r)

The lines from "The Resolve" follow the note.

THE MATCH.

   [1] George Herbert. See the Preface to the second part of *Silex*.
   [2] In "Obedience," lines 37–43 (*Works*, ed. F. E. Hutchinson
[Oxford, 1941], p. 105), Herbert speaks of his "poore paper" as a
deed whereby he passes his heart and all he has to God. He invites any other who would do the same to "set his hand / And
heart unto this Deed" and to "thrust his heart / Into these lines."

Two *Lifes* I hold from thee, my gracious Lord,
20   Both cost thee deer,
For one, I am thy Tenant here;
The other, the true life, in the next world
          And endless is,
     O let me still mind *that* in *this!*
25 To thee therefore my *Thoughts, Words, Actions*
          I do resign,
     Thy will in all be done, not mine.
Settle my *house*, and shut out all distractions
          That may unknit
30   My heart, and thee planted in it;
Lord *Jesu!* thou didst bow thy blessed head
          Upon a tree,
     O do as much, now unto me!
O hear, and heal thy servant! Lord, strike dead
35   All lusts in me,
     Who onely wish life to serve thee?
Suffer no more this dust to overflow
          And drown my eies,
     But seal, or pin them to thy skies.
40 And let this *grain* which here in tears I sow
          Though *dead*, and *sick*,
     Through thy *Increase* grow *new*, and *quick*.

[S–40]   Rules *and* Lessons.

When first thy Eies unveil, give thy Soul leave
To do the like; our Bodies but forerun
The spirits duty; True hearts spread, and heave
Unto their God, as flow'rs do to the Sun.
5   Give him thy first thoughts then; so shalt thou keep
     Him company all day, and in him sleep.

Yet, never sleep the Sun up; Prayer shou'd
Dawn with the day; There are set, awful hours
'Twixt heaven, and us; The *Manna* was not good
10 After Sun-rising,[1] far-day sullies flowres.
  Rise to prevent the Sun;[2] sleep doth sins glut,
  And heav'ns gate opens, when this world's is shut.

Walk with thy fellow-creatures: note the *hush*
And *whispers* amongst them. There's not a *Spring*,
15 Or *Leafe* but hath his *Morning-hymn*; Each *Bush*
And *Oak* doth know *I AM*; canst thou not sing?
  O leave thy Cares, and follies! go this way
  And thou art sure to prosper all the day.

Serve God before the world; let him not go
20 Until thou hast a blessing, then resigne
The whole unto him; and remember who
Prevail'd by *wrestling* ere the *Sun* did *shine*.[3]
  Poure *Oyle* upon the *stones*, weep for thy sin,
  Then journey on, and have an eie to heav'n.

25 *Mornings* are *Mysteries*; the first worlds *Youth*,
Mans *Resurrection*, and the futures *Bud*
Shrowd in their births: The Crown of life, light, truth
Is stil'd their *starre*, the *stone*, and *hidden food*.
  Three *blessings* wait upon them, two of which
30   Should move; They make us *holy*, *happy*, rich.

When the world's up, and ev'ry swarm abroad,
Keep thou thy temper, mix not with each Clay;
Dispatch necessities, life hath a load
Which must be carri'd on, and safely may.
35   Yet keep those cares without thee, let the heart
  Be Gods alone, and choose the better part.

RULES AND LESSONS.
 [1] Exod. 16.19–21.
 [2] Wisd. of Sol. 16.28, "we must prevent [i.e., go before] the sun, to give Thee thanks, and at the day spring pray unto Thee."
 [3] Jacob in Gen. 32.24–26. He poured oil upon the stone pillar set up at Bethel, Gen. 35.14.

Through all thy *Actions, Counsels,* and *Discourse,*
Let *Mildness,* and *Religion* guide thee out,
If truth be thine, what needs a brutish force?
40 But what's not *good,* and *just* ne'r go about.
    Wrong not thy Conscience for a rotten stick,
    That gain is dreadful, which makes spirits sick.

To God, thy Countrie, and thy friend be true,
If *Priest,* and *People* change, keep thou thy ground.
45 Who sels Religion, is a *Judas Jew,*
And, oathes once broke, the soul cannot be sound.
    The perjurer's a devil let loose: what can
    Tie up his hands, that dares mock God, and man?

Seek not the same steps with the *Crowd;* stick thou
50 To thy sure trot; a Constant, humble mind
Is both his own Joy, and his Makers too;
Let folly dust it on, or lag behind.
    A sweet *self-privacy* in a right soul
    Out-runs the Earth, and lines[4] the utmost pole.

55 To all that seek thee, bear an open heart;
Make not thy breast a *Labyrinth,* or *Trap;*
If tryals come, this wil make good thy part,
For honesty is safe, come what can hap;
    It is the good mans *feast;* The prince of flowres
60   Which thrives in *storms,* and smels best after
    showres.

Seal not thy Eyes up from the poor, but give
Proportion to their *Merits,* and thy *Purse;*
Thou mai'st in Rags a mighty Prince relieve
Who, when thy sins call for't, can fence[5] a Curse.
65   Thou shalt not lose one *mite.* Though waters stray,
    The Bread we cast returns in fraughts one day.

[4] Extends to.
[5] Repel, ward off.

Spend not an hour so, as to weep another,
For tears are not thine own; If thou giv'st words
Dash not thy *friend*, nor *Heav'n*; O smother
70 A vip'rous thought; some *Syllables* are *Swords*.
    Unbitted tongues are in their penance double,
    They shame their *owners*, and the *hearers* trouble.

Injure not modest bloud, whose *spirits* rise
In judgement against *Lewdness*; that's base wit
75 That voyds but *filth*, and *stench*. Hast thou no prize
But *sickness*, or *Infection*? stifle it.
    Who makes his jests of sins, must be at least
    If not a very *devill*, worse than a *Beast*.

Yet, fly no friend, if he be such indeed,
80 But meet to quench his *Longings*, and thy *Thirst*;
Allow your Joyes *Religion*; That done, speed
And bring the same man back, thou wert at first.
    Who so returns not, cannot pray aright,
    But shuts his door, and leaves God out all night.

85 To highten thy *Devotions*, and keep low
All mutinous thoughts, what busines e'r thou hast
Observe God in his works; here *fountains* flow,
Birds sing, *Beasts* feed, *Fish* leap, and th'*Earth* stands
    fast;
    Above are restles *motions*, running *Lights*,
90   Vast Circling *Azure*, giddy *Clouds*, days, nights.

When *Seasons* change, then lay before thine Eys
His wondrous *Method*; mark the various *Scenes*
In heav'n; *Hail*, *Thunder*, *Rain-bows*, *Snow*, and *Ice*,
Calmes, *Tempests*, *Light*, and *darknes* by his means;
95   Thou canst not misse his Praise; Each *tree*, *herb*,
    flowre
    Are shadows of his *wisedome*, and his Pow'r.

To *meales* when thou doest come, give him the praise
Whose *Arm* supply'd thee; Take what may suffice,
And then be thankful; O admire his ways
100   Who fils the worlds unempty'd granaries!
     A thankles feeder is a *Theif*, his feast
     A very *Robbery*, and himself no *guest*.

High-noon thus past, thy time decays; provide
Thee other thoughts; Away with friends, and mirth;
105   The Sun now stoops, and hasts his beams to hide
Under the dark, and melancholy Earth.
     All but preludes thy End. Thou art the man
     Whose *Rise, hight*, and *Descent* is but a span.

Yet, set as he doth, and 'tis well. Have all
110   Thy Beams home with thee: trim thy *Lamp*, buy *Oyl*,
And then set forth; who is thus drest, The *Fall*
Furthers his glory, and gives death the foyl.
     Man is a *Summers day*; whose *youth*, and *fire*
     Cool to a glorious *Evening*, and Expire.

115   When night comes, list thy deeds; make plain the way
'Twixt Heaven, and thee; block it not with delays,
But perfect all before thou sleep'st; Then say
Ther's one Sun more strung on my Bead of days.
     What's good score up for Joy; The bad wel scann'd
120   Wash off with tears, and get thy *Masters* hand.

Thy Accounts thus made, spend in the grave one houre
Before thy time; Be not a stranger there
Where thou may'st sleep whole ages; Lifes poor flowr
Lasts not a night sometimes. Bad spirits fear
125   This Conversation; But the good man lyes
     Intombed many days before he dyes.

Being laid, and drest for sleep, Close not thy Eys
Up with thy Curtains; Give thy soul the wing
In some good thoughts; So when the day shall rise
130   And thou *unrak'st* thy *fire*, those *sparks* will bring

New *flames*; Besides where these lodge vain *heats*
mourn
And die; That *Bush* where God is, shall not burn.[6]

When thy *Nap's* over, stir thy fire, unrake
In that *dead age*; one beam i'th' dark outvies
135 Two in the day; Then from the *Damps*, and *Ake*
Of night shut up thy *leaves*, be Chast; God prys
    Through thickest nights; Though then the Sun be far
    Do thou the works of *Day*, and rise a *Star*.

Briefly, *Doe as thou would'st be done unto,*
140 *Love God, and Love thy Neighbour; Watch, and Pray.*
These are the *Words*, and *Works* of life; This do,
And live; who doth not thus, hath lost *Heav'ns way.*
    O lose it not! look up, wilt Change those *Lights*
    For *Chains* of *Darknes*, and *Eternal Nights?*

[S–41]   Corruption.

    Sure, It was so. Man in those early days
        Was not all stone, and Earth,
    He shin'd a little, and by those weak Rays
        Had some glimpse of his birth.
5   He saw Heaven o'r his head, and knew from whence
        He came (condemned,) hither,
    And, as first Love draws strongest, so from hence
        His mind sure progress'd thither.
    Things here were strange unto him: Swet, and till
10   All was a thorn, or weed,
    Nor did those last, but (like himself,) dyed still
        As soon as they did *Seed*,
    They seem'd to quarrel with him; for that Act
        That fel[1] him, foyl'd them all,

[6] Exod. 3.2.
CORRUPTION.
  [1] Felled, ruined.

15 He drew the Curse upon the world, and Crackt
   The whole frame with his fall.
 This made him long for *home*, as loath to stay
   With murmurers, and foes;
 He sigh'd for *Eden*, and would often say
20   *Ah! what bright days were those?*
 Nor was Heav'n cold unto him; for each day
   The vally, or the Mountain
 Afforded visits, and still *Paradise* lay
   In some green shade, or fountain.[2]
25 Angels lay *Leiger*[3] here; Each Bush, and Cel,
   Each Oke, and high-way knew them,
 Walk but the fields, or sit down at some *wel*,
   And he was sure to view them.
 Almighty *Love!* where art thou now? mad man
30   Sits down, and freezeth on,
 He raves, and swears to stir nor fire, nor fan,
   But bids the thread be spun.
 I see, thy Curtains are Close-drawn; Thy bow
   Looks dim too in the Cloud,
35 Sin triumphs still, and man is sunk below
   The Center, and his shrowd;
 All's in deep sleep, and night; Thick darknes lyes
   And hatcheth o'r thy people;
 But hark! what trumpets that? what Angel cries
40   *Arise! Thrust in thy sickle.*[4]

[S–42]   H. Scriptures.

 Welcome dear book, souls Joy, and food! The feast
   Of Spirits, Heav'n extracted lyes in thee;
   Thou art lifes Charter, The Doves spotless neast
 Where souls are hatch'd unto Eternitie.

 [2] With these and the following lines compare the first five stanzas
of S–7.
 [3] See O–14, line 10.
 [4] Rev. 14.14–19.

5 In thee the hidden stone, the *Manna* lies,[1]
　　　　Thou art the great *Elixir*, rare, and Choice;
　　　　The Key that opens to all Mysteries,
　　The *Word* in Characters, God in the *Voice*.

　　O that I had deep Cut in my hard heart
10　　　　Each line in thee! Then would I plead in groans
　　　　Of my Lords penning, and by sweetest Art
　　Return upon himself the *Law*, and *Stones*.
　　　　Read here, my faults are thine. This Book, and I
　　　　Will tell thee so; *Sweet Saviour thou didst dye!*

[S–43]　　　　　　　Unprofitablenes.

How rich, O Lord! how fresh thy visits are!
'Twas but Just now my bleak leaves hopeles hung
　　　　Sullyed with dust and mud;
Each snarling blast shot through me, and did share
5 Their Youth, and beauty, Cold showres nipt, and wrung
　　　　Their spiciness, and bloud;
But since thou didst in one sweet glance survey
Their sad decays, I flourish, and once more
　　　　Breath all perfumes, and spice;
10 I smell a dew like *Myrrh*, and all the day
Wear in my bosome a full Sun; such store
　　　　Hath one beame from thy Eys.
But, ah, my God! what fruit hast thou of this?
What one poor leaf did ever I yet fall
15　　　　To wait upon thy wreath?
Thus thou all day a thankless weed doest dress,
And when th' hast done, a stench, or fog is all
　　　　The odour I bequeath.

H. SCRIPTURES.
[1] Rev. 2.17, quoted at the end of S–68; and see S–40, line 28.

[S–44]   CHRISTS
                          Nativity.

Awake, glad heart! get up, and Sing,
It is the Birth-day of thy King,
  Awake! awake*!*
  The Sun doth shake
5 Light from his locks, and all the way
Breathing Perfumes, doth spice the day.

2.

Awak, awak! heark, how th' *wood* rings,
Winds whisper, and the busie *springs*
  A Consort make;
10   Awake, awake!
Man is their high-priest, and should rise
To offer up the sacrifice.

3.

I would I were some *Bird*, or Star,
Flutt'ring in woods, or lifted far
15 Above this *Inne*
  And Rode of sin!
Then either Star, or *Bird*, should be
Shining, or singing still to thee.

4.

I would I had in my best part
20 Fit Roomes for thee! or that my heart
  Were so clean as
  Thy manger was!
But I am all filth, and obscene,
Yet, if thou wilt, thou canst make clean.

5.

25   Sweet *Jesu*! will then; Let no more
      This Leper haunt, and soyl thy door,
          Cure him, Ease him
          O release him!
      And let once more by mystick birth
30   The Lord of life be borne in Earth.

[S–45]   II.

      How kind is heav'n to man! If here
          One sinner doth amend
      Strait there is Joy, and ev'ry sphere
          In musick doth Contend;
5   And shall we then no voices lift?
          Are mercy, and salvation
      Not worth our thanks? Is life a gift
          Of no more acceptation?
      Shal he that did come down from thence,
10   And here for us was slain,
      Shal he be now cast off? no sense
          Of all his woes remain?
      Can neither Love, nor suff'rings bind?
          Are we all stone, and Earth?
15   Neither his bloudy passions mind,
          Nor one day blesse his birth?
      Alas, my God! Thy birth now here
      Must not be numbred in the year.[1]

CHRISTS NATIVITY, II.
[1] In 1644 Parliament abolished the religious observance of
Christmas.

[S–46]   The Check.

Peace, peace! I blush to hear thee; when thou art
   A dusty story
A speechlesse heap, and in the midst my heart
   In the same livery drest
5   Lyes tame as all the rest;
When six years thence digg'd up, some youthfull Eie
   Seeks there for Symmetry
But finding none, shal leave thee to the wind,
   Or the next foot to Crush,
10   Scatt'ring thy kind
And humble dust, tell then dear flesh
   Where is thy glory?

2.

As he that in the midst of day Expects
   The hideous night,
15 Sleeps not, but shaking off sloth, and neglects,
   Works with the Sun, and sets
   Paying the day its debts;
That (for Repose, and darknes bound,) he might
   Rest from the fears i'th' night;
20 So should we too. All things teach us to die
   And point us out the way
    While we passe by
And mind it not; play not away
   Thy glimpse of light.

3.

25 View thy fore-runners: Creatures giv'n to be
   Thy youths Companions,
Take their leave, and die; Birds, beasts, each tree
   All that have growth, or breath
   Have one large language, *Death.*

30   O then play not! but strive to him, who Can
         Make these sad shades pure Sun,
    Turning their mists to beams, their damps to day,
         Whose pow'r doth so excell
             As to make Clay
35   A spirit, and true glory dwell
             In dust, and stones.

4.

    Heark, how he doth Invite thee! with what voice
         Of Love, and sorrow
    He begs, and Calls; *O that in these thy days*
40   Thou knew'st but thy own good!
         Shall not the Crys of bloud,
    Of Gods own bloud awake thee? He bids beware
         Of drunknes, surfeits, Care,
    But thou sleep'st on; wher's now thy protestation,
45   Thy Lines, thy Love? Away,
             Redeem the day,
    The day that gives no observation,
         P rhaps to morrow.

[S–47]   Disorder *and* frailty.

    When first thou didst even from the grave
    And womb of darknes becken out
    My brutish soul, and to thy slave
    Becam'st thy self, both guide, and Scout;
5   Even from that hour
    Thou gotst my heart; And though here tost
         By winds, and bit with frost
             I pine, and shrink
             Breaking the link

10 'Twixt thee, and me; And oftimes creep
Into th' old silence, and dead sleep,
        Quitting thy way
        All the long day,
Yet, sure, my God! I love thee most.
15   *Alas, thy love!*

2.

I threaten heaven, and from my Cell
Of Clay, and frailty break, and bud
Touch'd by thy fire, and breath; Thy bloud
Too, is my Dew, and springing wel.
20   But while I grow
And stretch to thee, ayming at all
        Thy stars, and spangled hall,
        Each fly doth tast,
        Poyson, and blast
25 My yielding leaves; sometimes a showr
Beats them quite off, and in an hour
        Not one poor shoot
        But the bare root
Hid under ground survives the fall.
30   *Alas, frail weed!*

3.

Thus like some sleeping Exhalation
(Which wak'd by heat, and beams, makes up
Unto that Comforter, the Sun,
And soars, and shines; But e'r we sup
35   And walk two steps
Cool'd by the damps of night, descends,
        And, whence it sprung, there ends,)
        Doth my weak fire
        Pine, and retire,
40 And (after all my hight of flames,)
In sickly Expirations tames
        Leaving me dead
        On my first bed
Untill thy Sun again ascends.
45   *Poor, falling Star!*

4.

O, is!¹ but give wings to my fire,
And hatch my soul, untill it fly
Up where thou art, amongst thy tire
Of Stars, above Infirmity;
50   Let not perverse,
And foolish thoughts adde to my Bil
Of forward sins, and Kil
That seed, which thou
In me didst sow,
55   But dresse, and water with thy grace
Together with the seed, the place;
And for his sake
Who died to stake
His life for mine, tune to thy will
60   My heart, my verse.

Hosea Cap. 6. ver. 4.²
*O Ephraim what shall I do unto thee? O Judah how shall
I intreat thee? for thy goodness is as a morning Cloud, and
as the early Dew it goeth away.*

[S–48]   Idle Verse.

Go, go, queint folies, sugred sin,
        Shadow no more my door;
I will no longer Cobwebs spin,
        I'm too much on the score.¹

DISORDER AND FRAILTY.
    ¹ Martin (*Works*, 1957, pp. 703, 739) points out that *is* is a dia-
lectal form of *yes.*
    ² The Genevan version, substituting "thy" for "your" and "early"
for "morning."
IDLE VERSE.
    ¹ In debt.

5   For since amidst my youth, and night,
       My great preserver smiles,
    Wee'l make a Match, my only light,
       And Joyn against their wiles;

    Blind, desp'rate *fits*, that study how
10   To dresse, and trim our shame,
    That gild rank poyson, and allow
       Vice in a fairer name;

    The *Purles* of youthfull bloud, and bowles,[2]
       Lust in the Robes of Love,
15   The idle talk of feav'rish souls
       Sick with a scarf, or glove;

    Let it suffice my warmer days
       Simper'd, and shin'd on you,
    Twist not my Cypresse with your Bays,
20   Or Roses with my Yewgh;

    Go, go, seek out some greener thing,
       It snows, and freezeth here;
    Let Nightingales attend the spring,
       Winter is all my year.

[S–49]   Son-dayes.

Bright shadows of true Rest! some shoots of blisse,
          Heaven once a week;
The next worlds gladnes prepossest in this;
          A day to seek;

---

[2] *"Purles"* means the action or sound of purling as a rill (see OED, where Vaughan's use of the term is cited as an example); "bowles" means bowels, in the sense of the center of feeling or sensation.

5　Eternity in time; the steps by which
　　We Climb above all ages; Lamps that light
　　Man through his heap of dark days; and the rich,
　　And full redemption of the whole weeks flight.

2.

　　The Pulleys unto headlong man; times bower;
10　　　　　　　　The narrow way;
　　Transplanted Paradise; Gods walking houre;
　　　　　　　　The Cool o'th' day;

　　The Creatures *Jubile*; Gods parle with dust;
　　Heaven here; Man on those hills of Myrrh, and flowres;
15　Angels descending; the Returns of Trust;
　　A Gleam of glory, after six-days-showres.

3.

　　The Churches love-feasts; Times Prerogative,[1]
　　　　　　　　And Interest
　　Deducted from the whole; The Combs, and hive,
20　　　　　　　　And home of rest.

　　The milky way Chalkt out with Suns; a Clue
　　That guides through erring hours; and in full story
　　A taste of Heav'n on earth; the pledge, and Cue
　　Of a full feast; And the Out Courts of glory.

[S–50]　　　　　　Repentance.

　　Lord, since thou didst in this vile Clay
　　　　　That sacred Ray
　　Thy spirit plant, quickning the whole
　　With that one grains Infused wealth,
5　My forward flesh creept on, and subtly stole
　　Both growth, and power; Checking the health

SON-DAYES.
　[1] Mark or quality giving precedence, for its being the first day
of the week.

And heat of thine: That little gate
And narrow way, by which to thee
The Passage is, He[1] term'd a grate
10   And Entrance to Captivitie;
Thy laws but nets, where some small birds
(And those but seldome too) were caught,
Thy Promises but empty words
Which none but Children heard, or taught.

15   This I believed: And though a friend
Came oft from far, and whisper'd, *No*;
Yet that not sorting to my end
I wholy listen'd to my foe.
Wherefore, pierc'd through with grief, my sad
20   Seduced soul sighs up to thee,
To thee who with true light art Clad
And seest all things just as they be.
Look from thy throne upon this Rowl
Of heavy sins, my high transgressions,
25   Which I Confesse with all my soul,
My God, Accept of my Confession.

       It was last day
(Touch'd with the guilt of my own way)
I sate alone, and taking up
30   The bitter Cup,
Through all thy fair, and various store
Sought out what might outvie my score.[2]

     The blades of grasse, thy Creatures feeding,
     The trees, their leafs; the flowres, their seeding;
35   The Dust, of which I am a part,
     The Stones much softer than my heart,
     The drops of rain, the sighs of wind,
     The Stars to which I am stark blind,
     The Dew thy herbs drink up by night,
40   The beams they warm them at i'th' light,
     All that have signature or life,
     I summon'd to decide this strife,

REPENTANCE.
  [1] The flesh, or the natural man (Martin, *Works*, 1957, p. 739).
  [2] Exceed my debt.

And lest I should lack for Arrears,
A spring ran by, I told her tears,
45   But when these came unto the scale,
My sins alone outweigh'd them all.
O my dear God! my life, my love!
Most blessed lamb! and mildest dove!
Forgive your penitent Offender,
50   And no more his sins remember,
Scatter these shades of death, and give
Light to my soul, that it may live;
Cut me not off for my transgressions,
Wilful rebellions, and suppressions,
55   But give them in those streams a part
Whose spring is in my Saviours heart.
Lord, I confesse the heynous score,
And pray, I may do so no more,
Though then all sinners I exceed
60   O think on this; *Thy Son did bleed;*
O call to mind his wounds, his woes,
His Agony, and bloudy throws;
Then look on all that thou hast made,
And mark how they do fail, and fade,
65   The heavens themselves, though fair and bright
Are dark, and unclean in thy sight,
How then, with thee, Can man be holy
Who doest thine Angels charge with folly?[3]
O what am I, that I should breed
70   Figs on a thorne, flowres on a weed![4]
I am the gourd of sin, and sorrow
Growing o'r night, and gone to morrow,[5]
In all this *Round* of life and death
Nothing's more vile than is my breath,
75   Profanenes on my tongue doth rest,

[3] Job 4.17–18, "Behold, he put no trust in his servants; and his
angels he charged with folly."
[4] Luke 6.44, "For of thorns men do not gather figs, nor of a
bramble bush gather they grapes."
[5] Jonah 4.6–10. To shade Jonah, God provided a gourd, which
withered the next day.

Defects, and darknes in my brest,
Pollutions all my body wed,
And even my soul to thee is dead,
Only in him, on whom I feast,
80　Both soul, and body are well drest,
　　　His pure perfection quits all score,
　　　And fills the Boxes of his poor;
He is the Center of long life, and light,
I am but finite, He is Infinite.
85　O let thy *Justice* then in him Confine,
And through his merits, make thy mercy mine!

[S–51]　　　　　　The BURIAL
　　　　　　　　　Of an Infant.[1]

　　Blest Infant Bud, whose Blossome-life
　　Did only look about, and fal,
　　Wearyed out in a harmles strife
　　Of tears, and milk, the food of all;

5　　Sweetly didst thou expire: Thy soul
　　Flew home unstain'd by his new kin,
　　For ere thou knew'st how to be foul,
　　Death *wean'd* thee from the world, and sin.

　　Softly rest all thy Virgin-Crums![2]
10　*Lapt* in the sweets of thy young breath,
　　Expecting till thy Saviour Comes
　　To *dresse* them, and *unswadle* death.

THE BURIAL OF AN INFANT.
　[1] Perhaps one of Vaughan's own children. With the views of infancy here, compare S–21 and S–114.
　[2] Crum: a small particle of anything; a grain, as of dust (OED). Vaughan's phrase is cited in OED as an example of this meaning.

[S–52]   Faith.

    Bright, and blest beame! whose strong projection
         Equall to all,
    Reacheth as well things of dejection
         As th' high, and tall;
5   How hath my God by raying thee
         Inlarg'd his spouse,[1]
    And of a private familie
         Made open house?
    All may be now Co-heirs;[2] no noise
10   Of *Bond,* or *Free*[3]
    Can Interdict us from those Joys
         That wait on thee,
    The Law, and Ceremonies made
         A glorious night,
15   Where Stars, and Clouds, both light, and shade
         Had equal right;
    But, as in nature, when the day
         Breaks, night adjourns,
    Stars shut up shop, mists pack away,
20   And the Moon mourns;
    So when the Sun of righteousness
         Did once appear,
    That Scene was chang'd, and a new dresse
         Left for us here;
25   Veiles became useles, Altars fel,
         Fires smoking die;
    And all that sacred pomp, and shel
         Of things did flie;
    Then did he shine forth, whose sad fall,

FAITH.
  [1] The Church.
  [2] Cf. Eph. 3.6; Rom. 8.17.
  [3] I Cor. 12.13; Gal. 3.28.

30   And bitter fights
   Were figur'd in those mystical,
     And Cloudie Rites;
  And as i'th' natural Sun, these three,
     Light, motion, heat,[4]
35 So are now *Faith, Hope, Charity*
    Through him Compleat;
  Faith spans up blisse;[5] what sin, and death
     Put us quite from,
  Lest we should run for't out of breath,
40   Faith brings us home;
  So that I need no more, but say
     I do believe,
  And my most loving Lord straitway
    Doth answer, *Live.*

[S–53]   The Dawning.

  Ah! what time wilt thou come? when shall that crie
    The *Bridegroome's Comming*! fil the sky?[1]
    Shall it in the Evening run
    When our words and works are done?
5   Or wil thy all-surprizing light
     Break at midnight?
    When either sleep, or some dark pleasure
    Possesseth mad man without measure;
    Or shal these early, fragrant hours
10   Unlock thy bowres?
    And with their blush of light descry
    Thy locks crown'd with eternitie;
    Indeed, it is the only time
    That with thy glory doth best chime,

[4] Cf. S–62, line 32.
[5] Faith extends or stretches bliss (OED). Cf. S–38, line 20.
THE DAWNING.
[1] In Matt. 25.6 the cry came at midnight.

15 All now are stirring, ev'ry field
   Ful hymns doth yield,
  The whole Creation shakes off night,
  And for thy shadow looks the light,
  Stars now vanish without number,
20 Sleepie Planets set, and slumber,
  The pursie[2] Clouds disband, and scatter,
  All expect some sudden matter,
  Not one beam triumphs, but from far
   That morning-star;
25 O at what time soever thou
  (Unknown to us,) the heavens wilt bow,
  And, with thy Angels in the *Van*,
  Descend to Judge poor careless man,
  Grant, I may not like puddle lie
30 In a Corrupt securitie,
  Where, if a traveller water crave,
  He finds it dead, and in a grave;
  But as this restless, vocall *Spring*
  All day, and night doth run, and sing,
35 And though here born, yet is acquainted
  Elsewhere, and flowing keeps untainted;
  So let me all my busie age
  In thy free services ingage,
  And though (while here) of force I must
40 Have Commerce somtimes with poor dust,
  And in my flesh, though vile, and low,
  As this doth in her Channel, flow,
  Yet let my Course, my aym, my Love,
  And chief acquaintance be above;
45 So when that day, and hour shal come
  In which thy self wil be the Sun,
  Thou'lt find me drest and on my way,
  Watching the Break of thy great day.

[2] Swollen, heavy (OED; this example is cited).

[S–54]   Admission.

How shril are silent tears? when sin got head
    And all my Bowels turn'd
To brasse, and iron; when my stock lay dead,
    And all my powers mourn'd;
5   Then did these drops (for Marble sweats,
       And Rocks have tears,)
    As rain here at our windows beats,
      Chide in thine Ears;

2.

No quiet couldst thou have: nor didst thou wink,
10   And let thy Begger lie,
But e'r my eies could overflow their brink
    Didst to each drop reply;
    Bowels of Love! at what low rate,
      And slight a price
15   Dost thou relieve us at thy gate,
      And stil our Cries?

3.

Wee are thy Infants, and suck thee; If thou
    But hide, or turn thy face,
Because where thou art, yet, we cannot go,
20   We send tears to the place,
    These find thee out, and though our sins
      Drove thee away,
    Yet with thy love that absence wins
      Us double pay.

4.

25   O give me then a thankful heart! a heart
    After thy own, not mine;
So after thine, that all, and ev'ry part
    Of mine, may wait on thine;

O hear! yet not my tears alone,
30   Hear now a floud,
A floud that drowns both tears, and grones,
    My Saviours bloud.

[S-55]   Praise.

King of Comforts! King of life!
        Thou hast cheer'd me,
And when fears, and doubts were rife,
        Thou hast cleer'd me!

5   Not a nook in all my Breast
        But thou fill'st it,
Not a thought, that breaks my rest,
        But thou kill'st it;

Wherefore with my utmost strength
10   I wil praise thee,
And as thou giv'st line, and length,
        I wil raise thee;

Day, and night, not once a day
        I will blesse thee,
15   And my soul in new array
        I will dresse thee;

Not one minute in the year
        But I'l mind thee,
As my seal, and bracelet here
20   I wil bind thee;

In thy word, as if in heaven
        I wil rest me,
And thy promise 'til made even
        There shall feast me.

25   Then, thy sayings all my life
        They shal please me,
  And thy bloudy wounds, and strife
        They wil ease me;

  With thy grones my daily breath
30   I will measure,
  And my life hid in thy death
       I will treasure.

      Though then thou art
      Past thought of heart
35 All perfect fulness,
       And canst no whit
       Accesse admit
  From dust and dulness;

      Yet to thy name
40   (As not the same
  With thy bright Essence,)
       Our foul, Clay hands
       At thy Commands
  Bring praise, and Incense;

45   If then, dread Lord,
      When to thy board
  Thy wretch comes begging,
       He hath a flowre
       Or (to his pow'r,)
50 Some such poor Off'ring;

      When thou hast made
      Thy begger glad,
  And fill'd his bosome,
       Let him (though poor,)
55   Strow at thy door
  That one poor Blossome.

[S–56]   Dressing.

O Thou that lovest a pure, and whitend soul!
That feedst among the Lillies, 'till the day
Break, and the shadows flee;[1] touch with one Coal
My frozen heart; and with thy secret key

5   Open my desolate rooms; my gloomie Brest
With thy cleer fire refine, burning to dust
These dark Confusions, that within me nest,
And soyl thy Temple with a sinful rust.

Thou holy, harmless, undefil'd high-priest!
10   The perfect, ful oblation for all sin,
Whose glorious conquest nothing can resist,
But even in babes doest triumph still and win;

              Give to thy wretched one
           Thy mysticall *Communion,*
15   That, absent, he may see,
                  Live, die, and rise with thee;
     Let him so follow here, that in the end
     He may take thee, as thou doest him intend.

                 Give him thy private seal,
20   Earnest, and sign; Thy gifts so deal
                 That these forerunners here
                 May make the future cleer;
     Whatever thou dost bid, let faith make good,
     Bread for thy body, and Wine for thy blood.
25   Give him (with pitty) love,
              Two flowres that grew with thee above;
                  Love that shal not admit
                  Anger for one short fit,
     And pitty of such a divine extent
30   That may thy members, more than mine, resent.[2]

DRESSING.
    [1] Song of Sol. 2.16–17.
    [2] Possibly in the obsolete sense of to take favorably, to approve
of. See OED 8.c.

Give me, my God! thy grace,
The beams, and brightnes of thy face,
That never like a beast
I take thy sacred feast,
35   Or the dread mysteries of thy blest bloud
Use, with like Custome, as my Kitchin food.
Some sit to thee, and eat
Thy body as their Common meat,
O let not me do so!
40   Poor dust should ly still low,
Then kneel my soul, and body; kneel, and bow;
If *Saints*, and *Angels* fal down, much more thou.

[S–57]   Easter-day.

Thou, whose sad heart, and weeping head lyes low,
Whose Cloudy brest cold damps invade,
Who never feel'st the Sun, nor smooth'st thy brow,
But sitt'st oppressed in the shade,
5   Awake, awake,
And in his Resurrection partake,
Who on this day (that thou might'st rise as he,)
Rose up, and cancell'd two deaths due to thee.

Awake, awake; and, like the Sun, disperse
10   All mists that would usurp this day;
Where are thy Palmes, thy branches, and thy verse?
Hosanna! heark; why doest thou stay?
Arise, arise,
And with his healing bloud anoint thine Eys,
15   Thy inward Eys; his bloud will cure thy mind,
Whose spittle only could restore the blind.[1]

EASTER-DAY.
  [1] See John 9.6–7.

[S–58]   Easter Hymn.

                Death, and darkness get you packing,
                Nothing now to man is lacking,
                All your triumphs now are ended,
                And what *Adam* marr'd, is mended;
5   Graves are beds now for the weary,
                Death a nap, to wake more merry;
                Youth now, full of pious duty,
                Seeks in thee for perfect beauty,
                The weak, and aged tir'd, with length
10   Of daies, from thee look for new strength,
                And Infants with thy pangs Contest
                As pleasant, as if with the brest;
                    Then, unto him, who thus hath thrown
                    Even to Contempt thy kingdome down,
15   And by his blood did us advance
                Unto his own Inheritance,
                To him be glory, power, praise,
                From this, unto the last of daies.

[S–59]   The Holy Communion.

            Welcome sweet, and sacred feast; welcome life!
                Dead I was, and deep in trouble;
            But grace, and blessings came with thee so rife,
                That they have quicken'd even drie stubble;
5   Thus soules their bodies animate,
                And thus, at first, when things were rude,
                    Dark, void, and Crude
            They, by thy Word, their beauty had, and date;[1]

THE HOLY COMMUNION.
    [1] At the Creation.

All were by thee,
10   And stil must be,
Nothing that is, or lives,
But hath his Quicknings, and reprieves
As thy hand opes, or shuts;
Healings, and Cuts,
15   Darkness, and day-light, life, and death
Are but meer leaves turn'd by thy breath.
Spirits without thee die,
And blackness sits
On the divinest wits,
20   As on the Sun Ecclipses lie.
But that great darkness at thy death
When the veyl broke with thy last breath,[2]
Did make us see
The way to thee;
25   And now by these sure, sacred ties,
After thy blood
(Our sov'rain good,)
Had clear'd our eies,
And given us sight;[3]
30   Thou dost unto thy self betroth
Our souls, and bodies both
In everlasting light.

Was't not enough that thou hadst payd the price
And given us eies
35   When we had none, but thou must also take
Us by the hand
And keep us still awake,
When we would sleep,[4]
Or from thee creep,[5]
40   Who without thee cannot stand?

[2] See Matt. 27.45, 51.

[3] Cf. S–57, lines 14–15.

[4] Matt. 26.40, "And he cometh unto the disciples, and findeth them asleep, and saith unto Peter, What, could ye not watch with me one hour?"

[5] As Peter did when charged with being a follower of Jesus (Matt. 26.71).

Was't not enough to lose thy breath
And blood by an accursed death,
But thou must also leave
To us that did bereave
45   Thee of them both, these seals the means
That should both cleanse
And keep us so,
Who wrought thy wo?
O rose of *Sharon*! O the Lilly
50   Of the valley!⁶
How art thou now, thy flock to keep,
Become both *food*, and *Shepheard* to thy sheep!

[S–60]   Psalm 121.

Up to those bright, and gladsome hils
Whence flowes my weal, and mirth,
I look, and sigh for him, who fils
(Unseen,) both heaven, and earth.

5   He is alone my help, and hope,
That I shall not be moved,
His watchful Eye is ever ope,
And guardeth his beloved;

The glorious God is my sole stay,
10   He is my Sun, and shade,
The cold by night, the heat by day,
Neither shall me invade.

He keeps me from the spite of foes,
Doth all their plots controul,
15   And is a shield (not reckoning those,)
Unto my very soul.

⁶ Song of Sol. 2.1.

Whether abroad, amidst the Crowd,
Or els within my door,
He is my Pillar, and my Cloud,
20   Now, and for evermore.

[S–61]   Affliction.

Peace, peace; It is not so. Thou doest miscall
Thy Physick; Pils that change
Thy sick Accessions into setled health,
This is the great *Elixir*[1] that turns gall
5   To wine, and sweetness; Poverty to wealth,
And brings man home, when he doth range.
Did not he, who ordain'd the day,
Ordain night too?
And in the greater world display
10   What in the lesser he would do?
All flesh is Clay, thou know'st; and but that God
Doth use his rod,
And by a fruitfull Change of frosts, and showres
Cherish, and bind thy *pow'rs*,
15   Thou wouldst to weeds, and thistles quite disperse,
And be more wild than is thy verse;
Sickness is wholsome, and Crosses are but curbs
To check the mule, unruly man,
They are heavens husbandry, the famous fan
20   Purging the floor which Chaff disturbs.[2]

AFFLICTION.
 [1] The great Elixir is sometimes identified with the philosopher's
stone of the alchemists, used to turn baser metals into gold, but it
also designates an essence or tincture with the property of indefi-
nitely prolonging life.
 [2] Matt. 3.12, "Whose fan is in his hand, and he will throughly
purge his floor . . . but he will burn up the chaff with unquench-
able fire." And Luke 3.17.

Were all the year one constant Sun-shine, wee
    Should have no flowres,
All would be drought, and leanness; not a tree
    Would make us bowres;
25   Beauty consists in colours; and that's best
    Which is not fixt, but flies, and flowes;
The settled *Red* is dull, and *whites* that rest
    Something of sickness would disclose.
      Vicissitude plaies all the game,
30   Nothing that stirs,
        Or hath a name,
    But waits upon this wheel,
Kingdomes too have their Physick, and for steel,
    Exchange their peace, and furrs.
35   Thus doth God *Key* disorder'd man
      (Which none else can,)
    Tuning his brest to rise, or fall;
    And by a sacred, needfull art
    Like strings, stretch ev'ry part
40   Making the whole most Musicall.

[S–62]   The Tempest.

How is man parcell'd out? how ev'ry hour
    Shews him himself, or somthing he should see?
    This late, long heat may his Instruction be,
And tempests have more in them than a showr.

5   *When nature on her bosome saw*
        Her Infants die,
     And all her flowres wither'd to straw,
        Her brests grown dry;
    She made the Earth their nurse, & tomb,
10   *Sigh to the sky,*
     'Til to those sighes fetch'd from her womb
        Rain did reply,

So in the midst of all her fears
And faint requests
15   *Her Earnest sighes procur'd her tears*
And fill'd her brests.

O that man could do so! that he would hear
The world read to him! all the vast expence
In the Creation shed, and slav'd to sence
20 Makes up but lectures for his eie, and ear.

Sure, mighty love foreseeing the discent
Of this poor Creature, by a gracious art
Hid in these low things snares to gain his heart,
And layd surprizes in each Element.

25 All things here shew him heaven; *Waters* that fall
Chide, and fly up; *Mists* of corruptest fome
Quit their first beds & mount; trees, herbs, flowres, all
Strive upwards stil, and point him the way home.

How do they cast off grossness? only *Earth,*
30   And *Man* (like *Issachar*)[1] in lodes delight,
Water's refin'd to *Motion*, Aire to *Light,*
Fire to all[2] three, but man hath no such mirth.

Plants in the *root* with Earth do most Comply,
Their *Leafs* with water, and humiditie.
35   The *Flowres* to air draw neer, and subtiltie,
And *seeds* a kinred fire have with the sky.

THE TEMPEST.
   [1] In Gen. 49.14, Issachar, a son of Jacob, is called "a strong ass couching down between two burdens."
   [2] An asterisk appeared here in the 1650 edition, with this note in the right margin, alongside lines 31 and 32: *"Light, Motion, heat."* George Herbert ("The Starre," lines 17–18; *Works,* ed. Hutchinson, p. 74) has a "trinitie of light, / Motion, and heat." And see S–52, lines 34–35.

All have their *keyes*, and set *ascents*; but man
    Though he knows these, and hath more of his own,
    Sleeps at the ladders foot; alas! what can
40 These new discoveries do, except they drown?

Thus groveling in the shade, and darkness, he
    Sinks to a dead oblivion; and though all
    He sees, (like *Pyramids*,) shoot from this ball
And less'ning still grow up invisibly,

45 Yet hugs he stil his durt; The *stuffe* he wears
    And painted trimming takes down both his eies,
    Heaven hath less beauty than the dust he spies,
And money better musick than the *Spheres*.

Life's but a blast, he knows it; what? shal straw,
50   And bul-rush-fetters temper his short hour?
    Must he nor sip, nor sing? grows ne'r a flowr
To crown his temples? shal dreams be his law?

O foolish man! how hast thou lost thy sight?
    How is it that the Sun to thee alone
55   Is grown thick darkness, and thy bread, a stone?
Hath flesh no softness now? mid-day no light?

Lord! thou didst put a soul here; If I must
    Be broke again, for flints will give no fire
    Without a steel, O let thy power cleer
60 Thy gift once more, and grind this flint to dust![3]

[3] Cf. the engraved title page of *Silex Scintillans,* Part I (1650),
and S–1.

[S–63]   Retirement.

Who on yon throne of Azure sits,
    Keeping close house
    Above the morning-starre,
    Whose meaner showes,
5 And outward utensils these glories are
    That shine and share
    Part of his mansion; He one day
    When I went quite astray
    Out of meer love
10   By his mild Dove
Did shew me home, and put me in the way.

2.

Let it suffice at length thy fits
    And lusts (said he,)
    Have had their wish, and way;
15   Presse not to be
Still thy own foe, and mine; for to this day
    I did delay,
    And would not see, but chose to wink,
    Nay, at the very brink
20   .. And edge of all
    When thou wouldst fall
My *love-twist*[1] held thee up, my *unseen link*.

3.

I know thee well; for I have fram'd
    And hate thee not,
25   Thy spirit too is mine;
    I know thy lot,

RETIREMENT.
  [1] Cf. the "silk twist let down from heav'n to me" in George Herbert's "The Pearl," line 38 (*Works,* ed. Hutchinson, p. 89).

Extent, and end, for my hands drew the line
Assigned thine;
If then thou would'st unto my seat,
30   'Tis not th'applause, and feat
Of dust, and clay
Leads to that way,
But from those follies a resolv'd Retreat.[2]

4.

Now here below where yet untam'd
35   Thou doest thus rove
I have a house as well
As there above,
In it my *Name*, and *honour* both do dwell
And shall untill
40   I make all new; there nothing gay
In perfumes, or Array,
Dust lies with dust
And hath but just
The same Respect, and room, with ev'ry clay.

5.

45   A faithful school where thou maist see
In Heraldrie
Of stones, and speechless Earth
Thy true descent;
Where dead men preach, who can turn feasts, and mirth
50   To funerals, and *Lent*.
There dust that out of doors might fill
Thy eies, and blind thee still,
Is fast asleep;
Up then, and keep
55 Within those doors, (my doors) dost hear? *I will.*

2 Cf. S–21.

[S–64]   Love, and Discipline.

> Since in a land not barren stil
> (Because thou dost thy grace distil,)
> My lott is faln, Blest be thy will!

> And since these biting frosts but kil
> Some tares in me which choke, or spil[1]
> That seed thou sow'st, Blest be thy skil!

5

> Blest be thy Dew, and blest thy frost,
> And happy I to be so crost,
> And cur'd by Crosses at thy cost.

> The Dew doth Cheer what is distrest,
> The frosts ill weeds nip, and molest,
> In both thou work'st unto the best.

10

> Thus while thy sev'ral mercies plot,
> And work on me now cold, now hot,
> The work goes on, and slacketh not,

15

> For as thy hand the weather steers,
> So thrive I best, 'twixt joyes, and tears,
> And all the year have some grean Ears.

LOVE, AND DISCIPLINE.

[1] Kill or destroy. See the story of the tares and the wheat in Matt. 13.24–30.

[S–65]   The Pilgrimage.

As travellours when the twilight's come,
And in the sky the stars appear,
The past daies accidents do summe
With, *Thus wee saw there, and thus here.*

5   Then *Jacob*-like lodge in a place
           (A place, and no more, is set down,)[1]
           Where till the day restore the race
           They rest and dream homes of their own.

           So for this night I linger here,
10   And full of tossings too and fro,
           Expect stil when thou wilt appear
           That I may get me up, and go.

           I long, and grone, and grieve for thee,
           For thee my words, my tears do gush,
15   *O that I were but where I see!*
           Is all the note within my Bush.

           As Birds rob'd of their native wood,
           Although their Diet may be fine,
           Yet neither sing, nor like their food,
20   But with the thought of home do pine;

           So do I mourn, and hang my head,
           And though thou dost me fullnes give,
           Yet look I for far better bread
           Because by this man cannot live.

THE PILGRIMAGE.
   [1] In Gen. 28.11 Jacob is said only to have come upon "a certain
place" where he spent the night and dreamed of the ladder reach-
ing to heaven.

25   O feed me then! and since I may
        Have yet more days, more nights to Count,
        So strengthen me, Lord, all the way,
        That I may travel to thy Mount.

Heb. Cap. xi. ver. 13.[2]
*And they Confessed, that they were strangers, and Pilgrims
on the earth.*

[S–66]   The Law, and the Gospel.

        Lord, when thou didst on *Sinai* pitch
        And shine from *Paran*, when a firie Law
        Pronounc'd with thunder, and thy threats did thaw
        Thy Peoples hearts, when all thy weeds were rich
5   And Inaccessible for light,
                Terrour, and might,
        How did poor flesh (which after thou didst weare,)
                Then faint, and fear!
        Thy Chosen flock, like leafs in a high wind,
10   Whisper'd obedience, and their heads Inclin'd.[1]

2.

        But now since we to *Sion* came,
        And through thy bloud thy glory see,
        With filial Confidence we touch ev'n thee;
        And where the other mount all clad in flame,

[2] The King James and the Genevan versions of this portion of
Heb. 11.13 are identical. Vaughan supplies *"they"* before *"Confessed."*

THE LAW, AND THE GOSPEL.

[1] The stanza contains a series of allusions to the experiences of
Israel at Sinai when the Lord visited the mountain and issued the
Law through Moses. See, for example, Exod. 19 and 24, and Deut.
9.7–29; 10.1–5; 33.2.

15   And threatning Clouds would not so much
              As 'bide the touch,
        We Climb up this, and have too all the way
              Thy hand our stay,
        Nay, thou tak'st ours, and (which ful Comfort brings)
20 Thy Dove too bears us on her sacred wings.

3.

        Yet since man is a very brute
        And after all thy Acts of grace doth kick,
        Slighting that health thou gav'st, when he was sick,
        Be not displeas'd, If I, who have a sute
25   To thee each houre, beg at thy door
              For this one more;
        O plant in me thy *Gospel,* and thy *Law,*
              Both *Faith,* and *Awe;*
        So twist them in my heart, that ever there
30 I may as wel as *Love,* find too thy *fear!*

4.

        Let me not spil, but drink thy bloud,
        Not break thy fence, and by a black Excess
        Force down a Just Curse, when thy hands would bless;
        Let me not scatter, and despise my food,
35   Or nail those blessed limbs again
              Which bore my pain;
        So Shall thy mercies flow: for while I fear,
              I know, thou'lt bear,
        But should thy mild Injunction nothing move me,
40 I would both think, and Judge I did not love thee.

John Cap. 14. ver. 15.[2]
If ye love me, keep my Commandements.

---

[2] The King James and the Genevan versions of this verse are identical.

[S–67]   The World.

    I Saw Eternity the other night
    Like a great *Ring*[1] of pure and endless light,
        All calm, as it was bright,
    And round beneath it, Time in hours, days, years
5   Driv'n by the spheres
    Like a vast shadow mov'd, In which the world
        And all her train were hurl'd;
    The doting Lover in his queintest strain
        Did their Complain,
10 Neer him, his Lute, his fancy, and his flights,
        Wits sour delights,
    With gloves, and knots the silly snares of pleasure
        Yet his dear Treasure
    All scatter'd lay, while he his eys did pour
15   Upon a flowr.

2.

    The darksome States-man[2] hung with weights and woe
    Like a thick midnight-fog mov'd there so slow
        He did nor stay, nor go;

THE WORLD.
  [1] Cf. "this glorious Ring" of S–20, line 6.
  [2] Thought by some to represent Oliver Cromwell, but this is mere conjecture. Maren-Sofie Røstvig ("Casimire Sarbiewski and the English Ode," *SP*, LI [1954], 443–60) analyzes the poem in terms of the Hermetic notion of the seven spheres through which the soul ascends to the eighth and divine level. See *Hermetica,* Libellus I, 25–26a (ed. Walter Scott [Oxford, 1924–36], I, 129). Casimire Sarbiewski, some of whose odes Vaughan translated (O–37–43), gave the idea poetic treatment in his "E Rebus Humanis Excessus" (Book II, Ode 5, in *The Odes of Casimire,* The Augustan Reprint Society, No. 44 [Los Angeles, 1953], pp. 17–25). See T–9, lines 57–78, for another treatment of the ascent through the spheres.

Condemning thoughts (like sad Ecclipses) scowl
20   Upon his soul,
And Clouds of crying witnesses without
        Pursued him with one shout.
Yet dig'd the Mole, and lest his ways be found
        Workt under ground,
25 Where he did Clutch his prey, but one did see
        That policie,
Churches and altars fed him, Perjuries
        Were gnats and flies,
It rain'd about him bloud and tears, but he
30   Drank them as free.

3.

The fearfull miser on a heap of rust
Sate pining all his life there, did scarce trust
        His own hands with the dust,
Yet would not place one peece above, but lives
35   In feare of theeves.
Thousands there were as frantick as himself
        And hug'd each one his pelf,
The down-right Epicure plac'd heav'n in sense
        And scornd pretence
40 While others slipt into a wide Excesse
        Said little lesse;
The weaker sort slight, triviall wares Inslave
        Who think them brave,
And poor, despised truth sate Counting by
45   Their victory.

4.

Yet some, who all this while did weep and sing,
And sing, and weep, soar'd up into the *Ring*,[3]
        But most would use no wing.

[3] The *Hermetica*, Libellus I, 26a (ed. Scott, I, 129), says that those who have escaped the world by ascending through the seven spheres and have attained the eighth sphere sing, "hymning the Father," before entering into God "above the substance of the eighth sphere," where also there is singing. For the idea of singing

O fools (said I,) thus to prefer dark night
50   Before true light,
To live in grots, and caves, and hate the day
       Because it shews the way,
The way which from this dead and dark abode
       Leads up to God,
55 A way where you might tread the Sun, and be
       More bright than he.
But as I did their madnes so discusse
       One whisper'd thus,
This Ring the Bride-groome did for none provide
60   *But for his bride.*

John Cap. 2. ver. 16, 17.[4]
All that is in the world, the lust of the flesh, the lust of the Eys, and the pride of life, is not of the father, but is of the world.

And the world passeth away, and the lusts thereof, but he that doth the will of God abideth for ever.

[S–68]   The Mutinie.

Weary of this same Clay, and straw,[1] I laid
Me down to breath, and casting in my heart
The after-burthens, and griefs yet to come,
      The heavy sum
5 So shook my brest, that (sick and sore dismai'd)

---

and weeping, Vaughan may have identified these Hermetic souls with the "great multitude" of Revelation (7.9), "which came out of great tribulation" (7.14), from whose eyes "God shall wipe away all tears" (7.17; 21.4), and with the inhabitants of the New Jerusalem "prepared as a bride adorned for her husband" (21.2).

[4] Only minor variations from the King James version.

THE MUTINIE.

[1] As Martin (*Works,* 1957, p. 743) suggests, the imagery points to Israel's bondage in Egypt, Exod. 1.14 and 5.7 ff. And later in the poem, to Israel's wanderings in the wilderness.

My thoughts, like water which some stone doth start
Did quit their troubled Channel, and retire
Unto the banks, where, storming at those bounds,
They murmur'd sore; But I, who felt them boyl
10   And knew their Coyl,
Turning to him, who made poor sand to tire
And tame proud waves, If yet these barren grounds
          And thirstie brick must be (said I)
               My taske, and Destinie,

2.

15   Let me so strive and struggle with thy foes
(Not thine alone but mine too,) that when all
Their Arts and force are built unto the height
          That Babel-weight[2]
May prove thy glory, and their shame; so Close
20   And knit me to thee, That though in this vale
Of sin, and death I sojourn, yet one Eie
May look to thee, To thee the finisher
And Author of my faith;[3] so shew me home
          Tha all this fome
25   And frothie no se which up and down doth flie
May find no lodging in mine Eie, or Eare,
          O seal them up! that these may flie
               Like other tempests by.

3.

Not but I know thou hast a shorter Cut
30   To bring me home, than through a wildernes,
A Sea, or Sands and Serpents; Yet since thou
          (As thy words show)
Though in this desert I were wholy shut,
Canst light and lead me there with such redress
35   That no decay shal touch me; O be pleas'd
To fix my steps, and whatsoever path

---

[2] Gen. 11.1–9.
[3] Heb. 12.2, "Jesus the author and finisher of our faith."

Thy sacred and eternal wil decreed
> For thy bruis'd reed[4]
O give it ful obedience, that so seiz'd
40 Of all I have, I may nor move thy wrath
> Nor grieve thy *Dove*, but soft and mild
> Both live and die thy Child.

Revel. Cap. 2. ver. 17.[5]
To him that overcometh wil I give to eate of the hidden
Manna, and I wil give him a white stone, and in the stone a
new name written, which no man knoweth, saving he that re-
ceiveth it.

[S–69]   The Constellation.

Fair, order'd lights (whose motion without noise
> Resembles those true Joys
Whose spring is on that hil where you do grow
> And we here tast sometimes below,)

5 With what exact obedience do you move
> Now beneath, and now above,
And in your vast progressions overlook
> The darkest night, and closest nook!

Some nights I see you in the gladsome East,
10   Some others neer the West,
And when I cannot see, yet do you shine
> And beat about your endles line.

---

[4] Isa. 42.3, "A bruised reed shall he not break." And Matt. 12.20.

[5] The King James version, with the second *"I"* added, of this portion of the verse. See S–40, line 28, and S–42, line 5.

Silence, and light, and watchfulnes with you
Attend and wind the Clue,[1]
15 No sleep, nor sloth assailes you, but poor man
Still either sleeps, or slips his span.[2]

He grops beneath here, and with restless Care
First makes, then hugs a snare,
Adores dead dust, sets heart on Corne and grass
20 But seldom doth make heav'n his glass.

Musick and mirth (if there be musick here)
Take up, and tune his year,
These things are Kin to him, and must be had,
Who kneels, or sighs a life is mad.

25 Perhaps some nights hee'l watch with you, and peep
When it were best to sleep,
Dares know Effects, and Judge them long before,
When th' herb he treads knows much, much more.

But seeks he your *Obedience, Order, Light,*
30 Your calm and wel-train'd flight,
Where, though the glory differ in each star,[3]
Yet is there peace still, and no war?

Since plac'd by him who calls you by your names[4]
And fixt there all your flames,
35 Without Command you never acted ought
And then you in your Courses fought.[5]

THE CONSTELLATION.
[1] Literally, the thread; figuratively, the guide or key giving direction.
[2] Lets go of, or wastes, his life.
[3] I Cor. 15.41, "one star differeth from another star in glory."
[4] Ps. 147.4, "he calleth them [the stars] all by their names."
[5] Judg. 5.20, "the stars in their courses fought against Sisera."

But here Commission'd by a black self-wil
    The sons the father kil,
The Children Chase the mother, and would heal
40   The wounds they give, by crying, zeale.

Then Cast her bloud, and tears upon thy book
    Where they for fashion look,
And like that Lamb which had the Dragons voice[6]
    Seem mild, but are known by their noise.

45 Thus by our lusts disorder'd into wars
    Our guides prove wandring stars,
Which for these mists, and black days were reserv'd,
    What time we from our first love swerv'd.

Yet O for his sake who sits now by thee
50   All crown'd with victory,
So guide us through this Darknes, that we may
    Be more and more in love with day;

Settle, and fix our hearts, that we may move
    In order, peace, and love,
55 And taught obedience by thy whole Creation,
    Become an humble, holy nation.

Give to thy spouse her perfect, and pure dress,
    Beauty and *holiness,*
And so repair these Rents, that men may see
60   And say, *Where God is, all agree.*

[6] Rev. 13.11, "another beast . . . had two horns like a lamb, and he spake as a dragon."

[S–70]   The Shepheards.

    Sweet, harmles lives! (on whose holy leisure
        Waits Innocence and pleasure,)
    Whose leaders to those pastures, and cleer springs,
        Were *Patriarchs*, Saints, and Kings,
5 How happend it that in the dead of night
        You only saw true light,
    While *Palestine* was fast a sleep, and lay
        Without one thought of Day?
    Was it because those first and blessed swains
10   Were pilgrims on those plains
    When they receiv'd the promise, for which now
        'Twas there first shown to you?
    'Tis true, he loves that Dust whereon they go
        That serve him here below,
15 And therefore might for memory of those
        His love there first disclose;
    But wretched *Salem*[1] once his love, must now
        No voice, nor vision know,
    Her stately Piles with all their height and pride
20   Now languished and died,
    And *Bethlems* humble Cotts above them stept
        While all her Seers slept;
    Her Cedar, firr, hew'd stones and gold were all
        Polluted through their fall,
25 And those once sacred mansions were now
        Meer emptiness and show,
    This made the Angel call at reeds and thatch,
        Yet where the shepheards watch,
    And Gods own lodging (though he could not lack,)
30   To be a common *Rack*;[2]

THE SHEPHEARDS.
  [1] Jerusalem.
  [2] Manger.

No costly pride, no soft-cloath'd luxurie
    In those thin Cels could lie,
Each stirring wind and storm blew through their Cots
    Which never harbour'd plots,
35 Only Content, and love, and humble joys
    Lived there without all noise,
Perhaps some harmless Cares for the next day
    Did in their bosomes play,
As where to lead their sheep, what silent nook,
40   What springs or shades to look,
But that was all; And now with gladsome care
    They for the town prepare,
They leave their flock, and in a busie talk
    All towards *Bethlem* walk
45 To see their souls great shepheard, who was come
    To bring all straglers home,
Where now they find him out, and taught before
    That Lamb of God adore,
That Lamb whose daies great Kings and Prophets wish'd
50   And long'd to see, but miss'd.
The first light they beheld was bright and gay
    And turn'd their night to day,
But to this later light they saw in him,
    Their day was dark, and dim.

[S–71]   Misery.

    Lord, bind me up, and let me lye
    A Pris'ner to my libertie,
    If such a state at all can be
    As an Impris'ment serving thee;
5   The wind, though gather'd in thy fist,[1]
    Yet doth it blow stil where it list,[2]

MISERY.
  [1] Prov. 30.4, "who hath gathered the wind in his fists?"
  [2] John 3.8, "The wind bloweth where it listeth."

And yet shouldst thou let go thy hold
Those gusts might quarrel and grow bold.
  As waters here, headlong and loose
10   The lower grounds stil chase, and choose,
Where spreading all the way they seek
And search out ev'ry hole, and Creek;
So my spilt thoughts winding from thee
Take the down-rode to vanitie,
15   Where they all stray and strive, which shal
Find out the first and steepest fal;
I cheer their flow, giving supply
To what's already grown too high,
And having thus perform'd that part
20   Feed on those vomits of my heart.
I break the fence my own hands made
Then lay that trespasse in the shade,
Some fig-leafs stil I do devise[3]
As if thou hadst nor ears, nor Eyes.
25   Excesse of friends, of words, and wine
Take up my day, while thou dost shine
All unregarded, and thy book
Hath not so much as one poor look.
If thou steal in amidst the mirth
30   And kindly tel me, *I am Earth,*
I shut thee out, and let that slip,
Such Musick spoils good fellowship.
Thus wretched I, and most unkind,
Exclude my dear God from my mind,
35   Exclude him thence, who of that Cel
Would make a Court, should he there dwel.
He goes, he yields; And troubled sore
His holy spirit grieves therefore,
The mighty God, th' eternal King
40   Doth grieve for Dust, and Dust doth sing.
But I go on, haste to Devest
My self of reason, till opprest
And buried in my surfeits I
Prove my own shame and miserie.

[3] Gen. 3.7.

45   Next day I call and cry for thee
    Who shouldst not then come neer to me,
    But now it is thy servants pleasure
    Thou must (and dost) give him his measure.
    Thou dost, thou com'st, and in a showr
50   Of healing sweets thy self dost powr
    Into my wounds, and now thy grace
    (I know it wel,) fils all the place;
    I sit with thee by this new light,
    And for that hour th'art my delight,
55   No man can more the world despise
    Or thy great mercies better prize.
    I School my Eys, and strictly dwel
    Within the Circle of my Cel,
    That Calm and silence are my Joys
60   Which to thy peace are but meer noise.
    At length I feel my head to ake,
    My fingers Itch, and burn to take
    Some new Imployment, I begin
    To swel and fome and fret within.
65   *"The Age, the present times are not*
    "To snudge[4] in, and embrace a Cot,
    "Action and bloud now get the game,
    "Disdein treads on the peaceful name,
    "Who sits at home too bears a loade
70   *"Greater than those that gad abroad.*
    Thus do I make thy gifts giv'n me
    The only quarrellers with thee,
    I'd loose those knots thy hands did tie,
    Then would go travel, fight or die.
75   Thousands of wild and waste Infusions
    Like waves beat on my resolutions,
    As flames about their fuel run
    And work, and wind til all be done,
    So my fierce soul bustles about
80   And never rests til all be out.
    Thus wilded by a peevish heart
    Which in thy musick bears no part

---

[4] To remain snug and quiet; to nestle (OED cites this example).

I storm at thee, calling my peace
A Lethargy, and meer disease,
85   Nay, those bright beams shot from thy eys
To calm me in these mutinies
I stile meer tempers, which take place
At some set times, but are thy grace.
    Such is mans life, and such is mine
90   The worst of men, and yet stil thine,
Stil thine thou know'st, and if not so
Then give me over to my foe.
Yet since as easie 'tis for thee
To make man good, as bid him be,
95   And with one glaunce (could he that gain,)
To look him out of all his pain,
O send me from thy holy hil
So much of strength, as may fulfil
All thy delight (what e'r they be)
100   And sacred Institutes in me;
Open my rockie heart, and fil
It with obedience to thy wil,
Then seal it up, that as none see,
So none may enter there but thee.
105   O hear my God! hear him, whose bloud
Speaks more and better for my good!
O let my Crie come to thy throne!
My crie not pour'd with tears alone,
(For tears alone are often foul)
110   But with the bloud of all my soul,
With spirit-sighs, and earnest grones,
Faithful and most repenting mones,
With these I crie, and crying pine
Till thou both mend and make me thine.

[S–72]   The Sap.

    Come sapless Blossom, creep not stil on Earth
          Forgetting thy first birth;
    'Tis not from dust, or if so, why dost thou
          Thus cal and thirst for dew?
5   It tends not thither, if it doth, why then
          This growth and stretch for heav'n?
    Thy root sucks but diseases, worms there seat
          And claim it for their meat.
    Who plac'd thee here, did something then Infuse
10   Which now can tel thee news.
    There is beyond the Stars an hil of myrrh[1]
          From which some drops fal here,
    On it the Prince of *Salem* sits,[2] who deals
          To thee thy secret meals,
15   There is thy Country, and he is the way
          And hath withal the key.
    Yet liv'd he here sometimes, and bore for thee
          A world of miserie,
    For thee, who in the first mans loyns didst fal
20   From that hil to this vale,
    And had not he so done, it is most true
          Two deaths had bin thy due;
    But going hence, and knowing wel what woes
          Might his friends discompose,
25   To shew what strange love he had to our good
          He gave his sacred bloud
    By wil our sap, and Cordial; now in this
          Lies such a heav'n of bliss,

THE SAP.
  [1] See Song of Sol. 4.6 and 1.13.
  [2] Melchisedec was king of Salem and priest of God (Gen. 14.18), after whose order Jesus was made high priest (Heb. 6.20), and whose title, king of Salem, means king of peace (Heb. 7.2). He therefore becomes the type of Christ.

That, who but truly tasts it, no decay
30   Can touch him any way,
Such secret life, and vertue in it lies
          It wil exalt and rise
And actuate such spirits as are shed
          Or ready to be dead,
35   And bring new too. Get then this sap, and get
          Good store of it, but let
The vessel where you put it be for sure
          To all your pow'r most pure;
There is at all times (though shut up) in you
40   A powerful, rare dew,
Which only grief and love extract; with this
          Be sure, and never miss,
To wash your vessel wel: Then humbly take
          This balm for souls that ake,
45   And one who drank it thus, assures that you
          Shal find a Joy so true,
Such perfect Ease, and such a lively sense
          Of grace against all sins,
That you'l Confess the Comfort such, as even
50   Brings to, and comes from Heaven.

[S–73]   Mount of Olives.

When first I saw true beauty, and thy Joys
Active as light, and calm without all noise
Shin'd on my soul, I felt through all my powr's
Such a rich air of sweets, as Evening showrs
5 Fand by a gentle gale Convey and breath
On some parch'd bank, crown'd with a flowrie wreath;
Odors, and Myrrh, and balm in one rich floud
O'r-ran my heart, and spirited my bloud,
My thoughts did swim in Comforts, and mine eie
10 Confest, *The world did only paint and lie.*
And where before I did no safe Course steer
But wander'd under tempests all the year,

Went bleak and bare in body as in mind,
And was blow'n through by ev'ry storm and wind,
15 I am so warm'd now by this glance on me,
That, midst all storms I feel a Ray of thee;
So have I known some beauteous *Paisage*[1] rise
In suddain flowres and arbours to my Eies,
And in the depth and dead of winter bring
20 To my Cold thoughts a lively sense of spring.
    Thus fed by thee, who dost all beings nourish,
My wither'd leafs again look green and flourish,
I shine and shelter underneath thy wing
Where sick with love I strive thy name to sing,
25 Thy glorious name! which grant I may so do
That these may be thy *Praise,* and my *Joy* too.

[S–74]   Man.

    Weighing the stedfastness and state
    Of some mean things which here below reside,
    Where birds like watchful Clocks the noiseless date
        And Intercourse of times divide,
5   Where Bees at night get home and hive, and flowrs
        Early, aswel as late,
    Rise with the Sun, and set in the same bowrs;

              2.

    I would (said I) my God would give
    The staidness of these things to man! for these
10   To his divine appointments ever cleave,
        And no new business breaks their peace;
    The birds nor sow, nor reap, yet sup and dine,
        The flowres without clothes live,
    Yet *Solomon* was never drest so fine.[1]

MOUNT OF OLIVES.
  [1] Landscape.
MAN.
  [1] See Matt. 6.26, 28–29.

3.

15   Man hath stil either toyes, or Care,
He hath no root, nor to one place is ty'd,
But ever restless and Irregular
About this Earth doth run and ride,
He knows he hath a home, but scarce knows where,
20   He sayes it is so far
That he hath quite forgot how to go there.

4.

He knocks at all doors, strays and roams,
Nay hath not so much wit as some stones have
Which in the darkest nights point to their homes,[2]
25   By some hid sense their Maker gave;
Man is the shuttle, to whose winding quest
And passage through these looms
God order'd motion, but ordain'd no rest.

[S–75]   ¶

I Walkt the other day (to spend my hour,)
Into a field
Where I sometimes had seen the soil to yield
A gallant flowre,[1]
5   But Winter now had ruffled all the bowre
And curious store
I knew there heretofore.

[2] Loadstones, with magnetic properties.
"I WALKT THE OTHER DAY"
[1] In "Peace," lines 14–15 (ed. Hutchinson, p. 125), George Herbert calls "The Crown Imperiall" "A gallant flower." It was an English garden flower of Levantine origin (OED). Cf. T–42, line 28.

2.

Yet I whose search lov'd not to peep and peer
    I'th' face of things
10 Thought with my self, there might be other springs
    Besides this here
Which, like cold friends, sees us but once a year,
    And so the flowre
    Might have some other bowre.

3.

15 Then taking up what I could neerest spie
    I digg'd about
That place where I had seen him to grow out,
    And by and by
I saw the warm Recluse alone to lie
20   Where fresh and green
    He lived of us unseen.

4.

Many a question Intricate and rare
    Did I there strow,
But all I could extort was, that he now
25   Did there repair
Such losses as befel him in this air
    And would e'r long
    Come forth most fair and young.

5.

This past, I threw the Clothes quite o'r his head,
30   And stung with fear
Of my own frailty dropt down many a tear
    Upon his bed,
Then sighing whisper'd, *Happy are the dead!*
    What peace doth now
35   *Rock him asleep below?*

6.

And yet, how few believe such doctrine springs
   From a poor root
Which all the Winter sleeps here under foot
   And hath no wings
40 To raise it to the truth and light of things,
    But is stil trod
  By ev'ry wandring clod.

7.

O thou! whose spirit did at first inflame
   And warm the dead,
45 And by a sacred Incubation fed
   With life this frame
Which once had neither being, forme, nor name,[2]
   Grant I may so
  Thy steps track here below,

8.

50 That in these Masques and shadows I may see
   Thy sacred way,
And by those hid ascents climb to that day
   Which breaks from thee
Who art in all things, though invisibly;
55   Shew me thy peace,
  Thy mercy, love, and ease,

9.

And from this Care, where dreams and sorrows raign
   Lead me above
Where Light, Joy, Leisure, and true Comforts move
60   Without all pain,
There, hid in thee, shew me his life again
   At whose dumbe urn
  Thus all the year I mourn.

---

[2] According to Pettet (*Of Paradise and Light*, p. 79) this passage is "an unmistakable hermetic description of the Creation, of the Divine creative fire and the 'hatching' of the world."

[S–76]   Begging.

King of Mercy, King of Love,
In whom I live, in whom I move,
Perfect what thou hast begun,
Let no night put out this Sun;
5   Grant I may, my chief desire!
Long for thee, to thee aspire,
Let my youth, my bloom of dayes
Be my Comfort, and thy praise,
That hereafter, when I look
10   O'r the sullyed, sinful book,
I may find thy hand therein
Wiping out my shame, and sin.
O it is thy only Art
To reduce a stubborn heart,
15   And since thine is victorie,
Strong holds should belong to thee;
Lord then take it, leave it not
Unto my dispose or lot,
But since I would not have it mine,
20   O my God, let it be thine!

Jude ver. 24, 25.[1]

Now unto him that is able to keep us from falling, and to present us faultless before the presence of his glory with exceeding joy,

To the only wise God, our Saviour, be glory, and majesty, Dominion and power, now and ever, Amen.

FINIS.

BEGGING.

[1] Essentially the King James version of these verses, substituting *us* for *you*.

SILEX SCINTILLANS

Part Two

(1655)

A note on the title page of Silex Scintillans, 1655, on opposite page

This title page replaces the one which had appeared in 1650. This is not strictly a "second edition," inasmuch as Part I consists of the unsold sheets of the 1650 edition, with the exception of sigs. B2 and B3 which have been reset (see Textual Notes), and Part II appears for the first time.

The quotation from Job gives the King James version, with three words ("But none saith") omitted from the beginning of verse 10.

Silex Scintillans:

SACRED

POEMS

And private

EJACULATIONS.

The second Edition, In two Books;
By *Henry Vaughan*, Silurist.

Job chap. 35. ver. 10, 11.

*Where is God my Maker, who giveth Songs in
the night ?*
*Who teacheth us more then the beasts of the
earth, and maketh us wiser then the fowls
of heaven ?*

London, Printed for *Henry Crips*, and *Lodo-
wick Lloyd*, next to the Castle in *Cornhil*,
and in *Popes-head Alley*. 1655.

The Authors

PREFACE

To the following

HYMNS.

That this Kingdom hath abounded with those ingenious persons, which in the late notion are termed *Wits,*
is too well known. Many of them having cast away all
their fair portion of time, in no better imployments, then
5 a deliberate search, or excogitation of *idle words,* and a
most vain, insatiable desire to be reputed *Poets*; leaving
behind them no other Monuments of those excellent
abilities conferred upon them, but such as they may
(with a *Predecessor* of theirs) term *Parricides,*[1] and a
10 soul-killing Issue; for that is the Βραβεῖον,[2] and
Laureate *Crown,* which idle *Poems* will certainly bring
to their unrelenting Authors.

And well it were for them, if those willingly-studied
and wilfully-published vanities could defile no *spirits,*
15 but their own; but the *case* is far worse. These *Vipers*
survive their *Parents,* and for many ages after (like

THE AUTHORS PREFACE. . . .

[1] Grosart suggests (*Works,* I, 7) the predecessor may have been
Robert Greene, who urges (*Groats-worth of Witte,* ed. G. B. Harri-
son, Bodley Head Quartos [London, 1923], p. 40) his readers to
deal with his "vaine fantasies" and "follies" "as yee would deale
with so many parricides, cast them into the fire: call them *Tele-
gones* [from Telegonus, son of Ulysses by Circe, who unknowingly
killed his father], for now they kil their Father, and every lewd
line in them written, is a deepe piercing wound to my heart; every
idle houre spent by any in reading them, brings a million of sorrowes to my soule."

[2] Prize in the games.

Epidemic diseases) infect whole Generations, corrupting
always and unhallowing the best-gifted *Souls*, and the
most capable *Vessels*: for whose sanctification and well-
20 fare, the glorious *Son* of God laid down his *life*, and suffered the pretious *blood* of his blessed and innocent
heart to be poured out. In the mean time it cannot be
denyed, but these men are had in remembrance, though
we cannot say with any comfort, *Their memorial is*
25 *blessed;* for, that I may speak no more then the truth
(let their passionate *worshippers* say what they please)
all the commendations that can be justly given them,
will amount to no more, then what *Prudentius* the
Christian-sacred *Poet* bestowed upon *Symmachus*;

30   *Os dignum æterno tinctum quod fulgeat auro*
        Si mallet laudare deum: cui sordida monstra
        Prætulit, & liquidam temeravit crimine vocem;
        Haud aliter, quàm cum rastris qui tentat eburnis
        Cænosum versare solum, &c. ——[3]

35   In English thus,

        A wit most worthy in tryed Gold to shine,
        Immortal Gold: had he sung the divine
        Praise of his Maker: to whom he preferr'd
        Obscene, vile fancies, and prophanely marr'd
40   A rich, rare stile with sinful, lewd contents;
        No otherwise, then if with Instruments
        Of polish'd Ivory, some drudge should stir
        A dirty sink, &c. ——

This *comparison* is nothing odious, and it is as *true*,
45 as it is *apposite*; for a *good* wit in a *bad* subject, is (as
Solomon said of the *fair* and *foolish woman*) *Like a*
jewel of gold in a swines snowt, Prov. 11. 22. Nay, the
more acute the *Author is*, there is so much the more
danger and death in the *work*. Where the *Sun* is busie
50 upon a *dung-hill*, the *issue* is always some unclean *ver-*
mine. Divers persons of eminent piety and learning (I

---

[3] See *Contra Orationem Symmachi*, I, 635–39, in *Prudentius*, tr.
H. J. Thomson, Loeb Library (1949), I, 398. Line 638 of the
Loeb text reads *quis temptet* for Vaughan's *qui tentat*.

meddle not with the seditious and *Schismatical*) have, long before my time, taken notice of this *malady*; for the complaint against *vitious verse*, even by peaceful and
55 obedient *spirits*, is of some antiquity in this Kingdom. And yet, as if the evil consequence attending this inveterate *error*, were but a small thing, there is sprung very lately another prosperous *device* to assist it in the subversion of *souls*. Those that want the *Genius* of *verse*,
60 fall to *translating*; and the people are (every *term*) plentifully furnished with various *Foraign vanities*; so that the most lascivious compositions of *France* and *Italy* are here *naturalized* and made *English*: And this (as it is sadly observed) with so much favor and success,
65 that nothing *takes* (as they rightly phrase it) like a *Romance*. And very frequently (if that *Character* be not an *Ivy-bush*)[4] the *buyer* receives this lewd ware from *persons of honor*: who want not reason to forbear, much private misfortune having sprung from no other *seed*
70 at first, then some infectious and dissolving *Legend*.

To continue (after years of discretion) in this *vanity*, is an inexcusable desertion of *pious sobriety:* and to persist so to the end, is a wilful despising of Gods *sacred exhortations*, by a constant, sensual volutation[5] or wal-
75 lowing in *impure thoughts* and *scurrilous conceits*, which both defile their Authors, and as many more, as they are communicated to. If *every idle word shall be accounted for*,[6] and if *no corrupt communication should proceed out of our mouths*,[7] how desperate (I beseech you) is
80 their condition, who all their life time, and out of meer design, study *lascivious fictions*: then carefully record and publish them, that instead of *grace* and *life*, they *may minister sin and death*[8] unto their readers? It was wisely considered, and piously said by one,[9] *That he would*

[4] A means of concealment or deception.
[5] From Latin *volutatio*, a rolling about, wallowing.
[6] Matt. 12.36.
[7] Eph. 4.29.
[8] I Pet. 4.10–11.
[9] Owen Felltham, who has a much more compact version of the following passage in his essay "Of Idle Books," in his *Resolves*, II, 1 (ed. Cumming, London, 1820, p. 208).

85 *read no idle books; both in regard of love to his own
soul, and pity unto his that made them, for* (said he) *if
I be corrupted by them, their Composer is immediatly
a cause of my ill: and at the day of reckoning* (*though
now dead*) *must give an account for it, because I am*
90 *corrupted by his bad example, which he left behinde
him: I will write none, lest I hurt them that come after
me; I will read none, lest I augment his punishment that
is gone before me. I will neither write, nor read, lest I
prove a foe to my own soul: while I live, I sin too much;*
95 *let me not continue longer in wickedness, then I do in
life.* It is a sentence of sacred authority, that *he that is
dead, is freed from sin;*[10] because he cannot in that *state*,
which is without the *body*, sin any more; but he that
writes *idle books*, makes for himself another *body*, in
100 which he always *lives*, and *sins* (after *death*) as *fast* and
as *foul*, as ever he did in his *life*; which very consideration, deserves to be a sufficient *Antidote* against this evil
disease.

And here, because I would prevent a just *censure* by
105 my free *confession*, I must remember, that I my self have
for many years together, languished of this very *sickness*;
and it is no long time since I have recovered. But
(blessed be God for it!) I have by his saving assistance
supprest my *greatest follies*, and those which escaped
110 from me, are (I think) as innoxious, as most of that *vein*
use to be; besides, they are interlined with many virtuous, and some pious mixtures. What I speak of them, is
truth; but let no man mistake it for an *extenuation* of
faults, as if I intended an *Apology* for *them*, or my *self*,
115 who am conscious of so much *guilt* in *both*, as can never
be expiated without *special sorrows*, and that cleansing
and pretious *effusion* of my Almighty Redeemer: and
if the world will be so charitable, as to grant my request,
I do here most humbly and earnestly beg that none
120 would read them.

But an idle or sensual *subject* is not all the *poyson* in
these Pamphlets. Certain Authors have been so irrev-
erendly bold, as to dash *Scriptures*, and the *sacred Rela-*

[10] Rom. 6.7.

tives of *God*[11] with their impious conceits; And (which
125 I cannot speak without grief of heart) some of those
desperate *adventurers* may (I think) be reckoned
amongst the principal or most learned Writers of *English
verse.*

Others of a later *date*, being corrupted (it may be) by
130 that evil *Genius*, which came in with the publique distractions, have stuffed their books with *Oathes, horrid
Execrations*, and a most gross and studied *filthiness*. But
the *hurt* that ensues by the publication of *pieces* so
notoriously ill, lies heavily upon the *Stationers*[12] account,
135 who ought in conscience to refuse them, when they are
put into his hands. No *loss* is so doleful as that *gain*, that
will endamage the soul; he that *prints* lewdness and
impieties, is that mad man in the *Proverbs*, who *casteth
firebrands, arrows and death.*[13]

140   The suppression of this pleasing and prevailing *evil*,
lies not altogether in the power of the *Magistrate*; for it
will flie abroad in *Manuscripts*, when it fails of entertainment at the *press*. The true remedy lies wholly in
their bosoms, who are the gifted persons, by a wise ex-
145 change of *vain* and *vitious subjects*, for *divine Themes*
and *Celestial praise*. The *performance* is easie, and were
it the most difficult in the world, the *reward* is so glorious,
that it infinitely transcends it: for *they that turn many to
righteousness, shall shine like the stars for ever and
150 ever*[14]: whence follows this undenyable *inference*, That
the *corrupting of many*, being a contrary *work*, the
recompense must be so too; and then I know nothing
reserved for them, but *the blackness of darkness for
ever*;[15] from which (O God!) deliver all penitent and
155 reformed *Spirits!*

The first, that with any effectual success attempted a
diversion of this foul and overflowing *stream*, was the

[11] Holy things that relate to God.
[12] The Stationers' Company, with whom books had to be regis-
tered and approved before publication.
[13] Prov. 26.18.
[14] Dan. 12.3.
[15] Jude 13.

blessed man, Mr. *George Herbert*, whose holy *life* and
verse gained many pious *Converts*, (of whom I am the
160 least) and gave the first check to a most flourishing and
admired *wit* of his time.[16] After him followed diverse,—
Sed non passibus æquis;[17] they had more of *fashion*,
then *force:* And the *reason* of their so vast *distance* from
him, besides differing *spirits* and *qualifications* (for his
165 *measure* was eminent) I suspect to be, because they
aimed more at *verse*, then *perfection*; as may be easily
gathered by their frequent *impressions*, and numerous
pages: Hence sprang those wide, those weak, and lean
conceptions, which in the most inclinable *Reader* will
170 scarce give any nourishment or help to *devotion*; for not
flowing from a true, practick piety, it was impossible
they should effect those things abroad, which they never
had acquaintance with at home; being onely the produc-
tions of a common spirit, and the obvious ebullitions of
175 that light humor, which takes the pen in hand, out of
no other consideration, then to be seen in print. It is true
indeed, that to give up our thoughts to pious *Themes*
and *Contemplations* (if it be done for pieties sake) is
a great *step* towards *perfection*; because it will *refine*,
180 and *dispose* to devotion and sanctity. And further, it will
procure for us (so easily communicable is that *loving
spirit*) some small *prelibation* of those heavenly *refresh-
ments*, which descend but seldom, and then very spar-
ingly, upon *men* of an ordinary or indifferent *holyness*;
185 but he that desires to excel in this kinde of *Hagiography*,
or holy writing, must strive (by all means) for *perfection* and true *holyness*, that a *door may be opened to
him in heaven*, Rev. 4. 1. and then he will be able to
write (with *Hierotheus*[18] and holy *Herbert*) A *true*
190 *Hymn.*[19]

[16] Not positively identified. Donne and Herrick have been suggested.

[17] "But with unequal steps" (Virgil, *Aeneid*, II, 724).

[18] Supposed first-century bishop of Athens, mentioned by the
Pseudo-Dionysius as his teacher and author of hymns of love.

[19] The title of a Herbert poem (*Works*, ed. Hutchinson, p. 168).

To effect this in some measure, I have begged leave to communicate this my poor *Talent* to the *Church*, under the *protection* and *conduct* of her *glorious Head:* who (if he will vouchsafe to *own* it, and *go along* with it)
195 can make it as useful now in the *publick*, as it hath been to me in *private*. In the *perusal* of it, you will (peradventure) observe some *passages*, whose *history* or *reason* may seem something *remote*; but were they brought *nearer*, and plainly exposed to your view, (though that
200 (perhaps) might quiet your *curiosity*) yet would it not conduce much to your greater *advantage*. And therefore I must desire you to accept of them in that *latitude*, which is already alowed them. By the last *Poems* in the book (were not that *mistake* here prevented) you would
205 judge all to be *fatherless*, and the *Edition* posthume; for (indeed) *I was nigh unto death*,[20] and am still at no great distance from it; which was the necessary reason for that solemn and accomplished *dress*, you will now finde this *impression* in.

210   But *the God of the spirits of all flesh*,[21] hath granted me a further use of *mine*, then I did look for in the *body*; and when I expected, and had (by his assistance) prepared for a *message* of *death*, then did he *answer* me with *life*; I hope to his *glory*, and my great *advantage:*
215 that I may flourish not with *leafe* onely, but with some *fruit* also; which *hope* and earnest *desire* of his poor *Creature*, I humbly beseech him to perfect and fulfil for his dear *Sons* sake, unto *whom*, with *him* and the most holy and loving *Spirit*, be ascribed by *Angels*, by *Men*,
220 and by all his *Works*, All Glory, and Wisdom, and Dominion, in this the *temporal* and in the *Eternal* Being. *Amen.*

     Newton by *Usk*, near
     Sketh-rock,[22] Septem. 30.
225   1 6 5 4.

[20] Cf. Phil. 2.27, 30.
[21] Num. 16.22.
[22] I.e., Scethrog, a town on the Usk below Brecon. This Preface appears only in the "second edition" of *Silex*, 1655, sigs. A3–B4, with other introductory material, preceding the poems of Part I.

*O Lord, the hope of Israel, all they that forsake thee
shall be ashamed; and they that depart from thee, shall
be written in the earth, because they have forsaken the
Lord, the fountain of living waters.*

5 *Heal me, O Lord, and I shall be healed; save me, and
I shall be saved, for thou art my health, and my great
deliverer.*

*I said in the cutting off of my days, I shall go to the
gates of the grave; I have deprived my self of the residue*
10 *of my years.*

*I said, I shall not see the Lord, even the Lord in the
Land of the living: I shall behold man no more with the
Inhabitants of the world.*

O Lord! by thee doth man live, and from thee is the
15 *life of my spirit: therefore wilt thou recover me, and
make me to live.*

*Thou hast in love to my soul delivered it from the pit
of corruption; for thou hast cast all my sins behinde thy
back.*

20 *For thy names sake hast thou put off thine anger; for
thy praise hast thou refrained from me, that I should not
be cut off.*

*For the grave cannot praise thee, death cannot cele-
brate thee: they that go down into the pit, cannot hope*
25 *for thy truth.*

*The living, the living, he shall praise thee, as I do this
day: the Father to the children shall make known thy
truth.*

O Lord! thou hast been merciful, thou hast brought
30 *back my life from corruption: thou hast redeemed me
from my sin.*

They that follow after lying vanities, forsake their own mercy.

Therefore shall thy songs be with me, and my prayer
35 *unto the God of my life.*

I will go unto the altar of my God, unto God, the joy of my youth; and in thy fear will I worship towards thy holy temple.

I will sacrifice unto thee with the voice of thanksgiv-
40 *ing; I will pay that which I have vowed: salvation is of the Lord.*[1]

INTRODUCTORY VERSES.
[1] The above are either quotations or adaptations of the following passages: Jer. 17.13, 14; Isa. 38.10, 11, 16–19; 48.9; Jonah 2.6, 8, 9; Pss. 5.7; 42.8; 43.4. They first appear in the "second edition" of *Silex*, 1655, sigs. [B5–B6], with other introductory material, preceding the poems of Part I.

To my most merciful, my most
loving, and dearly loved Re-
deemer, the ever blessed,
the onely Holy and
JUST ONE,
JESUS CHRIST,
The Son of the living
GOD,
And the sacred
Virgin Mary.

I.

My God! thou that didst dye for me,[1]
These thy deaths fruits I offer thee;
Death that to me was life and light,
But dark and deep pangs to thy sight.
5   Some drops of thy all-quickning blood
Fell on my heart; those made it bud
And put forth thus, though Lord, before
The ground was curst, and void of store.
Indeed I had some here to hire
10   Which long resisted thy desire,
That ston'd thy servants, and did move
To have the murthred for thy love;
But Lord, I have expell'd them, and so bent,
Beg, thou wouldst take thy Tenants Rent.

DEDICATION.
   [1] With this, compare the 1650 dedication of *Silex,* Part I (S–2).

[S–77]   II.

Dear Lord, 'tis finished! and now he[2]
That copied it, presents it thee.
'Twas thine first, and to thee returns,
From thee it shin'd, though here it burns;
5   If the Sun rise on rocks, is't right,
To call it their inherent light?
No, nor can I say, this is mine,
For, dearest Jesus, 'tis all thine.
As thy cloaths, (when thou with cloaths wert clad)
10   Both light from thee, and virtue had,
And now (as then within this place)
Thou to poor rags dost still give grace.
This is the earnest thy love sheds,
The *Candle* shining on some heads,[3]
15   Till at thy charges they shall be,
Cloath'd all with immortality.

My dear Redeemer, the worlds light,
And life too, and my hearts delight!
For all thy mercies and thy truth
20   Shew'd to me in my sinful youth,
For my sad failings and my wilde
Murmurings at thee, when most milde:
For all my secret faults, and each
Frequent relapse and wilful breach,
25   For all designs meant against thee,
And ev'ry publish'd vanity
Which thou divinely hast forgiven,
While thy blood wash'd me white as heaven:

[2] This second dedication appears only in 1655.
[3] Job 29.3, "When his candle shined upon my head."

I nothing have to give to thee,
30   But this thy own gift, given to me;
Refuse it not! for now thy *Token*
Can tell thee where a heart is broken.

Revel. cap. 1. ver. 5, 6, 7.[4]

Unto him that loved us, and washed us from our sins in his own blood.

And hath made us Kings and Priests unto God and his Father; to him be glory and dominion, for ever and ever. Amen.

Behold, he cometh with clouds, and every eye shall see him, and they also which pierced him; and all kinreds of the earth shall wail because of him: even so. Amen.

[S–78]   ¶

Vain Wits and eyes[1]
Leave, and be wise:
Abuse not, shun not holy fire,
But with true tears wash off your mire.
5   Tears and these flames will soon grow kinde,
And mix an eye-salve for the blinde.
Tears cleanse and supple without fail,
And fire will purge your callous veyl.
Then comes the light! which when you spy,
10   And see your nakedness thereby,
Praise him, who dealt his gifts so free
In tears to you, in fire to me.

[4] Vaughan uses the King James version, retaining the early form "kinreds" as against the phonetic form "kindreds," which did not become common until the seventeenth century. See OED.

"VAIN WITS AND EYES"

[1] These lines appeared first in 1655, sig. [B8ᵛ], immediately preceding the poems of *Silex*, Part I.

Silex Scintillans, &c.

[S–79]   Ascension-day.

Lord Jesus! with what sweetness and delights,
Sure, holy hopes, high joys and quickning flights
Dost thou feed thine! O thou! the hand that lifts
To him, who gives all good and perfect gifts.
5   Thy glorious, bright Ascension (though remov'd
So many Ages from me) is so prov'd
And by thy Spirit seal'd to me, that I
Feel me a sharer in thy victory.
        I soar and rise
10   Up to the skies,
            Leaving the world their day,
        And in my flight,
        For the true light
            Go seeking all the way;
15 I greet thy Sepulchre, salute thy Grave,
That blest inclosure, where the Angels gave
The first glad tidings of thy early light,
And resurrection from the earth and night.
I see that morning in thy[1] Converts tears,
20 Fresh as the dew, which but this dawning wears?
I smell her spices, and her ointment yields,
As rich a scent as the now Primros'd-fields:
The Day-star smiles, and light with the deceast,
Now shines in all the Chambers of the East.
25 What stirs, what posting intercourse and mirth
Of Saints and Angels glorifie the earth?

ASCENSION-DAY.
   [1] An asterisk here in the 1655 edition designates the note,
"*St. Mary Magdalene.*" Mary Magdalene had been identified with
Mary of Bethany, who anointed the feet of Jesus (John 11.2; 12.3).
See S–104.

What sighs, what whispers, busie stops and stays;
Private and holy talk fill all the ways?
They pass as at the last great day, and run
30 In their white robes to seek the risen Sun;
I see them, hear them, mark their haste, and move
Amongst them, with them, wing'd with faith and love.
Thy forty days more secret commerce here,
After thy death and Funeral, so clear
35 And indisputable, shews to my sight
As the Sun doth, which to those days gave light.
I walk the fields of *Bethani*[2] which shine
All now as fresh as *Eden*, and as fine.
Such was the bright world, on the first seventh day,
40 Before man brought forth sin, and sin decay;
When like a Virgin clad in *Flowers* and *green*
The pure earth sat, and the fair woods had seen
No frost, but flourish'd in that youthful vest,
With which their great Creator had them drest:
45 When Heav'n above them shin'd like molten glass,
While all the Planets did unclouded pass;
And Springs, like dissolv'd Pearls their Streams did pour
Ne'r marr'd with floods, nor anger'd with a showre.
With these fair thoughts I move in this fair place,
50 And the last steps of my milde Master trace;
I see him leading out his chosen Train,
All sad with tears, which like warm Summer-rain
In silent drops steal from their holy eyes,
Fix'd lately on the Cross, now on the skies.
55 And now (eternal Jesus!) thou dost heave
Thy blessed hands to bless, these thou dost leave;
The cloud doth now receive thee, and their sight
Having lost thee, behold two men in white![3]
Two and no more: *what two attest, is true,*
60 Was thine own answer to the stubborn Jew.[4]
Come then thou faithful witness! come dear Lord
Upon the Clouds again to judge this world!

[2] Where Jesus ascended (Luke 24.50–51).
[3] Acts 1.9–10.
[4] Matt. 18.16; John 8.13–17.

[S–80]   Ascension-Hymn.

> Dust and clay
> Mans antient wear!
> Here you must stay,
> But I elsewhere;
> 5   Souls sojourn here, but may not rest;
> Who will ascend, must be undrest.

> And yet some
> That know to die
> Before death come,
> 10   Walk to the skie
> Even in this life; but all such can
> Leave behinde them the old Man.[1]

> If a star
> Should leave the Sphære,
> 15   She must first mar
> Her flaming wear,
> And after fall, for in her dress
> Of glory, she cannot transgress.

> Man of old
> 20   Within the line[2]
> Of *Eden* could
> Like the Sun shine
> All naked, innocent and bright,
> And intimate with Heav'n, as light;

ASCENSION-HYMN.
   [1] Col. 3.9, "ye have put off the old man with his deeds."
   [2] Within the boundaries.

25   But since he
        That brightness soil'd,
        His garments be
        All dark and spoil'd,
    And here are left as nothing worth,
30 Till the Refiners fire breaks forth.

        Then comes he!
        Whose mighty light
        Made his cloathes be
        Like Heav'n, all bright;
35 The Fuller, whose pure blood did flow
    To make stain'd man more white then snow.[3]

        Hee alone
        And none else can
        Bring bone to bone[4]
40   And rebuild man,
    And by his all subduing might
    Make clay ascend more quick then light.[5]

[S–81]   ¶

    They are all gone into the world of light!
        And I alone sit lingring here;
    Their very memory is fair and bright,
        And my sad thoughts doth clear.

5 It glows and glitters in my cloudy brest
        Like stars upon some gloomy grove,
    Or those faint beams in which this hill is drest,
        After the Sun's remove.

[3] Mark 9.3, "And his raiment became shining, exceeding white as snow; so as no fuller on earth can white them."
[4] Ezek. 37.7, "and the bones came together, bone to his bone."
[5] Phil. 3.21, "Who shall change our vile body . . . like unto his glorious body . . . whereby he is able even to subdue all things unto himself."

I see them walking in an Air of glory,
10   Whose light doth trample on my days:
My days, which are at best but dull and hoary,
       Meer glimering and decays.

O holy hope! and high humility,
       High as the Heavens above!
15 These are your walks, and you have shew'd them me
       To kindle my cold love,

Dear, beauteous death! the Jewel of the Just,
       Shining no where, but in the dark;
What mysteries do lie beyond thy dust;
20   Could man outlook that mark!

He that hath found some fledg'd birds nest, may know
       At first sight, if the bird be flown;
But what fair Well, or Grove he sings in now,
       That is to him unknown.

25 And yet, as Angels in some brighter dreams
       Call to the soul, when man doth sleep:
So some strange thoughts transcend our wonted theams,
       And into glory peep.

If a star were confin'd into a Tomb
30   Her captive flames must needs burn there;
But when the hand that lockt her up, gives room,
       She'l shine through all the sphære.

O Father of eternal life, and all
       Created glories under thee!
35 Resume thy spirit from this world of thrall
       Into true liberty.

Either disperse these mists, which blot and fill
       My perspective[1] (still) as they pass,
Or else remove me hence unto that hill,
40   Where I shall need no glass.

"THEY ARE ALL GONE . . ."
  [1] Magnifying glass, telescope.

[S–82]   White Sunday.[1]

> Wellcome white day! a thousand Suns,
> Though seen at once, were black to thee;
> For after their light, darkness comes,
> But thine shines to eternity.
>
> 5   Those flames which on the Apostles rush'd
> At this great feast, and in a tyre[2]
> Of cloven Tongues their heads all brush'd,
> And crown'd them with Prophetic fire:
>
> Can these new lights[3] be like to those,
> 10   These lights of Serpents like the Dove?
> Thou hadst no *gall*, ev'n for thy foes,
> And thy two wings were *Grief* and *Love*.
>
> Though then some boast that fire each day,
> And on Christs coat[4] pin all their shreds;
> 15   Not sparing openly to say,
> His candle shines upon their heads:[5]
>
> Yet while some rays of that great light
> Shine here below within thy Book,
> They never shall so blinde my sight
> 20   But I will know which way to look.

WHITE SUNDAY.

[1] The seventh Sunday after Easter, a festival commemorating the descent of the Holy Spirit at Pentecost. See Acts 2.1–4.

[2] Headdress or ornament.

[3] Novel doctrines, or the new sectaries.

[4] The seamless coat worn by Christ at the Crucifixion (John 19.23).

[5] Job 29.3, "When his candle shined upon my head."

For though thou doest that great light lock,
And by this lesser commerce keep:
Yet by these glances of the flock
I can discern Wolves from the Sheep.

25   Not, but that I have wishes too,
And pray, *These last may be as first,
Or better*; but thou long ago
Hast said, *These last should be the worst*.[6]

Besides, thy method with thy own,
30   Thy own dear people pens our times,
Our stories are in theirs set down
And penalties spread to our Crimes.

Again, if worst and worst implies
A State, that no redress admits,
35   Then from thy Cross unto these days
The *rule* without *Exception* fits.

And yet, as in nights gloomy page
One silent star may interline:
So in this last and lewdest age,
40   Thy antient love on some may shine.

For, though we hourly breath decays,
And our best *note* and highest *ease*
Is but meer changing of the *keys*,
And a *Consumption* that doth please;

45   Yet thou the great eternal Rock
Whose height above all ages shines,
Art still the same, and canst unlock
Thy waters to a soul that pines.

[6] Matt. 19.30, "But many that are first shall be last; and the last shall be first." And Matt. 12.45, "and the last state of that [wicked] man is worse than the first." Martin (*Works*, 1957, p. 745) cites II Tim. 3.13, "But evil men and seducers shall wax worse and worse."

Since then thou art the same this day
50   And ever, as thou wert of old,
And nothing doth thy love allay
But our hearts dead and sinful cold:

As thou long since wert pleas'd to buy
Our drown'd estate, taking the Curse
55   Upon thy self, so to destroy
The knots we tyed upon thy purse,

So let thy grace now make the way
Even for thy love; for by that means
We, who are nothing but foul clay,
60   Shal be fine gold, which thou didst cleanse.

O come! refine us with thy fire!
Refine us! we are at a loss.
Let not thy stars for *Balaams* hire[7]
Dissolve into the common dross!

[S–83]   The Proffer.

Be still black Parasites,
Flutter no more;
Were it still winter, as it was before,
You'd make no flights;
5   But now the dew and Sun have warm'd my bowres,
You flie and flock to suck the flowers.

But you would honey make:
These buds will wither,
And what you now extract, in harder weather
10   Will serve to take;
Wise husbands will (you say) there wants prevent,[1]
Who do not so, too late repent.

[7] A house full of silver and gold (Num. 22.18).
THE PROFFER.
[1] I.e., wise husbandmen will anticipate their wants.

O poys'nous, subtile fowls!
The flyes of hell
15   That buz in every ear, and blow on souls
Until they smell
And rot, descend not here, nor think to stay,
I've read, who 'twas, drove you away.[2]

Think you these longing eyes,
20   Though sick and spent,
And almost famish'd, ever will consent
To leave those skies,
That glass of souls and spirits, where well drest
They shine in white (like stars) and rest.

25   Shall my short hour, my inch,
My one poor sand,
And crum of life, now ready to disband
Revolt and flinch,
And having born the burthen all the day,
30   Now cast at night my Crown away?

No, No; I am not he,
Go seek elsewhere.
I skill[3] not your fine tinsel, and false hair,
Your Sorcery
35   And smooth seducements: I'le not stuff my story
With your Commonwealth and glory.

There are, that will sow tares
And scatter death
Amongst the quick, selling their souls and breath
40   For any wares;
But when thy Master comes, they'l finde and see
There's a reward for them and thee.[4]

[2] The Lord drove the flies from Egypt (Exod. 8.31).
[3] Care (for), reck.
[4] Back of the figures in this stanza is the parable of the tares and the wheat, Matt. 13.24–30, 37–40.

Then keep the antient way!
Spit out their phlegm
45   And fill thy brest with home; think on thy dream:
A calm, bright day!
A Land of flowers and spices! the word given,
If these be fair, O what is Heaven!

[S–84]   Cock-crowing.

Father of lights![1] what Sunnie seed,[2]
What glance of day hast thou confin'd
Into this bird? To all the breed
This busie Ray thou hast assign'd;
5   Their magnetisme works all night,
And dreams of Paradise and light.

Their eyes watch for the morning-hue,
Their little grain expelling night
So shines and sings, as if it knew
10   The path unto the house of light.
            It seems their candle, howe'r done,
Was tinn'd[3] and lighted at the sunne.

If such a tincture,[4] such a touch,
So firm a longing can impowre[5]
15   Shall thy own image think it much
To watch for thy appearing hour?
            If a meer blast so fill the sail,
Shall not the breath of God prevail?

COCK-CROWING.
[1] Jas. 1.17, "Every good gift . . . cometh down from the Father of lights."
[2] Seed, glance of light, and grain were three Hermetical terms for the soul's spiritual quality derived from the Father of lights.
[3] Kindled.
[4] Spirit or soul of a thing.
[5] Grosart suggests "in-pour" not "empower" as the meaning here.

O thou immortall light and heat!
20 Whose hand so shines through all this frame,
That by the beauty of the seat,
We plainly see, who made the same.
　　　Seeing thy seed abides in me,
　　　Dwell thou in it, and I in thee.

25 To sleep without thee, is to die;
Yea, 'tis a death partakes of hell:
For where thou dost not close the eye
It never opens, I can tell.
　　　In such a dark, Ægyptian border,[6]
30 　　　The shades of death dwell and disorder.

If joyes, and hopes, and earnest throws,[7]
And hearts, whose Pulse beats still for light
Are given to birds; who, but thee, knows
A love-sick souls exalted flight?
35 　　　Can souls be track'd by any eye
　　　But his, who gave them wings to flie?

Onely this Veyle[8] which thou hast broke,
And must be broken yet in me,
This veyle, I say, is all the cloke
40 And cloud which shadows thee from me.
　　　This veyle thy full-ey'd love denies,
　　　And onely gleams and fractions spies.

O take it off! make no delay,
But brush me with thy light, that I
45 May shine unto a perfect day,
And warme me at thy glorious Eye!
　　　O take it off! or till it flee,
　　　Though with no Lilie,[9] stay with me!

---

[6] A reference to the plague of darkness cast over Egypt (Exod. 10.21–22).

[7] Throes.

[8] The veil that obscures the meaning of the Old Testament, done away in Christ (II Cor. 3.13–16).

[9] "My beloved [Christ] . . . feedeth among the lilies" (Song of Sol. 2.16).

[S–85]   The Starre.

What ever 'tis, whose beauty here below
Attracts thee thus & makes thee stream & flow,
  And wind and curle, and wink and smile,
   Shifting thy gate and guile:

5 Though thy close commerce nought at all imbarrs
My present search, for Eagles eye not starrs,
  And still the lesser by the best
   And highest good is blest:

Yet, seeing all things that subsist and be,
10 Have their Commissions from Divinitie,
  And teach us duty, I will see
   What man may learn from thee.

First, I am sure, the Subject so respected
Is well disposed, for bodies once infected,
15 Deprav'd or dead, can have with thee
   No hold, nor sympathie.

Next, there's in it a restless, pure desire
And longing for thy bright and vitall fire,
  Desire that never will be quench'd,
20   Nor can be writh'd, nor wrench'd.

These are the Magnets which so strongly move
And work all night upon thy light and love,
  As beauteous shapes, we know not why,
   Command and guide the eye.

25   For where desire, celestiall, pure desire
      Hath taken root, and grows, and doth not tire,
            There God a Commerce states,[1] and sheds
            His Secret on their heads.

      This is the Heart he craves; and who so will
30   But give it him, and grudge not; he shall feel
            That God is true, as herbs unseen
            Put on their youth and green.

[S–86]   The Palm-tree.

      Deare friend sit down, and bear awhile this shade
      As I have yours long since; This Plant, you see
      So prest and bow'd, before sin did degrade
      Both you and it, had equall liberty

5   With other trees: but now shut from the breath
      And air of *Eden,* like a male-content
      It thrives no where. This makes these weights (like death
      And sin) hang at him; for the more he's bent

      The more he grows.[1] Celestial natures still
10 Aspire for home; This *Solomon* of old
      By flowers and carvings and mysterious skill
      Of Wings, and Cherubims, and Palms foretold.[2]

THE STARRE.
      [1] Establishes, or instates.
THE PALM-TREE.
      [1] Martin cites M. P. Tilley's *Proverbs in England in the Six-teenth and Seventeenth Centuries* (Ann Arbor, 1950), P 37: "The straighter (higher) grows the Palm the heavier the weight it bears." Cf. S–97, line 39.
      [2] See the description of the building of Solomon's temple in I Kings 6.

This is the life which hid above with Christ
In God,[3] doth always (hidden) multiply,
15 And spring, and grow, a tree ne'r to be pric'd,
A Tree, whose fruit is immortality.

Here Spirits that have run their race and fought
And won the fight, and have not fear'd the frowns
Nor lov'd the smiles of greatness, but have wrought
20 Their masters will, meet to receive their Crowns.

Here is the patience of the Saints:[4] this Tree
Is water'd by their tears, as flowers are fed
With dew by night; but One you cannot see
Sits here and numbers all the tears they shed.

25 Here is their faith too, which if you will keep
When we two part, I will a journey make
To pluck a Garland hence, while you do sleep
And weave it for your head against you wake.

[S–87]   Joy.

Be dumb course measures, jar no more; to me
There is no discord, but your harmony.
False, jugling sounds; a grone well drest, where care
Moves in disguise, and sighs afflict the air:
5 Sorrows in white; griefs tun'd; a sugerd Dosis[1]
Of Wormwood, and a Deaths-head crown'd with Roses.[2]
He weighs not your forc'd accents, who can have
A lesson plaid him by a winde or wave.

[3] Col. 3.3, "your life is hid with Christ in God."
[4] The patience of the saints is spoken of in Rev. 13.10 and
14.12.
JOY.
[1] Dose.
[2] In Wisd. of Sol. 2.8 the wicked say, "Let us crown ourselves
with rosebuds, before they be withered."

Such numbers tell their days, whose spirits be
10 Lull'd by those Charmers to a Lethargy.
    But as for thee, whose faults long since require
More eyes then stars; whose breath could it aspire
To equal winds: would prove too short: Thou hast
Another mirth, a mirth though overcast
15 With clouds and rain, yet full as calm and fine
As those *clear heights* which above tempests shine.
        Therefore while the various showers
        Kill and cure the tender flowers,
        While the winds refresh the year
20   Now with clouds, now making clear,
        Be sure under pains of death
        To ply both thine eyes and breath.
          As leafs in Bowers
          Whisper their hours,
25   And Hermit-wells
          Drop in their Cells:
      So in sighs and unseen tears
      Pass thy solitary years,
And going hence, leave written on some Tree,
30 *Sighs make joy sure, and shaking fastens thee.*

[S–88]   The Favour.

      O thy bright looks! thy glance of love
      Shown, & but shown me from above!
      Rare looks! that can dispense such joy
      As without wooing wins the coy,
5   And makes him mourn, and pine and dye
      Like a starv'd Eaglet, for thine eye.
      Some kinde herbs here, though low & far,
      Watch for, and know their loving star.
      O let no star compare with thee!
10   Nor any herb out-duty me!
      So shall my nights and mornings be
      Thy time to shine, and mine to see.

[S–89]   The Garland.

Thou, who dost flow and flourish here below,
To whom a falling star and nine dayes glory,
Or some frail beauty makes the bravest shew,
Hark, and make use of this ensuing story.

5   When first my youthfull, sinfull age
               Grew master of my wayes,
           Appointing errour for my Page,
               And darknesse for my dayes;
           I flung away, and with full crie
10   Of wild affections, rid
           In post for pleasures, bent to trie
               All gamesters that would bid.
           I played with fire, did counsell spurn,
               Made life my common stake;
15   But never thought that fire would burn,
               Or that a soul could ake.
           Glorious deceptions, gilded mists,
               False joyes, phantastick flights,
           Peeces of sackcloth with silk-lists,[1]
20   These were my prime delights.
           I sought choice bowres, haunted the spring,
               Cull'd flowres and made me posies:
           Gave my fond humours their full wing,
               And crown'd my head with Roses.[2]
25   But at the height of this Careire
               I met with a dead man,
           Who noting well my vain Abear,[3]
               Thus unto me began:

THE GARLAND.
   [1] Silk borders or edgings.
   [2] See S–87, line 6.
   [3] Bearing, behavior.

Desist fond fool, be not undone,
30   What thou hast cut to day
Will fade at night, and with this Sun
Quite vanish and decay.

Flowres gather'd in this world, die here; if thou
Wouldst have a wreath that fades not, let them grow,
35 *And grow for thee; who spares them here, shall find*
A Garland, where comes neither rain, nor wind.

[S–90]   Love-sick.

JESUS, my life! how shall I truly love thee?
O that thy Spirit would so strongly move me,
That thou wert pleas'd to shed thy grace so farr
As to make man all pure love, flesh a star!
5 A star that would ne'r set, but ever rise,
So rise and run, as to out-run these skies,
These narrow skies (narrow to me) that barre,
So barre me in, that I am still at warre,
At constant warre with them. O come and rend,
10 Or bow the heavens! Lord bow them and descend,
And at thy presence make these mountains flow,
These mountains of cold Ice in me! Thou art
Refining fire, O then refine my heart,
My foul, foul heart! Thou art immortall heat,
15 Heat motion gives; Then warm it, till it beat,
So beat for thee, till thou in mercy hear,
So hear that thou must open: open to
A sinfull wretch, A wretch that caus'd thy woe,
Thy woe, who caus'd his weal; so far his weal
20 That thou forgott'st thine own, for thou didst seal
Mine with thy blood, thy blood which makes thee mine,
Mine ever, ever; And me ever thine.

[S–91]   Trinity-Sunday.

> O Holy, blessed, glorious three,
> Eternall witnesses that be
> In heaven, One God in trinitie!
>
> As here on earth (when men with-stood,)
> 5   The Spirit, Water, and the Blood,
> Made my Lords Incarnation good:
>
> So let the *Anty-types* in me
> Elected, bought and seal'd for free,
> Be own'd, sav'd, *Sainted* by you three!

[S–92]   Psalme 104.

> Up, O my soul, and blesse the Lord. O God,
>   My God, how great, how very great art thou!
> Honour and majesty have their abode
>   With thee, and crown thy brow.
>
> 5 Thou cloath'st thy self with light, as with a robe,
>   And the high, glorious heav'ns thy mighty hand
> Doth spread like curtains round about this globe
>   Of Air, and Seà, and Land.
>
> The beams of thy bright Chambers thou dost lay
> 10   In the deep waters, which no eye can find;
> The clouds thy chariots are, and thy path-way
>   The wings of the swift wind.
>
> In thy celestiall, gladsome messages
>   Dispatch'd to holy souls, sick with desire
> 15 And love of thee, each willing Angel is
>   Thy minister in fire.

Thy arm unmoveable for ever laid
    And founded the firm earth; then with the deep
As with a vail thou hidst it, thy floods plaid
20   Above the mountains steep.

At thy rebuke they fled, at the known voice
    Of their Lords thunder they retir'd apace:
Some up the mountains past by secret ways,
      Some downwards to their place.

25 For thou to them a bound hast set, a bound
    Which (though but sand) keeps in and curbs whole
      seas:
There all their fury, fome and hideous sound
    Must languish and decrease.

And as thy care bounds these, so thy rich love
30   Doth broach the earth, and lesser brooks lets forth,
Which run from hills to valleys, and improve
    Their pleasure and their worth.

These to the beasts of every field give drink;
    There the wilde asses swallow the cool spring:
35 And birds amongst the branches on their brink
    Their dwellings have and sing.

Thou from thy upper Springs above, from those
    Chambers of rain, where Heav'ns large bottles lie,
Doest water the parch'd hills, whose breaches close
40   Heal'd by the showers from high.

Grass for the cattel, and herbs for mans use
    Thou mak'st to grow; these (blest by thee) the
    earth
Brings forth, with wine, oyl, bread: All which infuse
    To mans heart strength and mirth.

45 Thou giv'st the trees their greenness, ev'n to those
    Cedars in *Lebanon,* in whose thick boughs
The birds their nests build; though the Stork doth choose
    The fir-trees for her house.

To the wilde goats the high hills serve for folds,
50   The rocks give Conies a retyring place:
Above them the cool Moon her known course holds,
    And the Sun runs his race.

Thou makest darkness, and then comes the night;
    In whose thick shades and silence each wilde beast
55 Creeps forth, and pinch'd for food, with scent and sight
    Hunts in an eager quest.

The Lyons whelps impatient of delay
    Roar in the covert of the woods, and seek
Their meat from thee, who doest appoint the prey
60   And feed'st them all the week.

This past, the Sun shines on the earth, and they
    Retire into their dens; Man goes abroad
Unto his work, and at the close of day
    Returns home with his load.

65 O Lord my God, how many and how rare
    Are thy great works! In wisdom hast thou made
Them all, and this the earth, and every blade
    Of grass, we tread, declare.

So doth the deep and wide sea, wherein are
70   Innumerable, creeping things both small
And great: there ships go, and the shipmens fear
    The comely spacious Whale.

These all upon thee wait, that thou maist feed
    Them in due season: what thou giv'st, they take;
75 Thy bounteous open hand helps them at need,
    And plenteous meals they make.

When thou doest hide thy face (thy face which keeps
　　All things in being) they consume and mourn:
When thou with-draw'st their breath, their vigour sleeps,
80　　　　And they to dust return.

Thou send'st thy spirit forth, and they revive,
　　The frozen earths dead face thou dost renew.
Thus thou thy glory through the world dost drive,
　　And to thy works art true.

85 Thine eyes behold the earth, and the whole stage
　　Is mov'd and trembles, the hills melt & smoke
With thy least touch: lightnings and winds that rage
　　At thy rebuke are broke.

Therefore as long as thou wilt give me breath
90　　I will in songs to thy great name imploy
That gift of thine, and to my day of death
　　　Thou shalt be all my joy.

Ile *spice* my thoughts with thee, and from thy word
　　Gather true comforts; but the wicked liver
95 Shall be consum'd. O my soul, bless thy Lord!
　　Yea, blesse thou him for ever!

[S–93]　　　　　The Bird.

Hither thou com'st: the busie wind all night
Blew through thy lodging, where thy own warm wing
Thy pillow was. Many a sullen storm
　　(For which course[1] man seems much the fitter born,)
5　　　　Rain'd on thy bed
　　　　And harmless head.

THE BIRD.
　[1] Coarse.

And now as fresh and chearful as the light
Thy little heart in early hymns doth sing
Unto that *Providence*, whose unseen arm
10   Curb'd them, and cloath'd thee well and warm.
　　　All things that be, praise him; and had
　　　Their lesson taught them, when first made.

So hills and valleys into singing break,
And though poor stones have neither speech nor tongue,
15   While active winds and streams both run and speak,
Yet stones are deep in admiration.
Thus Praise and Prayer here beneath the Sun
Make lesser mornings, when the great are done.

For each inclosed Spirit is a star
20   　　Inlightning his own little sphære,
Whose light, though fetcht and borrowed from far,
　　Both mornings makes, and evenings there.

But as these Birds of light make a land glad,
Chirping their solemn Matins on each tree:
25   So in the shades of night some dark-fowls be,
Whose heavy notes make all that hear them, sad.

　　The Turtle then in Palm-trees mourns,
　　　While Owls and Satyrs howl;
　　The pleasant Land to brimstone turns
30   　　And all her streams grow foul.

Brightness and mirth, and love and faith, all flye,
Till the Day-spring breaks forth again from high.

[S–94]   The Timber.

Sure thou didst flourish once! and many Springs,
Many bright mornings, much dew, many showers
Past ore thy head: many light *Hearts* and *Wings*
Which now are dead, lodg'd in thy living bowers.

5 And still a new succession sings and flies;
Fresh Groves grow up, and their green branches shoot
Towards the old and still enduring skies,
While the low *Violet* thrives at their root.

But thou beneath the sad and heavy *Line*
10 Of death, dost waste all senseless, cold and dark;
Where not so much as dreams of light may shine,
Nor any thought of greenness, leaf or bark.

And yet (as if some deep hate and dissent,
Bred in thy growth betwixt high winds and thee,
15 Were still alive) thou dost great storms resent
Before they come, and know'st how near they be.

Else all at rest thou lyest, and the fierce breath
Of tempests can no more disturb thy ease;
But this thy strange resentment after death
20 Means onely those, who broke (in life) thy peace.

So murthered man, when lovely life is done,
And his blood freez'd, keeps in the Center still
Some secret sense, which makes the dead blood run
At his approach, that did the body kill.

25 And is there any murth'rer worse then sin?
Or any storms more foul then a lewd life?
Or what *Resentient*[1] can work more within,
Then true remorse, when with past sins at strife?

He that hath left lifes vain joys and vain care,
30 And truly hates to be detain'd on earth,
Hath got an house where many mansions are,[2]
And keeps his soul unto eternal mirth.

But though thus dead unto the world, and ceas'd
From sin, he walks a narrow, private way;
35 Yet grief and old wounds make him sore displeas'd,
And all his life a rainy, weeping day.

For though he should forsake the world, and live
As meer a stranger, as men long since dead;
Yet joy it self will make a right soul grieve
40 To think, he should be so long vainly lead.

But as shades set off light, so tears and grief
(Though of themselves but a sad blubber'd story)
By shewing the sin great, shew the relief
Far greater, and so speak my Saviors glory.

45 If my way lies through deserts and wilde woods;
Where all the Land with scorching heat is curst;
Better, the pools should flow with rain and floods
To fill my bottle, then I die with thirst.[3]

THE TIMBER.
    [1] That which causes a change of feeling (OED cites this example).
    [2] John 14.2, "In my Father's house are many mansions."
    [3] Martin (*Works*, 1957, p. 748) cites the story of Ishmael and Hagar in Gen. 21.9–19.

Blest showers they are, and streams sent from above
50 Begetting *Virgins* where they use to flow;
And trees of life no other waters love,[4]
These upper springs and none else make them grow.

But these chaste fountains flow not till we dye;
Some drops may fall before, but a clear spring
55 And ever running, till we leave to fling
Dirt in her way, will keep above the skie.

Rom. Cap. 6. ver. 7.[5]
He that is dead, is freed from sin.

[S–95]   The Jews.

When the fair year
Of your deliverer comes,
And that long frost which now benums
Your hearts shall thaw; when Angels here
5   Shall yet to man appear,
And familiarly confer
Beneath the Oke and Juniper:[1]
When the bright *Dove*[2]
Which now these many, many Springs
10   Hath kept above,
Shall with spread wings
Descend, and living waters flow
To make drie dust, and dead trees grow;

[4] The tree of life grew on either side of the river of the water of
life in Rev. 22.1–2.
[5] The King James and the Genevan versions are the same for
this verse.
THE JEWS.
[1] See S–7, lines 5, 7.
[2] The Holy Spirit (Matt. 3.16).

O then that I

15   Might live, and see the Olive bear
Her proper branches! which now lie
Scattered each where,
And without root and sap decay
Cast by the husband-man away.[3]

20   And sure it is not far!
For as your fast and foul decays
Forerunning the bright morning-star,
Did sadly note his healing rayes
Would shine elsewhere, since you were blind,

25   And would be cross, when God was kinde:
So by all signs
Our fulness too is now come in,
And the same Sun which here declines
And sets, will few hours hence begin

30   To rise on you again, and look
Towards old *Mamre* and *Eshcols* brook.[4]
For surely he
Who lov'd the world so, as to give
His onely Son to make it free,

35   Whose spirit too doth mourn and grieve
To see man lost, will for old love
From your dark hearts this veil remove.[5]

Faith sojourn'd first on earth in you,
You were the dear and chosen stock:

40   The *Arm* of God, glorious and true,
Was first reveal'd to be your rock.[6]

[3] Israel is a green olive tree whose branches are broken by the Lord (Jer. 11.16), who is the husbandman of John 15.1.

[4] The plain of Mamre was Abram's dwelling (Gen. 13.18); the brook of Eshcol was encountered in the land of Canaan by the spies sent by Moses (Num. 13.23–24).

[5] II Cor. 3.14.

[6] Deut. 32.4, "He is the Rock, his work is perfect."

You were the *eldest* childe, and when
Your stony hearts despised love,
The *youngest*, ev'n the Gentiles then
45   Were chear'd, your jealousie to move.

Thus, Righteous Father! doest thou deal
With Brutish men; Thy gifts go round
By turns, and timely, and so heal
The lost Son by the newly found.[7]

[S–96]   Begging.[1]

I,[2] Do not go! thou know'st, I'le dye!
My *Spring* and *Fall* are in thy book!
Or, if thou goest, do not deny
To lend me, though from far, one look!

5   My sins long since have made thee strange,
A very stranger unto me;
No morning-meetings since this change,
Nor evening-walks have I with thee.

Why is my God thus slow and cold,
10   When I am most, most sick and sad?
Well fare those blessed days of old
When thou didst hear the *weeping Lad!*[3]

[7] Cf. the story of the Prodigal Son (Luke 15.11–32), where it was the younger son who was lost and found, the elder who was faithful.

BEGGING.

[1] First published in *Flores Solitudinis* (1654) under the heading, "To the onely true and glorious God, the Sole disposer of Life and Death." Cf. M–23.

[2] Ay.

[3] Ishmael, miraculously saved from death by thirst (Gen. 21.14–19).

O do not thou do as I did,
Do not despise a Love-sick heart!
15   What though some clouds defiance bid
Thy Sun must shine in every part.

Though I have spoil'd, O spoil not thou!
Hate not thine own dear gift and token!
Poor birds sing best, and prettiest show,
20   When their nest is faln and broken.

Dear Lord! restore thy ancient peace,
Thy quikning friendship, mans bright wealth!
And if thou wilt not give me ease
From sicknesse, give my spirit health!

[S–97]   Palm-Sunday.

Come, drop your branches, strow the way
Plants of the day!
Whom sufferings make most green and gay.

The King of grief, the man of sorrow
5   Weeping still, like the wet morrow,
Your shades and freshness comes to borrow.

Put on, put on your best array;
Let the joy'd rode make holy-day,
And flowers that into fields do stray,
10   Or secret groves, keep the high-way.

Trees, flowers & herbs; birds, beasts & stones,
That since man fell, expect with groans[1]
To see the lamb, which all at once,
Lift up your heads and leave your moans!
15   For here comes he
Whose death will be
Mans life, and your full liberty.

PALM-SUNDAY.
   [1] Rom. 8.22, "For we know that the whole creation groaneth."

Hark! how the children shril and high
   Hosanna cry,
20 Their joys provoke the distant skie,
Where thrones and Seraphins reply,
And their own Angels shine and sing
   In a bright ring:
   Such yong, sweet mirth
25   Makes heaven and earth
Joyn in a joyful Symphony,
The harmless, yong and happy Ass,
Seen long before[2] this came to pass,
Is in these joys an high partaker
30 Ordain'd, and made to bear his Maker.

Dear feast of Palms, of Flowers and Dew!
Whose fruitful dawn sheds hopes and lights;
Thy bright solemnities did shew,
The third glad day through two sad nights.

35 I'le get me up before the Sun,
I'le cut me boughs off many a tree,
And all alone full early run
To gather flowers to wellcome thee.

Then like the *Palm*, though wrong, I'le bear,[3]
40 I will be still a childe, still meek
As the poor Ass, which the proud jear,
And onely my dear *Jesus* seek.

If I lose all, and must endure
The proverb'd griefs of holy *Job*,
45 I care not, so I may secure
But one *green Branch* and a *white robe*.[4]

---

[2] An asterisk appeared here in the 1655 edition, designating the following: "*Zechariah, chap.* 9. *ver.* 9." This verse foretells the coming of the King riding upon an ass.

[3] Cf. S–86, lines 8–9. "Wrong" means "bent."

[4] In Rev. 7.9 the multitude were clothed in white robes and had palms in their hands.

[S–98]   Jesus weeping.

S. *Luke* 19. *ver.* 41.[1]

 Blessed, unhappy City? dearly lov'd
 But still unkinde! art this day nothing mov'd!
   Art senseless still? O can'st thou sleep
   When God himself for thee doth weep!
5   Stiff-necked *Jews*! your fathers breed
   That serv'd the calf, not *Abr'ams* seed,[2]
   Had not the Babes *Hosanna* cryed,
   The stones had spoke, what you denyed.[3]

 Dear *Jesus* weep on! pour this latter
10 Soul-quickning rain, this living water
   On their dead hearts; but (O my fears!)
   They will drink blood, that despise tears.
   My dear, bright Lord! my Morning-star!
   Shed this live-dew on fields which far
15   From hence long for it! shed it there,
   Where the starv'd earth groans for one tear!

 This land, though with thy hearts blest extract fed,
 Will nothing yield but thorns to wound thy head.

JESUS WEEPING.
 [1] "And when he was come near, he beheld the city, and wept over it."
 [2] Exod. 32.4, 9.
 [3] Luke 19.40, "if these should hold their peace, the stones would immediately cry out."

[S–99]   The Daughter of *Herodias*.

St. Matth. chap. 14. *ver.* 6. *&c.*[1]

Vain, sinful Art! who first did fit
Thy lewd loath'd *Motions* unto *sounds,*
And made grave *Musique* like wilde *wit*
Erre in loose airs beyond her bounds?

5   What fires hath he heap'd on his head?
Since to his sins (as needs it must,)
His *Art* adds still (though he be dead,)
New fresh accounts of blood and lust.

Leave then[2] yong Sorceress; the *Ice*
10   Will those coy spirits cast asleep,
Which teach thee now to please[3] his eyes
Who doth thy lothsome mother keep.

But thou hast pleas'd so well, he swears,
And gratifies thy sin with vows:
15   His shameless lust in publick wears,
And to thy soft arts strongly bows.

Skilful Inchantress and true bred!
Who out of evil can bring forth good?
Thy mothers nets in thee were spred,
20   She tempts to *Incest*, thou to *blood*.

THE DAUGHTER OF HERODIAS.
[1] The passage tells the story of Salome and the beheading of
John the Baptist.
[2] An asterisk appeared here in the 1655 edition, designating the
following: "*Her name was* Salome; *in passing over a frozen river,
the ice broke under her, and chopt off her head*." [Vaughan's
note.] Don Cameron Allen, in *PQ*, XXIII (1944), 84–85, traces the
legend to Nikephoros Kallistos.
[3] An asterisk appeared here in the 1655 edition designating the
following: "*Herod Antipas*." [Vaughan's note.]

[S–100]   Jesus weeping.

St. John chap. 11. *ver.* 35.[1]

My dear, Almighty Lord! why dost thou weep?
    Why dost thou groan and groan again,
        And with such deep,
    Repeated sighs thy kinde heart pain,
5   Since the same sacred breath which thus
        Doth Mourn for us,
    Can make mans dead and scatter'd bones
Unite, and raise up all that dyed, at once?

    O holy groans! Groans of the Dove!
10   O healing tears! the tears of love!
    Dew of the dead! which makes dust move
And spring, how is't that you so sadly grieve,
        Who can relieve?

    Should not thy sighs refrain thy store
15   Of tears, and not provoke to more?
    Since two afflictions may not raign
    In one at one time, as some feign.
    Those blasts, which o'r our heads here stray,
    If showers then fall, will showers allay,
20   As those poor Pilgrims oft have tryed,
    Who in this windy world abide.

    Dear Lord! thou art all grief and love,
    But which thou art most, none can prove.
    Thou griev'st, man should himself undo,
25   And lov'st him, though he works thy wo.

JESUS WEEPING. [2]
  [1] "Jesus wept." This was at the death of Lazarus, when Jesus
also "groaned in the spirit" (vss. 33, 38).

'Twas not that vast, almighty measure
Which is requir'd to make up life,
(Though purchas'd with thy hearts dear treasure,)
          Did breed this strife
30   Of grief and pity in thy brest,
The throne where peace and power rest:
But 'twas thy love that (without leave,)
Made thine eyes melt, and thy heart heave;
For though death cannot so undo
35   What thou hast done, (but though man too
Should help to spoil) thou canst restore
All better far then 'twas before;
Yet, thou so full of pity art
(Pity which overflows thy heart!)
40   That, though the Cure of all mans harm
Is nothing to thy glorious arm,
Yet canst not thou that free Cure do,
But thou must sorrow for him too.
          Then farewel joys! for while I live,
45   My business here shall be to grieve:
A grief that shall outshine all joys
For mirth and life, yet without noise.
A grief, whose silent dew shall breed
Lilies and Myrrhe, where the curs'd seed
50   Did sometimes rule. A grief so bright
'Twill make the Land of darkness light;
And while too many sadly roam,
Shall send me (*Swan-like*) singing home.

Psal. 73. ver. 25.[2]

*Whom have I in heaven but thee? and there is none upon
earth, that I desire besides thee.*

[2] The King James version.

[S–101]   Providence.

        Sacred and secret hand!
    By whose assisting, swift command
    The *Angel* shewd that holy Well,
    Which freed poor *Hagar* from her fears,
5   And turn'd to smiles the begging tears
    Of yong, distressed *Ishmael.*[1]

        How in a mystick Cloud
    (Which doth thy strange sure mercies shroud)
    Doest thou convey man food and money
10   Unseen by him, till they arrive
    Just at his mouth, that thankless hive
    Which kills thy Bees, and eats thy honey!

        If I thy servant be
    (Whose service makes ev'n captives free,)
15   A fish shall all my tribute pay,[2]
    The swift-wing'd Raven shall bring me meat,[3]
    And I, like Flowers shall still go neat,
    As if I knew no moneth but *May.*

        I will not fear what man,
20   With all his plots and power can;
    Bags that wax old may plundered be,[4]
    But none can sequester or let
    A state that with the Sun doth set
    And comes next morning fresh as he.

PROVIDENCE.

  [1] Gen. 21.14–19.

  [2] In Matt. 17.27, on Christ's command, Peter caught a fish which had tribute money in its mouth.

  [3] A reference to Elijah's feeding, in I Kings 17.6.

  [4] In Luke 12.33 Christ instructs his disciples to "provide yourselves bags which wax not old, a treasure in the heavens."

25   Poor birds this doctrine sing,
And herbs which on dry hills do spring
Or in the howling wilderness
Do know thy dewy morning-hours,
And watch all night for mists or showers,
30   Then drink and praise thy bounteousness.

     May he for ever dye
Who trusts not thee! but wretchedly
Hunts gold and wealth, and will not lend
Thy service, nor his soul one day:
35   May his Crown, like his hopes, be clay,
And what he saves, may his foes spend!

     If all my portion here,
The measure given by thee each year
Were by my causeless enemies
40   Usurp'd; it never should me grieve
Who know, how well thou canst relieve,
Whose hands are open as thine eyes.

     Great King of love and truth!
Who would'st not hate my froward youth,
45   And wilt not leave me, when grown old;
Gladly will I, like *Pontick* sheep,[5]
Unto their wormwood-diet keep
Since thou hast made thy Arm my fold.

[5] Martin (*Works,* 1957, p. 749) cites Pliny, *Natural History,*
XXVII, 28, where Pontic wormwood is praised for its excellence
and where cattle fattening on it are said to be without gall.

[S–102]   The Knot.

> Bright Queen of Heaven! Gods Virgin Spouse!
>   The glad worlds blessed maid!
> Whose beauty tyed life to thy house,
>   And brought us saving ayd.
>
> 5   Thou art the true Loves-knot; by thee
>   God is made our Allie,
> And mans inferior Essence he
>   With his did dignifie.
>
> For Coalescent by that Band
> 10   We are his body grown,
> Nourished with favors from his hand
>   Whom for our head we own.
>
> And such a Knot, what arm dares loose,
>   What life, what death can sever?
> 15 Which us in him, and him in us
>   United keeps for ever.

[S–103]   The Ornament.

> The lucky world shewd me one day
> Her gorgeous Mart and glittering store,
> Where with proud haste the rich made way
> To buy, the poor came to adore.
>
> 5   Serious they seem'd and bought up all
> The latest Modes of pride and lust,
> Although the first must surely fall,
> And the last is most loathsome dust.

But while each gay, alluring wear
10   With idle hearts and busie looks
They viewd, (for idleness hath there
Laid up all her Archives and books.)

Quite through their proud and pompous file
Blushing, and in meek weeds array'd
15   With native looks, which knew no guile,
Came the sheep-keeping *Syrian* Maid.[1]

Whom strait the shining Row all fac'd
Forc'd by her artless looks and dress,
While one cryed out, We are disgrac'd!
20   For she is bravest, you confess.

[S–104]   St. Mary Magdalen.

Dear, beauteous Saint! more white then day,
When in his naked, pure array;
Fresher then morning-flowers which shew
As thou in tears dost, best in dew.
5   How art thou chang'd! how lively-fair,
Pleasing and innocent an air,
Not tutor'd by thy glass, but free,
Native and pure shines now in thee!
But since thy beauty doth still keep
10   Bloomy and fresh, why dost thou weep?
This dusky state of sighs and tears
Durst not look on those smiling years,

THE ORNAMENT.
[1] Rachel, "beautiful and well favored," kept her father Laban's
sheep (Gen. 29.9, 17).

When *Magdal*-castle was thy seat,[1]
Where all was sumptuous, rare and neat.
15   Why lies this *Hair* despised now
Which once thy care and art did show?
Who then did dress the much lov'd toy,
In *Spires*, *Globes*, angry *Curls* and coy,
Which with skill'd negligence seem'd shed
20   About thy curious, wilde, yong head?
Why is this rich, this *Pistic* Nard[2]
Spilt, and the box quite broke and marr'd?
What pretty sullenness did hast
Thy easie hands to do this waste?
25   Why art thou humbled thus, and low
As earth, thy lovely head dost bow?
    Dear *Soul!* thou knew'st, flowers here on earth
At their Lords foot-stool have their birth;
Therefore thy wither'd self in haste
30   Beneath his blest feet thou didst cast,
That at the root of this green tree
Thy great decays restor'd might be.
Thy curious vanities and rare;
Odorous ointments kept with care,
35   And dearly bought, (when thou didst see
They could not cure, nor comfort thee,)
Like a wise, early Penitent
Thou sadly didst to him present,
Whose interceding, meek and calm
40   Blood, is the worlds all-healing *Balm*.

ST. MARY MAGDALEN.
  [1] Legend identified Mary Magdalene with Mary of Bethany and gave her noble lineage. Her name reputedly came from the castle of Magdalo, two miles from Bethany and Nazareth, where she lived with her sister Martha and brother Lazarus.
  [2] The spikenard with which Mary anointed the feet of Jesus (John 12.3). "Pistic" is from the Greek νάρδος πιστική in John 12.3 and Mark 14.3, translated "spikenard." It may be a local name. Some equate it with "genuine," others with "liquid." A marginal note to Mark 14.3 in the 1612 edition of the King James version reads, *"Or, pure nard: or liquid nard."*

This, this Divine Restorative
Call'd forth thy tears, which ran in live
And hasty drops, as if they had
(Their Lord so near) sense to be glad.
45   Learn, *Ladies*, here the faithful cure
Makes beauty lasting, fresh and pure;
Learn *Marys* art of tears, and then
Say, *You have got the day from men.*
Cheap, mighty Art! her Art of love,
50   Who lov'd much, and much more could move;[3]

Her Art! whose memory must last
Till truth through all the world be past,
Till his abus'd, despised flame
Return to Heaven, from whence it came,
55   And send a fire down, that shall bring
Destruction on his ruddy wing.

Her Art! whose pensive, weeping eyes,
Were once sins loose and tempting spies,
But now are fixed stars, whose light
60   Helps such dark straglers to their sight.

Self-boasting *Pharisee*![4] how blinde
A Judge wert thou, and how unkinde?
It was impossible, that thou
Who wert all false, should'st true grief know;
65   Is't just to judge her faithful tears
By that foul rheum thy false eye wears?
This Woman (say'st thou) *is a sinner:*
And sate there none such at thy dinner?

[3] Luke 7.47, "Her sins, which are many, are forgiven; for she loved much."

[4] Simon the Pharisee, who invited Jesus to eat with him (Luke 7.36–50), taken by Vaughan to be the Simon the Leper of Matt. 26.6, and Mark 14.3.

Go Leper, go; wash till thy flesh
70   Comes like a childes, spotless and fresh;[5]
He is still leprous, that still paints:
Who Saint themselves, they are no *Saints*.

[S–105]   The Rain-bow.

Still yong and fine! but what is still in view
We slight as old and soil'd, though fresh and new.
How bright wert thou, when *Shems*[1] admiring eye
Thy burnisht, flaming *Arch* did first descry!
5   When *Terah, Nahor, Haran, Abram, Lot*,[2]
The youthful worlds gray fathers in one knot,
Did with intentive looks watch every hour
For thy new light, and trembled at each shower!
When thou dost shine darkness looks white and fair,
10   Storms turn to Musick, clouds to smiles and air:
Rain gently spends his honey-drops, and pours
Balm on the cleft earth, milk on grass and flowers.
Bright pledge of peace and Sun-shine! the sure tye
Of thy Lords hand, the[3] object of his eye.
15   When I behold thee, though my light be dim,
Distant and low, I can in thine see him,
Who looks upon thee from his glorious throne
And mindes the Covenant 'twixt *All* and *One*.

[5] When Naaman the leper had dipped himself seven times in
Jordan "his flesh came again like unto the flesh of a little child,
and he was clean" (II Kings 5.14).

THE RAIN-BOW.

[1] One of the sons of Noah.

[2] For their relationships see Gen. 11.24–27.

[3] An asterisk here in the 1655 edition designated the following:
"*Gen. chap.* 9 *ver.* 16" [Vaughan's note.] "And the bow shall be
in the cloud; and I will look upon it, that I may remember the everlasting covenant between God and every living creature, of all
flesh that is upon the earth."

O foul, deceitful men! my God doth keep
20 His promise still, but we break ours and sleep.
    After the *Fall*, the first sin was in *Blood*,[4]
    And *Drunkenness* quickly did succeed the flood;[5]
    But since *Christ* dyed, (as if we did devise
    To lose him too, as well as *Paradise*,)
25 These two grand sins we joyn and act together,
    Though blood & drunkeness make but foul, foul weather.
    Water (though both Heavens windows and the deep,
    Full forty days o'r the drown'd world did weep,)
    Could not reform us, and blood (in despight)
30 Yea Gods own blood we tread upon and slight.
    So those bad daughters, which God sav'd from fire,
    While *Sodom* yet did smoke, lay with their sire.[6]
    Then peaceful, signal bow, but in a cloud
    Still lodged, where all thy unseen arrows shrowd,
35 I will on thee, as on a Comet look,
    A Comet, the sad worlds ill-boding book;
    Thy light as luctual[7] and stain'd with woes
    I'le judge, where penal flames sit mixt and close.
    For though some think, thou shin'st but to restrain
40 Bold storms, and simply dost attend on rain,
    Yet I know well, and so our sins require,
    Thou dost but Court cold rain, till *Rain* turns *Fire*.

[4] Cain's murder of Abel (Gen. 4.8).

[5] Noah's (Gen. 9.21).

[6] The daughters of Lot (Gen. 19.30–36).

[7] Mournful, sorrowful (OED cites Vaughan's use of the word in this sense).

[S–106]   The Seed growing secretly.

S. Mark 4. 26.[1]

If this worlds friends might see but once
What some poor man may often feel,
Glory, and gold, and Crowns and Thrones
They would soon quit and learn to kneel.

5   My dew, my dew! my early love,[2]
My souls bright food, thy absence kills!
Hover not long, eternal Dove!
Life without thee is loose and spills.

Somthing I had, which long ago
10   Did learn to suck, and sip, and taste,
But now grown sickly, sad and slow,
Doth fret and wrangle, pine and waste.

O spred thy sacred wings and shake
One living drop! one drop life keeps!
15   If pious griefs Heavens joys awake,
O fill his bottle! thy childe weeps![3]

Slowly and sadly doth he grow,
And soon as left, shrinks back to ill;
O feed that life, which makes him blow
20   And spred and open to thy will!

For thy eternal, living wells
None stain'd or wither'd shall come near:
A fresh, immortal *green* there dwells,
And spotless *white* is all the wear.

THE SEED GROWING SECRETLY.

[1] "And he said, So is the kingdom of God, as if a man should cast seed into the ground." Verse 27 reads, ". . . and the seed should spring, and grow up he knoweth not how."

[2] Cf. "my first love" of S–21, line 8.

[3] See the story of Ishmael, Gen. 21.14–19.

25   Dear, secret *Greenness*! nurst below
       Tempests and windes, and winter-nights,
       Vex not, that but one sees thee grow,
       That *One* made all these lesser lights.

       If those bright joys he singly sheds
30   On thee, were all met in one Crown,
       Both Sun and Stars would hide their heads;
       And Moons, though full, would get them down.

       Let glory be their bait, whose mindes
       Are all too high for a low Cell:
35   Though Hawks can prey through storms and winds,
       The poor Bee in her hive must dwel.

       Glory, the Crouds cheap tinsel still
       To what most takes them, is a drudge;
       And they too oft take good for ill,
40   And thriving vice for vertue judge.

       What needs a Conscience calm and bright
       Within it self an outward test?
       Who breaks his glass to take more light,
       Makes way for storms into his rest.

45   Then bless thy secret growth, nor catch
       At noise, but thrive unseen and dumb;
       Keep clean, bear fruit, earn life and watch,
       Till the white winged Reapers come![4]

[S–107]   ¶

       As time one day by me did pass
          Through a large dusky glasse
          He held, I chanc'd to look
          And spyed his curious book
5   Of past days, where sad Heav'n did shed
       A mourning light upon the dead.

[4] Matt. 13.39, "the reapers are the angels."

Many disordered lives I saw
  And foul records which thaw
  My kinde eyes still, but in
10   A fair, white page of thin
And ev'n, smooth lines, like the Suns rays,
Thy name was writ, and all thy days.

O bright and happy Kalendar!
  Where youth shines like a star
15   All pearl'd with tears, and may
  Teach age, *The Holy way*;
Where through thick pangs, high agonies
Faith into life breaks, and death dies.

As some meek *night-piece* which day quails,
20   To candle-light unveils:
  So by one beamy line
  From thy bright lamp did shine,
In the same page thy humble grave
Set with green herbs, glad hopes and brave.

25   Here slept my thoughts dear mark! which dust
  Seem'd to devour, like rust;
  But dust (I did observe)
  By hiding doth preserve,
As we for long and sure recruits,
30   Candy with sugar our choice fruits.

O calm and sacred bed where lies
  In deaths dark mysteries
  A beauty far more bright
  Then the noons cloudless light;
35   For whose dry dust green branches bud
And robes are bleach'd in the *Lambs* blood.

Sleep happy ashes! (blessed sleep!)
 While haplesse I still weep;
 Weep that I have out-liv'd
40 My life, and unreliev'd
Must (soul-lesse shadow!) so live on,
Though life be dead, and my joys gone.

[S–108]   ¶

 Fair and yong light![1] my guide to holy
 Grief and soul-curing melancholy;
 Whom living here I did still shun
 As sullen night-ravens do the Sun,
5 And lead by my own foolish fire
 Wandred through darkness, dens and mire.
 How am I now in love with all
 That I term'd then meer bonds and thrall,
 And to thy name, which still I keep,
10 Like the surviving turtle, weep!
 O bitter curs'd delights of men!
 Our souls diseases first, and then
 Our bodies; poysons that intreat
 With fatal sweetness, till we eat;
15 How artfully do you destroy,
 That kill with smiles and seeming joy?
 If all the subtilties of vice
 Stood bare before unpractic'd eyes,
 And every act she doth commence
20 Had writ down its sad consequence,
 Yet would not men grant, their ill fate
 Lodged in those false looks, till too late.

"FAIR AND YONG LIGHT!"
 [1] Possibly Vaughan's first wife Catherine, the date of whose death is not known; she may have died between the two parts of *Silex*.

O holy, happy, healthy heaven,
Where all is pure, where all is even,
25   Plain, harmless, faithful, fair and bright,
But what Earth breaths against thy light!
How blest had men been, had their *Sire*[2]
Liv'd still in league with thy chaste fire,
Nor made life through her long descents,
30   A slave to lustful Elements!
I did once read in an old book
Soil'd with many a weeping look,
That the seeds of foul sorrows be
The finest things that are, to see.
35   So that fam'd fruit which made all dye
Seem'd fair unto the womans eye.[3]
If these supplanters in the shade
Of Paradise, could make man fade,
How in this world should they deter
40   This world, their fellow-murtherer!
And why then grieve we to be sent
Home by our first fair punishment,
Without addition to our woes
And lingring wounds from weaker foes?
45   Since that doth quickly freedom win,
For he that's dead, is freed from sin.[4]

O that I were winged and free
And quite undrest just now with thee,
Where freed souls dwel by living fountains
50   On everlasting, spicy mountains![5]
      Alas! my God! take home thy sheep;
      This world but laughs at those that weep.

[2] Adam.
[3] So the fruit seemed to Eve (Gen. 3.6).
[4] Rom. 6.7.
[5] Cf. "the mountains of spices" of Song of Sol. 8.14.

[S–109]   The Stone.

Josh. chap. 24. ver. 27.[1]

I have it now:
But where to act, that none shall know,
Where I shall have no cause to fear
            An eye or ear,
5   What man will show?
If nights, and shades, and secret rooms,
            Silent as tombs,
Will nor conceal nor assent to
My dark designs, what shall I do?
10   Man I can bribe, and woman will
Consent to any gainful ill,
But these dumb creatures are so true,
No gold nor gifts can them subdue.
Hedges have ears, said the old *sooth,*
15   *And ev'ry bush is somethings booth;*[2]
This cautious fools mistake, and fear
Nothing but man, when ambush'd there.

            But I (Alas!)
Was shown one day in a strange glass
20   That busie commerce kept between
God and his Creatures, though unseen.

            They hear, see, speak,
And into loud discoveries break,

THE STONE.

[1] "And Joshua said unto all the people, Behold, this stone shall
be a witness unto us; for it hath heard all the words of the Lord,
which he spake unto us; it shall be therefor a witness unto you,
lest yee deny your God."

[2] See G. L. Apperson, *English Proverbs and Proverbial Phrases:
a Historical Dictionary* (London, 1929), p. 296: "Hedges have eyes
(or ears)." There are several proverbs dealing with things (bears
or thieves) seen in bushes.

As loud as blood.[3] Not that God needs
25   Intelligence, whose spirit feeds
All things with life, before whose eyes,
Hell and all hearts stark naked lyes.
But[4] he that judgeth as he hears,
He that accuseth none, so steers
30   His righteous course, that though he knows
All that man doth, conceals or shows,
Yet will not he by his own light
(Though both all-seeing and all right,)
Condemn men; but will try them by
35   A process, which ev'n mans own eye
Must needs acknowledge to be just.

Hence sand and dust
Are shak'd for witnesses, and stones
Which some think dead, shall all at once
40   With one attesting voice detect
Those secret sins we least suspect.
For know, wilde men, that when you erre
Each thing turns Scribe and Register,
And in obedience to his Lord,
45   Doth your most private sins record.

The *Law* delivered to the *Jews*,
Who promis'd much, but did refuse
Performance, will for that same deed
Against them by a *stone* proceed;
50   Whose substance, though 'tis hard enough,
Will prove their hearts more stiff and tuff.
But now, since God on himself took
What all mankinde could never brook,

[3] In Gen. 4.10 Abel's blood is said to cry from the ground.

[4] An asterisk here in the 1655 edition designated the following: *"John chap.* 5. *ver.* 30. 45." [Vaughan's note.] Verse 30: "I can of mine own self do nothing: as I hear, I judge: and my judgement is just; because I seek not mine own will, but the will of the Father, which hath sent me." And verse 45: "Do not think that I will accuse you to the Father: there is one that accuseth you, even Moses, in whom ye trust."

If any (for he all invites)
55   His easie yoke rejects or slights,
The *Gospel* then (for 'tis his word
And not himself[5] shall judge the world)
Will by loose *Dust* that man arraign,
As one then dust more vile and vain.

[S–110]   The dwelling-place.

S. John, chap. 1. ver. 38, 39.[1]

What happy, secret fountain,
    Fair shade, or mountain,
Whose undiscover'd virgin glory
Boasts it this day, though not in story,
5   Was then thy dwelling? did some cloud
Fix'd to a Tent,[2] descend and shrowd
My distrest Lord? or did a star
Becken'd by thee, though high and far,
In sparkling smiles haste gladly down
10   To lodge light, and increase her own?
My dear, dear God! I do not know
What lodgd thee then, nor where, nor how;
But I am sure, thou dost now come
Oft to a narrow, homely room,
15   Where thou too hast but the least part,
My God, I mean *my sinful heart*.

[5] An asterisk here in the 1655 edition designated the following: "*St. John, chap.* 12. *ver.* 47, 48." [Vaughan's note.] "And if any man hear my words, and believe not, I judge him not; for I came not to judge the world, but to save the world. He that rejecteth me, and receiveth not my words, hath one that judgeth him: the word that I have spoken, the same shall judge him in the last day."

THE DWELLING-PLACE.

[1] "Then Jesus turned, and saw them following, and saith unto them, What seek yee? They said unto him, Rabbi . . . where dwellest thou? He sayeth unto them, Come and see. They came and saw where he dwelt, and abode with him that day. . . ."

[2] In the shape of a tent.

[S–111]   The Men of War.

S. *Luke, chap.* 23. *ver.* 11.[1]

If any have an ear
Saith holy[2] *John, then let him hear.*
He that into Captivity
Leads others, shall a Captive be.
5   *Who with the sword doth others kill,*
A sword shall his blood likewise spill.
Here is the patience of the Saints,
And the true faith, which never faints.

Were not thy word (dear Lord!) my light,
10   How would I run to endless night,
And persecuting thee and thine,
Enact for *Saints* my self and mine.
But now enlighten'd thus by thee,
I dare not think such villany;
15   Nor for a temporal self-end
Successful wickedness commend.
For in this bright, instructing verse
Thy Saints are not the Conquerers;
But patient, meek, and overcome
20   Like thee, when set at naught and dumb.
Armies thou hast in Heaven, which fight,
And follow thee all cloath'd in white,
But here on earth (though thou hast need)
Thou wouldst no legions, but wouldst bleed.
25   The sword wherewith thou dost command
Is in thy mouth, not in thy hand,[3]

THE MEN OF WAR.

[1] "And Herod with his men of war set him at naught, and mocked him, and arrayed him in a gorgeous robe, and sent him again to Pilate."

[2] An asterisk here in the 1655 edition designated the following: "*Revel. cap.* 13. *ver.* 10." [Vaughan's note.] Verse 9 also applies.

[3] See Rev. 19.14–15, 21.

And all thy Saints do overcome
By thy blood, and their Martyrdom.
But seeing Soldiers long ago
30 Did spit on thee, and smote thee too;
Crown'd thee with thorns, and bow'd the knee,
But in contempt, as still we see,
I'le marvel not at ought they do,
Because they us'd my Savior so;
35 Since of my *Lord* they had their will,
The servant must not take it ill.

Dear *Jesus* give me patience here,
And faith to see my Crown as near
And almost reach'd, because 'tis sure
40 If I hold fast and slight the *Lure*.
Give me humility and peace,
Contented thoughts, innoxious ease,
A sweet, revengeless, quiet minde,
And to my greatest haters kinde.
45 Give me, my God! a heart as milde
And plain, as when I was a childe;
That when *thy Throne is set*,[4] and all
These *Conquerors* before it fall,
I may be found (preserv'd by thee)
50 Amongst that chosen company,
Who by no blood (here) overcame
But the blood of the *blessed Lamb*.[5]

[4] Rev. 4.2, "and behold, a throne was set in the heaven, and one sat on the throne."

[5] Rev. 12.11, "And they overcame him [Satan] by the blood of the Lamb, and by the word of their testimony."

[S–112]   The Ass.

St. Matt. 21.[1]

Thou! who didst place me in this busie street
Of flesh and blood, where two ways meet:
The *One* of goodness, peace and life,
The *other* of death, sin and strife;
5   Where frail visibles rule the minde,
And present things finde men most kinde:
Where obscure cares the *mean* defeat,
And splendid vice destroys the *great*;
As thou didst set no law for me,
10   But that of perfect liberty,[2]
Which neither tyres, nor doth corrode,
But is a *Pillow*, not a *Load*:
So give me grace ever to rest,
And build on it, because the best;
15   Teach both mine eyes and feet to move
Within those bounds set by thy love;
Grant I may soft and lowly be,
And minde those things I cannot see;
Tye me to faith, though above reason,
20   Who question power, they speak treason:
Let me thy Ass[3] be onely wise
To carry, not search mysteries;
Who carries thee, is by thee lead,
Who argues, follows his own head.
25   To check bad motions, keep me still
Amongst the dead, where thriving ill
Without his brags and conquests lies,
And truth (opprest here) gets the prize.

THE ASS.

[1] Matt. 21.1–11, tells of Christ's ride into Jerusalem upon an ass.
[2] Jas. 1.25, "But whoso looketh into the perfect Law of liberty
. . . shall be blessed in his deed."
[3] Cf. S–119, line 11.

At all times, whatsoe'r I do,
30   Let me not fail to question, who
Shares in the *act*, and puts me to't?
And if not thou, let not me do't.
Above all, make me love the poor,
Those burthens to the rich mans door,
35   Let me admire those, and be kinde
To low estates, and a low minde.
If the world offers to me ought,
That by thy book must not be sought,
Or though it should be lawful, may
40   Prove not expedient for thy way;
To shun that peril, let thy grace
Prevail with me to shun the place.
Let me be wise to please thee still,
And let men call me what they will.

45   When thus thy milde, instructing hand
Findes thy poor *foal* at thy command,
When he from wilde is become wise,
And slights that most, which men most prize;
When all things here to thistles turn
50   Pricking his lips, till he doth mourn
And hang the head, sighing for those
Pastures of life, where the Lamb goes:
O then, just then! break or untye
These bonds, this sad captivity,
55   This leaden state, which men miscal
Being and life, but is dead thrall.
And when (O God!) the Ass is free,[4]
In a state known to none but thee;
O let him by his *Lord* be led,
60   To living springs, and there be fed
Where light, joy, health and perfect peace
Shut out all pain and each disease;
Where death and frailty are forgotten,
And bones rejoyce, which once were broken!

[4] Cf. Job 39.5, "Who hath sent out the wild ass free? or who hath loosed the bands of the wild ass?"

[S–113]   The hidden Treasure.

S. *Matt.* 13. 44.[1]

What can the man do that succeeds the[2] King?
Even what was done before, and no new thing.
Who shews me but one grain of sincere light?
False stars and fire-drakes,[3] the deceits of night
5 Set forth to fool and foil thee, do not boast;
Such Coal-flames shew but Kitchin-rooms at most.
And those I saw search'd through; yea those and all
That these three thousand years time did let fall
To blinde the eyes of lookers-back, and I
10 Now all is done, finde all is vanity.
Those secret searches, which afflict the wise,
Paths that are hidden from the *Vulturs* eyes[4]
I saw at distance, and where grows that fruit
Which others onely grope for and dispute.
15   The worlds lov'd wisdom (for the worlds friends think
There is none else) did not the dreadful brink
And precipice it leads to, bid me flie
None could with more advantage use, then I.
    Mans favorite sins, those tainting appetites
20 Which nature breeds, and some fine clay invites,
With all their soft, kinde arts and easie strains
Which strongly operate, though without pains,
Did not a greater beauty rule mine eyes,
None would more dote on, nor so soon entice.

THE HIDDEN TREASURE.
  [1] "The kingdom of heaven is like unto treasure hid in a field; the which when a man hath found, he hideth, and for joy thereof goeth and selleth all that he hath, and buyeth that field."
  [2] An asterisk here in the 1655 edition designated the following: "*Ecclesiastes, chap.* 2. 12." [Vaughan's note.]
  [3] Either fiery meteors or will-o'-the-wisps.
  [4] Job 28.7, "a path . . . which the vulture's eye hath not seen."

25 But since these sweets are sowre, and poyson'd here
Where the impure seeds flourish all the year,
And private Tapers will but help to stray
Ev'n those, who *by them* would finde out the day,
I'le seal my eyes up, and to thy commands
30 Submit my wilde heart, and restrain my hands;
I will do nothing, nothing know, nor see
But what thou bidst, and shew'st, and teachest me.
Look what thou gav'st; all that I do restore
But for one thing, though purchas'd once before.

[S–114]   Childe-hood.

I Cannot reach it; and my striving eye
Dazles at it, as at eternity.
    Were now that Chronicle alive,
Those white designs which children drive,
5   And the thoughts of each harmless hour,
With their content too in my pow'r,
Quickly would I make my path even,
And by meer playing go to Heaven.

            Why should men love
10 A Wolf, more then a Lamb or Dove?
Or choose hell-fire and brimstone streams
Before bright stars, and Gods own beams?
Who kisseth thorns, will hurt his face,
But flowers do both refresh and grace,
15 And sweetly living (*fie on men!*)
Are when dead, medicinal then.
If seeing much should make staid eyes,
And long experience should make wise;
Since all that age doth teach, is ill,
20 Why should I not love childe-hood still?
Why if I see a rock or shelf,
Shall I from thence cast down my self,

Or by complying with the world,
From the same precipice be hurl'd?
25   Those observations are but foul
Which make me wise to lose my soul.

And yet the *Practice* worldlings call
Business and weighty action all,
Checking the poor childe for his play,
30   But gravely cast themselves away.

Dear, harmless age! the short, swift span,
Where weeping virtue parts with man;
Where love without lust dwells, and bends
What way we please, without self-ends.

35   An age of mysteries! which he
Must live twice, that would Gods face see;[1]
Which *Angels* guard, and with it play,
Angels! which foul men drive away.

How do I study now, and scan
40   Thee, more then ere I studyed man,
And onely see through a long night
Thy edges, and thy bordering light!
O for thy Center and mid-day!
For sure that is the *narrow way*.[2]

CHILDE-HOOD.

[1] John 3.3, "Except a man be born again, he cannot see the kingdom of God."

[2] Matt. 7.14, "narrow is the way which leadeth unto life."

[S–115]   The Night.

John 2. 3.[1]

Through that pure *Virgin-shrine*,
That sacred vail drawn o'r thy glorious noon
That men might look and live as Glo-worms shine,
          And face the Moon:
5   Wise *Nicodemus* saw such light
          As made him know his God by night.

          Most blest believer he!
Who in that land of darkness and blinde eyes
Thy long expected healing wings could see,
10   When thou didst rise,[2]
          And what can never more be done,
          Did at mid-night speak with the Sun!

          O who will tell me, where
He found thee at that dead and silent hour!
15   What hallow'd solitary ground did bear
          So rare a flower,
          Within whose sacred leafs did lie
          The fulness of the Deity.

          No mercy-seat of gold,
20   No dead and dusty *Cherub*, nor carv'd stone,[3]
But his own living works did my Lord hold
          And lodge alone;
          Where *trees* and *herbs* did watch and peep
          And wonder, while the *Jews* did sleep.

THE NIGHT.

[1] This should read John 3.2, for the story of Nicodemus coming to Jesus by night.

[2] Mal. 4.2, "But unto you that fear my Name, shall the Sun of righteousness arise with healing in his wings."

[3] Cf. the description of the mercy seat and cherubim in Exod. 25.17 ff.

25   Dear night! this worlds defeat;
The stop to busie fools; cares check and curb;
The day of Spirits; my souls calm retreat
        Which none disturb!
    Christs⁴ progress, and his prayer time;
30   The hours to which high Heaven doth chime.

    Gods silent, searching flight:
When my Lords head is fill'd with dew, and all
His locks are wet with the clear drops of night;⁵
        His still, soft call;
35   His knocking time; The souls dumb watch,
    When Spirits their fair kinred catch.

    Were all my loud, evil days
Calm and unhaunted as is thy dark Tent,
Whose peace but by some *Angels* wing or voice
40   Is seldom rent;
        Then I in Heaven all the long year
    Would keep, and never wander here.

    But living where the Sun
Doth all things wake, and where all mix and tyre
45 Themselves and others, I consent and run
            To ev'ry myre,
        And by this worlds ill-guiding light,
        Erre more then I can do by night.

⁴ An asterisk in the 1655 edition designated the following:
"*Mark, chap.* 1. 35. *S. Luke, chap.* 21. 37." [Vaughan's note.]
⁵ Song of Sol. 5.2, "I sleep, but my heart waketh: it is the voice
of my beloved that knocketh, saying, Open to me, my sister, my
love, my dove, my undefiled: for my head is filled with dew, and
my locks with the drops of the night."

There is in God (some say)[6]
50   A deep, but dazling darkness; As men here
Say it is late and dusky, because they
See not all clear;
O for that night! where I in him
Might live invisible and dim.

[S–116]   Abels blood.

Sad, purple well! whose bubling eye
Did first against a Murth'rer cry;[1]
Whose streams still vocal, still complain
Of bloody *Cain,*
5   And now at evening are as red
As in the morning when first shed.
If single thou
(Though single voices are but low,)
Could'st such a shrill and long cry rear
10   As speaks still in thy makers ear,
What thunders shall those men arraign
Who cannot count those they have slain,
Who bath not in a shallow flood,
But in a deep, wide sea of blood?
15   A sea, whose lowd waves cannot sleep,
But *Deep* still calleth upon *deep:*[2]
Whose urgent *sound* like unto that
Of many waters,[3] beateth at
The everlasting doors above,
20   Where souls behinde the altar move,

[6] Martin (*Works,* 1957, p. 750) suggests Dionysius the Areopagite.

ABELS BLOOD.

[1] Gen. 4.10, "the voice of thy brother's blood crieth unto me from the ground."

[2] Ps. 42.7, "Deep calleth unto deep at the noise of thy water-spouts."

[3] See Rev. 19.6.

And with one strong, incessant cry
Inquire *How long?* of the most high.[4]
        Almighty Judge!
At whose just laws no just men grudge;
25   Whose blessed, sweet commands do pour
Comforts and joys, and hopes each hour
On those that keep them; O accept
Of his vow'd heart, whom thou hast kept
From bloody men! and grant, I may
30   That sworn memorial duly pay
To thy bright arm, which was my light
And leader through thick death and night!
        I,[5] may that flood,
That proudly spilt and despis'd blood,
35   Speechless and calm, as Infants sleep!
Or if it watch, forgive and weep
For those that spilt it! May no cries
From the low earth to high Heaven rise,
But what (like his, whose blood peace brings)
40   Shall (when they rise) *speak better things,*
Then *Abels* doth![6] may *Abel* be
Still single heard, while these agree
With his milde blood in voice and will,
Who pray'd for those that did him kill!

[S–117]   Righteousness.

Fair, solitary path! Whose blessed shades
The old, white Prophets planted first and drest:
Leaving for us (whose goodness quickly fades,)
A shelter all the way, and bowers to rest.

[4] Rev. 6.10.
[5] Aye.
[6] Heb. 12.24, "the blood of sprinkling, that speaketh better things than that of Abel."

5   Who is the man that walks in thee? who loves
Heav'ns secret solitude, those fair abodes
Where turtles build, and carelesse sparrows move
Without to morrows evils and future loads?

Who hath the upright heart, the single eye,
10   The clean, pure hand, which never medled pitch?
Who sees *Invisibles*, and doth comply
With hidden treasures that make truly rich?

He that doth seek and love
The things above,
15   Whose spirit ever poor, is meek and low;
Who simple still and wise,
Still homewards flies,
Quick to advance, and to retreat most slow.

Whose acts, words and pretence
20   Have all one sense,
One aim and end; who walks not by his sight:
Whose eyes are both put out,
And goes about
Guided by faith, not by exterior light.
25   Who spills no blood, nor spreds
Thorns in the beds
Of the distrest, hasting their overthrow;
Making the time they had
Bitter and sad
30   Like *Chronic* pains, which surely kill, though slow.

Who knows earth nothing hath
Worth love or wrath,
But in his *hope* and *Rock* is ever glad.
Who seeks and follows peace,
35   When with the ease
And health of conscience it is to be had.

Who bears his cross with joy
And doth imploy
His heart and tongue in prayers for his foes;
40   Who lends, not to be paid,
And gives full aid
Without that bribe which Usurers impose.

Who never looks on man
Fearful and wan,
45   But firmly trusts in God; the great mans measure
Though high and haughty must
Be ta'en in dust,
But the good man is Gods peculiar treasure.

Who doth thus, and doth not
50   These good deeds blot
With bad, or with neglect; and heaps not wrath
By secret filth, nor feeds
Some snake, or weeds,
Cheating himself; That man walks in this path.

[S–118]   Anguish.

My God and King! to thee
I bow my knee,
I bow my troubled soul, and greet
With my foul heart thy holy feet.
5   Cast it, or tread it! It shall do
Even what thou wilt, and praise thee too.

My God, could I weep blood,
Gladly I would;
Or if thou wilt give me that Art,
10   Which through the eyes pours out the hart,
I will exhaust it all, and make
My self all tears, a weeping lake.

O! 'tis an easie thing
                To write and sing;
15   But to write true, unfeigned verse
        Is very hard! O God, disperse
        These weights, and give my spirit leave
        To act as well as to conceive!

                O my God, hear my cry;
20   Or let me dye! ——

[S–119]   Tears.

            O When my God, my glory brings
                    His white and holy train,
            Unto those clear and living *Springs*,
                    Where comes no *stain*!

5   Where all is *light*, and *flowers*, and *fruit*,
                    And *joy*, and *rest*,
            Make me amongst them ('tis my suit!)
                    The last one, and the least.

            And when they all are fed, and have
10   Drunk of thy living stream,
            Bid thy poor Ass[1] (with tears I crave!)
                    Drink after them.

            Thy love claims highest thanks, my sin
                    The lowest pitch:
15   But if he pays, who *loves much*, then
                    Thou hast made beggers rich.

TEARS.
    [1] Cf. S–112, line 21.

[S–120]   Jacobs Pillow, and Pillar.[1]

I See the Temple in thy Pillar rear'd,
And that dread glory, which thy children fear'd,
In milde, clear visions, without a frown,
Unto thy solitary self is shown.
5 'Tis number makes a Schism: throngs are rude,
And God himself dyed by the multitude.
This made him put on clouds, and fire and smoke,
Hence he in thunder to thy Off-spring spoke;[2]
The small, still voice, at some low Cottage knocks,
10 But a strong wind must break thy lofty rocks.

    The first true worship of the worlds great King
From private and selected hearts did spring,
But he most willing to save all mankinde,
Inlarg'd that light, and to the bad was kinde.
15 Hence Catholick or Universal came
A most fair notion, but a very name.
For this rich Pearl, like some more common stone,
When once made publique, is esteem'd by none.
Man slights his Maker, when familiar grown,
20 And sets up laws, to pull his honor down.
This God foresaw: And when slain by the crowd
(Under that stately and mysterious cloud
Which his death scatter'd) he foretold the place,
And form to serve him in, should be true grace
25 And the meek heart, not in a Mount, nor at
Jerusalem,[3] with blood of beasts, and fat.
A heart is that dread place, that awful Cell,
That secret Ark, where the milde Dove doth dwell
When the proud waters rage: when Heathens rule
30 By Gods permission, and man turns a Mule.

JACOBS PILLOW, AND PILLAR.
  [1] Based on Gen. 28.11–22.
  [2] As at Mount Sinai (Exod. 19.16 ff.).
  [3] John 4.21–24.

This litle *Goshen*, in the midst of night,
And Satans seat, in all her Coasts hath light,[4]
Yea *Bethel* shall have Tithes (saith *Israels* stone)
And vows and visions, though her foes crye, None.
35 Thus is the solemn temple sunk agen
Into a Pillar, and conceal'd from men.
And glory be to his eternal Name!
Who is contented, that this holy flame
Shall lodge in such a narrow pit, till he
40 With his strong arm turns our captivity.

But blessed *Jacob*, though thy sad distress
Was just the same with ours, and nothing less,
For thou a brother, and blood-thirsty too
Didst flye,[5] whose children wrought thy childrens wo:
45 Yet thou in all thy solitude and grief,
On stones didst sleep and found'st but cold relief;
Thou from the Day-star a long way didst stand
And all that distance was Law and command.
But we a healing Sun by day and night,
50 Have our sure Guardian, and our leading light;
What thou didst hope for and believe, we finde
And feel a friend most ready, sure and kinde.
Thy pillow was but type and shade at best,
But we the substance have, and on him rest.

[4] During the plague of darkness in Egypt, only the Israelites in Goshen had light in their dwellings (Exod. 10.22–23).
[5] An asterisk here in the 1655 edition designated the following: "*Obadiah chap.* 1. 11. *Amos chap.* 1. 11." [Vaughan's note.] The Obadiah reference should read 1.10 (?).

[S–121]   The Agreement.

    I Wrote it down. But one that saw
    And envyed that Record, did since
    Such a mist over my minde draw,
    It quite forgot that purpos'd glimpse.
5   I read it sadly oft, but still
        Simply believ'd, 'twas not my Quill;

    At length, my lifes kinde Angel came,
    And with his bright and busie wing
    Scatt'ring that cloud, shewd me the flame
10   Which strait, like Morning-stars did sing,
        And shine, and point me to a place,
        Which all the year sees the Suns face.

    O beamy book! O my mid-day
    Exterminating fears and night!
15   The mount, whose white Ascendents may
    Be in conjunction with true light!
        My thoughts, when towards thee they move,
        Glitter and kindle with thy love.

    Thou art the oyl and the wine-house:
20   Thine are the present healing leaves,
    Blown from the tree of life to us
    By his breath whom my dead heart heaves.
        Each page of thine hath true life in't,
        And Gods bright minde exprest in print.

25   Most modern books are blots on thee,
    Their doctrine chaff and windy fits:
    Darken'd along, as their scribes be,
    With those foul storms, when they were writ;
        While the mans zeal lays out and blends
30   Onely self-worship and self-ends.

Thou art the faithful, pearly rock,
The Hive of beamy, living lights,
Ever the same, whose diffus'd stock
Entire still, wears out blackest nights.
35   Thy lines are rays, the true Sun sheds;
       Thy leaves are healing wings he spreads.[1]

For until thou didst comfort me,
I had not one poor word to say:
Thick busie clouds did multiply,
40   And said, I was no childe of day;
       They said, my own hands did remove
       That candle given me from above.

O God! I know and do confess
My sins are great and still prevail,
45   Most heynous sins and numberless!
But thy *Compassions* cannot fail.
       If thy sure mercies can be broken,
       Then all is true, my foes have spoken.

But while time runs, and after it
50   Eternity, which never ends,
Quite through them both, still infinite
Thy Covenant by *Christ* extends;
       No sins of frailty, nor of youth
       Can foil his merits, and thy truth.

55   And this I hourly finde, for thou
Dost still renew, and purge and heal:
Thy care and love, which joyntly flow
New Cordials, new *Cathartics* deal.
       But were I once cast off by thee
60   I know (my God!) this would not be.

THE AGREEMENT.
       [1] See note on S–115, line 10.

Wherefore with tears (tears by thee sent)
I beg, my faith may never fail!
And when in death my speech is spent,
O let that silence then prevail!
65   O chase in that *cold calm* my foes,
          And hear my hearts last private throws!

So thou, who didst the work begin
(For *I till*[2] *drawn came not to thee*)
Wilt finish it, and by no sin
70   Will thy free mercies hindred be.
          For which, O God, I onely can
          Bless thee, and blame unthankful man.

[S-122]   The day of Judgement.

O Day of life, of light, of love!
The onely day dealt from above!
A day so fresh, so bright, so brave
Twill shew us each forgotten grave,
5   And make the dead, like flowers, arise
          Youthful and fair to see new skies.
          All other days, compar'd to thee,
          Are but lights weak minority,
          They are but veils, and Cypers[1] drawn
10   Like Clouds, before thy glorious dawn.
          O come, arise, shine, do not stay
                    Dearly lov'd day!
          The fields are long since white,[2] and I

[2] An asterisk here in the 1655 edition designated the following:
"*St. John, chap.* 6. *ver.* 44. 65." [Vaughan's note.]
THE DAY OF JUDGEMENT.
    [1] Thus in 1655, an obsolete form of Cypres, or Cypress, a light
transparent material.
    [2] John 4.35, "look on the fields; for they are white already to
harvest."

With earnest groans for freedom cry,
15   My fellow-creatures too say, *Come!*[3]
And stones, though speechless, are not dumb.
When shall we hear that glorious voice
          Of life and joys?
That voice, which to each secret bed
20   Of my Lords dead,
Shall bring true day, and make dust see,
The way to immortality.
When shall those first white Pilgrims rise,
Whose holy, happy Histories
25   (Because they sleep so long) some men
Count but the blots of a vain pen?
          Dear Lord! make haste,
Sin every day commits more waste,
And thy old enemy, which knows
30   His time is short, more raging grows.[4]
Nor moan I onely (though profuse)
Thy Creatures bondage and abuse;
But what is highest sin and shame,
The vile despight done to thy name;
35   The forgeries, which impious wit
And power force on Holy Writ,
With all detestable designs
That may dishonor those pure lines.
O God! though mercy be in thee
40   The greatest attribute we see,
And the most needful for our sins;
Yet, when thy mercy nothing wins
But meer disdain, let not man say
Thy arm doth sleep;[5] but write this day
45   Thy judging one: Descend, descend!
Make all things new! and without end!

[3] Rev. 22.17.
[4] Rev. 12.12, "for the devil is come down unto you, having great wrath, because he knoweth that he hath but a short time."
[5] Isa. 51.9, "Awake, awake, put on strength, O arm of the Lord."

[S–123]   Psalm 65.

    Sions true, glorious God! on thee
    Praise waits in all humility.
    All flesh shall unto thee repair,
    To thee, O thou that hearest prayer!
5   But sinful words and works still spread
    And over-run my heart and head;
    Transgressions make me foul each day,
    O purge them, purge them all away!

      Happy is he! whom thou wilt choose
10   To serve thee in thy blessed house!
    Who in thy holy Temple dwells,
    And fill'd with joy, thy goodness tells!
    King of Salvation! by strange things
    And terrible, Thy Justice brings
15   Man to his duty. Thou alone
    Art the worlds hope, and but thee, none.
    Sailers that flote on flowing seas
    Stand firm by thee, and have sure peace.
    Thou still'st the loud waves, when most wild
20   And mak'st the raging people mild.
    Thy arm did first the mountains lay
    And girds their rocky heads this day.
    The most remote, who know not thee,
    At thy great works astonish'd be.

25   The *outgoings* of the *Even* and *Dawn*,
    In *Antiphones*[1] sing to thy Name.
    Thou visit'st the low earth, and then
    Water'st it for the sons of men,
    Thy upper river, which abounds
30   With fertil streams, makes rich all grounds,
    And by thy mercies still supplied
    The sower doth his bread provide.

PSALM 65.
  [1] Versicles or sentences sung by one choir in response to another.

Thou water'st every ridge of land
And settlest with thy secret hand
35   The furrows of it; then thy warm
And opening showers (restrain'd from harm)
Soften the mould, while all unseen
The blade grows up alive and green.
The year is with thy goodness crown'd,
40   And all thy paths drop fatness round,
They drop upon the wilderness,
For thou dost even the desarts bless,
And hills full of springing pride,
Wear fresh adornments on each side.
45   The fruitful flocks fill every Dale,
And purling[2] Corn doth cloath the Vale;
They shout for joy, and joyntly sing,
Glory to the eternal King!

[S–124]   The Throne.

Revel. chap. 20. ver. 11.[1]

When with these eyes clos'd now by thee,
            But then restor'd,
The great and white throne I shall see
            Of my dread Lord:
5   And lowly kneeling (for the most
            Stiff then must kneel)
Shall look on him, at whose high cost
            (Unseen) such joys I feel.

[2] Waving, rippling.
THE THRONE.
    [1] "And I saw a great white throne, and him that sat on it, from whose face the earth and the heaven fled away; and there was found no place for them."

What ever arguments, or skill
10   Wise heads shall use,
Tears onely and my blushes still
                        I will produce.
And should those speechless beggers fail,
                        Which oft have won;
15   Then taught by thee, I will prevail,
                        And say, *Thy will be done*!

[S–125]   Death.

Though since thy first sad entrance by
                        Just *Abels* blood,
'Tis now six thousand years well nigh,
And still thy sov'rainty holds good:
5   Yet by none art thou understood.

We talk and name thee with much ease
                        As a tryed thing,
And every one can slight his lease
As if it ended in a Spring,
10   Which shades & bowers doth rent-free bring.

To thy dark land these heedless go:
                        But there was *One*,
Who search'd it quite through to and fro,
And then returning, like the Sun,
15   Discover'd all, that there is done.

And since his death, we throughly see
                        All thy dark way;
Thy shades but thin and narrow be,
Which his first looks will quickly fray:
20   Mists make but triumphs for the day.

As harmless violets, which give
                    Their virtues here
For salves and syrups, while they live,
Do after calmly disappear,
25   And neither grieve, repine, nor fear:

So dye his servants; and as sure
                    Shall they revive.
Then let not dust your eyes obscure,
But lift them up, where still alive,
30   Though fled from you, their spirits hive.

[S–126]   The Feast.

O Come away,
Make no delay,
        Come while my heart is clean & steddy!
While Faith and Grace
5   Adorn the place,
            Making dust and ashes ready.

No bliss here lent
Is permanent,
        Such triumphs poor flesh cannot merit;
10   Short sips and sights
Endear delights,
            Who seeks for more, he would inherit.

Come then true bread,
Quickning the dead,
15   Whose eater shall not, cannot dye,
Come, antedate
On me that state
            Which brings poor dust the victory.

I,[1] victory
20   Which from thine eye
Breaks as the day doth from the east,
When the spilt dew,
Like tears doth shew
The sad world wept to be releast.

25   Spring up, O wine,
And springing shine
With some glad message from his heart,
Who did, when slain,
These means ordain
30   For me to have in him a part.

Such a sure part
In his blest heart,
The well, where living waters spring,
That with it fed
35   Poor dust though dead
Shall rise again, and live and sing.

O drink and bread
Which strikes death dead,
The food of mans immortal being!
40   Under veyls here
Thou art my chear,
Present and sure without my seeing.

How dost thou flye
And search and pry
45   Through all my parts, and like a quick
And knowing lamp
Hunt out each damp,
Whose shadow makes me sad or sick?

O what high joys
50   The Turtles voice
And songs I hear! O quickning showers

THE FEAST.
[1] Ay.

Of my Lords blood
You make rocks bud
    And crown dry hils with wells & flowers!

55   For this true ease
This healing peace,
    For this taste of living glory,
My soul and all,
Kneel down and fall
60   And sing his sad victorious story.

O thorny crown
More soft then down!
    O painful Cross, my bed of rest!
O spear, the key
65   Opening the way!
    O thy worst state, my onely best!

Oh! all thy griefs
Are my reliefs,
    And all my sins, thy sorrows were!
70   And what can I,
To this reply;
    What (O God!) but a silent tear?

Some toil and sow,
That wealth may flow,
75   And dress this earth for next years meat:
But let me heed,
Why thou didst bleed,
And what in the next world to eat.

Revel. chap. 19. ver. 9.[2]
Blessed are they, which are called unto the marriage Supper of the Lamb!

[2] The King James version.

[S–127]   The Obsequies.

Since dying for me, thou didst crave no more
        Then common pay,
    Some few true tears, and those shed for
        My own ill way;
5   With a cheap, plain remembrance still
        Of thy sad death,
    Because forgetfulness would kill
        Even lifes own breath:
I were most foolish and unkinde
10   In my own sense,
    Should I not ever bear in minde
If not thy mighty love, my own defense.
Therefore, those loose delights and lusts, which here
        Men call good chear,
15   I will close girt and tyed
For mourning sack-cloth wear, all mortified.

Not but that mourners too, can have
        Rich weeds and shrouds;
For some wore *White* ev'n in thy grave,[1]
20   And Joy, like light, shines oft in clouds:
But thou, who didst mans whole life earn,
Doest so invite, and woo me still,
That to be merry I want skill,
        And time to learn.
25   Besides, those Kerchiefs sometimes shed
        To make me brave,[2]
I cannot finde, but where thy head
Was once laid for me in thy grave.

THE OBSEQUIES.
  [1] The two angels at the tomb of Jesus (John 20.12).
  [2] Grosart suggests the kerchiefs bestowed by a lady on her knight.

Thy grave! To which my thoughts shal move
30   Like Bees in storms unto their Hive,
That from the murd'ring worlds false love
Thy death may keep my soul alive.

[S–128]   The Water-fall.

With what deep murmurs through times silent stealth
Doth thy transparent, cool and watry wealth
       Here flowing fall,
       And chide, and call,
5   As if his liquid, loose Retinue staid
Lingring, and were of this steep place afraid,
       The common pass
       Where, clear as glass,
       All must descend
10   Not to an end:
But quickned by this deep and rocky grave,
Rise to a longer course more bright and brave.[1]

       Dear stream! dear bank, where often I
       Have sate, and pleas'd my pensive eye,
15   Why, since each drop of thy quick[2] store
       Runs thither, whence it flow'd before,
       Should poor souls fear a shade or night,
       Who came (sure) from a sea of light?[3]
       Or since those drops are all sent back
20   So sure to thee, that none doth lack,
       Why should frail flesh doubt any more
       That what God takes, hee'l not restore?

THE WATER-FALL.
  [1] Resplendent.
  [2] Living.
  [3] A Hermetic concept.

O useful Element and clear!
My sacred wash and cleanser here,[4]
25   My first consigner unto those
Fountains of life, where the Lamb goes?[5]
What sublime truths, and wholesome themes,
Lodge in thy mystical, deep streams!
Such as dull man can never finde
30   Unless that Spirit lead his minde,
Which first upon thy face did move,
And hatch'd all with his quickning love.[6]
As this loud brooks incessant fall
In streaming rings restagnates[7] all,
35   Which reach by course the bank, and then
Are no more seen, just so pass men.
O my invisible estate,
My glorious liberty, still late![8]
Thou art the Channel my soul seeks,
40   Not this with Cataracts and Creeks.

[S–129]   Quickness.

False life! a foil and no more, when
                    Wilt thou be gone?
Thou foul deception of all men
That would not have the true come on.

5   Thou art a Moon-like toil; a blinde
                    Self-posing state;
A dark contest of waves and winde;
A meer tempestuous debate.

[4] In baptism.
[5] Rev. 7.17, "the Lamb . . . shall lead them unto living fountains of waters."
[6] The Spirit of God that moved upon the face of the waters
(Gen. 1.2). The idea of the "hatching" of the world appears in
Hermetic writings.
[7] Becomes or remains stagnant (OED; this place is cited).
[8] Cf. "the glorious liberty of the children of God," Rom. 8.21.

Life is a fix'd, discerning light,
10   A knowing Joy;
No chance, or fit: but ever bright,
And calm and full, yet doth not cloy.

'Tis such a blissful thing, that still
              Doth vivifie,
15   And shine and smile, and hath the skill
To please without Eternity.

Thou art a toylsom Mole, or less
              A moving mist.
But life is, what none can express,
20   A quickness, which my God hath kist.

[S–130]   The Wreath.

Since I in storms us'd most to be
              And seldom yielded flowers,
How shall I get a wreath for thee
              From those rude, barren hours?

5   The softer dressings of the Spring,
              Or Summers later store
I will not for thy temples bring,
              Which *Thorns*, not *Roses* wore.

But a twin'd wreath of *grief* and *praise*,
10   Praise soil'd with tears, and tears again
Shining with joy, like dewy days,
This day I bring for all thy pain,
Thy causless pain! and sad as death;
Which sadness breeds in the most vain,
15   (O not in vain!) now beg thy breath;
Thy quickning breath, which gladly bears
Through saddest clouds to that glad place,
Where cloudless Quires sing without tears,
Sing thy just praise, and see thy face.

[S–131]   The Queer.[1]

> O Tell me whence that joy doth spring
> Whose diet is divine and fair,
> Which wears heaven, like a bridal ring,
> And tramples on doubts and despair?

5
> Whose Eastern traffique deals in bright
> And boundless Empyrean themes,
> Mountains of spice, Day-stars and light,
> Green trees of life, and living streams?

> Tell me, O tell who did thee bring
10
> And here, without my knowledge, plac'd,
> Till thou didst grow and get a wing,
> A wing with eyes, and eyes that taste?

> Sure, *holyness* the *Magnet* is,
> And *Love* the *Lure*, that woos thee down;
15
> Which makes the high transcendent bliss
> Of knowing thee, so rarely known.

[S–132]   The Book.

> Eternal God! maker of all
> That have liv'd here, since the mans fall;
> The Rock of ages! in whose shade
> They live unseen, when here they fade.

THE QUEER.
  [1] I.e., the query or puzzle.

5   Thou knew'st this *papyr*, when it was
        Meer *seed*, and after that but *grass*;
        Before 'twas *drest* or *spun*, and when
        Made *linen*, who did *wear* it then:
        What were their lifes, their thoughts & deeds
10   Whither good *corn*, or fruitless *weeds*.

        Thou knew'st this *Tree*, when a green *shade*
        Cover'd it, since a *Cover* made,[1]
        And where it flourish'd, grew and spread,
        As if it never should be dead.

15   Thou knew'st this harmless *beast*, when he
        Did live and feed by thy decree
        On each green thing; then slept (well fed)
        Cloath'd with this *skin*, which now lies spred
        A *Covering* o're this aged book,
20   Which makes me wisely weep and look
        On my own dust; meer dust it is,
        But not so dry and clean as this.
        Thou knew'st and saw'st them all and though
        Now scatter'd thus, dost know them so.

25   O knowing, glorious spirit! when
        Thou shalt restore trees, beasts and men,
        When thou shalt make all new again,
        Destroying onely death and pain,
        Give him amongst thy works a place,
30   Who in them lov'd and sought thy face!

THE BOOK.
  [1] Many early books had wooden covers.

[S–133]   To the Holy Bible.

O Book! lifes guide! how shall we part,
And thou so long seiz'd[1] of my heart!
Take this last kiss, and let me weep
True thanks to thee, before I sleep.

5   Thou wert the first put in my hand,
When yet I could not understand,
And daily didst my yong eyes lead
To letters, till I learnt to read.
But as rash youths, when once grown strong
10   Flye from their Nurses to the throng,
Where they new Consorts choose, & stick
To those, till either hurt or sick:
So with that first light gain'd from thee
Ran I in chase of vanity,
15   Cryed dross for gold, and never thought
My first cheap Book had all I sought.
Long reign'd this vogue; and thou cast by
With meek, dumb looks didst woo mine eye,
And oft left open would'st convey
20   A sudden and most searching ray
Into my soul, with whose quick touch
Refining still, I strugled much.
By this milde art of love at length
Thou overcam'st my sinful strength,
25   And having brought me home, didst there
Shew me that pearl I sought elsewhere.[2]
Gladness, and peace, and hope, and love,
The secret favors of the Dove,
Her quickning kindness, smiles and kisses,
30   Exalted pleasures, crowning blisses,

TO THE HOLY BIBLE.
   [1] Put in possession.
   [2] The pearl of great price of Matt. 13.45–46.

Fruition, union, glory, life
Thou didst lead to, and still all strife.
Living, thou wert my souls sure ease,
And dying mak'st me go in peace:

35   Thy next *Effects* no tongue can tell;
Farewel O book of God! farewel!

S *Luke chap. 2. ver.* 14.[3]
*Glory be to God in the highest, and on
Earth peace, good will towards men.*

[S–134]   L'Envoy.

O The new worlds new, quickning Sun!
Ever the same, and never done!
The seers of whose sacred light
Shall all be drest in shining white,[1]

5   And made conformable to his
Immortal shape, who wrought their bliss,[2]
        Arise, arise!
And like old cloaths fold up these skies,
This long worn veyl: then shine and spread

10   Thy own bright self over each head,
And through thy creatures pierce and pass
Till all becomes thy cloudless glass,
Transparent as the purest day
And without blemish or decay,

15   Fixt by thy spirit to a state
For evermore immaculate.
A state fit for the sight of thy
Immediate, pure and unveil'd eye,

[3] The King James version, adding "be."
L'ENVOY.
   [1] Rev. 7.9.
   [2] Phil. 3.21, Christ "shall change our vile body, that it may be
fashioned like unto his glorious body."

A state agreeing with thy minde,
20   A state thy birth, and death design'd:
A state for which thy creatures all
Travel and groan, and look and call.[3]
O seeing thou hast paid our score,
Why should the curse reign any more?
25   But since thy number is as yet
Unfinish'd, we shall gladly sit
Till all be ready, that the train
May fully fit thy glorious reign.
Onely, let not our haters brag,
30   Thy seamless coat[4] is grown a rag,
Or that thy truth was not here known,
Because we forc'd thy judgements down.
Dry up their arms, who vex thy spouse,
And take the glory of thy house
35   To deck their own; then give thy saints
That faithful zeal, which neither faints
Nor wildly burns, but meekly still
Dares own the truth, and shew the ill.
Frustrate those cancerous, close[5] arts
40   Which cause solution[6] in all parts,
And strike them dumb, who for meer words
Wound thy beloved, more then swords.
Dear Lord, do this! and then let grace
Descend, and hallow all the place.
45   Incline each hard heart to do good,
And cement us with thy sons blood,
That like true sheep, all in one fold
We may be fed, and one minde hold.
Give watchful spirits to our guides!
50   For sin (like water) hourly glides

[3] Rom. 8.22, "the whole creation groaneth and travaileth in pain together until now." And see verse 19.
[4] John 19.23, Christ's coat "was without seam, woven from the top throughout."
[5] Secret.
[6] Dissolution.

By each mans door, and quickly will
Turn in, if not obstructed still.
Therefore write in their hearts thy law,
And let these long, sharp judgements aw
55   Their very thoughts, that by their clear
And holy lives, mercy may here
Sit regent yet, and blessings flow
As fast, as persecutions now.
So shall we know in war and peace
60   Thy service to be our sole ease,
With prostrate souls adoring thee,
Who turn'd our sad captivity!

S. Clemens apud Basil:[7]
Ζῆ ὁ Θεὸς, καὶ ὁ κύριος Ἰησοῦς Χριστὸς,
καὶ τὸ πνεῦμα τὸ ἅγιον.

FINIS.

[7] St. Basil the Great quotes St. Clement in *Liber de Spiritu Sancto*, XXIX (in Migne, *Patrologia Graeca*, XXXII, col. 201).

THALIA REDIVIVA

(1678)

A note on the title page opposite

The Thalia of the title (meaning "Thalia Renewed," or re-vived) was the Greek muse of pastoral poetry, also known as the muse of comedy. Hutchinson (*Works*, pp. 213–14) has the suggestion that the title may reflect the choice of Thomas Vaughan since he had named Thalia as his "Mistris" in *Lumen de Lumine* (in *The Works of Thomas Vaughan*, ed. A. E. Waite, pp. 245–47). It is also to be noted that only Thomas, not Henry, appears on the title page (as Eugenius Philalethes). Some twenty-four Latin poems by Thomas Vaughan, who had died in 1666, appear in this volume with a separate title page. The quotation from Virgil is from the *Eclogues*, VI, 2: "Thalia blushed not to dwell in the woods."

Thalia Rediviva:

THE
Pass-Times and *Diversions*
OF A
COUNTREY-MUSE,
In Choice
POEMS
On several Occasions.

WITH

Some Learned *Remains* of the Eminent
Eugenius Philalethes.

Never made Publick till now.

——Nec erubuit sylvas habitare Thalia. *Virgil.*

Licensed, *Roger L'Estrange.*

London, Printed for *Robert Pawlet* at the Bible in *Chancery-lane*, near *Fleetstreet*, 1 6 7 8.

TO THE
Most Honourable and truly Noble
HENRY
Lord Marquis and Earl of
WORCESTER, &c.[1]

My Lord,

Though *Dedications* are now become a kind of Tyranny over the Peace and Repose of great Men; yet I have
confidence I shall so manage the present Address as to
5 entertain your Lordship without much disturbance; and
because my purposes are govern'd by deep Respect and
Veneration, I hope to find your Lordship more facile
and accessible. And I am already absolv'd from a great
part of that fulsome and designing guilt, being sufficiently
10 remov'd from the causes of it: for I consider, my Lord!
that you are already so well known to the World in your
several Characters, and advantages of Honour; it was
yours by traduction, and the adjunct of your Nativity,
you were swaddl'd and rock'd in't, bred up and grew
15 in't to your now wonderful height and eminence: that
for me under pretence of the inscription to give you the
heraldry of your family, or to carry your person through
the fam'd Topicks of Mind Body, or Estate, were all one
as to perswade the World that Fire and Light were very

(DEDICATION)

[1] Henry Somerset, seventh earl and third marquis of Worcester,
later first duke of Beaufort. The Vaughans had a slight connection with the Somerset family, but Hutchinson (*Life,* p. 216) suggests that the Marquis may have been the choice of the editor
rather than of the author.

20 bright Bodies, or that the Luminaries themselves had
Glory. In point of Protection I beg to fall in with the
common wont, and to be satisfied by the reasonableness
of the thing, and abundant worthy precedents; and although I should have secret prophecy and assurance
25 that the ensuing Verse would live eternally, yet would I,
as I now do, humbly crave it might be fortifi'd with your
Patronage; for so the Sextile Aspects and Influences are
watch'd for, and applied to the actions of Life, thereby
to make the Scheme and good Auguries of the Birth pass
30 into Fate, and a success infallible.

My Lord! By a happy obliging Intercession, and your
own consequent Indulgence, I have now recourse to your
Lordship; hopeing, I shall not much displease by putting
these Twin Poets into your Hands. The Minion and
35 Vertical Planet of the Roman Lustre and Bravery was
never better pleased, than when he had a whole Constellation about him: not his finishing Five several Wars
to the promoting of his own Interest, nor particularly the
prodigious success at *Actium*, where he held in chase
40 the Wealth, Beauty and Prowess of the East; not the
Triumphs and absolute Dominions which followed, all
this gave him not half that serene Pride and Satisfaction
of Spirit as when he retir'd himself to umpire the different Excellencies of his insipid Friends, and to dis-
45 tribute Lawrels among his Poetick Heroes: If now upon
the Authority of this, and several such Examples I had
the Ability and Opportunity of drawing the Value and
strange Worth of a Poet, and withall of applying some
of the Lineaments to the following pieces; I should then
50 do my self a real Service, and attone in a great measure
for the present insolence. But best of all will it serve my
Defence and Interest to appeal to your Lordships own
conceptions and image of *Genuine* Verse; with which
so just, so regular Original, if these Copies shall hold
55 proportion and resemblance, then am I advanced very
far in your Lordships pardon: the rest will entirely be

supplied me by your Lordships Goodness, and my own
awful Zeal of being,

My Lord!

60   Your Lordships most
                    obedient, most humbly
                    devoted Servant
                          J. W.[2]

To the Reader.

The Nation of Poets *above all Writers has ever chal-
leng'd perpetuity of Name, or as they please by their
Charter of Liberty to call it,* Immortality. *Nor has the
World much disputed their claim, either easily resigning*
5 *a Patrimony in it self not very substantial; or, it may be,
out of despair to controule the authority of Inspiration
and Oracle. Howsoever the price as now quarrell'd for
among the* Poets *themselves is no such rich bargain: 'tis
only a vanishing interest in the Lees and Dreggs of*
10 *Time, in the Rear of those Fathers and Worthies in the
Art, who if they know any thing of the heats and fury of
their Successors must extreamly pity them.*

*I am to assure, that the Author has no portion of that
aiery happiness to lose by any injury or unkindness*
15 *which may be done to his Verse: his Reputation is better built in the sentiment of several judicious Persons,
who know him very well able to give himself a lasting
Monument, by undertaking any Argument of note in the
whole Circle of Learning.*

20   *But even these his Diversions*[1] *have been valuable*

[2] Probably John Williams, prebendary of St. David's in 1678,
the same as the "I. W." who signs the preface "To the Reader,"
and the commendatory poem "To my worthy Friend" of *Thalia.*
See Hutchinson, *Life,* p. 215.

TO THE READER.

[1] A reference to the subtitle of the volume, *"Diversions* of a
Countrey-Muse."

with the matchless Orinda,[2] *and since they deserv'd her
esteem and commendations; who so thinks them not
worth the publishing, will put himself in the opposite
Scale, where his own arrogance will blow him up.*

25   I. W.

[*Commendatory Poems.*]

To Mr. Henry Vaughan *the Silurist: upon these and his former* Poems.

Had I ador'd the Multitude, and thence
Got an Antipathy to wit and sence,
And hugg'd that Fate, in hope the World would grant
'Twas *good Affection* to the Ignorant:
5   Yet the least Ray of thy bright fancy seen
I had converted, or excuseless been.
For each Birth of thy Muse to after-times
Shall expiate for all this Ages Crimes.
First shines thy *Amoret*,[1] twice crown'd by thee:
10   Once by thy Love, next by thy Poetrie;
Where thou the best of Unions dost dispense
Truth cloath'd in Wit, and Love in Innocence.
So that the muddie Lover may learn here,
No Fountains can be sweet, that are not clear.
15   There *Juvenal*,[2] by thee reviv'd declares
How flat man's Joys are, and how mean his Cares;

[2] Mrs. Katherine Philips, a noted poet of her day. See her
commendatory poem on Vaughan following. And see O–12, O–16.
COMMENDATORY POEMS, "TO MR. HENRY VAUGHAN. . . ."

[1] An allusion to the Amoret of *Poems*, 1646, thought to have
been Catherine Wise, who became Vaughan's wife. See P–3.

[2] Whose tenth satire Vaughan translated in *Poems*, 1646 (P–14).

And wisely doth upbraid the World, that they
Should such a value for their ruine pay.
    But when thy sacred Muse diverts her Quill
20   The Landskip to design of *Sions* Hill,
As nothing else was worthy her, or thee:
So we admire almost t' Idolatrie.
What savage Breast would not be rap'd to find
Such Jewels in such Cabinets enshrin'd?
25   Thou fill'd with joys (too great to see or count:)
Descend'st from thence, like *Moses* from the Mount,
And with a candid, yet unquestion'd awe
Restor'st the Golden Age, when Verse was Law.
Instructing us, thou so secur'st thy Fame,
30   That nothing can disturb it, but my name.
Nay I have hopes, that standing so near thine
'Twill loose its dross, and by degrees refine.
Live! till the disabused World consent
All Truths of Use, of Strength or Ornament
35   Are with such Harmony by thee display'd
As the whole World was first by number made;
And from the charming rigour thy Muse brings
Learn, there's no pleasure but in serious things!

Orinda

Upon the Ingenious Poems *of his Learned Friend, Mr.* Henry Vaughan *the Silurist.*

Fairly design'd! to charm our *Civil* Rage
With *Verse*, and plant *Bayes* in an *Iron* Age.[1]
But hath steel'd *Mars* so ductible a Soul,
That *Love* and *Poesie* may it controule?

COMMENDATORY POEMS, "UPON THE INGENIOUS POEMS. . . ."
  [1] These lines have been taken to indicate that this poem was intended for a collection of Vaughan's poems written and designed to be published during the civil wars, perhaps in the late 1640s.

5　Yes: brave *Tyrtæus*,[2] as we read of old,
　　The *Grecian* Armies, as he pleas'd cou'd *mold*;
　　They march'd to his high *Numbers*, and did fight
　　With that *instinct* and *rage*, which he did write.
　　When he fell *lower*, they would strait *retreat*,
10　Grow soft and calm: and temper their bold heat.
　　Such *Magick* is in *Vertue!* See hear a young
　　Tyrtæus too, whose sweet persuasive Song
　　Can lead our *Spirits* any way, and move
　　To all *Adventures*: either *War* or *Love*.[3]

15　Then veil the bright *Etesia*,[4] that choice *She*,
　　Lest *Mars*, (*Timander's* Friend) his Rival be.
　　So fair a *Nymph*, drest by a *Muse* so neat,
　　Might warm the *North*, and thaw the frozen *Gete*.

Tho. Powel,[5] D.D.

To the ingenious *Author of* Thalia Rediviva.

Ode I.

　　Where Reverend Bards of old have sate
　And sung the pleasant enterludes of Fate,
　　　Thou takest the hereditary shade
　　　Which Natures homely Art had made,
5　And thence thou giv'st thy Muse her swing, and she
　　　　Advances to the Galaxie;

[2] Poet of Sparta (seventh century B.C.) whose verses were said to have affected notably the spirits of the Spartan army.

[3] If Vaughan ever wrote verses inciting to martial rage they have not survived. Some such poems may have been destroyed.

[4] See T–15–21.

[5] Thomas Powell. See T–1, O–14, O–46.

There with the sparkling *Cowley*[1] she above
Does hand in hand in graceful Measures move.
   We groveling Mortals gaze below,
10   And long in vain to know
Her wondrous paths, her wondrous flight
   In vaine; alas! we grope,
In vain we use our earthly Telescope,
   We'r blinded by an intermedial night:
15   Thine *Eagle-Muse* can only face
   The fiery Coursers in their race,
While with unequal paces we do try
To bear her train aloft, and keep her company.

II.

   The loud harmonious *Mantuan*[2]
20 Once charm'd the world, and here's the *Uscan* Swan
   In his declining years does chime,
And challenges the last remains of Time.
   Ages run on, and soon give o're,
   They have their Graves as well as we,
25   Time swallows all that's past and more,
Yet time is swallow'd in eternity:
This is the only profits Poets see.
There thy triumphant Muse shall ride in state
   And lead in Chains devouring Fate;
30   *Claudian's* bright Phœnix[3] she shall bring
   Thee an immortal offering;
Nor shall my humble tributary Muse
   Her homage and attendance too refuse,
   She thrusts her self among the Crowd
35 And joyning in th' applause she strives to clap aloud.

COMMENDATORY POEMS, "TO THE INGENIOUS AUTHOR. . . ."
[1] Abraham Cowley (1618–67), poet of the metaphysical school, whose amatory verse of *The Mistress* (1647), unfinished epic *Davideis* (1656), and *Pindarique Odes* (1656), along with his essays on literary and other topics, won him an extremely high reputation in his day.
[2] Virgil.
[3] See T–29.

III.

Tell me no more that Nature is severe
  Thou great Philosopher!
Lo she has laid her vast Exchequer here.
  Tell me no more that she has sent
40 So much already she is spent;
Here is a vast *America* behind
Which none but the great Silurist could find.
  Nature her last edition was the best,
  As big, as rich as all the rest
45 So will we here admit
  Another world of Wit.
No rude or savage fancy here shall stay
  The travailing Reader in his way,
But every coast is clear: go where he will
50 Vertu's the road *Thalia* leads him still:
Long may she live, and wreath thy sacred head
For this her happy resurrection from the dead.

       N. W.[4] Jes. Coll. *Oxon.*

To my worthy Friend, Mr. Henry Vaughan the Silurist.

See what thou wert! by what Platonick round
Art thou in thy first 'youth and Glories found!
Or from thy Muse does this Retrieve accrue,
Do's she which once inspir'd thee, now renew!
5 Bringing thee back those Golden years which time
Smooth'd to thy Lays, and polisht with thy Rhyme.
Nor is't to thee alone she do's convey
  Such happy change, but bountiful as day
On whatsoever Reader she do's shine
10 She makes him like thee, and for ever thine.

[4] Probably Nathaniel Williams, brother of John, who signed the dedication above.

And first thy manual op'ning gives to see
Ecclipse and suff'rings burnish Majesty,[1]
Where thou so artfully the draught hast made
That we best read the lustre in the shade,
15   And find our Sov'raign greater in that shroud:
So Lightning dazzles from its night and cloud;
So the *first Light himself* has for his Throne
Blackness, and Darkness his Pavilion.

Who can refuse thee company, or stay,
20   By thy next charming summons forc'd away,
If that be force which we can so resent
That only in its joys 'tis violent:
Upward thy *Eagle*[2] bears us e're aware
Till above Storms and all tempestuous Air
25   We radiant Worlds with their bright people meet,
Leaving this little *All* beneath our feet.
But now the pleasure is too great to tell,
Nor have we other bus'ness than to dwell
As on the hallow'd Mount th' Apostles meant
30   To build and fix their glorious banishment.
Yet we must know and find thy skilful Vein
Shall gently bear us to our homes again;
By which descent thy former flight's impli'd
To be thy extasie and not thy pride.
35   And here how well do's the wise *Muse* demeane
Her self, and fit her song to ev'ry Scene!
Riot of Courts, the bloody wreaths of War,
Cheats of the Mart, and clamours of the Bar,
Nay, life it self thou dost so well express
40   Its hollow Joyes, and real Emptiness,
That *Dorian* Minstrel never did excite,
Or raise for dying so much appetite.

COMMENDATORY POEMS, "TO MY WORTHY FRIEND. . . ."
   [1] See T–2.
   [2] See T–3.

Nor does thy other softer Magick move
Us less thy fam'd *Etesia*[3] to love;
45   Where such a *Character* thou giv'st that shame
Nor envy dare approach the Vestal Dame:
So at bright Prime *Idea's* none repine,
They safely in th' *Eternal Poet* shine.

Gladly th' *Assyrian Phœnix* now resumes
50   From thee this last reprizal of his Plumes;[4]
He seems another more miraculous thing
Brighter of Crest, and stronger of his Wing;
Proof against Fate in spicy Urns to come,
Immortal past all risque of Martyrdome.

55   Nor be concern'd, nor fancy thou art rude
T' adventure from thy Cambrian solitude,
Best from those lofty Cliffs thy *Muse* does spring
Upwards, and boldly spreads her Cherub-wing.

So when the *Sage* of *Memphis*[5] would converse
60   With boding Skies, and th' Azure Universe,
He climbs his starry Pyramid, and thence
Freely sucks clean prophetique influence,
And all Serene, and rap't and gay he pries
Through the Æthereal volum's Mysteries,
65   Loth to come down, or ever to know more
The *Nile's* luxurious, but dull foggy shore.

I. W. A.M. Oxon.

[3] See T–15–21.
[4] See T–29.
[5] Ancient Egypt was famed for her astrologer-philosophers. What particular *"Sage,"* if any, the poet had in mind is uncertain.

Choice POEMS on several
occasions.

[T–1] *To his Learned Friend and Loyal Fellow-
Prisoner,* Thomas Powel *of* Cant.
Doctor of Divinity.[1]

If sever'd Friends by *Sympathy* can joyn,
And absent *Kings* be honour'd in their *coin;*
May they do both, who are so curb'd! but we
Whom no such *Abstracts*[2] torture, that can see
5 And pay each other a full self-return,
May laugh, though all such *Metaphysics*[3] burn.
'Tis a kind Soul in *Magnets,* that attones[4]
Such two hard things as *Iron* are and *Stones,*
And in their dumb *compliance* we learn more
10 Of Love, than ever Books could speak before.
For though *attraction* hath got all the name,
As if that *power* but from one side came,
Which both unites; yet, where there is no *sence,*
There is no *Passion,* nor *Intelligence:*
15 And so by consequence we cannot state
A Commerce, unless both we animate.[5]

TO HIS LEARNED FRIEND . . . THOMAS POWEL. . . .
[1] Thomas Powell, rector of Cantref from 1635, was a long-time
friend of Vaughan. In what sense he was a *"Fellow-Prisoner"* is
not clear, whether literally or figuratively. See his commendatory
poem before *Olor Iscanus* and Vaughan's tributes to him, O–14,
O–46, T–45.
[2] Abstract ideas.
[3] Either those who deal in such esoteric "philosophies," or the
philosophies themselves.
[4] Conciliates or reconciles.
[5] We cannot explain the responses of apparently inanimate objects unless we attribute to them some kind of sence or life.

For senseless things, though ne'r so call'd upon,
Are deaf, and feel no Invitation;
But such as at the last day shall be shed
20 By the great Lord of Life into the Dead.
     'Tis then no *Heresie* to end the strife
With such rare Doctrine as gives *Iron* life.
     For were it otherwise (which cannot be,
And do thou judge my bold Philosophie:)
25 Then it would follow that if I were dead,
Thy love, as now in life, would in that Bed
Of Earth and darkness warm me, and dispense,
Effectual informing Influence.
Since then 'tis clear, that Friendship is nought else
30 But a Joint, kind propension: and excess
In none, but such whose equal easie hearts
Comply and meet both in their *whole* and *parts*:
And when they cannot meet, do not forget
To mingle Souls, but secretly reflect
35 And some third place their Center make, where they
Silently mix, and make an unseen stay:
Let me not say (though *Poets* may be bold,)
Thou art more hard than *Steel*, than *Stones* more cold,
But as the *Mary-gold* in Feasts of Dew
40 And early Sun-beams, though but thin and few
Unfolds its self, then from the Earths cold breast
Heaves gently, and salutes the hopeful *East*:
So from thy quiet *Cell*, the retir'd Throne
Of thy fair thoughts, which silently bemoan
45 Our sad distractions,[6] come: and richly drest
With reverend mirth and manners, check the rest
Of loose, loath'd men! why should I longer be
Rack't 'twixt two Ev'ls? *I see and cannot see.*[7]

[6] The disturbances of the civil wars and after.
[7] I.e., he sees his friend with his mind but not with his eye.

Thalia Rediviva.

[T–2]   The King Disguis'd.[1]

Written about the same time that Mr. John
Cleveland *wrote his.*[2]

A King and no King! Is he gone from us,
And stoln alive into his Coffin thus?
This was to ravish Death, and so prevent
The Rebells treason and their punishment.
5 He would not have them damn'd, and therefore he
Himself deposed his own Majesty.
Wolves did pursue him, and to fly the Ill
He wanders (Royal Saint!) in sheep-skin still.
Poor, obscure shelter! if that shelter be
10 Obscure, which harbours so much Majesty.
Hence prophane Eyes! the mysterie's so deep,
Like *Esdras* books,[3] the vulgar must not see't.
    Thou flying Roll,[4] written with tears and woe,
Not for thy Royal self, but for thy Foe:

THE KING DISGUIS'D.

[1] Charles I escaped from Oxford disguised as a servant on 27
April 1646.

[2] Cleveland's poem, *The Kings Disguise,* was printed in January
1647.

[3] The two books of Esdras are the first in the Apocrypha, or "hidden (books)," which were regarded as late as the seventeenth century as books of esoteric wisdom available only to a spiritually
gifted few. II Esdras has many references to secret writings not to
be exposed to the uninitiated.

[4] Cf. the "flying roll" of Zech. 5.1–3, which was "the curse that
goeth forth over the face of the whole earth," and the "roll of a
book" of Ezek. 2.9–10, in which were written "lamentations, and
mourning, and woe."

15 Thy grief is prophecy, and doth portend,
   Like sad *Ezekiel's* sighs,[5] the Rebells end.
   Thy robes forc'd off, like *Samuel's* when rent,[6]
   Do figure out anothers Punishment.
   Nor grieve thou hast put off thy self a while,
20 To serve as Prophet to this sinful Isle;
   These are our days of *Purim*,[7] which oppress
   The Church, and force thee to the Wilderness.
   But all these Clouds cannot thy light confine,
   The Sun in storms and after them, will shine.
25 Thy day of life cannot be yet compleat,
   'Tis early sure; thy shadow is so great.
      But I am vex'd, that we at all can guess
   This change, and trust great *Charles* to such a dress.
   When he was first obscur'd with this coarse thing,
30 He grac'd *Plebeians*,[8] but prophan'd the King.
   Like some fair Church, which Zeal[9] to Charcoals burn'd,
   Or his own Court now to an Ale-house turn'd.
      But full as well may we blame Night, and chide
   His wisdom, who doth light with darkness hide:
35 Or deny Curtains to thy Royal Bed,
   As take this sacred cov'ring from thy Head.
   Secrets of State are points we must not know;
   This vizard is thy privy Councel now,
      Thou Royal Riddle, and in every thing
40 The true white Prince, our Hieroglyphic[10] King!
   Ride safely in his shade, who gives thee Light:

[5] Ezekiel sighed at the grievous prophecy he was commanded to deliver (Ezek. 21.6–7).

[6] Samuel rent his garments as a sign that Israel had been rent from Saul (I Sam. 15.27–28).

[7] It has been suggested that Vaughan had in mind not the feast of Purim (Esther 9.26–28), which was a feast of rejoicing over the deliverance of the Jews from the threat of Haman, but the day of the Atonement (Lev. 16.7–10), when the scapegoat was let go into the wilderness.

[8] Common people, or Parliamentarians.

[9] I.e., Puritan zeal which burned Anglican churches.

[10] Hidden, secret.

And can with blindness thy pursuers smite.
O may they wander all from thee as farr
As they from peace are, and thy self from Warr!
45 And wheresoe're thou do'st design to be
With thy (now spotted) spottles Majestie,
Be sure to look no Sanctuary there,
Nor hope for safety in a temple, where
Buyers and Sellers trade: O strengthen not
50 With too much trust the Treason of a Scot![11]

[T–3]   *The Eagle*

'Tis madness sure; And I am in the *Fitt*,
To dare an *Eagle* with my *unfledg'd* witt.
For what did ever *Rome* or *Athens* sing
In all their *Lines*, as loftie as his wing?
5   He that an Eagles *Powers* would rehearse
Should with his plumes first feather all his Verse.
    I know not, when into thee I would prie,
Which to admire, thy *Wing* first: or thine *Eye*;
Or whether Nature at thy birth design'd
10   More of her *Fire* for thee, or of her *Wind*.
When thou in the clear *Heights* and upmost *Air*
Do'st face the Sun, and his dispersed Hair,
Ev'n from that distance thou the *Sea* do'st spie
And sporting in its deep, wide Lap the *Frie*.
15   Not the least *Minoe* there, but thou can'st see;
Whole Seas are narrow spectacles to thee.
    Nor is this Element of water here
Below, of all thy miracles the sphere.
If Poets ought may add unto thy store,
20   Thou hast in Heav'n of wonders many more.
For when just *Jove* to Earth his thunder bends
And from that bright, eternal Fortress sends

---

[11] Charles had escaped from Oxford to the camp of the Scots, whom Vaughan likens to the money-changers in the temple (Matt. 21.12–13).

His louder vollies: strait this Bird doth fly
To *Ætna*, where his Magazine doth lye:
25   And in his active Talons brings him more
Of ammunition, and recruits his store.
Nor is't a low, or easie *Lift*. He soares
'Bove *Wind* and *Fire*; gets to the *Moon*, and pores
With scorn upon her duller face; for she
30   Gives him but shadows and obscurity.
Here much displeas'd, that any thing like night
Should meet him in his proud and loftie flight,
That such dull *Tinctures*[1] should advance so farr,
And rival in the glories of a star:
35   Resolv'd he is a nobler Course to try
And measures out his voyage with his Eye.
Then with such furie he begins his flight,
As if his *Wings* contended with his sight.
Leaving the Moon, whose humble light doth trade
40   With *Spotts*, and deals most in the *dark* and *shade*:
To the day's Royal *Planet* he doth pass
With daring Eyes, and makes the Sun his glass.
Here doth he plume and dress himself, the Beams
Rushing upon him, like so many Streams;
45   While with direct looks he doth entertain
The thronging flames, and shoots them back again.
And thus from star to star he doth repaire
And wantons in that pure and peaceful air.
Sometimes he frights the starrie *Swan*, and now
50   *Orion*'s fearful *Hare* and then the Crow.[2]
Then with the *Orbe* it self he moves, to see
Which is more swift th' *Intelligence*[3] or *He*.
Thus with his wings his body he hath brought
Where man can travell only in a thought.
55   I will not seek, rare bird, what *Spirit* 'tis

THE EAGLE.
    [1] Hues or colors.
    [2] All constellations; respectively, Cygnus, Orion, Lepus, and Corvus.
    [3] I.e., the angel governing the orb or sphere.

That mounts thee thus; I'le be content with this;
To think, that Nature made thee to express
Our souls bold *Heights* in a material dress.

[T–4]   To Mr. M. L.[1] *upon his reduction of the*
Psalms *into Method.*[2]

SIR,
You have oblig'd the *Patriarch.*[3] And tis known
He is your Debtor now, though for his own.
What he wrote, is a *Medley.* We can see
Confusion trespass on his Piety.
5 Misfortunes did not only Strike at him;
They charged further, and oppress'd his pen.
For he wrote as his *Crosses* came, and went
By no safe *Rule,* but by his *Punishment.*
His *quill* mov'd by the *Rod;* his witts and he
10 Did know no *Method,* but their *Misery.*
You brought his *Psalms* now into *Tune.* Nay, all
His measures thus are more than musical.
Your *Method* and his *Aires* are justly sweet,
And (what's *Church-musick* right) like *Anthems* meet.
15 You did so much in this, that I believe
He gave the *Matter,* you the *form* did give.
And yet I wish you were not understood,
For now *'tis a misfortune to be good!*
Why then, you'l say, all I would have, is this;
20 None must be good, because the time's amiss.
For since wise Nature did ordain the *Night,*
I would not have the *Sun* to give us Light.
Whereas this doth not take the *Use* away:
But urgeth the *Necessity* of day.

TO MR. M. L. . . .
  [1] Not positively identified. Grosart's suggestion of Matthew Locke
is now seriously questioned. See Hutchinson, *Life,* p. 217, n. 2.
  [2] Metrical form, not necessarily musical form.
  [3] To Vaughan this would be David.

25 Proceed to make your pious work as free,
   Stop not your seasonable charity.
   Good works despis'd, or censur'd by bad times,
   Should be sent out to aggravate their Crimes.
   They[4] should first *Share* and then *Reject* our store:
30 Abuse our *Good*, to make their *Guilt* the more.
   'Tis *Warr* strikes at our *Sins*, but it must be
   A *Persecution* wounds our *Pietie*.[5]

[T–5]   *To the pious memorie of* C. W. Esquire[1]
        *who finished his Course here, and made
        his Entrance into Immortality upon
        the* 13 *of* September, *in the year
        of* Redemption 1653.

Now, that the publick Sorrow doth subside,
And those slight tears which *Custom* Springs, are dried;
While all the rich & *out-side-Mourners* pass
Home from thy *Dust* to empty their own *Glass*:[2]
5 I (who the throng affect not, nor their state:)
Steal to thy grave undress'd,[3] to meditate
On our sad loss, accompanied by none,
An obscure mourner that would weep alone.
   So when the world's great Luminary setts,
10 Some scarce known Star into the *Zenith* gets,
Twinkles and curls a weak but willing spark:
As Gloworms here do glitter in the dark.

[4] The perpetrators of the evils of the times become additionally guilty by first sharing in the good of the old established order and then rejecting it.

[5] War can be a just punishment for sins, but whatever injures true good ("wounds our *Pietie*") is persecution.

TO THE PIOUS MEMORIE OF C. W. . . .

[1] Charles Walbeoffe, Vaughan's cousin.

[2] Either hourglass, as measuring out their lives, or drink.

[3] Without affectation.

Yet, since the dimmest flame that kindles there,
An humble love unto the light doth bear,
15 And true devotion from an Hermits Cell
Will Heav'ns kind King as soon reach and as well
As that which from rich Shrines and Altars flyes
Lead by ascending Incense to the Skies:
'Tis no malicious rudeness, if the might
20 Of love makes dark things wait upon the bright,
And from my sad retirements calls me forth
The Just Recorder of thy death and worth.
    Long did'st thou live (if length be measured by
The tedious Reign of our Calamity[4]:)
25 And Counter to all storms and changes still
Kept'st the same temper, and the self same will.
Though trials came as duly as the day,
And in such mists, that none could see his way:
Yet thee I found still virtuous, and saw
30 The Sun give Clouds: and *Charles* give both the Law.
When private Interest did all hearts bend
And wild dissents the public peace did rend:
Thou neither won, nor worn wer't still thy self;
Not aw'd by force, nor basely brib'd with pelf.
35   What the insuperable stream of times
Did dash thee with, those *Suff'rings* were, not *Crimes*.
So the bright *Sun* Ecclipses bears; and we
Because then passive, blame him not, should he
For inforc'd shades, and the *Moon's* ruder veile
40 Much nearer us, than him; be Judg'd to fail?
Who traduce thee, so erre. As poisons by
Correction are made Antidotes, so thy
Just Soul did turn ev'n hurtful things to Good;
Us'd bad Laws so, they drew not Tears, nor Blood.[5]
45 Heav'n was thy Aime, and thy great rare Design
Was not to Lord it here, but there to shine.

[4] The defeat of the Royalists in the civil wars.
[5] Walbeoffe held various appointments to official posts by the
Parliament, whose "bad Laws" he so administered that the Royalist
Welsh would not suffer unduly.

Earth nothing had, could tempt thee. All that e're
Thou pray'dst for here, was *Peace*; and *Glory* there.
For though thy Course in times long progress fell
50 On a sad age, when Warr and open'd Hell
Licens'd all Artes and Sects, and made it free
To thrive by fraud and blood and blasphemy:
Yet thou thy just Inheritance did'st by
No sacrilege, nor pillage multiply;
55 No rapine swell'd thy state: no bribes, nor fees
Our new oppressors best Annuities.
Such clean, pure hands had'st thou! And for thy heart
Man's secret region and his noblest part;
Since I was privy to't, and had the Key
60 Of that faire Room, where thy bright Spirit lay:
I must affirm, it did as much surpass
Most I have known, as the clear Sky doth glass.
Constant and kind, and plain and meek and Mild
It was, and with no new Conceits defil'd.
65 Busie, but sacred thoughts (like *Bees*) did still
Within it stirr, and strive unto that Hill,[6]
Where redeem'd Spirits evermore alive
After their Work is done, ascend and *Hive*.
No outward tumults reach'd this inward place,
70 'Twas holy ground: where peace, and love and grace
Kept house: where the immortal restles life
In a most dutiful and pious strife
Like a fix'd *watch*,[7] mov'd all in order, still;
The *Will* serv'd God, and ev'ry *Sense* the Will!
75   In this safe state death mett thee. Death which is
But a kind Usher of the good to bliss.
Therefore to Weep because thy Course is run,
Or droop like Flow'rs, which lately lost the *Sun:*
I cannot yield,[8] since faith will not permitt,
80 A *Tenure* got by *Conquest* to the *Pitt*.[9]

[6] The holy hill of Zion (Ps. 2.6), i.e., the heavenly city.
[7] Military watch.
[8] Consent.
[9] Hell.

For the great Victour[10] fought for us, and Hee
Counts ev'ry dust, that is lay'd up of thee.
Besides, Death now grows decrepit and hath
Spent the most part both of its time and wrath.
85 That thick, black night which mankind fear'd, is torn
By *Troops* of Stars, and the bright day's *Forlorn*.[11]
The next glad news (most glad unto the Just!)
Will be the Trumpet's summons from the dust.
Then Ile not grieve; nay more, I'le not allow
90 My Soul should think thee absent from me now.
Some bid their Dead *good night!* but I will say
Good morrow to dear Charles! for it is day.

[T–6]   *In Zodiacum Marcelli Palingenii.*[1]

It is perform'd! and thy great *Name* doth run
Through ev'ry *Sign* an everlasting *Sun*.
Not Planet-like, but *fix'd*; and we can see
Thy *Genius* stand still in his *Apogie*.[2]
5   For how canst thou an *Aux*[3] eternal miss,
Where ev'ry *House*[4] thine *Exaltation*[5] is?

[10] Christ.

[11] Short for Forlorn Hope, a term for troops sent in advance of
the main body, a vanguard (OED).

IN ZODIACUM MARCELLI PALINGENII.

[1] Marcellus Palingenius (Pier Angelo Manzolli) was an early
sixteenth-century Italian humanist whose *Zodiacus Vitae* appeared
in the early 1530s (1531 or 1535). It was translated (1560–65)
by Barnabe Googe and appeared in England in several later editions, both Latin and English. It became a well-known textbook for
schools. In twelve parts, each marked by a sign of the zodiac, it
contains comments on social and ecclesiastical conditions, and speculations in philosophy and science. Vaughan's interest was obviously
in the astrological, or astronomical, lore the book contained.

[2] The highest point in a planet's orbit.

[3] Or auge, another term for apogee.

[4] Sign of the zodiac.

[5] Position of greatest influence.

Here's no *Ecclyptic*[6] threatens thee with night,
Although the wiser few take in thy light.
They are not at that glorious *pitch*, to be
10   In a *Conjunction* with *Divinitie*.
Could we partake some oblique *Ray* of thine,
Salute thee in a *Sextile*,[7] or a *Trine*,[8]
It were enough; but thou art flown so high,
The *Telescope* is turn'd a Common Eye.
15   Had the grave *Chaldee*[9] liv'd thy Book to see,
He had known no *Astrologie*, but thee;
Nay more, (for I believ't,) thou shouldst have been
Tutor to all his Planets, and to him.
Thus whosoever reads thee, his charm'd sense
20   Proves captive to thy *Zodiac's* influence.
Were it not foul to erre so, I should look
Here for the *Rabbins* universal Book:[10]
And say, their fancies did but dream of thee,
When first they doted on that mystery.
25   Each line's a *via lactea*,[11] where we may
See thy fair steps, and tread that happy way
Thy *Genius* lead thee in. Still I will be
Lodg'd in some *Sign*, some *Face* and some *Degree*
Of thy bright *Zodiac*, Thus I'le teach my *Sense*
30   To move by that, and thee th' *Intelligence*.[12]

[6] A conjunction that would produce an eclipse.
[7] Aspect of two planets which are 60 degrees, or one-sixth part of the zodiac, distant from each other.
[8] Aspect of two planets which are 120 degrees, or one-third part of the zodiac, distant from each other.
[9] Marilla (*Secular Poems*, p. 293) suggests Galileo. *Chaldee* was a term for an astrologer or astronomer.
[10] The Cabala?
[11] Milky way.
[12] The controlling spirit or angel.

[T–7] *To* Lysimachus,[1] *the Author being with him in* London.

Saw not, *Lysimachus,* last day, when wee
Took the pure Air in its simplicity,
And our own too: how the trim'd *Gallants* went
Cringing, & past each step some Complement?
5   What strange, phantastic *Diagrams* they drew
With Legs and Arms; the like we never knew
In *Euclid, Archimed:*[2] nor all of those
Whose learned lines are neither Verse nor Prose?
What store of *Lace* was there? how did the *Gold*
10   Run in rich *Traces,* but withall made bold
To measure the proud *things,* and so deride
The *Fops* with that, which was part of their pride?
How did they point at us, and boldly call,
As if we had been Vassals to them all,
15   Their poor *Men-mules* sent thither by hard fate
To yoke our selves for their *Sedans* and State?
Of all ambitions, this was not the least,
Whose drift translated man into a beast.
What blind discourse the *Heroes* did afford?
20   This *Lady* was their Friend, and such a *Lord.*
How much of *Blood* was in it? one could tell
He came from *Bevis*[3] and his *Arundel*;
Morglay was yet with him, and he could do
More feats with it, than his old Grandsire too.
25   Wonders my Friend at this? what is't to thee,
Who canst produce a nobler Pedigree,
And in meer truth affirm thy Soul of kin
To some bright *Star,* or to a *Cherubin?*

TO LYSIMACHUS. . . .
   [1] Unidentified.
   [2] Archimedes.
   [3] Sir Bevis of Hampton, hero of a famous romance; his horse was Arundel, his sword Morglay.

When these in their profuse *moods* spend the night
30 With the same sins, they drive away the light,
Thy learned *thrift* puts her to use; while she
Reveals her firy Volume unto thee;
And looking on the separated skies
And their clear Lamps with careful thoughts & eyes
35 Thou break'st through Natures upmost rooms & bars
To Heav'n, and there conversest with the Stars.
    Well fare such harmless, happy *nights* that be
Obscur'd with nothing but their *privacie:*
And missing but the false world's *glories,* do
40 Miss all those *vices,* which attend them too!
Fret not to hear their ill-got, ill-giv'n praise;
Thy darkest nights outshine their brightest dayes.

[T–8]   *On Sir* Thomas Bodley's *Library;*[1]
         the Author being then in Oxford.

Boast not proud *Golgotha:*[2] that thou can'st show
The ruines of mankind, and let us know
How fraile a thing is flesh! though we see there
But empty Skulls, the *Rabbins*[3] still live here.
5 They are not dead, but full of *Blood* again,
I mean the *Sense,* and ev'ry *Line* a *Vein.*
Triumph not o're their Dust; whoever looks
In here, shall find their *Brains* all in their Books.
    Nor is't old *Palestine* alone survives,
10 *Athens* lives here, more than in *Plutarch's* lives.
The stones which sometimes danc'd unto the strain

ON SIR THOMAS BODLEY'S LIBRARY. . . .
   [1] Sir Thomas Bodley (1545–1613) established the Bodleian Library, Oxford, in 1598.
   [2] Meaning "skull," the place of execution outside Jerusalem where Christ was crucified.
   [3] Jewish authorities on law and doctrine.

Of *Orpheus*,[4] here do lodge his muse again.
And you the *Roman* Spirits, learning has
Made your lives longer, than your Empire was.
15 *Cæsar* had perish'd from the World of men,
Had not his *Sword* been rescu'd by his *pen*.
Rare *Seneca*![5] how lasting is thy breath?
Though *Nero* did, thou could'st not bleed to Death.
How dull the expert Tyrant was, to look
20 For that in thee, which lived in thy Book?
Afflictions turn our *Blood* to *Ink*, and we
Commence when *Writing*, our *Eternity*.
Lucilius[6] here I can behold, and see
His *Counsels* and his *Life* proceed from thee.
25 But what care I to whom thy *Letters* be?
I change the *Name*, and thou do'st write to me;
And in this Age, as sad almost as thine,
Thy stately *Consolations*[7] are mine.
Poor Earth! what though thy viler dust enrouls
30 The frail Inclosures of these mighty Souls?
Their graves are all upon Record; not one
But is as bright, and open as the Sun.
And though some part of them obscurely fell
And perish'd in an unknown, private Cell:
35 Yet in their books they found a glorious way
To live unto the Resurrection-day.
    Most noble *Bodley*! we are bound to thee
For no small part of our *Eternity*.
Thy treasure was not spent on *Horse* and *Hound*,
40 Nor that new Mode, which doth old *States* confound.[8]

[4] Orpheus' music was said to have moved rocks, trees, and beasts.
[5] Seneca, the philosopher, at one time tutor to Nero, was allowed
to take his life by opening his veins. Nero died a similar death but
left no written works behind him, as Seneca did.
[6] Lucilius the younger, to whom Seneca addressed many letters
and other writings.
[7] Seneca left three formal *consolationes*.
[8] Presumably the political activities of revolutionary character
which overthrew the old order in the civil wars.

Thy legacies another way did go:
Nor were they left to those would spend them so.
Thy safe, discreet Expence on us did flow;
Walsam[9] is in the mid'st of *Oxford* now.
45 Th' hast made us all thine *Heirs*: whatever we
Hereafter write, 'tis thy *Posterity*.
This is thy *Monument*! here thou shalt stand
Till the times fail in their last grain of Sand.
And wheresoe're thy silent *Reliques* keep,
50 This *Tomb* will never let thine honour sleep.
Still we shall think upon thee; all our fame
Meets here to speak one *Letter* of thy name.[10]
Thou can'st not dye! here thou art more than safe
Where every *Book* is thy large *Epitaph*.

[T–9] *The importunate Fortune, written to Doctor Powel of* Cantre.[1]

For shame desist, why should'st thou seek my fall?
It cannot make thee more Monarchical.
Leave off; thy Empire is already built;
To ruine me were to inlarge thy guilt,
5   Not thy Prerogative. I am not he
Must be the measure to thy victory.
The Fates hatch more for thee; 'twere a disgrace
If in thy Annals I should make a Clause.[2]
The future Ages will disclose such men,
10 Shall be the glory, and the end of them.

[9] Walsingham, formerly a place of pilgrimage. Oxford has now become the center for pilgrims (to books).

[10] Hutchinson (*Life,* p. 31) suggests the T-shape of the building which housed the library as Bodley's first initial. But *B* for both Bodley and Books would also be appropriate. See line 54.

THE IMPORTUNATE FORTUNE. . . .

[1] On Thomas Powell, see T–1, O–14, O–46. Although written to Powell, the poem is addressed to Fortune, or wealth.

[2] I.e., if I should constitute the smallest entry in your history.

Nor do I flatter. So long as there be
Descents in Nature, or Posterity,
There must be Fortunes; whether they be good,
As swimming in thy Tide and plenteous Flood,
15 Or stuck fast in the shallow Ebb, when we
Miss to deserve thy gorgeous charity.
Thus, Fortune, the great World thy period is;
Nature and you are *Parallels* in this.
     But thou wilt urge me still. Away, be gone;
20 I am resolv'd, I will not be undone.
I scorn thy trash and thee: nay more, I do
Despise my self, because thy Subject too.
Name me Heir to thy malice, and I'le be;
Thy hate's the best Inheritance for me.
25 I care not for your wondrous *Hat* and *Purse:*
Make me a *Fortunatus*[3] with thy Curse.
How careful of my self then should I be,
Were I neglected by the world and thee?
Why do'st thou tempt me with thy dirty Ore,
30 And with thy Riches make my Soul so poor?
My Fancy's pris'ner to thy Gold and thee,
Thy favours rob me of my liberty.
I'le to my Speculations. Is't best
To be confin'd to some dark narrow chest
35 And Idolize thy Stamps,[4] when I may be
Lord of all Nature, and not slave to thee?
The world's my Palace. I'le contemplate there,
And make my progress into ev'ry Sphere.
The Chambers of the *Air* are mine; those three
40 Well furnish'd *Stories* my possession be.[5]

---

[3] Hero of a popular series of fifteenth-century German tales showing the miseries wealth brings. His magic hat enabled him to move about at will, and his purse provided an endless supply of gold pieces. See Dekker's comedy *Old Fortunatus.*

[4] Coins.

[5] Air existed in three levels or storeys: terrestrial, celestial or astral, and empyrean.

I hold them all *in Capite*,[6] and stand
Propt by my Fancy there. I scorn your Land,
It lies so far below me. Here I see
How all the Sacred Stars do circle me.
45   Thou to the *Great* giv'st rich Food, and I do
Want no Content; I feed on *Manna* too.
They have their *Tapers*; I gaze without fear
On flying *Lamps*, and flaming *Comets* here.
Their wanton flesh in *Silks* and *Purple* Shrouds,
50   And Fancy wraps me in a *Robe* of *Clouds*.
There some delicious beauty they may woo,
And I have *Nature* for my Mistris too.
     But these are mean; the *Archtype* I can see,
And humbly touch the *hem* of Majestie.
55   The power of my Soul is such, I can
Expire, and so *analyse* all that's man.
First my dull Clay I give unto the *Earth*,
Our common Mother, which gives all their birth.[7]
My growing Faculties I send as soon
60   Whence first I took them, to the humid *Moon*.
All Subtilties and every cunning Art
To witty *Mercury* I do impart.
Those fond Affections which made me a slave
To handsome Faces, *Venus* thou shalt have.
65   And saucy Pride (if there was ought in me,)
Sol, I return it to thy Royalty.
My daring Rashness and Presumptions be
To *Mars* himself an equal Legacy.
My ill-plac'd Avarice (sure 'tis but small;)
70   *Jove*, to thy Flames I do bequeath it all.
And my false *Magic*, which I did believe,
And mystic Lyes to *Saturn* I do give.
My dark Imaginations rest you there,
This is your grave and Superstitious Sphære.
75   Get up my disintangled Soul, thy fire
Is now refin'd & nothing left to tire,   1

[6] Directly from the king.
[7] The process of divesting oneself of limitations, described in this and the following lines, follows a Hermetic pattern. See S–67.

Or clog thy wings. Now my auspicious flight
Hath brought me to the *Empyrean* light.
I am a sep'rate *Essence*,[8] and can see
80   The *Emanations*[9] of the Deitie,
And how they pass the *Seraphims*, and run
Through ev'ry *Throne* and *Domination*.[10]
So rushing through the Guard, the Sacred streams
Flow to the neighbour Stars, and in their beams
85   (A glorious Cataract!) descend to Earth
And give Impressions unto ev'ry birth.
With Angels now and Spirits I do dwell.
And here it is my Nature to do well,
Thus, though my Body you confined see,
90   My boundless thoughts have their *Ubiquitie*.
And shall I then forsake the *Stars* and *Signs*
To dote upon thy dark and cursed *Mines?*
Unhappy, sad exchange! what, must I buy
Guiana[11] with the loss of all the skie?
95   *Intelligences*[12] shall I leave, and be
Familiar only with mortalitie?
Must I know nought, but thy Exchequer? shall
My purse and fancy be Symmetrical?
Are there no Objects left but one? must we
100   In gaining that, lose our Varietie?
     Fortune, this is the reason I refuse
Thy Wealth; it puts my Books all out of use.
'Tis poverty that makes me wise; my mind
Is big with speculation, when I find
105   My purse as *Randolph's* was,[13] and I confess
There is no Blessing to[14] an Emptiness!
The *Species* of all things to me resort

[8] Pure individual being.
[9] Plotinian and Hermetic thought envisioned the divine creative power as exerting itself through emanations or radiations.
[10] Seraphim, Thrones, and Dominations were orders of angels.
[11] Symbol of great wealth.
[12] Spirits that governed the spheres.
[13] Thomas Randolph wrote a poem on his empty purse.
[14] Compared with.

And dwell then in my breast, as in their port.
Then leave to Court me with thy hated store,
110   Thou giv'st me that, to rob my Soul of more.

[T–10]   *To* I. Morgan *of* White-hall Esq;[1]
upon his sudden
Journey and succeeding Marriage.

So from our cold, rude World, which all things tires
To his warm *Indies* the bright sun retires.
Where in those provinces of Gold and spice
Perfumes his progress: *pleasures* fill his Eyes.
5   Which so refresh'd in their return convey
Fire into *Rubies,* into *Chrystalls* day;
And prove, that *Light* in kinder Climates can
Work more on senseless *Stones,* than here on *man.*
But you, like one ordain'd to shine, take in
10   Both *Light* and *Heat:* can *Love* and *Wisdom* spin
Into one thred, and with that firmly tye
The same bright Blessings on posterity;
Which so intail'd, like *Jewels* of the Crown,
Shall with your *Name* descend still to your own.
15   When I am dead, and malice or neglect
The worst they can upon my dust reflect,
(For *Poets* yet have left no names, but such
As men have *envied,* or *despis'd* too much;)
You above both (and what *state* more excells
20   Since a just Fame like *Health,* nor *wants,* nor *swells?*)
To after ages shall remain Entire,
And shine still spottles, like your planets Fire.
No single lustre neither; the access
Of your fair *Love* will yours adorn and bless;

TO I. MORGAN OF WHITE-HALL ESQ. . . .
[1] John Morgan of Wenallt (or White Hill, not White *Hall*), a
relative of Vaughan, lived across the Usk from Newton. The date of
his marriage is not known.

25 Till from that bright *Conjunction*, men may view
      A *Constellation* circling her and you:
          So two sweet *Rose-buds* from their *Virgin-beds*
      First peep and blush, then kiss and couple heads;
      Till yearly blessings so increase their store
30 Those two can number two and twenty more,
      And the fair *Bank* (by heav'ns free bounty Crown'd)
      With choice of *Sweets* and *Beauties* doth abound;
      Till time, which *Familys* like *Flowers* far spreads;
      Gives them for *Garlands* to the best of heads.
35 Then late posterity (if chance, or some
      Weak *Eccho*, almost quite expir'd and dumb
      Shall tell them, who the *Poet* was, and how
      He liv'd and lov'd thee too; which thou do'st know)
      Strait to my grave will *Flowers* and *spices* bring
40 With *Lights* and *Hymns*, and for an *Offering*
      There vow this truth; That *Love* (which in old times
      Was censur'd *blind*, and will contract worse Crimes
      If hearts mend not) did for thy sake in me
      Find both his *Eyes*, and all foretell and see.

[T–11]   F I D A : *Or The Country-beauty*:
                    to Lysimachus.

      Now I have seen her; And by *Cupid*
      The young *Medusa*[1] made me stupid!
      A face, that hath no Lovers slain,
      Wants forces, and is near disdain.
5   For every *Fop* will freely peep
      At Majesty that is asleep.
      But she (fair Tyrant!) hates to be
      Gaz'd on with such impunity.

FIDA: OR THE COUNTRY-BEAUTY. . . .
      [1] Woman in Greek mythology, one of the three Gorgons, whose
sight turned men to stone.

Whose prudent Rigor bravely bears
10   And scorns the trick of whining tears:
Or sighs, those false All-arms of grief,
Which kill not, but afford relief.
Nor is it thy hard fate to be
Alone in this Calamity,
15   Since I who came but to be gone,
Am plagu'd for meerly looking on.
     Mark from her forhead to her foot
What charming *Sweets* are there to do't.
A *Head* adorn'd with all those glories
20   That *Witt* hath shadow'd in quaint stories:
Or *pencill* with rich colours drew
In imitation of the true.
     Her *Hair* lay'd out in curious *Setts*
And *Twists,* doth shew like silken *Nets,*
25   Where (since he play'd at *Hitt* or *Miss:*)
The God of *Love* her pris'ner is,
And fluttering with his skittish Wings
Puts all her locks in Curls and Rings.
     Like twinkling Stars her *Eyes* invite
30   All gazers to so sweet a light,
But then two *arched Clouds* of brown
Stand o're, and guard them with a frown.
     Beneath these rayes of her bright Eyes
Beautie's rich *Bed* of *blushes* lyes.
35   Blushes, which lightning-like come on,
Yet stay not to be gaz'd upon;
But leave the *Lilies* of her Skin
As fair as ever, and run in:
Like swift *Salutes* (which dull *paint* scorn,)
40   Twixt a *white* noon, and *Crimson* Morne.
     What *Corall* can her *Lips* resemble?
For hers are warm, swell, melt and tremble:
And if you dare contend for *Red,*
This is *alive,* the other *dead.*
45   Her equal *Teeth* (above, below:)
All of a *Cise,*[2] and *Smoothness* grow.

[2] Size.

Where under close restraint and awe
(Which is the Maiden, Tyrant law:)
Like a cag'd, sullen *Linnet,* dwells
50   Her *Tongue,* the *Key* to potent spells.
      Her *Skin,* like heav'n when calm and bright,
Shews a rich *azure* under *white,*
With *touch* more soft than heart supposes,
And *Breath* as sweet as new blown *Roses.*
55   Betwixt this *Head-land* and the *Main,*
Which is a rich and flowry *Plain:*
Lyes her fair *Neck,* so fine and slender
That (gently) how you please, 'twill bend her.
      This leads you to her *Heart,* which ta'ne
60   Pants under *Sheets* of whitest *Lawn,*
And at the first seems much distrest,
But nobly treated, lyes at rest.
      Here like two *Balls* of new fall'n snow,
Her *Breasts,* Loves native *pillows* grow;
65   And out of each a *Rose-bud* Peeps
Which *Infant* beauty sucking, sleeps.

      Say now my *Stoic,* that mak'st soure faces
At all the *Beauties* and the *Graces,*
That criest *unclean!* though known thy self
70   To ev'ry coorse, and dirty shelfe:
Could'st thou but see a *piece* like this,
A piece so full of *Sweets* and *bliss*:
In *shape* so rare, in *Soul* so rich,
Would'st thou not swear she is a witch?

[T–12]   *Fida forsaken.*

Fool that I was! to believe blood
While swoll'n with greatness, then most good;
And the false thing, forgetful man:
To trust more than our true God, *Pan,*
5   Such swellings to a dropsie tend,
And meanest things such great ones bend.

Then live deceived! and *Fida* by
That life destroy fidelity.
For living wrongs will make some wise,
10   While death chokes lowdest Injuries:
And skreens the *faulty*, making Blinds
To hide the most unworthy minds.

And yet do what thou can'st to hide
A bad trees fruit will be descri'd.
15   For that foul guilt which first took place
In his dark heart, now damns his face:
And makes those Eyes, where life should dwell,
Look like the pits of Death and Hell.

Bloud, whose rich *purple* shews and seals
20   Their faith in *Moors*, in him reveals
A blackness at the heart, and is
Turn'd *Inke*, to write his faithlesness.
Only his lips with bloud look *red*,
As if asham'd of what they sed.

25   Then, since he wears in a dark skin
The shadows of his hell within,
Expose him no more to the light,
But thine own *Epitaph* thus write.
Here burst, and dead and unregarded
30   *Lyes Fida's heart! O well rewarded!*

[T–13] *To the Editor of the matchless* Orinda.[1]

Long since great witts have left the Stage
Unto the *Drollers*[2] of the age,
And noble numbers with good sense
Are like good works, grown an offence.
5   While much of verse (worse than old story,)
Speaks but *Jack-Pudding*, or *John-Dory*.[3]
Such trash-admirers made us poor,
And *Pyes*[4] turn'd *Poets* out of door.
For the nice Spirit of rich verse
10   Which scorns absurd and low commerce,
Although a flame from heav'n, if shed
On *Rooks* or *Daws*: warms no such head.
Or else the Poet, like bad priest,
Is seldom good, but when opprest:
15   And wit, as well as piety
Doth thrive best in adversity;
For since the thunder[5] left our air
Their *Laurels* look not half so fair.
    However 'tis 'twere worse than rude
20   Not to profess our gratitude
And debts to thee, who at so low
An Ebbe do'st make us thus to flow:
And when we did a Famine fear,
Hast blest us with a fruitful year.

TO THE EDITOR OF THE MATCHLESS ORINDA.

[1] Sir Charles Cotterel edited Mrs. Katherine Philips' poems in 1667, three years after her death, but this poem does not appear in the edition.

[2] Jesters, buffoons.

[3] Jack Pudding was a buffoon or clown. John Dory was the subject of a popular seventeenth-century song or catch. His name came to be applied to any light, foolish fellow.

[4] Magpies.

[5] Of the civil wars.

25   So while the world his absence mourns
        The glorious Sun at last returns,
        And with his kind and vital looks
        Warms the cold Earth and frozen brooks:
        Puts drowsie nature into play
30   And rids impediments away,
        Till Flow'rs and Fruits and spices through
        Her pregnant lap get up and grow.
        But if among those sweet things, we
        A miracle like that could see
35   Which nature brought but once to pass:
        A *Muse,* such as *Orinda* was,
        Phœbus himself won by these charms
        Would give her up into thy arms;
        And recondemn'd to kiss his *Tree,*[6]
40   Yield the young *Goddess* unto thee.

[T–14] *Upon sudden news of the much lamented death of Judge* Trevers.[1]

        Learning and *Law* your *Day* is done,
        And your *work* too; you may be gone!
        Trever, that lov'd you, hence is fled:
        And *Right,* which long lay *Sick,* is *dead.*
5   *Trever!* whose rare and envied *part*
        Was both a wise and winning heart,
        Whose sweet civilitys could move
        Tartars and *Goths* to noblest love.
        Bold *Vice* and *blindness* now dare act,
10   And (like the *gray groat,*)[2] pass, though crack't;

[6] Daphne, turned into a tree to avoid the embraces of Phoebus Apollo.

UPON SUDDEN NEWS OF THE MUCH LAMENTED DEATH OF JUDGE TREVERS.

[1] Arthur Trevor, Puisne Judge of the Brecknock circuit, 1661–67 (Hutchinson, *Life,* pp. 217–18).

[2] English coin worth about four pence. A cracked groat meant something worthless.

While those sage lips lye dumb and cold,
Whose words are well-weigh'd and tried gold.
O how much to descreet desires
Differs pure *Light* from foolish *fires*!
15   But nasty *Dregs* out last the *Wine*,
And after Sun-set *Gloworms* shine.

[T–15]   *To* Etesia[1] (*for* Timander,)
                the first Sight.

What smiling *Star* in that fair Night,
Which gave you *Birth* gave me this *Sight*,
And with a kind *Aspect* tho keen
Made me the *Subject*: you the *Queen*?
5   That sparkling *Planet* is got now
Into your Eyes, and shines below;
Where nearer force, and more acute
It doth dispence, without dispute,
For I who yesterday did know
10   Loves fire no more, than doth cool Snow
With one bright look am since undone;
Yet must adore and seek my Sun.
    Before I walk'd free as the wind,
And if but stay'd (like it,) unkind.
15   I could like daring Eagles gaze
And not be blinded by a face;
For what I saw, till I saw thee,
Was only not deformity.
Such shapes appear (compar'd with thine,)
20   In *Arras*, or a tavern-sign,

TO ETESIA (FOR TIMANDER,). . . .
    [1] Etesia has sometimes been regarded as identical with the
Amoret of *Poems* (1646), but with little real evidence. See P–3.
The name comes from a Greek term for the winds that blew dur-
ing a period of the summer.

And do but mind me to explore
A fairer piece, that is in store.
So some hang *Ivy* to their Wine,
To signify, there is a *Vine*.[2]
25   Those princely Flow'rs (by no storms vex'd,)
Which smile one day, and droop the next:
The gallant *Tulip* and the *Rose*,
Emblems which some use to disclose
Bodyed *Idea*'s: their weak grace
30   Is meer imposture to thy face.
For nature in all things, but thee,
Did practise only *Sophistry*;
Or else she made them to express
How she could vary in her dress:
35   But thou wert form'd, that we might see
Perfection, not Variety.
Have you observ'd how the Day-star
Sparkles and smiles and shines from far:
Then to the gazer doth convey
40   A silent, but a piercing Ray?
So wounds my love, but that her Eys
Are in *Effects*, the better Skys.
A brisk bright *Agent* from them Streams
Arm'd with no arrows, but their beams,
45   And with such stillness smites our hearts,
No noise betrays him, nor his darts.
He working on my easie Soul
Did soon persuade, and then controul;
And now he flyes (and I conspire)
50   Through all my blood with wings of fire,
And when I would (which will be never)
With cold despair allay the fever:
The spiteful thing *Etesia* names,
And that new-fuells all my flames.

---

[2] Referring to the custom of draping ivy over a tavern sign to indicate wine within.

[T–16]   *The Character, to* Etesia

Go catch the *Phœnix,* and then bring
A *quill* drawn for me from his wing.
Give me a Maiden-beautie's *Bloud,*
A pure, rich *Crimson,* without mudd:
5   In whose sweet *Blushes* that may live,
Which a dull verse can never give.
Now for an untouch'd, spottles *white,*
For blackest things on paper write;
Etesia at thine own Expence
10   Give me the *Robes* of innocence.
     Could we but see a *Spring* to run
Pure *Milk,* as sometimes Springs have done,
And in the *Snow-white* streams it sheds
Carnations wash their *bloudy* heads.
15   While ev'ry *Eddy* that came down
Did (as thou do'st,) both *smile* and *frown.*
Such objects and so fresh would be
But dull Resemblances of thee.
     Thou art the dark worlds Morning-star,
20   Seen only, and seen but from far;
Where like Astronomers we gaze
Upon the glories of thy face,
But no acquaintance more can have,
Though all our lives we watch and Crave.
25   Thou art a world thy self alone,
Yea three great worlds refin'd to one.
Which shews all those, and in thine Eyes
The shining *East,* and *Paradise.*
     Thy Soul (a *Spark* of the first *Fire,*)
30   Is like the *Sun,* the worlds desire;
And with a nobler influence
Works upon all, that claim to sense;
But in *Summers* hath no *fever,*
And in frosts is chearful ever.

35   As *Flowr's*, besides their curious *dress*
        Rich *odours* have, and *Sweetnesses*.
        Which tacitely infuse desire
        And ev'n oblige us to admire:
        Such and so full of innocence
40   Are all the *Charms*, thou do'st dispence;
        And like fair *Nature*, without *Arts*
        At once they seize, and please our hearts.
        O thou art such, that I could be
        A lover to Idolatry!
45   I could, and should from heav'n stray,
        But that thy life shews mine the way,
        And leave a while the *Diety*,
        To serve his *Image* here in thee.

[T-17]   *To* Etesia *looking from her Casement
          at the full* Moon.

        See you that beauteous *Queen*, which no age tames?
        Her Train is *Azure*, set with *golden* flames.
        My brighter *fair*, fix on the *East* your Eyes,
        And view that bed of Clouds, whence she doth rise.
5   Above all others in that one short hour
        Which most concern'd me, she had greatest pow'r.
        This made my *Fortunes* humorous as wind,
        But fix'd *Affections* to my constant mind.
        She fed me with the *tears* of *Starrs*, and thence
10   I suck'd in *Sorrows* with their *Influence*.
        To some in *smiles*, and store of *light* she broke:
        To me in sad *Eclipses* still she spoke.
        She bent me with the motion of her *Sphere*,
        And made me feel, what first I did but fear.
15   But when I came to Age, and had o'regrown
        Her Rules, and saw my freedom was my own,
        I did reply unto the Laws of Fate,
        And made my Reason, my great Advocate:

I labour'd to inherit my just right;
20 But then (O hear *Etesia!*) lest I might
Redeem my self, my unkind Starry Mother
Took my poor Heart, and gave it to another.

[T–18]   *To* Etesia *parted from him, and
looking back.*

O Subtile Love! thy Peace is War;
It wounds and kills without a scar:
It works unknown to any sense,
Like the Decrees of Providence,
5   And with strange silence shoots me through:
The *Fire* of Love doth fall like *Snow.*
        Hath she no *Quiver,* but my Heart?
Must all her Arrows hit that part?
Beauties like Heav'n, their Gifts should deal
10   Not to destroy us, but to heal.
        Strange *Art* of Love! that can make sound,
And yet exasperates the wound;
That *look* she lent to ease my heart,
Hath pierc't it, and improv'd the smart.

[T–19]   In Etesiam lachrymantem.

*O Dulcis luctus, risuque potentior omni!
        Quem decorant lachrymis Sydera tanta suis.
Quam tacitæ spirant auræ! vultusque nitentes
        Contristant veneres, collachrymantque suæ!*
5   *Ornat gutta genas, oculisque simillima gemma:
        Et tepido vivas irrigat imbre rosas.
Dicite* Chaldæi! *quæ me fortuna fatigat,
        Cum formosa dies & sine nube perit?*

[On Etesia Weeping

O sweet grief, more potent than any laughter, which
such bright stars as these grace with their tears! How
quiet her sobs are! Yet they quite overcloud the bright
charms of her face, and weep themselves in sympathy.
Teardrops adorn her cheeks, jewels that shine like her
eyes, and sprinkle the natural roses of her complexion
with a warm shower. Say, Chaldeans, what ill-fortune
plagues me, when a beautiful, cloudless day is suddenly
ruined?]

[T–20]   *To* Etesia *going beyond Sea.*

Go, if you must! but stay—and know
And mind before you go, my vow.
    To ev'ry thing, but *Heav'n* and *you,*
With all my Heart, I bid Adieu!
5   Now to those happy *Shades* I'le go
Where first I saw my beauteous Foe.
I'le seek each silent *path,* where we
Did walk, and where you sate with me
I'le sit again, and never rest
10   Till I can find some *flow'r* you prest.
That near my dying Heart I'le keep,
And when it wants *Dew,* I will weep:
Sadly I will repeat past Joyes,
And Words, which you did sometimes voice:
15   I'le listen to the *Woods,* and hear
The *Eccho* answer for you there.
But famish'd with long absence I
Like *Infants* left, at last shall cry,
And Tears (as they do *Milk*) will sup
20   Until you come, and take me up.

[T–21]   Etesia *absent*.

  Love, the Worlds Life! what a sad death
  Thy absence is? to lose our breath
  At once and dye, is but to live
  Inlarg'd, without the scant reprieve
5 Of *Pulse* and *Air*: whose dull *returns*
  And narrow *Circles*[1] the Soul mourns.
   But to be dead alive, and still
  To wish, but never have our will:
  To be possess'd, and yet to miss;
10 To wed a true but absent bliss:
  Are lingring tortures, and their smart
  Dissects and racks and grinds the Heart!
  As Soul and Body in that state
  Which unto us seems separate,
15 Cannot be said to live, until
  Reunion; which dayes fulfill
  And slow-pac'd seasons: So in vain
  Through hours and minutes (Times long *train*,)
  I look for thee, and from thy sight,
20 As from my Soul, for life and light.
  For till thine Eyes shine so on me,
  Mine are fast-clos'd and will not see.

ETESIA ABSENT.
 [1] Thought to indicate Vaughan's awareness of Harvey's discovery
of the circulation of the blood, which first appeared in print in 1628.

Translations.

Some *Odes* of the Excellent and Knowing *Severinus*,[1] Englished.

[T–22]   *Metrum 12. Lib. 3.*[2]

    Happy is he, that with fix'd Eyes
    The Fountain of all goodness spies!
    Happy is he, that can break through
    Those Bonds, which tie him here below!
5   The *Thracian* Poet long ago
    Kind *Orpheus,* full of tears and wo
    Did for his lov'd *Euridice*
    In such sad Numbers mourn, that he
    Made the *Trees* run in to his mone,
10   And *Streams* stand still to hear him grone.
    The *Does* came fearless in one throng
    With *Lyons* to his mournful Song,
    And charm'd by the harmonious sound
    The *Hare* stay'd by the quiet *Hound.*
15   But when *Love* heightned by *despair*
    And deep *reflections* on his *Fair*
    Had swell'd his Heart, and made it rise
    And run in Tears out at his Eyes:

TRANSLATIONS. SOME ODES . . . METRUM 12. LIB. 3.

[1] Anicius Manlius Severinus Boethius, parts of whose *Consolation of Philosophy* Vaughan had translated in *Olor Iscanus.* Here, as elsewhere in his translations, Vaughan takes considerable liberties with his text. The quality of his verse rendering is apparently more important to him than faithfulness to his original, and he does not hesitate to add to Boethius or to paraphrase very loosely indeed. For specific examples of his departures from the text, see Martin, *Works* (1957), p. 759.

[2] *De Consolatione,* III, Met. xii, Loeb Library, pp. 294–97.

And those sweet *Aires*, which did appease
20   Wild Beasts, could give their Lord no ease;
Then vex'd, that so much grief and Love
Mov'd not at all the gods above,
With desperate thoughts and bold intent,
Towards the *Shades* below he went;
25   For thither his fair Love was fled,
And he must have her from the dead.
There in such *Lines*, as did well suit
With sad *Aires* and a Lovers *Lute*,
And in the richest Language drest
30   That could be thought on, or exprest,
Did he complain, whatever *Grief*,
Or *Art*, or *Love* (which is the chief,
And all innobles,) could lay out;
In well-tun'd woes he dealt about.
35   And humbly bowing to the *Prince*
Of Ghosts, begg'd some Intelligence
Of his *Euridice*, and where
His beauteous *Saint* resided there.
Then to his *Lutes* instructed grones
40   He sigh'd out new melodious mones;
And in a melting charming *strain*
Begg'd his dear *Love* to life again.
   The *Music* flowing through the shade
And darkness, did with ease invade
45   The silent and attentive Ghosts;
And *Cerberus*, which guards those coasts
With his lowd barkings, overcome
By the sweet *Notes*, was now struck dumb.
The *Furies*, us'd to rave and howl
50   And prosecute each guilty Soul,
Had lost their rage, and in a deep
Transport did most profusely weep.
Ixion's wheel stopt, and the curst
Tantalus almost kill'd with thirst,
55   Though the *Streams* now did make no haste,
But waited for him, none would taste.

That *Vultur*, which fed still upon
Tityus his liver, now was gone
To feed on *Air*, and would not stay
60   Though almost famish'd, with her prey.
 Won with these wonders, their fierce Prince
At last cry'd out, *We yield! and since
Thy merits claim no less, take hence
Thy Consort for thy Recompence.*
65   *But,* Orpheus, *to this law we bind
Our grant, you must not look behind,
Nor of your fair Love have one Sight,
Till out of our Dominions quite.*
 Alas! what laws can Lovers awe?
70   *Love is it self the greatest Law!*
Or who can such hard bondage brook
To be in Love, and not to Look?
Poor *Orpheus* almost in the light
Lost his dear Love for one short sight;
75   And by those Eyes, which Love did guide,
What he most lov'd unkindly dyed!
 This tale of *Orpheus* and his *Love*
Was meant for you, who ever move
Upwards, and tend into that light,
80   Which is not seen by mortal sight.
For if, while you strive to ascend,
You droop, and towards Earth once bend
Your seduc'd Eyes, down you will fall
Ev'n while you look, and forfeit all.

[T–23]   *Metrum* 2. Lib. 3.[1]

What fix'd *Affections,* and lov'd *Laws*
(Which are the hid, magnetic *Cause*;)
Wise *Nature* governs with, and by
What fast, inviolable *tye*

TRANSLATIONS. SOME ODES . . . METRUM 2. LIB. 3.
 [1] *De Consolatione*, III, Met. ii, Loeb Library, pp. 232–35.

5   The whole Creation to her ends
For ever provident she bends:
All this I purpose to rehearse
In the sweet *Airs* of solemn Verse.
     Although the *Lybian Lyons* should
10   Be bound with chains of purest Gold,
And duely fed, were taught to know
Their keepers voice, and fear his blow:
Yet, if they chance to taste of bloud,
Their rage which slept, stirr'd by that food
15   In furious roarings will awake,
And fiercely for their freedom make.
No chains, nor bars their fury brooks,
But with inrag'd and bloody looks
They will break through, and dull'd with fear
20   Their keeper all to pieces tear.
     The *Bird*, which on the *Woods* tall boughs
Sings sweetly, if you Cage or house,
And out of kindest care should think
To give her honey with her drink,
25   And get her store of pleasant meat,
Ev'n such as she delights to Eat:
Yet, if from her close prison she
The *shady-groves* doth chance to see,
Straitway she loaths her pleasant food
30   And with sad looks longs for the *Wood*.
The wood, the wood alone she loves!
And towards it she looks and moves:
And in sweet *notes* (though distant from,)
Sings to her first and happy home!
35   That *Plant*, which of it self doth grow
Upwards, if forc'd, will downwards bow;
But give it freedom, and it will
Get up, and grow erectly still.
     The *Sun*, which by his prone descent
40   Seems westward in the Evening bent,
Doth nightly by an unseen way
Haste to the *East*, and bring up day.

Thus all things long for their first State,
And gladly to't return, though late.
45   Nor is there here to any thing
A *Course* allow'd, but in a *Ring*;
Which, where it first *began*, must *end:*
And to that *Point* directly tend.

[T–24]   *Metrum* 6 Lib. 4.[1]

Who would unclouded see the Laws
Of the supreme, eternal *Cause*,
Let him with careful thoughts and eyes
Qbserve the high and spatious Skyes.
5   There in one league of Love the *Stars*
Keep their old peace, and shew our wars.
The *Sun*, though flaming still and hot,
The cold, pale *Moon* annoyeth not.
Arcturus with his *Sons* (though they
10   See other stars go a far way,
And out of sight,) yet still are found
Near the *North-pole*, their noted bound.
Bright *Hesper* (at set times) delights
To usher in the dusky nights:
15   And in the *East* again attends
To warn us, when the day ascends,
So alternate *Love* supplys
Eternal Courses still, and vies
Mutual kindness; that no Jars
20   Nor discord can disturb the Stars.
     The same sweet *Concord* here below
Makes the fierce *Elements* to flow
And *Circle* without quarrel still,
Though temper'd diversly; thus will
25   The *Hot* assist the *Cold*: the *Dry*
Is a friend to *Humidity*.

TRANSLATIONS. SOME ODES . . . METRUM 6. LIB. 4.
     [1] *De Consolatione*, IV, Met. vi, Loeb Library, pp. 352–57.

And by the *Law* of *kindness* they
The like relief to them repay.
The *fire*, which active is and bright,
30 Tends upward, and from thence gives light.
The *Earth* allows it all that space
And makes choice of the lower place;
For things of weight hast to the Center
A fall to them is no adventure.

35 From these kind *turns* and *Circulation*
Seasons proceed and *Generation*.
This makes the *Spring* to yield us flow'rs,
And melts the Clouds to gentle show'rs.
The *Summer* thus matures all seeds
40 And ripens both the Corn and weeds.
This brings on *Autumn*, which recruits
Our old, spent store with new fresh fruits.
And the cold *Winters* blustring Season
Hath snow and storms for the same reason.

45 This *temper* and wise *mixture* breed
And bring forth ev'ry living *seed*.
And when their *strength* and *substance* spend
(For while they *live*, they drive and tend
Still to a *change*,) it takes them hence
50 And shifts their *dress*; and to our sense
Their *Course* is over, as their *birth*:
And hid from us, they turn to Earth.

But all this while the *Prince* of life
Sits without *loss*, or *change*, or *strife*:
55 Holding the *Rains*, by which all move;
(And those his *wisdom*, *power*, *Love*
And *Justice* are;) And still what he
The *first life* bids, that needs must be,
And live on for a time; that done
60 He calls it back, meerly to shun
The mischief, which his *creature* might
Run into by a further flight.
For if this dear and tender sense
Of his preventing providence
65 Did not restrain and call things back:

Both heav'n and earth would go to wrack.
And from their great *preserver* part,
As *blood* let out forsakes the *Heart*
And perisheth; but what returns
70 With fresh and Brighter spirits burns.
　　This is the *Cause* why ev'ry living
Creature affects an *endless being*.
A *grain* of this bright *love* each thing
Had giv'n at first by their great King;
75 And still they creep (drawn on by this:)
And look back towards their *first bliss*.
For otherwise, it is most sure,
Nothing that liveth could *endure*:
Unless it's Love turn'd retrograde
80 Sought that *first life*, which all things made.

[T–25]　　　　　　　*Metrum* 3. Lib. 4.[1]

If old tradition hath not fail'd,
Ulysses, when from *Troy* he sail'd,
Was by a tempest forc'd to land
Where beauteous *Circe* did command.
5 *Circe*, the daughter of the Sun,
Which had with *Charms* and *Herbs* undone
Many poor strangers, and could then
Turn into Beasts, the bravest Men.
Such *Magic* in her potions lay
10 That whosoever past that way
And drank, his shape was quickly lost;
Some into *Swine* she turn'd, but most
To *Lyons* arm'd with teeth and claws;
Others like *Wolves*, with open Jaws
15 Did howl; But some (more savage) took
The *Tiger's* dreadful shape and look.

TRANSLATIONS. SOME ODES . . . METRUM 3. LIB. 4.
[1] *De Consolatione*, IV, Met. iii, Loeb Library, pp. 320–23.

But wise *Ulysses* by the *Aid*
Of *Hermes*, had to him convey'd
A *Flow'r*, whose virtue did suppress
20   The force of charms, and their success.
While his *Mates* drank so deep, that they
Were turn'd to *Swine*, which fed all day
On *Mast*, and humane food had left;
Of shape and voice at once bereft.
25   Only the *Mind* (above all charms,)
Unchang'd, did mourn those monstrous harms.
        O worthless *herbs*, and weaker *Arts*
To change their *Limbs*, but not their *Hearts*!
Mans *life and vigor* keep within,
30   Lodg'd in the *Center*, not the *Skin*.
Those piercing charms and poysons, which
His *inward parts* taint and bewitch,
More fatal are, than such, which can
Outwardly only spoile the man.
35   Those change his *shape* and make it foul;
But these deform and kill his soul.

[T–26]   *Metrum* 6. Lib. 3.[1]

All *sorts* of men, that live on Earth,
Have one *beginning* and one *birth*.
For all things there is one *Father*,
Who *lays out* all, and all doth *gather*.
5   He the warm Sun with rays adorns,
And fils with brightness the Moon's horns.
The azur'd heav'ns with stars he burnish'd
And the round world with creatures furnish'd.
But *Men* (made to inherit all,)
10   His *own Sons* he was pleas'd to call,
And that they might be so indeed,
He gave them *Souls* of divine seed.

TRANSLATIONS. SOME ODES . . . METRUM 6. LIB. 3.
[1] *De Consolatione*, III, Met. vi, Loeb Library, pp. 248–51.

A noble *Offspring* surely then
Without distinction, are all men.
15   O why so vainly do some boast
Their *Birth* and *Blood*, and a great *Hoste*
Of Ancestors, whose *Coats* and *Crests*
Are some rav'nous *Birds* or *Beasts*!
If *Extraction* they look for
20   And *God*, the great *Progenitor*:
No man, though of the meanest state
Is *base*, or can *degenerate*;
Unless to *Vice* and *lewdness* bent
He leaves and *taints* his true *descent*.

[T–27] *The old man of* Verona *out of* Claudian.[1]

Fælix, qui propriis ævum transegit in arvis,
Una domus puerum &c.

Most happy man! who in his own sweet *fields*
Spent all his time, to whom one *Cottage* yields
In *age* and *youth* a lodging: who grown *old*
Walks with his *staff* on the same *soil* and *mold*
5   Where he did creep an *infant*, and can tell
Many fair years spent in one quiet *Cell*!
No *toils* of fate made him from home far known,
Nor forreign *waters* drank, driv'n from his own.
No loss by *Sea*, no wild *lands* wastful war
10   Vex'd him; not the brib'd *Coil*[2] of *gowns* at bar.

THE OLD MAN OF VERONA OUT OF CLAUDIAN.
    [1] See "De sene Veronensi qui Suburbium numquam egressus est,"
in *Claudian*, tr. Maurice Platnauer, Loeb Library (1922), II, 194–
97. The second line of the Loeb text reads *ipsa* instead of *Una*.
Both Abraham Cowley and Thomas Randolph made translations of
this poem.
    [2] Turmoil, bustle.

Exempt from *cares*, in *Cities* never seen
The fresh *field-air* he loves, and rural *green*.
The years set *turns* by *fruits*, not *Consuls* knows;
Autumn by apples: *May* by blossom'd boughs.

15 Within one hedg his *Sun* doth set and rise,
The world's wide day his short Demeasnes comprise.
Where he observes some known, concrescent[3] *twig*
Now grown an *Oak*, and old, like him, and big.
Verona he doth for the *Indies* take,

20 And as the *red Sea* counts *Benacus* lake.[4]
Yet are his *limbs* and *strength* untir'd, and he
A lusty *Grandsire* three *descents* doth see.
Travel and sail who will, search sea, or shore;
This man hath *liv'd*, and that hath *wander'd* more.

[T–28] *The Sphere of* Archimedes *out of*
Claudian.[1]

Jupiter *in parvo cum cerneret æthera vitro*
Risit, & ad superos &c.

When *Jove* a heav'n of small glass did behold,
He smil'd, and to the Gods these words he told.
Comes then the power of mans *Art* to this?
In a fraile *Orbe* my work new acted is.

5 The *poles* decrees, the *fate* of things: *God's* laws
Down by his *Art* old *Archimedes* draws.
Spirits inclos'd the sev'ral *Stars* attend,
And orderly the *living work* they bend.

---

[3] Growing by assimilation.
[4] Modern Lago di Garda in northern Italy.

THE SPHERE OF ARCHIMEDES OUT OF CLAUDIAN.

[1] See "In sphaeram Archimedis," in *Claudian*, Loeb Library, II,
278–81. Thomas Randolph also translated this poem.

A feigned *Zodiac* measures out the year,
10   Ev'ry new *month* a false *Moon* doth appear.
And now bold *industry* is proud, it can
Wheel round its *world*, and rule the *Stars* by man.
Why at *Salmoneus*[2] thunder do I stand?
Nature is rivall'd by a *single hand*.

[T–29]   *The* Phœnix *out of* Claudian.[1]

Oceani summo circumfluus æquore lucus
Trans Indos, Eurumque viret &c,

A grove there grows round with the *Sea* confin'd
Beyond the *Indies*, and the *Eastern* wind.
Which, as the *Sun* breaks forth in his first beam,
Salutes his *steeds*, and hears him whip his *team*.
5   When with his dewy *Coach* the *Eastern* Bay
Crackles, whence blusheth the approaching day;
And blasted with his burnish'd *wheels*, the night
In a pale dress doth vanish from the light.
This the blest *Phœnix* Empire is, here he
10   Alone exempted from mortality,
Enjoys a land, where no diseases raign;
And ne'r afflicted, like our world, with pain.
A *Bird* most equal to the Gods, which vies
For length of life and durance, with the skyes;
15   And with renewed limbs tires ev'ry age,
His appetite he never doth asswage
With common food. Nor doth he use to drink
When thirsty, on some *River*'s muddy brink.

[2] A son of Aeolus who imitated Zeus' lightning and thunder, whom Zeus eventually destroyed.
THE PHOENIX OUT OF CLAUDIAN.
[1] See "Phoenix," in *Claudian*, Loeb Library, II, 222–31.

A purer, vital *heat* shot from the Sun
20 Doth nourish him, and *airy sweets* that come
From *Tethis* lap,[2] he tasteth at his need;
On such *abstracted Diet* doth he feed.
    A secret *Light* there streams from both his Eyes
A firy *hue* about his *cheeks* doth rise.
25 His *Crest* grows up into a glorious *Star*
Giv'n t' adorn his head, and shines so far,
That piercing through the bosom of the night
It rends the darkness with a gladsome light.
His thighs like *Tyrian* scarlet, and his wings
30 (More swift than *Winds* are,) have skie-colour'd *rings*
Flowry and rich: and round about inroll'd
Their utmost *borders* glister all with gold.
Hee's not conceiv'd, nor springs he from the Earth,
But is himself the *Parent*, and the *birth*.
35 None him begets; his fruitful death reprieves
Old age, and by his funerals he lives.
For when the tedious *Summer*'s gone about
A thousand times: so many *Winters* out,
So many *Springs*: and *May* doth still restore
40 Those leaves, which *Autumn* had blown off before;
Then prest with years his vigour doth decline
Foil'd with the number; as a stately *Pine*
Tir'd out with storms, bends from the top & height
Of *Caucasus*, and falls with its own weight:
45 Whose part is torn with dayly *blasts*, with *Rain*
Part is consum'd, and part with *Age* again.
So now his Eyes grown dusky, fail to see
Far off, and drops of colder rheums there be
Fall'n slow and dreggy from them; such in sight
50 The cloudy *Moon* is, having spent her light.
And now his *wings*, which used to contend
With *Tempests*, scarce from the low Earth ascend.
He knows his time is out! and doth provide
New principles of life; herbs he brings dried
55 From the hot hills, and with rich spices frames

2 I.e., the sea.

A *Pile* shall burn, and *Hatch* him with its flames.
On this the *weakling* sits; salutes the Sun
With pleasant noise, and prays and begs for some
Of his own fire, that quickly may restore
60 The youth and vigour, which he had before.
Whom soon as *Phœbus* spyes, stopping his rayns,
He makes a stand and thus allayes his pains.
O thou that buriest old age in thy grave,
And art by seeming funerals to have
65 A new return of life! whose custom 'tis
To rise by ruin, and by death to miss
Ev'n death it self: a new beginning take,
And that thy wither'd body now forsake!
Better thy self by this thy change! This sed,
70 He shakes his *locks*, and from his golden *head*
Shoots one bright *beam*, which smites with vital fire
The willing bird; to burn is his desire,
That he may live again: he's proud in death,
And goes in haste to gain a better breath.
75 The spicie heap fir'd with cœlestial rays
Doth burn the aged *Phœnix*, when strait stays
The Chariot of th' amazed *Moon*; the *pole*
Resists the wheeling, swift *Orbs*, and the whole
Fabric of *Nature* at a stand remains,
80 Till the old bird a new, young being gains.
All stop and charge the faithful flames, that they
Suffer not nature's glory to decay.
    By this time, *life* which in the ashes lurks
Hath fram'd the *Heart*, and taught new *bloud* new *works*;
85 The whole *heap* stirs, and ev'ry *part* assumes
Due vigour; th' *Embers* too are turn'd to *plumes*.
The parent in the Issue now revives,
But young and brisk; the bounds of both these lives
With very little space between the same,
90 Were parted only by the middle flame.
    To *Nilus* straight he goes to consecrate
His parents ghoste; his mind is to translate
His dust to *Egypt*. Now he hastes away
Into a distant land, and doth convey

95 The ashes in a turf. Birds do attend
His Journey without number, and defend
His pious flight like to a guard; the sky
Is clouded with the Army, as they fly.
Nor is there one of all those thousands dares
100 Affront his leader: they with solomn cares
Attend the progress of their youthful king;
Not the rude hawk, nor th' Eagle that doth bring
Arms up to *Jove*, fight now; lest they displease;
The miracle enacts a common peace.
105 So doth the *Parthian* lead from *Tigris* side
His barbarous troops, full of a lavish pride
In pearls and habit, he adorns his head
With royal tires[3]: his steed with gold is lead.
His robes, for which the scarlet fish is sought,
110 With rare *Assyrian* needle work are wrought.
And proudly reigning o're his rascal bands,
He raves and triumphs in his large Commands.
A City of *Egypt* famous in all lands
For rites, adores the *Sun*, his temple stands
115 There on a hundred pillars by account
Dig'd from the quarries of the *Theban* mount.
Here, as the Custom did require (they say,)
His happy parents dust down he doth lay;
Then to the Image of his *Lord* he bends
120 And to the flames his burden strait commends.
Unto the *Altars* thus he destinates
His own Remains: the light doth gild the gates;
Perfumes divine the *Censers* up do send:
While th' *Indian* odour doth it self extend
125 To the *Pelusian*[4] fens, and filleth all
The men it meets with the sweet storm. A gale
To which compar'd, *Nectar* it self is vile:
Fills the seav'n channels of the misty *Nile*.
O happy bird! sole heir to thy own dust!
130 Death, to whose force all other Creatures must

[3] Headdresses.
[4] From Pelusium, a city located on the easternmost mouth of the Nile amid noted marshes.

Submit, saves thee. Thy ashes make thee rise;
'Tis not thy nature, but thy age that dies.
Thou hast seen All! and to the times that run
Thou art as great a witness, as the Sun.
135 Thou saw'st the *deluge*, when the sea outvied
The land, and drown'd the mountains with the tide.
What year the stragling *Phaeton* did fire
The world, thou know'st. And no plagues can conspire
Against thy life; alone thou do'st arise
140 Above mortality; the Destinies
Spin not thy days out with their fatal Clue;[5]
They have no Law, to which thy life is due.

Pious thoughts and Ejaculations.

[T–30]   *To his Books.*

Bright books! the *perspectives*[1] to our weak sights:
The clear *projections* of discerning lights.
Burning and shining *Thoughts*; man's posthume *day*:
The *track* of fled souls, and their *Milkie-way*.
5   The dead *alive* and *busie*, the still *voice*
Of inlarg'd Spirits, kind heav'ns white *Decoys*.
Who lives with you, lives like those knowing *flow'rs*,
Which in commerce with *light*, spend all their hours:
Which shut to *Clouds*, and *shadows* nicely shun;
10   But with glad haste unveil to *kiss* the Sun.
Beneath you all is dark and a dead night;
Which whoso lives in, wants both health and sight.
     By sucking you, the wise (like *Bees*) do grow
Healing and rich, though this they do most slow:
15   Because most choicely,[2] for as great a store
Have we of *Books*, as Bees of *herbs*, or more.

[5] Thread.

TO HIS BOOKS.
[1] Telescopes, magnifying glasses.
[2] With special care.

And the great task to *try*, then know the good:
To discern *weeds*, and Judge of wholsome *Food*,
Is a rare, scant performance; for *Man* dyes
20   Oft e're 'tis done, while the *bee* feeds and flyes.
But you were all choice *Flow'rs*, all set and drest
By old, sage *florists*, who well knew the best.
And I amidst you all am turn'd a *weed*!
Not wanting knowledge, but for want of heed.
25   Then thank thy self *wild fool*, that would'st not be
Content to know——what was to much for thee!

[T–31]   *Looking back.*

Fair, shining *Mountains* of my pilgrimage,
    And flow'ry *Vales*, whose flow'rs were stars:
The *days* and *nights* of my first, happy age;
    An age without distast and warrs:
5   When I by thoughts ascend your *Sunny heads*,
    And mind those sacred, *midnight* Lights:
By which I walk'd, when curtain'd Rooms and Beds
    Confin'd, or seal'd up others sights:
        O then how bright
10   And quick a light
    Doth brush my heart and scatter night;
        Chasing that shade
        Which my sins made,
    While I so *spring*, as if I could not *fade*!

15   How brave a prospect is a bright *Back-side*![1]
    Where flow'rs and palms refresh the Eye:
And days well spent like the glad *East* abide,
    Whose morning-glories cannot dye!

LOOKING BACK.
  [1] The region behind him (figuratively, his past life) to which he
looks back from the *"Sunny heads"* of the *"shining Mountains."*
The OED has no definition of the word which quite fits this use.
Cf. O–17, line 34.

[T–32]   *The Shower.*

    Waters above! eternal Springs!
    The dew, that silvers the *Doves* wings!
    O welcom, welcom to the sad:
    Give dry dust drink; drink that makes glad!
5   Many fair *Ev'nings*, many *Flowr's*
    Sweeten'd with rich and gentle showers
    Have I enjoy'd, and down have run
    Many a fine and shining *Sun*;
    But never till this happy hour
10   Was blest with such an *Evening-shower*!

[T–33]   *Discipline.*

    Fair prince of life, lights living well!
    Who hast the keys of death and hell!
    If the mule[1] man despise thy day,
    Put chains of darkness[2] in his way.
5   Teach him how deep, how various are
    The Councels of thy love and care.
    When Acts of grace and a long peace
    Breed but rebellion and displease;
    Then give him his own way and will,
10   Where lawless he may run until
    His own choice hurts him, and the sting
    Of his foul sins full sorrows bring.

DISCIPLINE.

  [1] Vaughan elsewhere refers to "the mule, unruly man" (S–61, line 18), but here the sense would seem to require "mole." All copies of *Thalia* (1678), however, read "mule."

  [2] II Pet. 2.4, "God spared not the angels that sinned, but . . . delivered them into chains of darkness, to be reserved unto judgment."

If Heav'n and Angels, hopes and mirth
Please not the *mole* so much as Earth:
15   Give him his *Mine* to dig, or dwell;
And one sad *Scheme* of hideous hell.

[T–34]   *The Ecclipse.*

Whither, O whither did'st thou fly
When I did grieve thine holy Eye?
When thou did'st mourn to see me lost,
And all thy Care and Councels crost.
5   O do not grieve where e'er thou art!
Thy grief is an undoing smart.
Which doth not only pain, but break
My heart, and makes me blush to speak.
Thy anger I could kiss, and will:
10   But (O!) thy grief, thy grief doth kill.

[T–35]   *Affliction.*

O Come, and welcom! Come, refine;
For *Moors* if wash'd by thee, will shine.
Man *blossoms* at thy touch; and he
When thou draw'st blood, is thy *Rose-tree.*
5   *Crosses* make strait his *crooked* ways,
And *Clouds* but cool his *dog-star* days.
Diseases too, when by thee blest,
Are both *restoratives* and *rest.*
    Flow'rs that in *Sun-shines* riot still,
10   Dye scorch'd and sapless; though *storms* kill.
The fall is fair ev'n to desire,
Where in their *sweetness* all expire.
O come, pour on! what *calms* can be
So fair as *storms*, that appease thee?

[T–36]   *Retirement.*

Fresh *fields* and *woods*! the Earth's fair *face*,
God's *foot-stool*, and mans *dwelling-place.*
I ask not why the first *Believer*[1]
Did love to be a Country liver?
5   Who to secure pious content
Did pitch by *groves* and *wells* his tent;
Where he might view the boundless *skie*,
And all those glorious *lights* on high:
With flying *meteors, mists* and *show'rs*,
10   Subjected *hills, trees, meads* and *Flow'rs*:
And ev'ry minute bless the King
And wise Creatour of each thing.
        I ask not why he did remove
To happy *Mamre*'s holy grove,
15   Leaving the *Citie*'s of the plain
To *Lot* and his successless train?
All various Lusts in *Cities* still
Are found; they are the *Thrones* of Ill.
The dismal *Sinks*, where blood is spill'd,
20   *Cages* with much uncleanness fill'd.
But *rural shades* are the sweet fense[2]
Of piety and innocence.
They are the *Meek*'s calm region, where
Angels descend, and rule the sphere:
25   Where heav'n lyes *Leiguer*,[3] and the *Dove*
Duely as *Dew*, comes from above.
If *Eden* be on Earth at all,
'Tis that, which we the *Country* call.

RETIREMENT.
  [1] Abraham, the first great example of faith. See Gen. 12 ff.
  [2] Defense.
  [3] Resides as agent or ambassador. Cf. O–14, line 10.

[T–37]   *The Revival.*

    Unfold, unfold! take in his light,
    Who makes thy Cares more short than night.
    The Joys, which with his *Day-star* rise,[1]
    He deals to all, but drowsy Eyes:
5   And what the men of this world miss,
    Some *drops* and *dews* of future bliss.
       Hark! how his *winds* have chang'd their *note*,
    And with warm *whispers* call thee out.
    The *frosts* are past, the *storms* are gone:
10   ·And backward *life* at last comes on.
    The lofty *groves* in express Joyes
    Reply unto the *Turtles* voice,
    And here in *dust* and *dirt*, O here
    The *Lilies* of his love appear![2]

[T–38]   *The Day-spring.*[1]

    Early, while yet the *dark* was gay,
    And *gilt* with stars, more trim than day:
    Heav'ns *Lily*, and the Earth's chast *Rose*:[2]

THE REVIVAL.

[1] II Pet. 1.19, "take heed, as unto a light that shineth in a dark place, until the day dawn, and the day star arise in your hearts."

[2] The lines are filled with echoes of Song of Sol. 2.1, 2, 10–13.

THE DAY-SPRING.

[1] Means both the dawn and Christ (Luke 1.78, where "branch" is given as an alternate reading for "day spring").

[2] Song of Sol. 2.1, "I am the rose of Sharon, and the lily of the valleys." In the 1678 edition, alongside lines 3 and 4, the following citation appeared: "S. *Mark c.* 1. *v.* 35." Mark 1.35: "And in the morning, rising up a great while before day, he went out, and departed into a solitary place, and there prayed."

The green, immortal B R A N C H arose;
5   And in a solitary place
Bow'd to his father his bless'd face.
    If this calm season pleas'd my *Prince,*
Whose *fullness* no need could evince,
Why should not I poor, silly sheep
10   His *hours,* as well as *practice* keep?
Not that his hand is tyed to these,
From whom *time* holds his transient *Lease:*
But *mornings,* new Creations are,
When men all night sav'd by his Care,
15   Are still reviv'd; and well he may
Expect them grateful with the day.
So for that first *drawght* of his hand,[3]
Which finish'd heav'n and sea and land,
The *Sons* of God their thanks did bring,
20   And all the *Morning-stars* did sing.
Besides, as his part heretofore
The *firstlings* were of all, that bore:[4]
So now each day from all he saves,
Their Soul's *first thoughts* and fruits he craves.
25   This makes him daily shed and shower
His graces at this early hour;
Which both his Care and Kindness show,
Chearing the good: quickning the slow.
As holy friends mourn at delay,
30   And think each minute an hour's stay:
So his divine and loving *Dove*
With longing throws[5] doth heave and move,
And soare about us, while we sleep:
Sometimes quite through that *lock* doth peep,
35   And shine; but always without fail
Before the slow Sun can unveile,

[3] In the 1678 edition, alongside lines 18–20, the following citation appeared: "Job. *c.* 38. *v.* 7." See also vss. 4–6.
[4] Abel brought the firstlings of his flock to the Lord (Gen. 4.4).
And see Exod. 13.12.
[5] Throes.

In new *Compassions* breaks like light,
And *Morning-looks*, which scatter night.
    And wilt thou let thy *creature* be
40   When *thou* hast watch'd, asleep to thee?
Why to unwellcome, loath'd surprises
Do'st leave him, having left his vices?
Since these, if suffer'd, may again
Lead back the *living*, to the *slain*.
45   O change this *Scourge*! or, if as yet
None less will my transgressions fit:
Dissolve, dissolve! death cannot do
What I would not submit unto.

[T–39]   *The Recovery.*

Fair *Vessell* of our daily light, whose proud
And previous *glories* gild that blushing Cloud:
Whose lively *fires* in swift projections glance
From hill to hill, and by refracted chance
5 Burnish some neighbour-*rock*, or tree, and then
Fly off in coy and winged *flams* agen:
       If thou this day
       Hold on thy way,
Know, I have got a greater *light* than thine;
10 A light, whose *shade* and *back-parts*[1] make thee shine.
    Then get thee down: then get thee down;
    I have a *Sun* now of my own.

II.

Those nicer livers, who without thy Rays
Stirr not abroad, those may thy lustre praise:
15 And wanting light (*light*, which no *wants* doth know!)
To thee (weak *shiner*!) like blind *Persians* bow;

THE RECOVERY.
[1] God protected Moses from the fullness of His glory by allowing
him to see only His back parts (Exod. 33.23).

But where that *Sun*, which tramples on thy head,
From his own bright, eternal *Eye* doth shed
One living *Ray*,
20   There thy dead day
Is needless, and man to a *light* made free,
Which shews what thou can'st neither shew, nor see.
Then get thee down, Then get thee down;
I have a *Sun* now of my own.

[T–40]   *The Nativity.*

Written in the year 1656.

Peace? and to all the world? sure, one
And he the prince of peace, hath none.
He travels[1] to be born, and then
Is born to travel more agen.
5   Poor *Galile!* thou can'st not be
The place for his Nativity.
His restless mother's call'd away,
And not deliver'd, till she pay.
   A *Tax*? 'tis so still![2] we can see
10   The Church thrive in her misery;
And like her head at *Bethlem*, rise
When she opprest with troubles, lyes.
Rise? should all fall, we cannot be
In more extremities than he.
15   Great *Type* of passions! come what will,
Thy grief exceeds all *copies* still.
Thou cam'st from heav'n to earth, that we
Might go from Earth to Heav'n with thee.

THE NATIVITY.
  [1] Travails.
  [2] Martin (*Works*, 1957, p. 760) suggests that Vaughan had reference to the Decimation Tax imposed on Royalists in 1655, and extended in 1656.

And though thou found'st no welcom here,
20   Thou did'st provide us *mansions* there.[3]
A *stable* was thy *Court*, and when
Men turn'd to *beasts*; Beasts would be *Men*.
They were thy *Courtiers*, others none;
And their poor *Manger* was thy *Throne*.
25   No swadling *silks* thy Limbs did fold,
Though thou could'st turn thy Rays to gold.
No *Rockers*[4] waited on thy birth,
No *Cradles* stirr'd: nor songs of mirth;
But her chast *Lap* and sacred *Brest*
30   Which lodg'd thee first, did give thee *rest*.
     But stay: what light is that doth stream,
And drop here in a gilded beam?
It is thy Star runs *page*, and brings
Thy tributary *Eastern* Kings.
35   Lord! grant some *Light* to us, that we
May with them find the way to thee.
Behold what mists eclipse the day:
How dark it is! shed down one *Ray*
To guide us out of this sad night,
40   And say once more, *Let there be Light*.

[T–41]   *The true Christmas.*

So stick up *Ivie* and the *Bays*,
And then restore the *heathen* ways.
Green will remind you of the spring;
Though this great day denies the thing.
5   And mortifies the Earth and all
But your wild *Revels*, and loose *Hall*.
Could you wear *Flow'rs*, and *Roses* strow
Blushing upon your breasts *warm Snow*,
That very *dress* your lightness will
10   Rebuke, and wither at the Ill.

[3] John 14.2, "In my Father's house are many mansions."
[4] Nurses.

The brightness of this day we owe
Not unto *Music, Masque* nor *Showe*:
Nor gallant *furniture,* nor *Plate*;
But to the *Manger's* mean Estate.
His *life* while here, as well as *birth,*
Was but a check to *pomp* and *mirth*;
And all mans *greatness* you may see
Condemn'd by his *humility.*
    Then leave your open *house* and *noise,*
To welcom him with *holy Joys,*
And the poor *Shepherd's* watchfulness:
Whom *light* and *hymns* from Heav'n did bless.
What you *abound* with, cast abroad
To those that *want,* and ease your loade.
Who empties thus, will bring more in;
But riot is both *loss* and *Sin.*
Dress finely what comes not in sight,[1]
And then you keep your *Christmas* right.

15

20

25

[T–42]   *The Request.*

O Thou! who did'st deny to me
This world's ador'd felicity,
And ev'ry big, imperious lust,
Which fools admire in sinful Dust;
With those fine, subtile *twists,* that tye
Their *bundles* of foul gallantry:
Keep still my weak Eyes from the *shine*
Of those gay things, which are not thine,
And shut my Ears against the noise
Of wicked, though applauded *Joys.*
For thou in any land hast store
Of shades and Coverts for thy poor,
Where from the busie dust and heat,
As well as storms, they may retreat.

5

10

THE TRUE CHRISTMAS.
  [1] The inner man, the soul.

15   A Rock, or Bush are douny beds,
         When thou art there crowning their heads
         With secret blessings: or a *Tire*
         Made of the *Comforter's* live-fire.[1]
         And when thy goodness in the *dress*
20   Of anger, will not seem to bless:
         Yet do'st thou give them that rich *Rain,*
         Which as it drops, clears all again.[2]
           O what kind *Visits* daily pass
         'Twixt thy great self and such poor *grass,*
25   With what sweet looks doth thy love shine
         On those low *Violets* of thine!
         While the tall *Tulip* is accurst,
         And *Crowns Imperial*[3] dye with thirst.
         O give me still those secret meals,
30   Those rare *Repasts,* which thy love deals!
         Give me that Joy, which none can grieve,
         And which in all griefs doth relieve.
         This is the portion thy Child begs,
         Not that of rust, and rags and dregs.

[T–43]   *Jordanis*

Quid celebras auratam undam, Et combusta pyropis
    Flumina, vel Medio quæ serit æthra salo?
Æternùm refluis si pernoctaret in undis
    Phœbus, & incertam sydera suda Tethyn
5 *Si colerent, tantæ gemmæ! nil cærula librem:*
    Sorderet rubro in littore dives Eos.

THE REQUEST.

[1] A crown or headpiece of fire, such as sat upon the disciples on the day of Pentecost (Acts 2.3).

[2] Deut. 32.2, "My doctrine shall drop as the rain, my speech shall distil as the dew, as the small rain upon the tender herb, and as the showers upon the grass."

[3] An English garden flower of Levantine origin. Cf. S–75, line 4.

Pactoli *mea lympha macras ditabit arenas,*
    Atq; Universum gutta minuta Tagum.
O charum caput! O cincinnos unda beatos
10   *Libata! O domini balnea Sancta mei!*
Quod fortunatum voluit spectare Canalem,
    Hoc erat in laudes area parva tuas.
Jordanis *in medio perfusus flumine lavit,*
    Divinoq; tuas ore beavit aquas.
15   Ah! Solyma *infœlix rivis obsessa prophanis!*
    Amisit Genium porta Bethesda *suum.*
Hic Orientis *aquæ currunt, & apostata* Pharpar,
    Atq; Abana *immundo turbidus amne fluit.*
Ethnica te totam cum fœdavere fluenta,
20   *Mansit Christicolâ* Jordanis *unus aqua.*

[The Jordan

Why sing of a golden wave or of rivers ablaze with gilt, or
of jewels which heaven sows in the depths of the salt sea? If
the sun were to sleep forever among the ebbing waves, instead
of merely spending the night there, or if the bright stars were
to go down and dwell in Tethys' turbid realm, then what
jewels these would make! But I should still not think the sea
worth anything, and the orient riches of the Arabian coast
would still seem mere trash. I could enrich Pactolus' poor
sands and the whole of the river Tagus with just one little drop
of my water. O precious spring! O water which was poured
over those blessed locks! My Lord's holy bath! That He was
willing to favor you with a look—lucky river—was only a
small part of your glory. Dripping with river water He bathed
in the middle of Jordan and blessed your currents with His
divine mouth. Ah, wretched Jerusalem, surrounded by un-
holy streams! Bethesda's gate has lost its angel. Now the
waters of the East and apostate Pharpar rush along, and
muddy Abana flows by with its defiling stream. Since heathen
rivers have polluted you, Jordan alone is still Christian water.]

[T–44]   Servilii Fatum, *sive* Vindicta divina.[1]

> *Et sic in cythara, sic in dulcedine vitæ*
> *Et facti & luctus regnat amarities.*
> *Quàm subitò in fastum extensos atq; effera vultus*
> *Ultrici oppressit vilis arena sinu!*
5 > *Si violæ, spiransque crocus: si lilium ἄεινον*
> *Non nisi Justorum nascitur è cinere:*
> *Spinarum, tribuliq; atq; infœlicis avenæ*
> *Quantus in hoc tumulo & qualis acervus erit?*
> *Dii superi! damnosa piis sub sydera longum*
10 > *Mansuris stabilem conciliate fidem!*
> *Sic olim in cœlum post nimbos clariùs ibunt,*
> *Supremo occidui tot velut astra die.*
> *Quippe ruunt horæ, qualisq; in Corpore vixit,*
> *Talis it in tenebras bis moriturus homo.*

[The Fate of Servilius, or Divine Vengeance

As in the lute's music, so in the sweetness of life, the bitterness of the inevitable and of our grief is dominant. How quickly the base earth crushes with its avenging embrace those features once drawn awry by scorn and fierce looks. If violets and the fragrant crocus and the never-fading lily spring from the remains only of just men, then what monstrous growth of brambles and thistle and barren wild oats will be found on this grave? You gods, grant a strong and stable

SERVILII FATUM, SIVE VINDICTA DIVINA.

[1] E. K. Chambers suggested (*The Athenaeum*, March 29, 1902, p. 403) that the Servilius of the title is P. Servilius Casca, one of the murderers of Julius Caesar, and that the seventeenth-century person alluded to is either Bradshaw or Ireton, not Cromwell, as Miss L. I. Guiney contended in the same number of *The Athenaeum* ("Cromwell and Henry Vaughan," pp. 402–3).

faith to right-minded men who are destined to remain long
beneath injurious stars! Thus, when the clouds have passed,
they will go up to heaven more brightly, setting like so many
constellations at their last day. For the hours fly by, and the
man who has two deaths to die will go down into the dark as
he lived in the body.]

[T–45]   De Salmone.[1]

Ad virum optimum, & sibi familiariùs notum: D. *Thomam
Poellum* Cantrevensem: S. S. Theologiæ Doctorem.

> *Accipe prærapido Salmonem in gurgite captum,*
>   *Ex imo in summas cum penetrâsset aquas.*
> *Mentitæ culicis quem forma elusit inanis:*
>   *Picta coloratis plumea musca notis.*
> 5 *Dum captat, capitur; vorat inscius, ipse vorandus;*
>   *Fitq; cibi raptor grata rapina mali.*
> *Alma quies! miseræ merces ditissima vitæ,*
>   *Quàm tutò in tacitis hic latuisset aquis!*
> *Qui dum spumosi fremitus & murmura rivi*
> 10   *Quæritat, hamato fit cita præda cibo.*
> *Quam grave magnarum specimen dant ludicra rerum?*
>   *Gurges est mundus: Salmo, homo: pluma, dolus.*

DE SALMONE.
  [1] For other poems on Powęll see O–14, O–46, and T–1.

[On a Salmon

To that most worthy gentleman, his especial
friend, Mr. Thomas Powell of Cantref,
Doctor of Divinity

Accept this salmon, caught above a rushing weir when he
had fought his way up from the bottom to the waters at the
top. The empty beauty of a seeming insect was his downfall:
a fly made of feathers, dyed in colors which he recognized.
Catching it, he is caught. All unawares he swallows it, doomed
to be swallowed himself. As he plunders the unlucky bait he
too becomes a tasty plunder. Blessed peace! The richest prize
of this wretched life! How safely he could have lurked in
silent pools. But when he seeks the roar and bellow of the
foaming torrent he quickly succumbs to my hooked bait. How
impressively these playful trifles symbolize great affairs! The
weir is the world: the salmon, man: the feathers, falsehood.]

[T–46]   *The World.*

Can any tell me what it is? can you,
    That wind your thoughts into a *Clue*[1]
To guide out others, while your selves stay in,
           And hug the Sin?
5   I, who so long have in it liv'd,
          That if I might,

THE WORLD.
  [1] Ball of thread.

In truth I would not be repriev'd:
                        Have neither sight,
                        Nor sense that knows
10   These *Ebbs* and *Flows*.
But since of all, all may be said,
And *likelines*[2] doth but upbraid,
And mock the *Truth*, which still is lost
In fine *Conceits*, like streams in a sharp frost:
15   I will not strive, nor the *Rule* break
Which doth give Loosers leave to speak.[3]
Then false and foul World, and unknown
                        Ev'n to thy own:
Here I renounce thee, and resign
20   Whatever thou can'st say, is thine.
    Thou art not *Truth*; for he that tries
Shall find thee all deceit and lyes.
Thou art not *friendship*; for in thee
'Tis but the *bait* of policy.
25   Which, like a *Viper* lodg'd in *Flow'rs*,
Its venom through that sweetness pours.
And when not so, then always 'tis
A fadeing *paint*; the short-liv'd bliss
Of *air* and *Humour*: out and in
30   Like *Colours* in a *Dolphin*'s skin.[4]
But must not live beyond *one day*,
Or *Convenience*; then away.
Thou art not *Riches*; for that *Trash*
Which one age hoords, the next doth wash
35   And so severely sweep away;
That few remember, where it lay.
So rapid *streams* the wealthy *land*

[2] Semblance, similarity (of false and true, evil and good).

[3] An old proverb, Give Losers leave to speak (talk)—apparently as some comfort or compensation for their losses. See Tilley, *Proverbs in England*, L 458.

[4] Like the changeable, iridescent colors of the dolphin, more probably the dorado, a fish noted for its beautiful colors which change rapidly when the fish is taken out of water or is dying. The dorado is often confused with the common dolphin.

About them, have at their command:
And shifting *channels* here restore,
40   There break down, what they bank'd before.
Thou art not *Honour*; for those gay
Feathers will wear, and drop away;
And princes to some upstart *line*
Give new ones, that are full as fine.
45   Thou art not *pleasure*; for thy *Rose*
Upon a *thorn* doth still repose;
Which if not cropt, will quickly shed;
But soon as cropt, grows dull and dead.
Thou art the *sand*, which fills one *glass*,
50   And then doth to another pass;
And could I put thee to a stay,
Thou art but *dust*! then go thy way,
And leave me *clean* and bright, though *poor*;
Who stops thee, doth but *dawb* his floor,
55   And *Swallow*-like, when he hath done,
To *unknown dwellings* must be gone![5]
Welcom pure thoughts and peaceful hours
Inrich'd with *Sunshine* and with *show'rs*;
Welcom fair hopes and holy Cares,
60   The not to be repented *shares*
Of time and business: the sure *rode*
Unto my last and lov'd *Abode*!
O supreme *Bliss*!
The Circle, Center and Abyss
65   Of blessings, never let me miss
Nor leave that *Path*, which leads to thee:
Who art alone all things to me!
I hear, I see all the long day
The noise and pomp of the *broad way*;
70   I note their Course and proud approaches:
Their silks, perfumes and glittering Coaches.

[5] Swallows were known as notoriously temporary (and dirty)
tenants around a house. See Tilley, *Proverbs in England,* S 1026:
"Swallows, like false friends, fly away upon the approach of
winter."

But in the *narrow way* to thee
I observe only poverty,
And despis'd things: and all along
75   The ragged, mean and humble throng
Are still on foot, and as they go,
They sigh and say; *Their Lord went so*!
    Give me my *staff* then, as it stood
When green and growing in the Wood.
80   (Those *stones*, which for the *Altar* serv'd,
Might not be smooth'd, nor finely carv'd:)
With this *poor stick* I'le pass the *Foord*
As *Jacob* did;[6] and thy dear *word*,
As thou hast dress'd it: not as *Witt*
85   And *deprav'd tastes* have poyson'd it:
Shall in the passage be my meat,
And none else will thy Servant eat.
Thus, thus and in no other sort
Will I set forth, though laugh'd at for't;
90   And leaving the wise *World* their way,
Go through; though Judg'd to go astray.

[T–47]   *The Bee.*

From fruitful *beds* and flowry *borders*
Parcell'd to wastful Ranks and Orders,
Where *state*[1] grasps more than plain *Truth* needs
And wholesome *Herbs* are starv'd by *Weeds*:
5   To the wild Woods I will be gone,

[6] Gen. 32.10, "for with my staff I [Jacob] passed over this Jordan." The stones of the altar probably constitute a reference to the altar that Jacob built at Bethel (Gen. 35.7) which, Vaughan supposes, was made not of carved but of natural stones.
THE BEE.
[1] Estate, or pomp, costly display.

And the course Meals of great *Saint John*.[2]
　　When truth and piety are mist
　Both in the Rulers and the Priest;
　When pity is not cold, but dead,
10　And the rich eat the Poor like bread;
　While factious heads with open Coile[3]
　And force first make, then share the spoile:
　To *Horeb* then *Elias* goes,[4]
　And in the *Desert* grows the *Rose*.[5]
15　　　Hail Christal Fountains and fresh shades,
　　　　　　Where no proud look invades.
　No busie worldling hunts away
　The sad Retirer all the day:
　Haile happy harmless solitude,
20　Our Sanctuary from the rude
　And scornful world: the calm recess
　Of faith, and hope and holiness!
　Here something still like *Eden* looks,
　Hony in Woods, *Julips* in Brooks:
25　And *Flow'rs*, whose rich, unrifled *Sweets*
　With a chast kiss the cool dew greets.
　When the toyls of the Day are done
　And the tir'd world sets with the Sun,
　Here *flying* winds and *flowing* Wells
30　Are the wise, watchful Hermits *Bells*;
　Their buisie *murmurs* all the night
　To *praise* or *prayer* do invite,
　And with an awful sound arrest
　And piously employ his breast.
35　　When in the *East* the Dawn doth blush,
　Here cool, fresh *Spirits* the air brush;
　Herbs (strait) get up, *Flow'rs* peep and spread:
　Trees whisper praise, and bow the head.

[2] The coarse meals of John the Baptist were locusts and wild honey (Matt. 3.4).

[3] Bustle, confusion.

[4] I Kings 19.8 ff.

[5] Isa. 35.1, "the desert shall rejoice, and blossom as the rose."

Birds from the shades of night releast
40   Look round about, then quit the neast,
And with united gladness sing
The glory of the morning's King.
The *Hermit* hears, and with meek voice
Offers his own up, and their Joys:
45   Then prays, that all the world may be
Blest with as sweet an unity.
      If sudden storms the day invade,
They flock about him to the shade:
Where wisely they expect the end,
50   Giving the tempest time to spend;
And hard by shelters on some bough
Hilarion's servant, the sage *Crow*.[6]
      O purer years of light, and grace!
The *diff'rence* is great, as the *space*
55   'Twixt you and us: who blindly run
After *false-fires*, and leave the *Sun*.
Is not fair *Nature* of her self
Much richer than dull *paint*, or *pelf*?
And are not *streams* at the *Spring-head*
60   More sweet than in carv'd *Stone*, or *Lead*?
But *fancy* and some *Artist's* tools
Frame a Religion for fools.
      The *truth*, which once was plainly taught,
With *thorns* and *briars* now is fraught.
65   Some part is with bold *Fables* spotted,
Some by strange *Comments* wildly blotted:
And *discord* (old Corruption's Crest,)
With *blood* and *blame* hath stain'd the rest.

[6] Vaughan confuses Hilarion with Paul the Hermit. Jerome, who wrote the lives of both hermits, tells of a crow who fed Paul a half-loaf of bread for sixty years, and brought a full loaf when Paul received Anthony as a visitor. But no crow appears in the life of Hilarion. In Vaughan's prose *The Mount of Olives* (Martin, *Works*, 1957, pp. 183–84) there occurs the same association of the crow with Hilarion rather than with Paul.

So *Snow*, which in its first descents
70   A whiteness, like pure heav'n presents,
When touch'd by *Man* is quickly soil'd
And after trodden down, and spoil'd.
     O lead me, where I may be free
In *truth* and *Spirit* to serve thee!
75   Where undisturb'd I may converse
With thy great self, and there rehearse
Thy gifts with thanks, and from thy store
Who art all blessings, beg much more!
Give me the Wisdom of the *Bee*,
80   And her unwearied Industry:
That from the *wild Gourds*[7] of these days
I may extract Health and thy praise;
Who can'st turn darkness into light,
And in my weakness shew thy might!
85   Suffer me not in any want
To seek refreshment from a *Plant*,
Thou did'st not *set*! since all must be
Pluck'd up, whose *growth* is not from thee.
'Tis not the *garden* and the *Bowrs*,
90   Nor *fense* and *forms* that give to flow'rs
Their *wholsomness*: but thy *good will*,
Which *truth* and *pureness* purchase still.
     Then since corrupt man hath driv'n hence
Thy kind and saving *Influence*,
95   And *Balm* is no more to be had
In all the Coasts of *Gilead*:[8]
Go with me to the *shade* and *cell*,
Where thy best *Servants* once did dwell.
There let me know thy *Will*, and see
100 Exil'd *Religion* own'd by thee.
For thou can'st turn dark *Grots* to *Halls*,
And make *Hills* blossome like the *vales*:

[7] A wild vine of bitter taste which by a miracle of Elisha was turned to edible food (II Kings 4.38–41).

[8] Jer. 8.22, "Is there no balm in Gilead? is there no physician there?"

Decking their untill'd *heads* with flow'rs
And fresh delights for all sad hours:
105   Till from them, like a laden *Bee*,
I may fly home, and *hive* with thee.

[T–48]   *To Christian Religion.*

Farewel thou true and tried Refection
Of the still poor and meek *Election*![1]
Farewel Souls *Joy*, the quickning *health*
Of Spirits, and their secret *wealth*!
5   Farewel my *Morning-star*, the bright
And dawning *looks* of the true Light!
O blessed *shiner*! tell me whither
Thou wilt be gone, when night comes hither?
A *Seer*,[2] that observ'd thee in
10   Thy Course, and watch'd the growth of Sin,
Hath giv'n his Judgment and foretold,
That *West-ward* hence thy *Course* will hold:
And when the day with us is done,
There fix, and shine a glorious Sun.
15   O hated *shades* and *darkness*! when
You have got here the Sway agen,
And like unwholsome *fogs* withstood
The light, and blasted all that's good:
Who shall the happy *shepherds* be
20   To watch the next *Nativity*
Of Truth and brightness, and make way
For the returning, rising day?

TO CHRISTIAN RELIGION.
    [1] The body of the elect.
    [2] George Herbert, who in "The Church Militant" traces the westward progress of the Christian religion, pursued by sin and darkness, eventually to pass "to the *American* strand" (line 235) and finally to a place of judgment in the East where it began.

O! what year will bring back our bliss,
Or who shall live, when God doth this?[3]

25   Thou *Rock* of Ages, and the *Rest*
Of all, that for thee are opprest!
Send down the *Spirit* of thy truth,
That Spirit, which the tender *Youth*
And first *growths* of thy *Spouse*[4] did spread

30   Through all the world, from one small *head*!
Then, if *to blood we must resist*[5]
Let thy mild *Dove*, and our high *Priest*
Help us, when man proves false, or frowns,
To bear the *Cross*, and save our *Crowns*.[6]

35   O! honour those, that honour thee!
Make *Babes* to still the Enemy:
And teach an *Infant* of few days
To perfect by his death, thy praise!
Let none defile what thou did'st *wed*,

40   Nor tear the *garland* from her head:
But chast and chearful let her dye,
And pretious in the *Bridegrooms* Eye!
So to thy glory, and her praise
These last shall be her brightest dayes.

Revel. Chap. last, vers. 17.[7]
The Spirit and the Bride say, Come.

[3] Num. 24.23.

[4] The Church.

[5] Heb. 12.4, "Ye have not yet resisted unto blood, striving against sin."

[6] Rev. 2.10, "be thou faithful unto death, and I will give thee a crown of life." And Rev. 3.11, "hold that fast which thou hast, that no man take thy crown."

[7] Rev. 22.17.

[T–49]   *DAPHNIS.*[1]

An Elegiac *Eclogue.*

The Interlocutors,
Damon, Menalcas.

    Da. What clouds, *Menalcas*, do oppress thy brow?
Flow'rs in a Sunshine never look so low.
Is *Nisa* still cold Flint? or have thy Lambs
Met with the Fox by straying from their Dams?

5   *Men.* Ah! *Damon*, no; my Lambs are safe, & she
Is kind, and much more white than they can be.
But what doth life, when most serene, afford
Without a worm, which gnaws her fairest gourd?
Our days of gladness are but short reliefs,
10 Giv'n to reserve us for enduring griefs.
So smiling Calms close Tempests breed, wch break
Like spoilers out, and kill our flocks, when weak.
    I heard last *May* (and *May* is still high Spring,)
The pleasant *Philomel* her Vespers sing.
15 The green wood glitter'd with the golden Sun
And all the West like Silver shin'd; not one
Black cloud, no rags, nor spots did stain
The Welkins beauty: nothing frown'd like rain;
But e're night came, that Scene of fine sights turn'd
20 To fierce dark showrs; the Air with lightnings burn'd;

DAPHNIS.
  [1] Hutchinson (*Life,* pp. 220–21) gives reasons for thinking that this poem was originally written to commemorate the death of William Vaughan, Henry's younger brother (died 1648), but was later revised as a tribute to Thomas Vaughan (died 1666).

The woods sweet Syren rudely thus opprest,
Gave to the Storm her weak and weary Breast.
I saw her next day on her last cold bed;
And *Daphnis* so, just so is *Daphnis* dead!

25   *Da.* So Violets, so doth the Primrose fall,[2]
At once the Springs pride and its funeral.
Such easy sweets get off still in their prime,
And stay not here, to wear the soil of Time.
While courser Flow'rs (which none would miss, if past)
30 To scorching Summers, and cold Autumns last.

   Men. Souls need not time, the early forward things
Are always fledg'd,[3] and gladly use their Wings,
Or else great parts, when injur'd quit the Crowd,
To shine above still, not behind the Cloud.
35 And is't not just to leave those to the night,
That madly hate, and persecute the light?
Who doubly dark, all *Negroes* do exceed,
And inwardly are true black Moores indeed.[4]

   Da. The punishment still manifests the Sin,
40 As outward signs shew the disease within.
While worth opprest mounts to a nobler height,
And Palm-like bravely overtops the weight.[5]
So where swift Isca[6] from our lofty hills
With lowd farewels descends, and foming fills
45 A wider Channel, like some great port-vein,[7]
With large rich streams to feed the humble plain:
I saw an Oak, whose stately height and shade

[2] Vaughan had referred, probably to his brother William, as "this *Prim-rose*" in S–19, line 10.
[3] Feathered for flight.
[4] Reference to Henry More, the Cambridge Platonist, who engaged in a bitter pamphlet exchange with Thomas Vaughan in the late 1640s and 50s. See Hutchinson, *Life*, pp. 26, 96–97, 146–47.
[5] See note to "S–86," lines 8–9.
[6] The Usk River.
[7] A large vein opening from the liver.

Projected far, a goodly shelter made,
And from the top with thick diffused Boughs
50 In distant rounds grew, like a Wood-nymphs house.
Here many Garlands won at Roundel-lays[8]
Old shepheards hung up in those happy days,
With knots and girdles, the dear spoils and dress
Of such bright maids, as did true lovers bless.
55 And many times had old *Amphion*[9] made
His beauteous Flock acquainted with this shade;
A Flock, whose fleeces were as smooth and white
As those, the wellkin shews in Moonshine night.
Here, when the careless world did sleep, have I
60 In dark records and numbers noblie high
The visions of our black, but brightest Bard[10]
From old *Amphion*'s mouth full often heard;
With all those plagues poor shepheards since have known,
And Ridles more, which future times must own.
65 While on his pipe young *Hylas* plaid, and made
Musick as solemn as the song and shade.
But the curs'd owner from the trembling top
To the firm brink, did all those branches lop,
And in one hour what many years had bred,
70 The pride and beauty of the plain lay dead.
The undone Swains in sad songs mourn'd their loss,
While storms & cold winds did improve the Cross.[11]
But Nature, which (like vertue) scorns to yield
Brought new recruits and succours to the Field;
75 For by next Spring the check'd Sap wak'd from sleep
And upwards still to feel the Sun did creep,
Till at those wounds, the hated Hewer made,
There sprang a thicker and a fresher shade.

Men. So thrives afflicted Truth! and so the light,
80 When put out, gains a value from the Night.

8 Singing matches.
9 Matthew Herbert, his old tutor?
10 Perhaps Merlin, the Black Bard of Welsh legend.
11 I.e., inflicted more suffering than the Cross.

How glad are we, when but one twinkling Star
Peeps betwixt clouds, more black than is our Tar?
And Providence was kind, that order'd this
To the brave Suff'rer should be solid bliss;
85 Nor is it so till this short life be done,
But goes hence with him, and is still his Sun.

    Da. Come Shepherds then, and with your greenest
        Bays
Refresh his dust, who lov'd your learned Lays.
Bring here the florid glories of the Spring,
90 And as you strew them pious *Anthems* sing,
Which to your children and the years to come
May speak of *Daphnis*, and be never dumb.
While prostrate I drop on his quiet Urn
My Tears, not gifts; and like the poor, that mourn
95 With green, but humble Turfs; write o're his Hearse
For false, foul Prose-men this fair Truth in Verse.

"Here *Daphnis* sleeps! & while the great watch goes
"Of loud and restless Time, takes his repose.
"Fame is but noise, all Learning but a thought:
100 "Which one admires, another sets at nought.
"Nature mocks both, and Wit still keeps adoe;
"But Death brings knowledge and assurance too.

    Men. Cast in your Garlands, strew on all the flow'rs
Which *May* with smiles, or *April* feeds with show'rs.
105 Let this days Rites as stedfast as the Sun
Keep pace with Time, and through all Ages run,
The publick character and famous Test
Of our long sorrows and his lasting rest;
And when we make procession on the plains,
110 Or yearly keep the Holyday of Swains,
Let *Daphnis* still be the recorded name
And solemn honour of our feasts and fame.

For though the *Isis* and the prouder *Thames*[12]
Can shew his reliques lodg'd hard by their streams,
115 And must for ever to the honour'd name
Of Noble *Murrey*[13] chiefly owe that fame:
Yet, here his Stars first saw him, and when fate
Beckon'd him hence, it knew no other date.
Nor will these vocal Woods and Valleys fail,
120 Nor *Isca*'s lowder Streams this to bewail,
But while Swains hope and Seasons change, will glide
With moving murmurs, because *Daphnis* di'd.

Da. A fatal sadness, such as still foregoes,
Then runs along with publick plagues and woes,
125 Lies heavy on us, and the very light
Turn'd Mourner too, hath the dull looks of Night.
Our vales like those of Death, a darkness shew
More sad than Cypress, or the gloomy Yew,
And on our hills, where health with height complied,
130 Thick drowsie Mists hang round and there reside.
Not one short parcel of the tedious year
In its old dress and beauty doth appear;
Flowr's hate the Spring, and with a sullen bend
Thrust down their Heads, which to the Root still tend,
135 And though the Sun like a cold Lover, peeps
A little at them, still the Days-eye[14] sleeps.
But when the Crab and Lion[15] with acute
And active Fires their sluggish heat recruit,
Our grass straight russets, and each scorching day
140 Drinks up our Brooks as fast as dew in May.
Till the sad Heardsman with his Cattel faints,
And empty Channels ring with loud Complaints.

[12] The Thames about Oxford is called the Isis. Thomas Vaughan
was actually buried at Albury, several miles from the Thames, but
very near the Thame, with which Vaughan evidently confused the
Thames. See Hutchinson, *Life*, pp. 144–45.

[13] Sir Robert Moray, friend and patron of Thomas Vaughan in
his chemical studies.

[14] Daisy.

[15] The constellations Cancer and Leo are ascendant in the summer months.

Men. Heaven's just displeasure & our unjust ways
Change Natures course, bring plagues dearth and decays.
145 This turns our lands to Dust, the skies to Brass,
Makes old kind blessings into curses pass.
And when we learn unknown and forraign Crimes,
Brings in the vengeance due unto those Climes.
The dregs and puddle of all ages now
150 Like Rivers near their fall, on us do flow.
Ah happy *Daphnis!* who, while yet the streams
Ran clear & warm (though but with setting beams,)
Got through: and saw by that declining light
His toil's and journey's end before the Night.

155   *Da.* A night, where darkness lays her chains and Bars,
And feral[16] fires appear instead of Stars.
But he along with the last looks of day
Went hence, and setting (Sun-like) past away.
What future storms our present sins do hatch
160 Some in the dark discern, and others watch;
Though foresight makes no Hurricane prove mild;
Fury that's long fermenting, is most wild.
    But see, while thus our sorrows we discourse,
Phœbus hath finish'd his diurnal course.
165 The shades prevail, each Bush seems bigger grown:
Darkness (like State,)[17] makes small things swell and
    frown.
The Hills and Woods with Pipes and Sonnets round
And bleating sheep our Swains drive home, resound.

    Men. What voice from yonder Lawn tends hither?
    heark!
170 'Tis *Thyrsis* calls, I hear *Lycanthe* bark.
His Flocks left out so late, and weary grown
Are to the Thickets gone, and there laid down.

[16] Funereal, gloomy.
[17] Position of importance, estate.

     Da. Menalcas, haste to look them out, poor sheep
     When day is done, go willingly to sleep.
175 And could bad Man his time spend, as they do,
     He might go sleep, or die, as willing too.

     Men. Farewel kind *Damon!* now the Shepheards Star[18]
     With beauteous looks smiles on us, though from far.
     All creatures that were favourites of day
180 Are with the Sun retir'd and gone away.
     While feral Birds[19] send forth unpleasant notes,
     And night (the Nurse of thoughts,) sad thoughts pro-
          motes.
     But Joy will yet come with the morning-light,
     Though sadly now we bid good night! *Da.* good night!

[18] The evening star Hesperus.
[19] "Fatal" or night birds, because they were supposed to threaten death.

MISCELLANEOUS POEMS

A note on the Miscellaneous Poems

The majority of the following verses appear scattered through Vaughan's prose works. They are for the most part translations or paraphrases of bits of verse Vaughan found in the Latin works he was turning into English. Few if any of them will enhance Vaughan's reputation as a poet, but they provide additional material for a study of his methods and practices as a translator. They belong in any edition of the complete poetry of Vaughan, as it has now been identified. Other verses of dubious attribution (see Martin, *Works* [1957], pp. 685–86) have not been included because of reasonable doubt of Vaughan's authorship.

The Miscellaneous Poems are divided into eleven sections, each group being preceded by a headnote indicating the location of the verse in Vaughan's works and the source Vaughan was using. Examples of Vaughan's verse translation are identified by page references to the prose translation in which they appear, followed by the original in brackets, also identified whenever possible by title and page of the larger work from which it comes. When, however, Vaughan gives in his text the original Latin or Greek followed by his translation, his order is used. Often he will give only a part of the Latin passage he is translating, followed by the translation itself. In such cases only the remainder of the Latin, in brackets, is normally given after his translation. The order of the verses is that of publication.

I.

From *Of The Benefit Wee may get by our Enemies*. A Discourse Written originally in the Greek by *Plutarchus Chaeronensis*, translated in to Latin by *I. Reynolds* Dr. of Divinitie, and lecturer of the Greeke Tongue in *Corpus Christi* College In *Oxford*. *Englished By* H: V: *Silurist*. (London, 1651).

This essay appeared in *Olor Iscanus* (1651), pp. 65–95. The Latin original, "Plutarchi Libellus, Quo Modo ex Inimicis Prepiatur *utilitas*," may be found in John Rainolds, *Orationes Duodecem* (London, 1628), pp. 471–93.

[M–1]   *Sure* Priam *will to mirth incline,*
         And all that are of Priam's *line.*

                              —Olor, p. 75.

        [Laetetur certè Priamus, Priamoq; creati.]
                —Rainolds, *Orationes*, p. 476;
                from *Iliad*, I, 255.

[M–2]   *Feeding on fruits which in the heavens doe grow,*
         Whence all divine and holy Counsells flow.
                              —Olor, p. 77.

        [Fructus ab alto mente capientem solo.
        Ex quo sacrata consilia progerminant?]
                —Rainolds, *Orationes*, p. 478.

[M–3]   *Excell then if thou canst, be not withstood,*
         But strive, and overcome the evill with good.
                              —Olor, p. 78.

[Ergo antecelle tu malis; si quidem potes.]
—Rainolds, *Orationes*, p. 478.

[M-4] *You minister to others wounds a Cure,*
      But leave your own all rotten and impure.
                                        —*Olor*, p. 78.

[Aliis medetur ipsus ulceribus scatens.]
—Rainolds, *Orationes*, p. 479.

[M-5] *Chance taking from me things of highest price*
      At a deare rate hath taught me to be wise.
                                        —*Olor*, p. 84.

[Fortuna tollens res mihi charissimas
Mercede docuit me gravi sapientiam.]
—Rainolds, *Orationes*, p. 484.

[M-6] *Knaves tongues, and calumnies no more doth price*
      Then the vaine buzzing of so many flies.
                                        —*Olor*, p. 86.

[Non magis ac Muscam convitia tetra movebant.]
—Rainolds, *Orationes*, p. 485.

[M-7] *His deepe, dark heart (bent to supplant)*
      Is Iron, or else Adamant.
                                        —*Olor*, p. 88.

[Habet cor atrum, lividum, aut ferreum,
aut adamantinum.]
—Rainolds, *Orationes*, p. 487.

[M-8] *What though they boast their riches unto us?*
      Those cannot say, That they are virtuous.
                                        —*Olor*, p. 94.

[At virtutis opus nos illis nos tribuemus
Propter opes.]
—Rainolds, *Orationes*, p. 492.

II.

From *Of The Diseases Of The Mind And the Body*. A Discourse Written originally in the Greek by *Plutarchus Chaeronensis,* put into latine by *I. Reynolds D.D.* Englished by *H: V:* Silurist. (London, 1651). This essay appeared in *Olor Iscanus* (1651), pp. 97–106. The Latin original, "Plutarchi Chaeronensis, Utrum Animi an Corporis morbi sint *graviores,"* may be found in John Rainolds, *Orationes Duodecem* (London, 1628), pp. 495–502.

[M–9]   *That man for misery excell'd*
          All creatures which the wide world held.

                                        —*Olor,* p. 99.

          [——Hominem miserandâ vincere sorte
          Omnia, quae latis vivunt, animantia, terris.]
                              —Rainolds, *Orationes,* p. 495.

[M–10]   *A tender Kid (see, where 'tis put,)*
          I on the Hils did slay,
          Now drest, and into quarters cut,
          A pleasant, daintie prey.

                                        —*Olor,* p. 104.

          [Tenerum ad aedes ecce capreolum, Ferimus celso
          vertice montium. Modò discerptum, felix spolium.]
                              —Rainolds, *Orationes,* p. 499.

III.

From *Of The Diseases Of The Mind, And The Body, And which of them is most pernicious*. The Question stated, and decided by *Maximus Tirius* a Platonick Philosopher, written originally in the Greek, put into Latine by *John Reynolds* D.D. *Englished by* Henry Vaughan *Silurist*. (London, 1651). This essay also appeared in *Olor Iscanus* (1651), pp. 107–23. The Latin original, "Maximi Tyrii Philosophi Platonici Disputatio, Utri sint graviores, morbi corporis, an *animi*," is in John Rainolds, *Orationes Duodecem* (London, 1628), pp. 537–48.

[M–11]   *O Coelestium princeps Sanitas!*
           Utinam tecum degere possim
           Quod mihi tempus superest vitae!

           O health the chief of gifts divine*!*
           I would I might with thee and thine
           Live all those days appointed mine!
                                    —*Olor*, p. 109.

           [O coelestum princeps, Sanitas,
           Utinam tecum degere possim,
           Quod mi tempus superest vitae.]
                           —Rainolds, *Orationes*, p. 537.

IV.

From *Man In Darkness, Or, A Discourse Of* Death, which appeared in *The Mount of Olives*: *Or,* Solitary Devotions (London, 1652), pp. 71–131.

[M–12]   Draw neer, fond man, and dresse thee by this glasse,
        Mark how thy bravery and big looks must passe
        Into corruption, rottennesse and dust;
        The fraile Supporters which betray'd thy trust.
5   O weigh in time thy last and loathsome state,
        To purchase heav'n for tears is no hard rate.
        Our glory, greatnesse, wisdome, all we have,
        If misimploy'd, but adde hell to the grave:
        Onely a faire redemption of evill Times
10   Finds life in death, and buryes all our Crimes.[1]
                  —*Mount of Olives*, p. 48 [72].

[M–13]   Animula vagula, blandula,
        Hospes comésque corporis,
        Quae nunc abibis in loca?
        Pallidula, querula, nudula,
        Nec, ut soles, dabis jocos.[2]

SECTION IV.

[1] Apparently an original composition by Vaughan. Martin (*Works,* 1957, p. 714) points out that line 6 echoes Herbert's "Vanity," II, lines 9–10.

[2] Attributed to Hadrian. See *Minor Latin Poets,* ed. J. Wight Duff and A. M. Duff, Loeb Library, p. 444.

My soul, my pleasant soul and witty,
The guest and consort of my body,
Into what place now all alone
Naked and sad wilt thou be gone?
No mirth, no wit, as heretofore,
Nor Jests wilt thou afford me more.
                    —*Mount of Olives*, p. 85.

[M–14]   Nam mihi quid prodest quod longo flumina cursu
         Semper inexhaustis prona feruntur aquis?
         Ista manent: nostri sed non mansêre parentes,
         Exigui vitam temporis hospes ago.

What is't to me that spacious rivers run
Whole ages, and their streams are never done?
Those still remain: but all my fathers di'd,
And I my self but for few dayes abide.[3]
                    —*Mount of Olives*, p. 88.

[M–15]   𝕸is maſurddh rhyddhig Adar,
                   Poh peth y ddhaſu trſux ddhayar,
                   Ond y marſu maur by garchar.

In March birds couple, a new birth
Of herbs and flowers breaks through the earth,
But in the grave none stirs his head;
Long is th' Impris'ment of the dead.
                    —*Mount of Olives*, p. 89.

[M–16]   *Sic nostros casus solatur mundus in astris.*[5]

So our decays God comforts by
The Stars concurrent state on high.
                    —*Mount of Olives*, p. 95.

---

[3] Cf. M–69, lines 33–38, for a different rendering of these lines.
[4] Attributed to Aneurin, the great sixth-century Welsh warrior
and poet.
[5] Manilius, *Astronomicon*, II, 261.

[M–17] Sunt qui in fortunae jam casibus omnia ponunt,
        Et nullo credunt mundum rectore moveri,
        Naturâ volvente vices & lucis & anni.[6]

        There are that do believe all things succeed
        By chance or fortune, & that nought's decreed
        By a divine, wise will; but blindly call
        Old time and nature rulers over all.
                              —*Mount of Olives*, pp. 97–98.

[M–18]   *Ex quo poli sunt perfecti*
                    Aude numero complecti
                    Stellas cœli, stillas roris,
                    Undas aquei fluoris,
                    Guttas imbris pluvialis,
                    Floccos velleris nivalis.
                    Quot sunt vere novo flores,
                    Quot odores, quot colores,
                    Quot vinacios Autumnus,
                    Poma legit & vertumnus;
                    Quot jam grana tulit æstas,
                    Frondes hyemis tempestas,
                    Totus orbis animantes,
                    Aër atomos volantes,
                    Pilos feræ, pecus villos,
                    Vertex hominum capillos;
                    Adde littoris arenas,
                    Adde graminis verbenas,
                    Tot myriades Annorum,
                    Quot momenta sæculorum:
                    Heus adhuc æternitatis
                    Portus fugit à damnatis![7]

        Æternum, æternum! quanta hæc duratio, quanta!
        Quàm speranda bonis, quámque tremenda malis!

---

[6] Juvenal, *Satires*, XIII, 86–88.
[7] An ancient hymn of uncertain authorship, once attributed to
St. Hildebert.

From the first hour the heav'ns were made
Unto the last, when all shall fade,
Count (if thou canst) the drops of dew,
The stars of heav'n and streams that flow;
5   The falling snow, the dropping showres,
And in the moneth of *May* the flowres,
Their sents and colours, and what store
Of grapes and apples Autumne bore;
How many grains the Summer beares,
10   What leaves the wind in Winter tears;
Count all the creatures in the world,
The motes which in the air are hurl'd,
The haires of beasts and mankind, and
The shores innumerable sand,
15   The blades of grasse, and to these last
Adde all the yeers which now are past,
With those whose course is yet to come,
And all their minutes in one summe.
When all is done, the damneds state
20   Out-runs them still, and knows no date.
                —*Mount of Olives*, pp. 100–2.

[M–19]   *Virg. lib. 4. Georgic.*

Namque sub Oebaliæ memini me turribus altis
Corycium vidisse senem: cui pauca relicti
Jugera ruris erant, nec fertilis illa juvencis,
Nec pecori opportuna seges, nec commoda Baccho.
Hic rarum tamen in dumis holus, albáque circum
Lilia, verbenásque premens, vescúmque papaver,
Regum æquabat opes animo, seráque revertens
Nocte domum, dapibus mensas onerabat inemptis.
Primus vere rosam, atque Autumno carpere poma:
Et cum tristis hyems etiamnum frigore saxa
Rumperet, & glacie cursus frænaret aquarum,
Ille comam mollis jam tum tondebat Acanthi
Æstatem increpitans seram, Zephirósque morantes.

Englished thus.

> *I saw beneath* Tarentum's *stately towers*
> *An old* Cilician *spend his peaceful houres:*
> *Some few bad* acres *in a waste, wild* field,
> *Which neither* Grasse, *nor* Corne, *nor* Vines *would*
>   *yield,*
> 5   *He did possesse; There (amongst* thorns *and* weeds)
> *Cheap Herbs and* Coleworts,[8] *with the common*
>   Seeds
> *Of* Chesboule[9] *or* tame poppeys *he did sowe,*
> *And* Verveyne[10] *with* white Lilies *caus'd to grow.*
> *Content he was, as are successeful* Kings,
> 10 *And late at night come home* (for long work brings
> The night still home,) *with* unbought messes *layd*
> *On his* low table, *he his* hunger *stayd.*
> Roses *he gather'd in the* youthful Spring;
> *And* Apples *in the* Autumn *home did bring;*
> 15 *And when the* sad, cold winter *burst with frost*
> *The* stones, *and the* still streams *in* Ice *were lost,*
> *He would soft leaves of* Beares-foot[11] *crop, and*
>   *chide*
> *The slow West-winds, and lingring Summer tyde!*
>   —*Mount of Olives,* pp. 114–15;
>   Virgil, *Georgics,* IV, 125, 127–38.

[M–20]   Sydera cuncta notat tacito labentia coelo.
                     [Virgil, *Aen.,* III, 515]

> *And rising at midnight the Stars espi'd*
> *All posting Westward in a silent glide.*
>   —*Mount of Olives,* p. 122.

[8] Plants of the cabbage family.

[9] Or chesboll, a poppy (OED).

[10] Plant of the genus *Verbena.* Incorrectly used as translation of Latin *verbena* (OED), as Vaughan does here.

[11] Hellebore.

[M–21]   *The trees, we set, grow slowly, and their shade*
           Stays for our sons, while (we the Planters) fade.
                             Virg. Georg. [II, 58]

Tarda venit, serísque futura nepotibus umbra.
                             —*Mount of Olives*, p. 123.

V.

From *Man In Glory: Or, A Discourse of the blessed state of the Saints in the New Jerusalem*. Written in Latin by the most Reverend and holy Father *ANSELMUS* Archbishop of *Canterbury*, and now done into English. (1652).

This translation appeared with *The Mount of Olives*, pp. 133–89.

[M–22]   Here holy *Anselme*[1] lives in ev'ry page,
    And sits Arch-bishop still, to vex the age.
    Had he foreseen (and who knows but he did?)
    This fatal wrack,[2] which deep in time lay hid,
5   'Tis but just to believe, that little hand[3]
    Which clouded him, but now benights our land,
    Had never (like *Elias*[4]) driv'n him hence,
    A sad retirer for a slight offence.
    For were he now, like the returning year,
10   Restor'd to view these desolations here,
    He would do penance for his old complaint,
    And (weeping) say, That *Rufus*[5] was a Saint.

—*Mount of Olives*, p. 138.

SECTION V.

[1] St. Anselm was Archbishop of Canterbury 1093–1109. This poem is Vaughan's own composition.

[2] The ruin, in Vaughan's judgment, which came to England by the civil wars.

[3] The cloud that was to break the drought in the land first appeared to Elijah's servant rising out of the sea like a man's hand (I Kings 18.44).

[4] Elijah fled the threatened vengeance of Jezebel (I Kings 19.1–14). Anselm withdrew to the Continent during his contention with William II over the spiritual authority of Canterbury.

[5] William II, called Rufus, reigned 1087–1100. He was notorious for confiscating the revenues of the church and denying its prerogatives.

VI.

From *Flores Solitudinis*. Certaine Rare and Elegant Pieces; *Viz*. Two Excellent Discourses Of 1. *Temperance, and Patience*; 2. *Life and Death*. By *I. E.* Nierembergius. The World Contemned; By Eucherius, Bp of Lyons. And the Life of Paulinus, Bp of *Nola*. Collected in his Sicknesse and Retirement, By *Henry Vaughan*, Silurist. (London, 1654).

Juan Eusebio Nieremberg (1595–1658), born in Madrid of German parents, was a noted theologian, a prolific writer widely read and translated. His *De Arte Voluntatis, Libri Sex* provided Vaughan with material for "two excellent discourses." The Paris edition of 1639, Book II, Appendix I, "Tolerantia, & temperantia rerum" (pp. 105–41) supplies most of the material for Vaughan's first essay, although he drew on other parts of the volume also. Book VI, Diorismus V, of *De Arte Voluntatis*, entitled "Ex comparatione vitae, & mortis" (pp. 472–505) is the basis of Vaughan's second essay. Since the two translations are paginated consecutively in *Flores Solitudinis*, the page references are to *Flores* rather than to the separate essays. On Eucherius and Paulinus see below, headnote VII.

[M–23]   To the onely true and glorious
              God, the Sole disposer of
              Life and Death.[1]

> O Doe not goe, thou know'st I'le dye,
> My *Spring* and *Fall* are in thy Booke!
> Or if thou goest, doe not deny
> To lend me, though from far, one looke!

SECTION VI.

[1] Vaughan's own composition, which appears in *Silex*, Part II, as "Begging." See S–96 for annotations and variants.

5   My sinnes long since have made thee strange,
    A very stranger unto me;
    No *morning-meetings* (since this change)
    Nor *Evening-walkes* have I with thee.

    Why is my God thus hard and cold,
10   When I am most, most sick and sad?
    Well-fare those blessed dayes of old,
    When thou did'st heare the *weeping Lad!*

    O doe not thou doe as I did,
    Doe not despise a love-sick heart!
15   What though some *Clouds* defiance bid!
    Thy *Sun* must shine in every part.

    Though I have spoyl'd, O spoyle not thou,
    Hate not thine owne deere gift and token!
    Poore *Birds* sing best, and prettiest show,
20   When their *neast* is fallen and broken.

    Deare Lord! restore thy Ancient peace,
    Thy quickning friendship, mans bright wealth;
    And if thou wilt not give *me* Ease
    From sicknes, Give my *Spirit* health!
               —*Flores*, following title page
               in BM copy.

[M–24]   *Puella tota quanta, nil erat aliud*
        Quàm Illecebra picta, delicatus harpago, &c.
    The whole wench[2] (*how compleat soe'r*) *was but*
    A *specious* baite; *a soft, sly, tempting* slut;
    A *pleasing witch*; *a living* death; *a faire,*
    Thriving disease; *a fresh,* infectious aire;
    A *pretious* plague; *a* furie *sweetly drawne*;
    Wild fire *laid up and finely drest in* Lawne.
               —*Flores*, sigs. A1ᵛ–A2ʳ.

[2] I.e., this world.

[The two lines of Latin followed by:
Flexanima Furia, viva mors, valens lues,
Pretiosa pestis, linteatum Incendium!]

—Bisselius, *Icaria* (Ingolstadt,
1637), pp. 215–16.

[M–25]   Amaena, Petre, cum vides, &c.

Peter, *when thou this pleasant world dost see,*
Beleeve, thou seest meere Dreames *and* vanitie;
Not reall *things, but* false: *and through the* Aire
Each where, an empty, slipp'rie Scene, *though*
faire.
Each where, an empty, slipp'rie Scene, *though faire.*
5   *The chirping* birds, *the fresh* woods *shadie boughes,*
The leaves *shrill whispers, when the* west-wind
blowes.
The swift, fierce Greyhounds *coursing on the*
plaines,
The flying hare *distrest 'twixt feare and paines;*
The bloomy Mayd *decking with* flowers *her head,*
10   *The gladsome, easie* youth *by light* love *lead;*
And whatsoe'r heere with admiring eyes
Thou seem'st to see, 'tis but a fraile disguise
Worne by eternall *things, a passive* dresse
Put on by beings *that are passiveles.*

—*Flores,* sig. A3ʳ–ᵛ.

[Amaena Petre quae vides vagus loca
Putato vana te videre somnia,
Nec esse quippe, sed videri & undique
Per altum inane lubricumque prospici.
Aves canorae, & arborum leves comae,
Et acre murmur insonansque frondium:
Eas movente leniter Favonio,
Canes per aequa fervidi, fugax lepus,
Puella flore vinciens novo caput,
Amore laetus ac vagans levi puer;
Et omne, quod videris hic alacriter

Videre, prorsus umbra sunt perennium
Inanis, ac valentium esse perpete
In omne tempus.]
> —Augurellus, *Geronticon*, I, Ad
> Petrum Lipomanum in Obitu Clarae
> Sororis (Antwerp, 1582), p. 92.

[M–26]   —*The naked man too getts the field,*
And often makes the armed foe to yeeld.
> —*Flores*, p. 2.

[vincit inermis,
Armatósque solet vincere saepè viros.]
> —*De Arte Voluntatis*, p. 106.

[M–27]   *Struggle & grone as if by* Panthers *torne*
Or Lyons *teeth, which makes them lowdly mourn.*
Some others seem unto themselves to dy.
Some clime steep solitudes & Mountains high,
From whence they seeme to fall inanely[3] *down,*
Panting with fear, till wak'd, and scarce their owne,
They feel about them if in bed they lye,
Deceiv'd with dreams, and nights Imagerie.
> —*Flores*, p. 34.

[Multi depugnant, gemitusque doloribus edunt,
Et quasi Pantherae morsu, saevive leonis
Mendantur: magnis clamoribus omnia complent.
Multi mortem obeunt: multi de montibus altis,
Ut quasi praecipitent ad terram corpore toto,
Exterrentur; & ex somno quasi mentibus capti
Vix ad se redeunt permoti corporis aestu.]
> —*De Arte Voluntatis*, p. 123; from
> Lucretius, *De Rerum*, IV, 1015–17,
> 1020–23.

[3] Senselessly.

[M–28]   *In vain with earnest struglings they contend*
To ease themselves: for when they stir & bend
Their greatest force to do it, even then most
Of all they faint, and in their hopes are crost.
Nor tongue, nor hand, nor foot will serve their turne,
But without speech and strength within they
mourne.

—*Flores,* p. 34.

[Nec quicquam avidos extendere cursus
Velle videmur, & in mediis conatibus agri
Succidimus: non lingua valet, non corpore notae
Sufficiunt vires: nec vox, aut verba sequuntur.]

—*De Arte Voluntatis,* p. 123; from
Virgil, *Aen.,* XII, 909–12.

[M–29]   παυσίπονον νηπενθὲς ἔφυς, ἔυαλθες ὄνειαρ.
Thou the Nepenthe[4] *easing griefe*
Art, and the minds healing reliefe.

—*Flores,* p. 40.
[The Greek from Nieremberg, *De Arte Voluntatis,*
p. 126.]

[M–30]   *Base man! & couldst thou think Cato alone*
Wants courage to be dry, &, but him, none?
Look'd I so soft? breath'd I such base desires,
Not proofe against this Libyc Sun's weak fires?
That shame and plague on thee more justly lye!
To drinke alone, when all our troops are dry.

—*Flores,* p. 46.

[Méne, inquit, degener unum
Miles in hac turba vacuum virtute parasti?
Usque adeo mollis, primisque caloribus impar
Sum visus? Quantò poena tu dignior ista es,
Qui populo sitiente bibas.]

—*De Arte Voluntatis,* p. 129.

───────────

[4] Drink or drug supposed to induce forgetfulness.

[M–31]   *For, with brave rage he*[5] *flung it on the Sand,*
         And the spilt draughts suffic'd each thirsty band.
                                              —Flores, p. 47.

                    [Sic concitus ira
         Excussit galeam, sufficitque omnibus unda.]
                              —De Arte Voluntatis, p. 129.

[M–32]   *——And will not hear the Crie*
         Of distrest man, not shut his weeping Eye.
                                              —Flores, p. 52.

         [mors . . . saeva in flentes oculos,
              Surda miseros avertitur aure.]
                              —De Arte Voluntatis, p. 133.

[M–33]   *Like some faire* Oke, *that when her boughes*
         Are cut by rude hands, thicker growes:
         And from those wounds the Iron made,
         Resumes a rich and fresher shade.
                                              —Flores, p. 63.

         [Duris ut ilex tonsa bipennibus,
         Nigrae feraci frondis in algido,
         Per damna, per cedes ab ipso
         Ducis opes, animumque ferro.]
                              —De Arte Voluntatis, p. 139.

[M–34]   ——Τροφὴ μία πᾶσιν ἀρίστη
         Δαίνυσθαι μεγάλοιο Θεοῦ νόον ἠδὲ φαεινῆς
         Ε῎λκειυ ἐκ Τρίαδος σελας ἄπλετον.——

         ——one food the best for all
         Is to feed on the great Gods mind, & draw
         An Immense light from the bright Trinity.
                                              —Flores, p. 64.

              [The Greek from *De Arte Voluntatis*, p. 139.]

[5] Cato.

[M–35]   *——They faine would (if they might)*
Descend to hide themselves in Hell. So light
Of foot is vengeance, and so near to sin,
That soon as done, the Actors do begin
To fear and suffer by themselves: Death moves
Before their Eyes; Sad dens, and duskie groves
They haunt, and hope (vain hope which fear doth
        guide!)
That those dark shades their inward guilt can hide.
                                    —Flores, p. 72.

[Cuperent, si fortè pateret,
Condere se barathro: usque adeò contermina poenae
Culpa suae est, ut iam miseros mortale paventes
Mortis imago iuvet; sylvas, umbrosáque lustra
Obtendunt, vanis solatia salsa tenebris.]
                                —De Arte Voluntatis, p. 144.

[M–36]   *But night and day doth his owne life molest,*
And bears his Judge and witnesse in his brest.
                                    —Flores, p. 75.

[Nocte, diéque suum gestare in pectore testem.]
                                —De Arte Voluntatis, p. 145.

[M–37]   *Virtues faire cares some people measure*
For poys'nous works, that hinder pleasure.
                                    —Flores, p. 81.

λοίγια δ'ὠρώξει τοῖσιν μεμεληωφία ἔργα.
                                —De Arte Voluntatis, p. 149.

[M–38]   *Man should with Virtue arm'd, and hearten'd be,*
And innocently watch his Enemy:
For fearlesse freedom, which none can controule,
Is gotten by a pure and upright Soul.
                                    —Flores, p. 83.

[Virum vera virtute vivere animatum addecet.
Fortiter, cumque innoxium vacare adversùs adver-
   sarios.
Ea libertas est, quae pectus purum & firmum
   gestitat.]
                —*De Arte Voluntatis*, p. 149.

[M–39]   *Whose guilty soul with terrours fraught, doth frame*
       New torments still, and still doth blow that flame
       Which still burns him: nor sees what end can be
       Of his dire plagues, and fruitful penalty?
       But fears them living, and fears more to dye.
       Which makes his life a constant Tragedy.
                   —*Flores*, p. 83.

             [mens, sibi conscia facti,
Praemetuens adhibet stimulos, terrétque flagellis:
Nec videt intereà, qui terminus esse malorum
Possit, nec qui sit poenarum denique finis.
Atque eadem metuit magis; haec, ne in morte
   gravescant.
Hinc Acherusia fit stultorum denique vita.]
                —*De Arte Voluntatis*, p. 150.

[M–40]   *And for lifes sake to lose the crown of life?*
                 —*Flores*, p. 86.

[Et propter vitam vivendi perdere causas?]
                —*De Arte Voluntatis*, p. 151.

[M–41]   *Nature even for her self doth lay a snare,*
       And handsome faces their own traitours are.
                 —*Flores*, p. 86.

        [Laqueos natura tetendit:
Ipsa suas facies fabricat insidias.]
                —*De Arte Voluntatis*, p. 152.

[M–42]   —*True life in this is shown,*
To live for all mens good, not for our own.
—*Flores*, p. 103.

τοῦτ' ἐστὶ τὸ ζῆν οὐχ ἑαντῷ ζῆν μόνον.
—*De Arte Voluntatis*, p. 94; from
Menander, Frag. 646 (Teubner ed.).

[M–43]   *As* Egypts *drought by* Nilus *is redrest,*
So thy wise tongue doth comfort the opprest.
—*Flores*, p. 105.

[defectum fortè labore,
Nilus ut Ægyptum, sic tua lingua fovet.]
—*De Arte Voluntatis*, p. 95.

[M–44]   [Like] *To speedy posts,*[6] *bear hence the Lamp of*
life.
—*Flores*, p. 111.

[Et quasi cursores vitaï lampada tradunt.]
—*De Arte Voluntatis*, p. 98; from Lucretius, II, 79.

[M–45]   *All worldly things, even while they grow, decay,*
As smoke doth, by ascending, wast away.
—*Flores*, p. 115.

[Omnia praetereunt, ut inanis in aëre fumus.]
—*De Arte Voluntatis*, p. 100.

[M–46]   *Whose*[7] *hissings fright all Natures monstrous Ills,*
His eye darts death, more swift then poison kils.
All Monsters by instinct to him give place,
They fly for life, for death lives in his face;
And hee alone by Natures hid commands
Reigns Paramont, *and* Prince *of all the sands.*
—*Flores*, p. 130.

[6] Couriers, bearers of express mail.
[7] The basilisk's.

[Sibiláque effundens cunctas terrentia pestes
Ante venena nocens, latè sibi submovet omne
Vulgus, & in vacua regnat basilicus arena.]
　　　　　　　　—*De Arte Voluntatis*, p. 476.

[M–47]　*The plenteous Evills of frail life fill the old:*
　　　　Their wasted Limbs the loose skin in dry folds
　　　　Doth hang about; their joynts are numm'd and
　　　　　　　through
　　　　Their veines not blood, but rheumes and waters
　　　　　　　flow.
　　　　Their trembling bodies with a staffe they stay,
　　　　Nor doe they breath, but sadly sigh all day:
　　　　Thoughts tire their hearts, to them their very mind
　　　　Is a disease; their Eyes no sleep can find.
　　　　　　　　　　　　—*Flores*, p. 136.

[Multa senem fragilis vexant incommoda carnis:
Non macie turpit abescunt languida membra,
Tunc ienuum iunctura riget, venasque per omnes
Illius in toto frigescit corpore sanguis:
Sic baculonitens artus sustentat inertes.
Quid tristes memorem gemitus? quid taedia mentis?
Somnus abest oculis.]
　　　　　　　　—*De Arte Voluntatis*, p. 479.

[M–48]　*Against the Virtuous man we all make head,*
　　　　And hate him while he lives, but praise him dead.
　　　　　　　　　　　　—*Flores*, p. 158.

Δεινοὶ γου ἀνδρὲι πάντες εσμοῦ ἐυχλεῶ
Ζῶντι φρονήσαι κατρανόντα δ΄ ἀινέσου.
　　　　　　　　—*De Arte Voluntatis*, p. 490,
　　　　　　　　quoting Mimnermus.

[M–49]　*Long life, opprest with many woes,*
　　　　Meets more, the further still it goes.
　　　　　　　　　　　　—*Flores*, p. 174.

[Longa, tument multis tempora foeta malis.]
—*De Arte Voluntatis*, p. 497.

[M–50] *What   greater   good   had   deckt   great* Pompey's
       Crown
       Then death, if in his honours fully blown,
       And mature glories he had dyed? those piles
       Of huge successe, lowd fame & lofty stiles
5   *Built in his active youth, long, lazie life*
       Saw quite demolished by ambitious strife:
       He lived to weare the weake and melting snow
       Of lucklesse Age, where garlands seldom grow.
       But by repining fate torne from the head
10   *Which wore them once, are on another shed.*
                                        —*Flores*, p. 176.

[Quid felicius Pompeio accidisset, quàm antè, aut
in sua felicitate perire, cùm sui desiderium relinque-
ret, si non expectaret fastidium fortunae?]
                            —*De Arte Voluntatis*, pp. 497–98.

[M–51] *Whome God doth take care for and love,*
       He dies young here, to live above.
                                        —*Flores*, p. 178.

[Nam, quem tuetur, atque diliget Deus,
Juvenis supremum mortis intrat limitem.]
                            —*De Arte Voluntatis*, p. 498.

[M–52] *Sickness and death, you are but sluggish things,*
       And cannot reach, a heart that hath got wings.[8]
                                        —*Flores*, p. 191.

[8] There is no source for this in the original.

VII.

From *Primitive Holiness, Set forth in the Life of blessed Paulinus, The most Reverend, and Learned Bishop of Nola*: Collected out of his own Works, and other Primitive Authors by *Henry Vaughan*, Silurist (London, 1654).

This essay appeared in *Flores Solitudinis* (1654), with pagination (pp. 57–159) that is consecutive with the Eucherius essay, "The World Contemned," (pp. 1–55) which Vaughan translated from *D. Eucherii Episcopi Lugdunensis De Contemptu Mundi Epistola paraenetica ad Valerianum cognatum* (Antwerp, 1621), which also contains the *Vita* of Paulinus. The pagination of these two essays is separate from the two Nieremberg essays (see above, Section VI), which also appeared in *Flores*. For his Life of Paulinus, Vaughan seems to have relied most heavily on *Divi Paulini Episcopi Nolani Opera*, containing the *Vita*, edited with notes by Heribertus Rosweydus and Ducaeus and published in Antwerp, 1622. Page references following Vaughan's translations given below are to the *Life* in *Flores*. Page references following passages from the *Vita* are to the *Opera*, 1622. Passages from Ausonius that occur in the *Vita* or that are the sources of some of Vaughan's translations are identified in both the *Opera* (actually reads *OPBRA*) of Ausonius published in Bordeaux, 1604, and, for ease of reference, in the modern Loeb edition, although numbering of the verse epistles in the Loeb differs from that of the Bordeaux edition. Some of the Paulinus epistles to Ausonius also appear in the Loeb *Ausonius*.

[M–53]   *Which silently, and by none seen,*
         Grow great and green.

                                                    —*Life*, p. 63.

[Crescit occulto velut arbor aevo
Fama Marcelli.]
— Horace, *Odes*, I, xii, 45–46.[1]

[M–54]   *Ne raptam sparsamq; domum, &c.*

Let me not weep to see thy ravish'd house
All sad & silent, without Lord or Spouse,
And all those vast dominions once thine owne,
Torn 'twixt a hundred slaves to me unknown.
— *Life*, p. 66.

[Ne raptam sparsamque domum, lacerataq; centum
Per dominos veteris Paulini regna fleamus.]
— *Vita*, p. 654; from Ausonius, Epist. 27, 115-16.

[M–55]   *Undè istam meruit non fœlix Charta repulsam?*
          Hostis ab hoste tamen, &c.

—— how could that paper sent,
That luckless paper, merit thy contempt?
Ev'n foe to fo (though furiously) replies;
And the defied, his Enemy defies:
5   Amidst the swords and wounds ther's a Salute.
Rocks answer man, and though hard, are not mute.
Nature made nothing dumb, nothing unkind:
The trees and leaves speak trembling to the wind.
If thou doest feare discoveries, and the blot
10   Of my love, *Tanaquil*[2] shal know it not.
— *Life*, p. 72.

[Unde istam meruit non felix charta repulsam?
Spernit tam longo cessatio quam tua fastu.
Hostis ab hoste tamen per barbara verba salutem
Accipit: & Salve mediis intervenit armis.

SECTION VII.
[1] Cited by L. I. Guiney, ed. *The Mount of Olives and Primitive Holiness* (London, 1902), p. 88.
[2] Wife of the elder Tarquin, a type of the strong, overbearing woman.

Respondent & saxa homini. percussus ab antris
Sermo redit. reboat nemorum vocalis imago.

. . . .

Nil mutum natura dedit.

. . . .

Atque arguta suis loquitur coma pinea ventis,
Incubuit foliis quotiens levis eurus acutis.

. . . .

Si prodi, Pauline, times: nostraeque vereris
Crimen amicitiae, Tanaquil tua nesciat istud.]
            —Ausonius, *Ep.* xxv, lines 5–10, 17,
                14–15; *Ep.* xxiv, lines 30–31, in
                    Opera, 1604; Loeb Library, II, 112, 114.

[M–56]   *Continuata meæ durare silentia linguæ,*
          Te nunquam tacito memoras; placitamq; latebris
          Desidiam exprobras; neglectæq; insuper addis
          Crimen amicitiæ; formidatamq; Jugalem
          Objicis, & durum iacis in mea viscera versum, &c.

          Obdurate still, and tongue-tyed you accuse
          (Though yours is ever vocall) my dull muse;
          You blame my Lazie, lurking life, and adde
          I scorne your love, a Calumny most sad;
5   Then tell me, that I fear my wife, and dart
          Harsh, cutting words against my dearest heart.
              Leave, learned Father, leave this bitter Course,
          My studies are not turn'd unto the worse;
          I am not mad, nor idle; nor deny
10   Your great deserts, and my debt, nor have I
          A wife like *Tanaquil,* as wildly you
          Object, but a *Lucretia,*[3] chast and true.
                              —*Life,* pp. 72–73.

[3] Wife of Lucius Tarquinus Collatinus, noted in legend and story
for her exemplary life, celebrated by Shakespeare, among others.

[To the above five lines of Latin add:
Parce, precor, lacerare tuum, nec amara paternis
Admiscere velis, ceu melli absinthia, verbis.]
—Paulinus, *Poemata* xi, in *Opera*,
p. 471; *Ausonius*, Loeb Library, II, 118.

[Ne me igitur, venerande parens, his ut malè versum
Increpites studiis, neque me vel conjuge carpas,
Vel mentis vitio: non anxia Bellerophontis
Mens est, nec Tanaquil mihi, sed Lucretia conjunx.]
—Paulinus, *Poemata* xii, in *Opera*,
p. 476; *Ausonius*, Loeb Library, II, 136.

[M–57]   *Hoc pignus commune superno in lumine Celsum*
Credite vivorum lacte favisq; frui.
Aut cum Bethlæis infantibus in Paradiso
(Quos malus Herodes perculit invidiâ,)
Inter odoratum ludit nemus, &c.

This pledge of your joint love, to Heaven now fled,
With honey-combs and milk of life is fed.
Or with the *Bethlem*-Babes (whom *Herods* rage
Kill'd in their tender, happy, holy age)[4]
5   Doth walk the groves of Paradise, and make
Garlands, which those young Martyrs from him
take.
With these his Eyes on the mild lamb are fixt,
A Virgin-Child with Virgin-infants mixt.
Such is my *Celsus* too, who soon as given,
10   Was taken back (on the eighth day) to Heaven,
To whom at *Alcala*[5] I sadly gave
Amongst the Martyrs Tombes a little grave.
Hee now with yours (gone both the blessed way,)
Amongst the trees of life doth smile and play;
15   And this one drop of our mixt blood may be
A light for my *Therasia*,[6] and for me.
—*Life*, pp. 74–75.

[4] Matt. 2.16.
[5] Alcalá de Henares in Spain, where Paulinus lived at one time.
[6] Wife of Paulinus.

[To the above five lines of Latin add:

        . . . atque coronas
Texit honorandis praemia Martyribus.
Talibus immistus Regem comitabitur Agnum,
    Virgineis infans additus agminibus.
Celse, Beatorum castae puer incola terrae,
    Celse dolor patribus, gloria Celse patrum,
Celse, amor & desiderium, lumenque tuorum,
    Celse, brevis nobis gratia, longa tibi.
Sed tamen & nobis poterit tua gratia longùm
    Vivere, si nostri sis memor ad Dominum.
Namque in te parvi meritis ingentibus aevi
    Tempore vita brevis, sed pietate potens.
Talium enim coeli regnum Deus esse profatur,
    Qualis eras aevo, mente fideque puer;
Qualis & ille fuit noster, tuus ille beati
    Nominis, accitus tempore quo datus est,
Exoptata diu soboles, nec praestita nobis,
    Guadere indignis posteritate pia:
Credimus aeternis illum tibi, Celse, viretis
    Laetitiae & vitae ludere participem,
Quem Complutensi mandavimus urbe, propinquis
    Conjunctum tumuli foedere Martyribus;
Ut de vicino Sanctorum sanguine ducat;
    Quo nostras illo purget in igne animas.
Fortè etenim nobis quoque peccatoribus olim,
    Sanguinis haec nostri guttula lumen erit.
Celse, iuva fratrem socia pietate laborans,
    Ut vestra nobis sit locus in requie.
Vivite participes, aeternùm vivite fratres,
    Et laetos dignum par habitate locos.
Innocuisque pares meritis peccata parentum
    Infantes castis vincite suffragiis.
Quot tibi, Celse, annis, totidem illi vita diebus
    Hausta; sed ille minor, quà prior est senior.
Nam minor est, in quo vixit minùs; attamen idem
    Quà prior abscessit, nunc ibi te senior.
Celse, tuo cum fratre tuis (quibus addimur) adsta,
    Nam tua de patrio sanguine vena sumus.

Cum patre Pneumatio, simul & cum matre Fideli
Dic & Paulinum Therasiamque tuos.
Ut precibus commune tuis miserante habeamus
Praesidium Christo nos quoque, Celse, tui.
Sed tamen & nobis superest operam dare, qua te
Possimus simili simplicitate sequi.
Tum nostro socii possimus vivere Celso,
Dulcis & aeternùm pignoris esse pares.]

—Paulinus, *Poemata* xv, De Obitu Celsi
Pueri Panegyricus, lines 623–24,
627–75, in *Opera*, pp. 533–34.

[M–58]   *Vertisti*, Pauline, *tuos dulcissime mores?* &c.

Sweet Paulinus, *is thy nature turn'd?*
Have I so long in vaine thy absence mourn'd?
Wilt thou, my glory, and great Romes *delight,*
The Senates prop, their oracle, and light,
In Bilbilis *and* Calagurris[7] *dwel,*
Changing thy Ivorie-chair for a dark Cell?
Wilt bury there thy Purple, and contemn
All the great honours of thy noble stem?

—*Life*, pp. 82–83.

[Vertisti Pauline tuos dulcissime mores.
Vasconis hoc saltus, & ninguida Pyrenaei
Hospitia, & nostri facit hoc oblivio caeli.
Imprecer ex merito quid non tibi, Hiberica tellus?
Te populent Poeni: te perfidus Hannibal urat:
Te belli sedem repetat Sertorius exul.
Ergo meum, patriaeque decus, columénque senatus,
Bilbilis, aut haerens scopulis Calagorris habebit?
Aut quae dejectis juga per scruposa ruinis
Arida torrentem Sicorim despectat Hilerda?
Hìc trabeam Pauline tuam, Latiámque curulem
Constituis? patriósque istic sepelibis honores?][8]

—Ausonius, *Ep.* xxv, lines 50–61, in
Opera, 1604; Loeb Library, II, 116.

[7] Towns in Spain.
[8] Lines 51–55, 58–59 are omitted in the *Vita*, as they are from Vaughan's translation.

[M–59]   ———*Revocandum me tibi credam,*
Cum steriles fundas non ad divina precatus?
Castalidis supplex averso numine musis, &c.

Shall I beleeve you can make me return,
Who pour your fruitless prayers when you mourn,
Not to your Maker? Who can hear you cry:
But to the fabled Nymphs of *Castalie?*
5   You never shall by such false Gods bring me
Either to *Rome,* or to your company.
As for those former things you once did know,
And which you still call mine, I freely now
Confesse, I am not he, whom you knew then;
10   I have dyed since, and have been borne agen.[9]
Nor dare I think my sage instructor can
Believe it errour, for redeemed man
To serve his great redeemer. I grieve not,
But glory so to erre. Let the wise knot
15   Of worldlings call me fool; I slight their noise,
And heare my God approving of my choice.
Man is but glass, a building of no trust,
A moving shade, and, without *Christ,* meer dust:
His choice in life concerns the Chooser much:
20   For when he dyes, his good or ill (just such
As here it was) goes with him hence, and staies
Still by him, his strict Judge in the last dayes.
These serious thoughts take up my soul, and I
While yet 'tis day-light, fix my busie eye
25   Upon his sacred Rules, lifes precious sum,
Who in the twilight of the world shall come
To judge the lofty looks, and shew mankind
The diff'rence 'twixt the ill and well inclin'd.
This second coming of the worlds great King
30   Makes my heart tremble, and doth timely bring
A saving care into my watchfull soul,
Lest in that day all vitiated and foul
I should be found: That day, times utmost line,
When all shall perish, but what is divine.

[9] Referring to his conversion to Christianity.

35   When the great Trumpets mighty blast shall shake
       The earths foundations, till the hard Rocks quake,
       And melt like piles of snow, when lightnings move
       Like hail, and the white thrones are set above.
       That day, when sent in glory by the Father,
40   The Prince of life his blest Elect shall gather;
       Millions of Angels round about him flying,
       While all the kindreds of the earth are crying,
       And he enthron'd upon the clouds shall give
       His last just sentence, who must die, who live.
45   This is the fear, this is the saving care,
       That makes me leave false honours, and that share
       Which fell to mee of this fraile world; lest by
       A frequent use of present pleasures I
       Should quite forget the future, and let in
50   Foul Atheism, or some presumptuous sin.
       Now by their loss I have secur'd my life,
       And bought my peace ev'n with the cause of strife.
       I live to him, who gave me life & breath,
       And without feare expect the houre of death.
55   If you like this, bid joy to my rich state,
       If not, leave me to *Christ* at any rate.

                                   —*Life,* pp. 83–86.

              [Revocandum me tibi credam,
        Cùm steriles fundas non ad divina precatus,
        Castalidis supplex averso numine Musis?
        Non his numinibus tibi me patriaeque reduces.
        .   .   .   .
        Nam mea si reputes quae pristina, quae tibi nota,
        Spontè fatebor eum modò me non esse sub illo
        Tempore qui fuerim, quo non perversus habebar.

        .   .   .   .
        Agnosci datur, à summo Genitore novari,

        .   .   .   .
        Non reor id sano sic displicuisse parenti,
        Mentis ut erro rem credat, sic vivere Christo,
        Ut Christus sanxit. Juvat hoc, nec poenitet huius
        Erroris; stultus diversa sequentibus esse

Nil moror, aeterno mea dum sententia Regi
Sit sapiens. Breve quidquid homo est, ut corporis
     aegri,
Temporis occidui, & sine Christo pulvis & umbra:
Quod probat aut damnat, tanti est, quanti arbiter
     ipse.
Ipse obit, atque illi suus est comitabilis error,
Cumque suo moriens sententia iudice transit.
     At nisi, dum tempus praesens datur, anxia nobis
Cura sit, ad Domini praeceptum vivere Christi,
Sera erit exutis homini querimonia membris,
Dum levia humanae metuit convitia linguae,
Non timuisse graves divini judicis iras,
Quem Patris aeterni solio dextraque sedentem
Omnibus impositum Regem, & labentibus annis
Venturum, ut cunctas aequato examine gentes
Judicet, & variis referat sua praemia gestis,
Credo equidem, & metuo: studio properante laboro,
Si qua datur, ne morte priùs quam crimine solvar.
     Huius in adventum trepidis mihi credula fibris.
Corda tremunt, gestitq; anima, haec iam cauta
     futuri,
Praemetuens, ne vincta aegris pro corpore curis,
Ponderibusque gravis rerum, si fortè recluso
Increpitet tuba vasta polo, non possit in auras
Regis ad occursum levibus se tollere pennis,
Inter honora volans Sanctorum millia coelo;
Qui per inane leves, neque mundi compede vinctos
Ardua in astra pedes facili molimine tollent,
Et teneris vecti per sidera nubibus ibunt,
Coelestem ut medio venerentur in aëre Regem,
Claraque adorato conjungant agmina Christo.
     Hic metus est, labor iste, dies ne me ultimus atris
Sopitum tenebris sterili deprendat in actu,
Tempora sub vacuis ducentem perdita curis.
Nam quid agam? lentis si dum conniveo votis,
Christus ab aetheria mihi proditus arce coruscet,
Et subitis Domini coelo venientis aperto
Praestrictus radiis, obscura & tristia noctis

Subfugia illato confusus lumine quaeram?
   Quod mihi ne pareret vel diffidentia veri,
Vel praesentis amor vitae, rerumque voluptas,
Curarúmve labor, placuit praevertere casus
Proposito, & curas finire superstite vita.
Comissisque Deo ventura in saecula rebus,
Expectare trucem securo pectore mortem.
Si placet hoc, gratare tui spe divite amici:
Si contrà est, Christo tantùm me linque probari.]
    —Paulinus, *Poemata* xii, the Fourth
      Epistle to Ausonius, lines 8–11, 29–
      31, 35, 181–229, in *Opera*, pp. 473–
      74, 479–80; *Ausonius*, Loeb Library, II,
      130, 132, 144–46.

[M–60]   _____ *Et res magna videtur,*
Mercari propriam de re pereunte salutem?
Perpetuis mutare caduca? &c.

_____ And is the bargain thought too dear,
To give for Heaven our fraile subsistence here?
To change our mortall with immortall homes,
And purchase the bright Stars with darksome stones?
Behold! my God (a rate great as his breath!)
On the sad crosse bought me with bitter death,
Did put on flesh, and suffer'd for our good,
For ours, (vile slaves!) the losse of his dear blood.
             —*Life*, p. 91.

    [& res magna putatur,
Mercari propriam de re pereunte salutem?
Perpetuis mutare caduca, & vendere terram,
Coelum emere? Ecce Deus quanto me cariùs emit
Morte crucis? passus, dejectus imagine servi,
Ut viles emeret pretioso Sanguine servos.]
        —Paulinus, *Poemata* xxiv, Natalis
          Nonus, in *Opera*, p. 607; also in
          Vita, p. 703.

[M–61]   *Marcellina, tuos cum vita resolveret artus;*
                    Sprevisti patriis, &c.

Life, *Marcellina*, leaving thy faire frame,
Thou didst contemne those Tombes of costly fame,
Built by thy Roman Ancestours, and lyest
At *Millaine*, where great *Ambrose* sleeps in Christ.
Hope, the deads life, and faith, which never faints,
Made thee rest here, that thou may'st rise with
     Saints.

—*Life*, p. 97.

[Marcellina, tuos cùm vita resolveret artus,
Sprevisti patriis corpus sociare sepulcris,
Dum pia fraterni speras consortia somni,
Sanctorumq́; cupis charâ requiescere terrâ.]
          —From a note of
               Rosweydus in Paulinus, *Opera*, p. 847.

[M–62]   *Abluitis quicunq; animas & membra lavacris,*
               Cernite propositas ad bona facta vias, &c.

You that to wash your flesh and Soules draw near,
Ponder these two examples set you here.
Great *Martin* shewes the holy life, and white;
Paulinus to repentance doth invite.
5   *Martins* pure, harmlesse life tooke Heaven by force,
Paulinus tooke it by teares and remorse.
Martin leads through victorious palms and flowers,
Paulinus leades you through the pooles and showres.
You that are sinners, on *Paulinus* look,
10   You that are Saints, great *Martin* is your book.
The first example bright and holy is,
The last, though sad and weeping, leads to blisse.[10]
                    —*Life*, pp. 118–19.

[10] A fusion of the two Latin verses that follow.

[Abluitis quicumque animas & membra lavacris,
    Cernite propositas ad bona facta vias.
Adstat perfectae Martinus regula vitae:
    Paulinus veniam quo mereare docet.
Hunc peccatores, illum spectate beati:
    Exemplar sanctis ille sit, iste reis.
            Item de eodem:
Dives opum Christo, pauper sibi, pulchra Severus
    Culmina sacratis fontibus instituit.
Et quia coelestes aulam condebat in actus,
    Qua renovarentur fonte Deóque homines:
Digna Sacramentis gemina sub imagine pinxit,
    Disceret ut vitae dona renatus homo.
Martinum veneranda viri testatur imago:
    Altera Paulinum forma refert humilem.
Ille fidem exemplis & dictis fortibus armat,
    Ut meriti palmas intemerata ferat.
Iste docet fusis redimens sua crimina nummis,
    Vilior ut sit res quàm sua cuique salus.]
                —Paulinus, *Epistle* xii, Ad Severum,
                    in *Opera*, pp. 142–43.

[M–63]   *Hic reparandarum generator fons animarum*
        Vivum viventi lumine flumen agit, &c.

    Here the great well-spring of wash'd Soules, with
            beams
    Of living light quickens the lively streams;
    The Dove descends, and stirs them with her wings,
    So weds these waters to the upper springs,
5   They strait conceive: A new birth doth proceede
    From the bright streams by an immortall seed.
    O the rare love of God! sinners wash'd here,
    Come forth pure Saints, all justified and clear.
    So blest in death and life, man dyes to sins,
10   And lives to God; Sin dyes, and life begins
    To be reviv'd: Old *Adam* falls away,
    And the new lives, born for eternal sway.
                —*Life,* pp. 119–20.

[Hic reparandarum generator fons animarum
  Vivum divino lumine flumen agit.
Sanctus in hunc coelo descendit Spiritus amnem,
Coelestiq́; sacras fonte maritat aquas.
Concipit unda Deum: sanctamq́; liquoribus almis
  Edit ab aeterno semine progeniem.
Mira Dei pietas! Peccator mergitur undis,
  Mox eadem emergit justificatus aqua.
Sic homo & occasu felici functus & ortu,
  Terrenis moritur, perpetuis oritur.
Culpa perit, sed vita redit; vetus interit Adam,
  Et novus aeternis nascitur imperiis.]
                    —Paulinus, *Epistle* xii, Ad Severum,
                      in *Opera*, p. 144.

[M–64] *Coelestes intrate vias per amoena vireta,* &c.

Through pleasant green fields enter you the way
To blisse; and wel through shades and blossoms
  may
The walkes leade here, from whence directly lyes
The good mans path to sacred *Paradise*.
                              —*Life*, p. 141.

[Coelestes intrate vias per amoena vireta
Christicolae; & laetis decet huc ingressus ab hortis,
Unde sacrum meritis datur exitus in paradisum.]
                    —Paulinus, *Epistle* xii, Ad Severum,
                      in *Opera*, p. 151.

[M–65] *Ardua floriferae Crux,* &c.

The painfull Crosse with flowers and Palms is
  crown'd,
Which prove, it springs; though all in blood 'tis
  drown'd:
The Doves above it shew with one consent,
Heaven opens onely to the innocent.
                              —*Life*, p. 142.

[Ardua floriferae Crux cingitur orbe coronae,
  Et Domini fuso tincta cruore rubet.
Quaeq́; super signum resident coeleste columbae
  Simplicibus produnt regna patere Dei.]
                    —Paulinus, *Epistle* xii, Ad Severum,
                      in *Opera*, p. 152.

[M–66]   *Ecce vidès quantus splendor velut æde renatâ*
          Rideat, insculptum camerâ crispante lacunar
          In ligno mentitur ebur; tectoque supernè
          Pendentes lychni spiris retinentur ahenis,
          Et medio in vacuo laxis vaga lumina nutant
          Funibus, undantes flammas levis aura fatigat, &c.

          You see what splendour through the spatious Isle,[11]
          As if the Church were glorified, doth smile.
          The Ivory-wrought beams seem to the sight
          Ingraven, while the carv'd roofe looks curl'd and
            bright.
          On brasse hoopes to the upmost vaults we tie
          The hovering Lamps, which nod and tremble by
          The yeelding Cords; fresh Oyle doth still repair
          The waving flames, vex'd with the fleeting aire.
                    —*Life*, pp. 143–44. Latin
                      identical with Paulinus,
                      Poemata xxiv, Natalis Nonus,
                      in *Opera*, p. 609.

[M–67]   *Sanctorum labor & merces sibi rite cohærent,*
          Ardua Crux, pretiumque crucis sublime, corona, &c.

          The paines of Saints, and Saints rewards are twins,
          The sad Crosse, and the Crowne which the Crosse
            wins.
          Here *Christ* the Prince both of the Cross and Crown
          Amongst fresh Groves and Lillies fully blown,
  5   Stands, a white Lamb bearing the purple Crosse,
          White shewes his purenesse, *Red* his bloods dear
            losse:

[11] I.e., the aisle.

To ease his sorrowes the Chast *Turtle*[12] sings,
And fans him swetting blood with her bright wings;
While from a shining Cloud the *Father* Eyes
10   His Sons sad conflict with his Enemies,
And on his blessed head lets gently down
Eternal glory made into a Crown.
About him stand two flocks of differing notes,
One of white sheepe, and one of speckled goates,
15   The first possesse his right hand, and the last
Stand on his left: The spotted Goates are cast
All into thick, deep shades, while from his right
The white sheepe passe into a whiter light.

                              —*Life*, pp. 144–46.

[Sanctorum labor & merces sibi ritè cohaerent,
Ardua Crux, pretiúmq; Crucis sublime, corona.
Ipse Deus, nobis princeps crucis atque coronae,
Inter floriferi coeleste nemus paradisi,
Sub cruce sanguinea niveo stat Christus in agno,
Agnus ut innocua injusto datus hostia leto.
Alite quem placida sanctus perfundit hiantem
Spiritus, & rutila Genitor de nube coronat.
Et quia praecelsa quasi iudex rupe superstat,
Bis geminae pecudis discors agnis genus hoedi
Circumstant solium: laevos avertitur hoedos
Pastor, & emeritos dextra complectitur agnos.]
                         —Paulinus, *Epistle* xii, Ad Severum,
                            in *Opera*, p. 155.

[M–68]   —*hos per longa morantes*
         Tempora, dum tardi splendens rota vertitur anni
         Sustineo intentis affecto pectore votis:
         Quos cupio totis mihi praelucere diebus,
         Vel quando veniunt ita compensare moras, ut
         Æstivis possent spatiis producere lucem,
         Aut illum pensare diem, qui sistere Jussis
         Syderibus, longo lassavit lumine mundum,
         Humanos duplicans dilatâ nocte labores.

[12] Turtledove.

Ergo velut cælum stellis, & floribus arva
Temporibusque annos dominus, sic ipse diebus
Tempora distinxit festis, ut pigra diurnis
Ingenia obsequiis, saltem discrimine facto,
Post intervallum reduci sollemnia voto
Sancta libenter agant, residesque per annua mentes
Festa parent domino, quia jugiter intemeratos
Justitiæ servare piget: delinquere suetis,
Parcere peccato labor est: decurritur omni
Valle, per ascensum non est evadere cursu.

Inde bonus dominus cunctos pietatis ut alis
Contegat, invalidis niti virtutis ad arcem
Congrua sanctorum dedit intervalla dierum,
Ut saltem officiis mediocribus ultima Christi
Vestimenta legant, & eos sacra fimbria sanet.

Primus enim gradus est cælo pertexere cunctos
Continuâ bonitate dies, & tempore toto
Pascha sacrum Christi Cultu celebrare pudico.
Quod si mista seges tribulis mihi germinat, & cor
Incultum stimulat terreni spina laboris,
Vel festis domino studeam me offere diebus,
Ut vel parte mei tanquam confinia Vitæ,
Corpore ne toto trahar in Consortia mortis.

Englished thus.

Those sacred daies by tedious time delai'd
While the slow years bright line about is laid,
I patiently expect, though much distrest
By busie longing, and a love-sicke brest:
5   I wish, they may outshine all other daies,
Or when they come, so recompence delaies
As to outlast the Summer-hours bright length,
Or that fam'd day, when stopt by Divine strength,
The Sun did tyre the World with his long light,
10   Doubling mens labours, and adjourning night.[13]

[13] At the siege of Jericho (Josh. 10.12–13).

As the bright Skye with stars, the fields with
flowers,
The years with diff'ring seasons, months and houres
God hath distinguished and mark'd; so he
With sacred feasts did ease and beautifie
15 The working dayes: because that mixture may
Make men (loath to be holy ev'ry day,)
After long labours with a freer will
Adore their maker, and keepe mindfull still
Of holynesse, by keeping holy daies:
20 For otherwise they would dislike the wayes
Of piety as too severe. To cast
Old customes quite off, and from sinne to fast
Is a great work. To runne which way we will,
On plaines is easie, not so up a hill.
25   Hence 'tis our good God (who would all men
bring
Under the Covert of his saving wing,)
Appointed at set times his solemne feasts,
That by mean services, men might at least
Take hold of Christ as by the hemme, and steal
30 Help from his lowest skirts their Soules to heal.[14]
   For the first step to Heaven, is to live well
All our life long, and each day to excel
In holynesse; but since that tares are found
In the best Corn, and thistles will Confound
35 And prick my heart with vaine cares, I will strive
To weed them out on feast-daies, and so thrive
By handfuls, 'till I may full life obtaine,
And not be swallow'd of Eternall paine.

> —*Life*, pp. 148–52. The Latin has
> minor variations from that in
> Paulinus, *Poemata* xxiv, Natalis
> Nonus, lines 3–11, 107–16, 119–
> 23, 127–34, in *Opera*, pp. 598 ff.

[14] As did the woman who touched the hem of Christ's garment
(Matt. 9.20–22).

[M–69]   St. *Paulinus* to his Wife
                    Therasia.[15]

    Come my true Consort in my Joyes and Care!
    Let this uncertaine and still wasting share
    Of our fraile life be giv'n to God. You see
    How the swift dayes drive hence incessantlie,
5   *And the fraile, drooping World (though still*
        thought gay,)
    In secret, slow consumption weares away.
    All that we have, passe from us: and once past
    Returne no more; like clouds, they seeme to last,
    And so delude loose, greedy mindes. But where
10   *Are now those trim deceits? to what darke sphere*
    Are all those false fires sunck, which once so shin'd
    They captivated Soules, and rul'd mankind?
    He that with fifty ploughes his lands did sow,
    Will scarse be trusted for two Oxen now,
15   *His rich, lowd Coach known to each crowded street*
    Is sold, and he quite tir'd walkes on his feet.
    Merchants that (like the Sun) their voyage made
    From East to West, and by whole-sale did trade,
    Are now turn'd Sculler-men,[16] *or sadly swett*
20   *In a poore fishers boat with line and nett.*
    Kingdomes and Cities to a period tend,
    Earth nothing hath, but what must have an end:
    Mankind by plagues, distempers, dearth and warre,
    Tortures and prisons dye both neare and farre;
25   *Furie and hate rage in each living brest,*
    Princes with Princes, States with States contest;
    An Universall discord mads each land,
    Peace is quite lost, the last times are at hand;

[15] This poem appears in the *Opera* (1622) of Paulinus under the title, "Ad Conjugem Suam Exhortatio," (p. 643) with a marginal note, "Ex Prospero, creditur enim esse Paulini." Vaughan chose to regard it as clearly belonging to Paulinus. The poem does not appear in the *Vita,* either 1621 or 1622.

[16] Operators of small boats, using sculls.

But were these dayes from the last day secure,
30   *So that the world might for more yeares endure,*
Yet we (like hirelings) should our terme expect,
And on our day of death each day reflect.
For what (Therasia!) doth it us availe
That spatious streames shall flow and never faile,
35   *That aged forrests live to tyre the Winds,*
And flowers each spring returne and keepe their
      kinds?
Those still remaine: but all our Fathers dyed,
And we our selves but for few dayes abide.[17]
   This short time then was not giv'n us in vaine,
40   *To whom tyme dyes, in which we dying gaine,*
But that in time eternall life should be
Our care, and endlesse rest our industrie.
And yet, this Taske which the rebellious deeme
Too harsh, who god's mild lawes for chaines esteem,
45   *Suites with the meeke and harmelesse heart so right*
That 'tis all ease, all comfort and delight.
"To love our God with all our strength and will;
"To covet nothing; to devise no ill
"Against our neighbours; to procure or doe
50   *"Nothing to others, which we would not to*
"Our very selves; not to revenge our wrong;
"To be content with little; not to long
"For wealth and greatnesse; to despise or feare
"No man, and if we be despised, to bear;
55   *"To feede the hungry; to hold fast our Crown;*
"To take from others naught; to give our owne;
These are his precepts: and (alas!) in these
What is so hard, but faith can doe with ease?
He that the holy Prophets doth beleeve,
60   *And on Gods words relies, words that still live*
And cannot dye; that in his heart hath writ
His Saviour's death and tryumph, and doth yet
With constant care, admitting no neglect,
His second, dreadfull comming still expect:

---

[17] With lines 33–38 compare the rendering, shortened by two lines, of M–14, above.

65   *To such a liver earthy things are dead,*
With Heav'n alone, and hopes of heav'n hee's fed;
He is no Vassall unto worldly trash,
Nor that black knowledge, which pretends to wash,
But doth defile: A knowledge, by which Men
70   *With studied care loose Paradise agen.*
Commands and titles, the vaine worlds device,
With gold, the forward seed of sin and vice,
He never minds: his Ayme is farre more high,
And stoopes to nothing lower than the skie;
75   *Nor griefe, nor pleasures breede him any pain,*
He nothing feares to loose, would nothing gaine;
What ever hath not God, he doth detest:
He lives to Christ, is dead to all the rest.
This Holy one sent hither from above
80   *A Virgin brought forth, shadow'd by the Dove;*
His skin with stripes, with wicked hands his face,
And with foule spittle soyl'd and beaten was;
A Crown of thornes his blessed head did wound,
Nayles pierc'd his hands and feet, and he fast bound
85   *Stuck to the painefull Crosse, where hang'd till*
       dead
With a cold speare his hearts dear blood was shed.
All this for man, for bad, ungratefull Man
The true God suffer'd! not that sufferings can
Adde to his glory ought, who can receive
90   *Accesse from nothing, whom none can bereave*
Of his all-fullnesse: but the blest designe
Of his sad death was to save me from mine;
He dying bore my sins, and the third day
His early rising rais'd me from the clay.
95   *To such great mercies what shall I preferre,*
Or who from loving God shall me deterre?
Burne me alive, with curious, skilfull paine
Cut up and search each warme and breathing
       vaine:
When all is done, death brings a quick release,
100   *And the poore mangled body sleepes in peace.*
Hale me to prisons, shut me up in brasse:

My still free Soule from thence to God shall passe;
Banish or bind me, I can be no where
A stranger, nor alone; My God is there.
105   I feare not famine; how can he be sed
To sterve, who feedes upon the living bread?
And yet this courage springs not from my store,
Christ gave it me, who can give much, much more;
I of my selfe can nothing dare or doe,
110   He bids me fight, and makes me conquer too:
If (like great Abr'ham,[18]) I should have command
To leave my fathers house and native Land,
I would with joy to unknown regions run,
Bearing the Banner of his blessed Son.
115   On worldly goods I will have no designe,
But use my owne, as if mine were not mine;
Wealth I'le not wonder at, nor greatnesse seeke,
But chuse (though laugh'd at,) to be poore &
         meeke.
In woe and wealth I'le keepe the same stay'd mind,
120   Griefe shall not breake me, nor joyes make me
         blind:
My dearest Jesus I'le still praise, and he
Shall with Songs of Deliverance compasse me.
     Then come my faithfull Consort! joyne with me
In this good fight, and my true helper be;
125   Cheare me when sad; advise me when I stray;
Let us be each the others guide and stay;
Be your Lords Guardian: give joynt ayde and due;
Helpe him when falne; rise, when he helpeth you;
That so we may not onely one flesh be,
130   But in one Spirit, and one Will agree.
                              —Life, pp. 161–65.

[Age iam precor mearum
Comes irremota rerum,
Trepidam brevemque vitam
Domino Deo dicemus.

[18] Gen. 12.1.

Celeri vides rotatu
Rapidos dies meare,
Fragilisque membra mundi
Minui, perire, labi.
Fugit omne, quod tenemus,
Neque fluxa habent recursum:
Cupidas vagasque menteis
Specie trahunt inani.
Ubi nunc imago rerum?
Ubi sunt opes potentum?
Quibus occupare captas
Animas fuit voluptas?
Qui centum quondam terram vertebat aratris,
    Æstuat, ut geminos possit habere boves.
Vectus magnificis carpentis saepè per urbeis,
    Rus vacuum fessis aeger adit pedibus.
Ille decem celsis sulcans maria alta carinis,
    Nunc lembum exiguum scandit, & ipse regit.
Non idem status est agris, non urbibus ullis,
    Omniaque in finem praecipitata ruunt.
Ferro, peste, fame, vinclis, algore, calore,
    Mille modis miseros mors rapit una homines.
Undiq; bella fremunt, omneis furor excitat, armis
    Incumbunt reges regibus innumeris.
Impia confuso saevit discordia mundo,
    Pax abiit terris, ultima quaeque vides.
Et si concluso superessent tempora saeclo,
    Ut posset longos mundus habere dies:
Nos tamen occasum nostrum observare deceret,
    Et finem vitae quemque videre suae.
Nam mihi quid prodest, quòd longo flumina cursu
    Semper inexhaustis prona feruntur aquis?
Multa quòd annosae vicerunt saecula silvae,
    Quodque suis durant florea rura locis?
Ista manent, nostri sed non mansere parentes:
    Exigui vitam temporis hospes ago.
Non ergo sumus hîc nequidquam in saecula nati,
    Quae pereunt nobis, & quibus occidimus:

Sed vitam aeternam vita ut mereamur in ista,
  Ut subeat requies longa labore brevi.
Et tamen iste labor sit fortè rebellibus asper,
  Ac rigidas leges effera corda putent:
Non tamen haec gravis est mansueto sarcina dorso:
  Nec laedit blandum mitia colla jugum.
Tota mente Deus, tota vi cordis amari
  Praecipitur: vigeat cura secunda hominis.
Quod sibi quis nolit fieri, non inferat ulli,
  Vindictam laesus nesciat exigere.
Contentus modicis vitet sublimis haberi,
  Sperni non timeat, spernere non libeat.
Parcus, vera loquens, & mente & corpore castus,
  Insontem vitam pacis amator agat.
Et proprio pascat loculo quos norit egenteis,
  Non sua non cupiat: quae sua sunt, tribuat.
Quid, rogo, mandatis durum censetur in istis?
  Aut quid erit, quod non possit obire fides?
Qui credunt sacros verum cecinisse Prophetas,
  Et qui non dubitant verba manere Dei,
Qui Christum passum poenas crucis, ultima mortis
  In toto excelsi Patris honore vident,
Quíque ipsum multa cum majestate tremendum
  Expectant, pingui lampade pervigiles:
His sordent terrena, patent caelestia, nec se
  Captivos servos temporis huius agunt.
Non illos fallax cepit sapientia mundi,
  Nec curae steriles inservere polis.
Imperia & fasceis, indocti munera vulgi,
  Quásque orbis scelerum semina fecit opes,
Calcarunt, sancta caelum ambitione petentes,
  Suffragiis Christi, & plausibus Angelicis.
Nec labor hos durus vincit, nec blanda voluptas,
  Quaerere nil cupiunt, perdere nil metuunt.
Omnia non Christi, qui Christi est, odit, in illo
  Se statuens, in se qui gerere optat eum.
Ille Deus, caeli rerum terraéque creator,
  Me propter sacra Virgine natus homo est.

Flagris dorsa, alapis maxillas, ora salivis
    Praebuit, & figi se cruce non renuit.
Non ut tanta Deo quidquam patientia ferret,
    Cuius nec crescunt nec minuuntur opes:
Sed quod erat vitiatum in me, ut superaret in illo,
    Factus sum Christi corporis, ille mei.
Me gessit moriens, me victa morte resurgens,
    Et secum ad Patrem me super astra tulit.
Quidnam igitur tanta pro spe tolerare recusem?
    Aut quid erit quod me separet à Domino?
Ignem adhibe, rimare manu mea viscera tortor,
    Effugient poenas membra soluta tuas.
Carcare si caeco claudar, nectarque catenis,
    Liber in excessu mentis adibo Deum.
Si mucrone paret cervicem abscindere lictor,
    Impavidum inveniet: mors cita, poena brevis.
Non metuo exilium, mundus domus omnibus una
    est,
    Sperno famem, Domini sit mihi sermo cibus.
Nec tamen ista mihi de me fiducia surgit,
    Tu das Christe loqui, tuque pati tribuis.
In nobis nihil audemus, sed fidimus in te,
    Quos pugnare jubes, & superare facis.
Spes igitur mea sola Deus, quem credere vita est,
    Qui patriae civem me dedit alterius.
Sorte patrum occiduum jussus transcurrere mun-
    dum,
    Sub Christi sacris advena miles eo,
Nec dubius me jure brevi terrena tenere,
    Sic utar propriis, ceu mea non mea sint.
Non mirabor opes, nullos sectabor honores,
    Pauperiem Christo divite non metuam.
Qua stetero adversis, hac utar mente secundis:
    Nec mala me vincent, nec bona me capient.
Semper agam grates Christo, dabo semper honores,
    Laus Domini semper vivet in ore meo.
Tu modò, fida comes, mecum isti accingere pugnae,
    Quam Deus infirmo praebuit auxilium.

Sollicita elatum cohibe, solare dolentem:
    Exemplum vitae simus uterque piae.
Custos esto tui custodis, mutua redde,
    Erige labentem, surge levantis ope.
Ut caro non eadem tantùm, sed mens quoq; nobis
    Una sit, atque duos spiritus unus alat.]
                   —Paulinus, *Opera,* pp. 643–47.

VIII.

From *Hermetical Physick: Or, The right way to preserve, and to restore Health.* By That famous and faithfull Chymist, *Henry Nollius.* Englished by Henry Vaughan, Gent. (London, 1655). This is a translation of a part of Heinrich Nolle's *Systema Medicinae Hermeticae Generale* (Frankfort, 1613).

[M–70]   *Quo me cunq; rapit tempestas, deferor hospes,*
             Nullius addictus jurare in verba Magistri.

Where-e'r my fancy calls, there I goe still,
Not sworne a slave to any Masters will.
                         —*Herm. Phys.*, p. 8; from
                         Horace, *Epistle*, I, i, 15, 14,
                         quoted in *Systema*, p. 63.

[M–71]   *There's need (betwixt his clothes, his bed and*
                 bord,)
             Of all that Earth and Sea, and Air afford.
                         —*Herm. Phys.*, p. 13.

[Quod pontus, quod terra, quod educat aer.]
                         —*Systema*, p. 65.

[M–72]   *With restless cares they wast the night and day,*
             To compasse great Estates, and get the sway.
                         —*Herm. Phys.*, p. 14.

[Noctes atq; dies niti praestante labore,
Ad summas emergere opes, rerumq; potiri.]
                         —*Systema*, p. 66.

[M–73]   —*When ever did (I pray,)*
One Lyon take anothers life away?
Or in what Forrest did a wild Bore by
The tusks of his owne fellow wounded, die?
Tygers with Tygers never have debate,
And Beares amongst themselves abstain from hate.

—*Quando Leoni,*
Fortior eripuit vitam leo? quo nemore unquam,
Expiravit Aper, &c.
                              —*Herm. Phys.*, pp. 14–15.

[Quando leoni
Fortior eripuit vitam leo? quo nemore unquam
Expiravit aper majoris dentibus apri?
Indica tigris agit rabida cum tigride pacem
Perpetuam, saevis inter se convenit ursis.]
                    —*Systema*, p. 66; from
                    Juvenal, *Satires*, XV, 160–64.

[M–74]   *Esteem it no point of revenge to kill,*
Unless they may drinke up the blood they spill;
Who do believe that hands, & hearts, and heads,
Are but a kind of meat, &c.

—*Quorum non sufficit iræ,*
Occidisse aliquem, sed pectora, brachia, vultus
Crediderint genus esse cibi, &c.
                              —*Herm. Phys.*, pp. 16–17.

[Invenias populos quorum non sufficit irae,
Occidisse aliquem, sed pectora, brachia, vultum
Crediderint genus esse cibi.]
                         —*Systema*, p. 67; from Juvenal,
                         Satires, XV, 169–71.

IX.

From *The Chymists Key To shut, and to open: Or The true doctrin of* Corruption *and* Generation, . . . By that *Judicious & Industreous* Artist *Henry Nollius.* Published by *Eugenius Philalethes.* (London, 1657).

This is based on Heinrich Nolle's *De Generatione Rerum Naturalium* (Frankfort, 1615), which appeared with the *Systema* of 1613 in one volume, with continuous pagination (pp. 141–52). In a letter to Aubrey of 15 June 1673 (Martin, *Works,* 1957, p. 688), Vaughan lists a translation of *De Generatione* among his printed works.

[M–75]   *The greedy cheat with impure hands may not*
   Attempt this Art,[1] nor is it ever got
   By the unlearn'd and rude: the vitious mind
   To lust and softnesse given, it strikes stark blind,
5 *So the slye, wandring factour, &c.*

      And shortly after.
  But the sage, pious man, who stil adores
  And loves his Maker, and his love implores,
  Who ever joyes to search the secret cause
  And series of his works, their love and lawes,
10 *Let him draw near, and joyning will with strength*
  Study this Art in all her depth and length;
  Then grave experience shall his consort be
  Skill'd in large nature's inmost mysterie.
  The knots and doubts his busie course and cares
15 *Will oft disturb, till time the truth declares,*
  And stable patience (through all trials past)
  Brings the glad end and long hop'd for, at last.
      —*Chymists Key,* Epistle Dedicatory.

SECTION IX.
 [1] Of chemistry.

[Hanc non impuris manibus fraudator avarus
Attingat, decoctor item, quisquisve fabrili
Arte valet, mollisve etiam cum perdita cordi
Otia Mercatorq; vagus, &c.
               Et paulo post:
Ast sapiens superos in primis qui colat, & qui
Noscendis penitus causis modo gaudeat; huc se
Conferat & totis sectetur viribus artem.
Tunc Comes haerebit gravis exploratio rerum
Intima naturae passim vestigia servans.
Tunc mora sollicitos cursus remorata sequetur,
Et visura olim stabilis patientia finem.]

> —*De Generatione*, pp. 134–35;
> from Augurellus, *Chrysopoeiae*,
> II (Antwerp, 1582), pp. 31–32,
> with minor variations in the Latin.

X.

From Thomas Powell's *Humane Industry: Or, A History Of most Manual Arts . . . shewing forth the excellency of Humane Wit . . .* (London, 1661, but the Thomason copy in the BM is dated Decemb. 1660). The Latin and the Vaughan translations are given in the order in which they appear in the Powell volume.

[M–76]   Of a portable Clock or Watch, take this ensuing Epigram of our Countryman *Thomas Campian, de Horologio Portabili.*[1]

> *Temporis interpres parvum congestus in orbem.*
> *Qui memores repetis nocte dieq́; sonos.*
> *Ut semel instructus jucundè sex quater horas*
> *Mobilibus rotulis irrequietus agis.*
> *Nec mecum (quocunq́; feror) comes ire gravaris*
> *Annumerans vitae damna, levansq́; meae:*

> Times-Teller[2] wrought into a little round,
> Which count'st the days and nights with watchful sound;

SECTION X.

[1] Thomas Campion (1567–1619) was known as a poet before he gained fame as a musician and physician. This epigram appears as No. 151, Book I, of his *Epigrammatum Libri II* (London, 1619). See *Campion's Works*, ed. Percival Vivian (Oxford, 1909), p. 257. Vivian's note (p. 372) reads rather curiously: "This epigram must refer not to a striking clock, which was no novelty, but, as the word *portabili* implies, a form of repeating watch." To Powell, at least, it meant simply a portable watch, since he was discussing a watch mounted on a saddle.

[2] A note in the left margin here reads, "Translated H.V."

How (when once fixt) with busie Wheels dost
    thou
The twice twelve useful hours drive on and show.
And where I go, go'st with me without strife,
The Monitor and Ease of fleeting life.

                         —Pp. 11–12.

[M–77]   Of this Microcosme or Representation of the World
        . . . the excellent *Grotius*[3] hath framed this Epi-
        gram following.

> *In organum motus perpetui quod est penes*
>   *Maximum* Britanniacum *Regem* Jacobum.

Perpetui motus indelassata potestas
    Absq́; quiete quies, absq; labore labor,
Contigerant cœlo, tunc cùm Natura caducis,
    Et solidis unum noluit esse locum.
Et geminas partes Lunæ dispescuit orbe,
    In varias damnans inferiora vices.
Sed quod nunc Natura suis è legibus exit
    Dans terris semper quod moveatur opus?
Mira quidem res est sed non nova (maxime Regum)
    Hoc fieri docuit mens tua posse prius.
Mens tua quæ semper tranquilla & torpida nun-
    quam,
    Tramite constanti per sua regna meat.
Ut tua mens ergò motûs cœlestis Imago:
    Machina sic hæc est mentis Imago tuæ.

                Translated thus.

The untired strength of never-ceasing motion,
A restless rest a toyl-less operation,
Heaven then had given it, when wise Nature did[4]
To frail & solid things one place forbid;

---

[3] Hugo Grotius (1583–1645), the great Dutch humanist, whose
associations with England were numerous. This epigram appears in
his *Poemata* (London, 1639), p. 371.

[4] A note in the right margin identifies the translator as "H.V."

5   And parting both, made the Moons Orb their bound,
       Damning to various change this lower ground.
       But now what Nature hath those Laws transgrest,
       Giving to earth a work that ne're will rest?
       Though 'tis most strange, yet (great King) 'tis not
           new;
10   This Work was seen and found before in You.
       In You, whose minde (though still calm) never
           sleeps,
       But through your Realms one constant motion
           keeps:
       As your minde (then) was Heavens type first, so
           this
       But the taught *Anti-type* of your mind is.

                                        —Pp. 20–21.

[M–78]   . . . *Juvenal* in his third *Satyr* thus:[5]

       —— *Quoties nos descendentis Arenæ*
       Vidimus in partes, ruptâq; voragine terræ
       Emersisse feras & iisdem sæpe latebris
       Aurea cum Croceo creverunt Arbuta libro?
       Nec solum nobis Sylvestria cernere monstra
       Contigit, Æquoreos ego cum certantibus Ursis
       Spectavi vitulos & equorum nomine dignum
       Sed deforme pecus——

                   Translated by *H. V.*

       How oft have we beheld wilde Beasts appear
       From broken gulfs of earth, upon some part
       Of sand that did not sink? How often there
       And thence did golden boughs ore saffron'd start?
       Nor only saw we monsters of the wood,
       But I have seen Sea-Calves whom Bears withstood;

    [5] Not by Juvenal at all. The author is Calpurnius Siculus,
Eclogue VII, lines 69–72, 64–67. See *Minor Latin Poets*, Loeb
Library, pp. 282–84.

And such a kinde of Beast as might be named
A horse, but in most foul proportion framed.

—Pp. 40–41.

[M–79]   . . . *Martial* in his Book of Shows, the 105th
Epigr.[6] which I have here annexed, with the Translation of M. *Hen. Vaughan Silurist,* whose excellent Poems are publique.

Picto quod juga delicata collo
Pardus sustinet, improbæq̃; Tygres
Indulgent patientiam flagello,
Mordent aurea quod lupata Cervi;
Quod Frænis Lybici domantur Ursi,
Et quantum Caledon *tulisse fertur*
Paret purpureis Aper Capistris.
Turpes[a] *esseda quod trahunt Bisontes*[b],
Et molles dare jussa quod choreas:
Nigro[c] *Bellua*[d] *nil negat Magistro,*
Quis spectacula non putet Deorum?
Hæc transit tamen ut minora, quisquis
Venatus humiles videt Leonum, &c.[7]

That the fierce Pard doth at a beck
Yield to the Yoke his spotted neck,
And the untoward Tyger bear
The whip with a submissive fear;
5   That Stags do foam with golden bits
And the rough Lybic bear submits
Unto the Ring; that a wild Boar
Like that which *Caledon* of Yore
Brought forth, doth mildly put his head
10   In purple Muzzles to be lead:
That the vast strong-limb'd Buffles draw
The *Brittish* Chariots with taught awe.

[6] Martial, *Epigrams,* I, civ, 1–13.
[7] Marginal notes read: "*a* Brittish Chariots. *b* Wild Oxen in the
Hercynian Forrest called Buffles. *c* The Negro or Black-Moor, that
rides him. *d* The Elephant."

And the Elephant with Courtship falls
To any dance the *Negro* calls:
15   Would not you think such sports as those
Were shews which the Gods did expose;
But these are nothing, when we see
That Hares by Lions hunted be, &c.

—Pp. 175–76.

XI.

From Ezekiel Polsted's Καλῶς Τελωνήσανται *Or, The Excise-Man* (London, 1697), sig. a4ᵛ.

[M–80]   *ALIUD,*
                                To The
                    Officers *of the* Excise[1]

>   *We own'd your* Power, *and the* Pleasures *too*
>   *That, as their* Center, *ever meet in you*;
>   *But your* monopolizing Sense, *affords*
>   *A* Ravishment, *beyond the* Pow'r *of Words:*
>   *To* Silence *thus* confin'd, *I must obey,*
>   *And only* freely say, *that I can* nothing say.
>   *Henry Vaughan* Silurist.

SECTION XI.

[1] Men appointed to collect the very unpopular excise tax, first introduced into England in 1643.

TEXTUAL NOTES

TEXTUAL NOTES

The texts of the four major collections of Vaughan's poetry —*Poems*, 1646; *Olor Iscanus*, 1651; *Silex Scintillans*, Part I, 1650, and Part II, 1655; and *Thalia Rediviva*, 1678—are based on first editions in the Huntington Library, which have been collated with microfilms of first editions in the British Museum (of all four collections), Harvard University Library (of *Poems*, *Olor*, and *Silex*), the University of Illinois Library (of *Poems*, *Olor*, and *Silex*), and Yale University Library (of *Olor*). These have been carefully checked against such modern editions as L. C. Martin's *Works* and E. L. Marilla's *Secular Poems*, and the older editions of H. F. Lyte (1847), A. B. Grosart (1871), and E. K. Chambers (1896).

In the following notes wherever a date alone is given for an edition, it stands for the Huntington Library copy. Other copies are distinguished by an appropriate letter before the date—e.g., H 1646 for the Harvard copy of *Poems*, 1646; BM 1646 for the British Museum copy; and I 1646 for the Illinois copy. Y 1651 identifies the Yale copy of *Olor Iscanus*, 1651. And so on for the other volumes of verse. When all examined copies agree with the reading of the Huntington copy, distinguishing letters before dates of editions are not used. *Er* indicates a reading from the list of errata which appears in some, not all, copies of *Olor*, 1651.

I have attempted to present a reasonable replica of the first editions in matters of indentation of lines, distribution of titles and headings, use of capital letters, and retention of italics even when they seem to be the eccentricity of the printer rather than the intention of the author. One exception was made in the use of capitals. The printer invariably set the second letter of the first line of a poem in capitals, even when it appeared within a word. The capital has been retained when the second letter begins a new word, but when it appears within the first word of the line it has been reduced to lower case. The attention to italics may seem overscrupulous at times, but as Edmund Blunden points out, Vaughan often had a special purpose in italicizing certain words and phrases, and it was deemed best to retain even stray italic letters although no purpose was evident. The few contractions and abbreviations that occur in the first editions have been retained, but i and j, u and v, and long s have been silently altered to conform to modern usage. Certain eccentricities in the type setting (e.g., inverted u's or n's, or other obvious errors) have been corrected in the text, but they have been recorded in the textual variants.

All of Vaughan's poems, but not the commendatory poems of others, have been numbered consecutively within the major divisions of his poetry with a preceding capital letter to identify the division within which the poem occurs: P for the *Poems*, 1646; O for *Olor*; S for *Silex*; T for *Thalia*; and M for Miscellaneous Poems.

Poems, 1646

P–1   34 Lovers / Looers [1646]. 43 greene, / greene; [1646].

P–2   22 spring / spring: [1646]. 23 Of / If [1646]. 24 beds: / heads: [1646].

P–3   3 sings, / sings. [1646]. 5 thou / thon [1646].

P–4   7 tyranny, / tyranny: [1646].

P–5   [Martin lists a number of manuscript alterations in an early hand in the BM copy (C. 56. b. 16) of the *Poems*, 1646, for this poem and for P–6 and P–8. The authority of the alterations is dubious.]

P–7   8 streames; / streames [1646].

P–9   6 Metamorphosis [I 1646 and 1646] / Metempsuchosis [H 1646 and BM 1646].

P–10   [Title] Rhapsodie / Rhapsodis [1646]. 52 to; he! / to he! [1646].

P–11   14 Eyes. [H 1646 and BM 1646] / Eyes: [I 1646 and 1646].

P–14   2 unto / unro [1646]. 62 (for / for [1646]. 172 equall / eqnall [1646]. 218 chime / chine [1646]. 227 seeke. / seeke [1646]. 245 fam'd / fram'd [1646]. 252 stay, / stay [1646]. 262 sight / slight [1646]. 316 sav'd, / sav'd [1646]. 355 lost / low [1646]. 395 nature, / nature. [1646]. 398 had lost, how / had low, host [1646]. 489 Ring / King [1646]. 546 what can / what [1646].

Olor Iscanus

O–1   2 qualisq; / qualisq, [Y 1651]. 25 *nusquàm* / *uusquàm* [1651].

Upon the following *Poems*   11 thy [Er] / my [1651].

O–2   6 *proud* / *prou'd* [1651]. 9 swoln [Er] / sworn [1651]. 83 *safety* / *fafety* [1651].

O–3   14 blast / blaff [1651]. 37 of a face [Er] / of face [1651]. 52 Phantastick / Phautastick [1651]. 66 One [Er] / On [1651].

O–6   24 ta'ne / t'ane [1651].

O–7   18 beat / heat [1651].

O–8   42 purs't / pur'st [1651].

O–10   49 *raves,*) / *raves,* [1651].

O–13   34 *Gown,* / *Gown* [1651].

O–16   11 no [Er] / not [1651]. 17 God [Er] / good [1651].

O–18   36 *smiles* / *similes* [1651].

O–22   80 Eye,) / Eye, [1651].

O–23   29 *Procris* / *Pocris* [1651]. 62 *Ecclyps'd* / *Ecelyps'd* [1651]. 63 they / thy [1651].

O–24   5 fate [Er and BM 1651] / *faith* [H, Y 1651 and 1651].

O–25   28 Mysterie. / Mysterie, [1651].

O–27   42 find, / find. [1651].

O–34   31 worse / worst [1651].

O–43   64 rest, / rest [1651].

O–45   2 *fluet* / *fluat* [1651].

O–47   4 *relatu* [Er] / *relatus* [1651]. 5 *Te per* [Er] / *Per te* [1651].

Silex Scintillans, Part I, 1650 and 1655.

With the exceptions noted below under S–8, the text of *Silex*, Part I, is the same in the 1650 and 1655 editions. The variants marked 1650 will also apply, therefore, to the 1655 edition unless otherwise stated. Variants in Part II will of course refer only to the 1655 edition.

S–1   [This poem only in 1650; missing from I 1650.] 4 *præmonuit.* / *præmonuit* [1650]. 10 Lapis. / Lapis [1650].

S–8   75 [From this point through S–10 (sigs. B2ʳ–B3ᵛ in 1650 and 1655) the original leaves have been cancelled and new ones printed, with substantial variants from the 1650 readings. I have followed BM 1655 (11626. b. 52) in most of its revisions of 1650, noting the variants between 1650 and 1655. The running head of 1650 sig. B2ᵛ reads, *Silex Scintillans*; that of 1655 sig. B2ᵛ reads, *Silix Scintillans*. The running head of 1650 sig. B3ʳ reads, *Or Sacred Poems.*; that of 1655 sig. B3ʳ reads, *Of Sacred Poems.* The running head of 1650 sig. B3ᵛ reads, *Silex Scintillans*; that of 1655 sig. B3ᵛ reads, *Silix Scintillans.*]

75 leave, / leave [1650]. 84 pray'r / Pray'r [1650]. 86 meer Despair / meere Despaire [1650]. 89 or Dust / Or Dust; [1650]. 94 just / Just [1650]. 96 seeks / seekes [1650]. [Bible verse] ver. / ve. [1650]. *seek . . . feel . . . finde* / *seeke . . . feele . . . find* [1650].

S–9   [Title] *Isaacs* / *Isaac's* [catchword 1650 and 1655]. *Marriage* / *Marriage.* [1650]. [Bible verse] *coming* / *comming* [1650]. 3 date, [1650] / date. [1655]. 4 renew't / renew't, [1650]. 6 And [1650] / And [1655]. 8 beams / beames [1650]. 9 multipli'd / multiply'd, [1650]. 11 But / [1650 indented one space]. 11–12. But being for a bride, prayer was such | A decryed course, sure it prevail'd not much. | But being for a bride, sure, prayer was | Very strange stuffe wherewith to court thy lasse, [1650]. 13 Complement?

[1650] / Complement? [1655]. 14 odde dull / odde, corse [1650]. 16 sev'ral / sev'rall [1650]. 17 wilde / wild [1650]. 18 dayes [1650] / daye [1655]. expose! / expose! [1650]. 19 Conscience by lew'd use / sinne, by sinning oft, [1650]. sense / sence [1650]. 21 train / traine [1650]. 22 needlesse / needless [1650]. 23 Retinue; [1650] / Retinue [1655]. 24 calm / calme [1650]. 25 wind / wind, [1650]. 26 And [1650] / And [1655]. minde / mind [1650]. 28 do / doe [1650]. 32 look / looke [1650]. 33 plain / plaine [1650]. truth: [1650] / truth: [1655]. 34 *rowles* / *rowles,* [1650]. mincing / mincing, [1650]. dumb / dumbe [1650]. 35–36 Virgins native blush and fears . . . those roses, which the day-spring wears. / frighted, virgin-blush approach'd . . . the morning, when 'tis newly Coach'd; [1650]. 42 drink / drinke [1650]. 43 And [1650] / And [1655]. knewest her coming / knewst her comming [1650]. 47 undress / undresse [1650]. 48 soul / soule [1650]. refresh [1650] / refrsh [1655]. 49 restor'd did flye [1650] / resto'd did flee [1655]. 51 And [1650] / and [1655]. ayer / ayre [1650]; ayer. [1655]. 52 incense / Incense [1650]. pray'r. [1650] / pray'r [1655]. 53 Well / Well, [1650]. 58 thirstie [1650] / thirst [1655]. 59 thankful / thankfull [1650]. self / selfe [1650]. 61 returns / returnes [1650]. 62 sacrifice. [1650] / sacrifice [1655]. [Marg. note opposite line 62] *well* / *wel* [1650]. 65 zeal / zeale [1650]. tried / tryed [1650]. 66 Infancie. / Infancie, [1650]. 67 to't / to't, [1650]. 68 Diddst / Didst [1650]. yeers / years [1650]. 69 Age [1650] / Age [1655]. 72 *marri'd* / *marry'd* [1650].

S–10   2 *shadows* / *shadowes* [1650]. 3 head [1650] / head. [1655]. 4 Mirrhe / Myrrhe [1650]. 5 Haste / Hast [1650]. dear / deare [1650]. 7 lots again / lotts againe [1650]. 8 seamlesse / seamless [1650]. 9 Jews / Iewes [1650]. 10 stain / staine [1650]. 12 Or / Ot [1650]. yet [1650] / yet [1655]. until / untill [1650]. 18 hast / haste [1650]. 19 As [1650] / As [1655]. 20 [1655, line set even with preceding line; 1650, line set two spaces left of preceding line]. [Latin] *Aprorum!* [1650] / *Aprorum!* [1655].

S–18   11 How / how [1650].

S–20   21 Which / Wich [1650].

S–21   10 see / fee [in BM 1655].

S–40   63 Prince / Prlnce [1650]. 76 stifle / stiflle [1650 and 1655]. 82 at / all [1650]. 125 Conversation / Coversation [1650].

S–44   10 Awake / A wake [1650].

S–46   42 thee / thet [1650].

S–47   23 tast, / tast [1650].

S–52   44 Doth / doth [1650].

S–55   40 As / as [1650].

S–56   3 flee / ssee [1650].

S–60   6 That / that [1650].

S–61   22 Should / should [1650]. 24 Would / would [1650]. 26 flowes; / flowes [punctuation blurred in 1650]. 30 Nothing / nothing [1650]. 36 Which / which [1650].

S–67   11 sour / so our [1650].

S–70   12 'Twas / 'Iwas [1650].

S–71   58 Cel, / Cel [1650].

S–75   32 Upon / upon [1650].

Silex Scintillans, Part II, 1655.

[Preface] 93 *neither* / *ne ther* [1655]. 109 escaped / e caped [1655]. 149 *like* / *l ke* [1655].

S–77   [Bible verses] 6 *of* / *af* [1655].

S–79   30 risen / tisen [1655].

S–81   24 unknown. / unknown [1655].

S–83   11 husbands / husband [1655]. 26 My / my [1655].

S–86   15 pric'd / prick'd [1655].

S–88   6 eye. / eye [1655].

S–89   1 below, / below. [1655]. 21 bowres, / bowres [1655]. 23 their / the r [1655]. 31 Will / Whll [1655].

S–93   23 But / but [1655].

S–94   13 if / is [1655].

S–96   [For textual variants, see this same poem among the Miscellaneous Poems, M–23, as it first appeared in *Flores Solitudinis*, 1654.]

S–98   8 denyed. / denyed [1655].

S–103   19 one / once [1655].

S–104   6 an / and [1655].

S–105   10 Storms / Forms [1655]. 26 weather. / weather [1655].

S–107   10 [Indentation follows 1655 edition.] 22 shine, / shine; [1655]. 36 blood. / blood [1655].

S–108   5–8 [These lines, the last on p. 43 of 1655, are repeated at the top of p. 44 thus:] And led by my own foolish fire, | Wandred through darkness dens and mire. | How am I now in love withal | That I term'd then mere bonds and thrall,.

S–112   39 though / thought [1655]. 48 prize; / prize [1655].

S–115   23 *herbs* / *herhs* [1655]. 27 retreat / retaeat [1655]. 42 [Indentation follows 1655 edition.]

S–116   33 I, / I [1655]. 40 *things,* / *things.* [1655].

S–117   6 Heav'ns / Heav ns [1655]. 7 carelesse / carelese [1655]. 20 Have / have [1655]. 30 pains / prayers [1655]. 35 When / when [1655].

S–120   31 night, [BM 1655] / night. [I 1655, H 1655, 1655].

S–121   6 Quill; [BM 1655, I 1655(?)] / Quill, [H 1655, 1655]. 58 *Cathartics* / *Catharties* [1655].

S–126   19 I, / I [1655]. 65 Opening / opening [1655].

S–128   16 before, / before. [1655].

S–132   16 live / liee [1655]. 18 *skin* / *skln* [1655].

S–134   58 fast, / fast. [1655].

Thalia Rediviva

Dedication 32 Indulgence / Iudulgence [1678].

To the Reader 7 *Howsoever the* / *Howsoevert he* [1678].

To the ingenious Author   12 vaine / raine [1678].

To my worthy Friend   7 is't / i'st [1678]. 11 manual / manu'al [1678]. 51 another / anothet [1678].

T–1   [Title] several / seve-veral [1678].

T–2   15 portend, / portend. [1678]. 43 wander / wonder [1678].

T–3   20 Heav'n / Heav n [1678].

T–5   53 did'st / di'dst [1678].

T–6   8 wiser / wiser, [1678].

T–10   37 Shall / shall [1678]. 43 not) / not; [1678].

T–11   3 slain / stain [1678]. 32 Stand / stand [1678]. 49 dwells / dwells. [1678].

T–12   14 descri'd. / describ'd. [1678].

T–14   4 *Sick,* / *Sick* [1678].

T–15   11 With / with [1678].

T–17   6 me / in [1678].

T–19   8 *perit* / *peruit* [1678].

T–22   30 exprest, / exprest. [1678].

T–23   2 (Which . . . *Cause;*) / (which . . . *Cause;* [1678].

T–27   10 *gowns* / *growns* [1678].

T–29   26 far, / far. [1678]. 44 *Caucasus* / *Causacus* [1678].

T–30   18 *Food,* / *Food.* [1678].

T–38   15 reviv'd / reviv d [1678].

T–40   26 Rays / rags [Manuscript alteration in 1678].

T–41   16 check / cheek [1678].

T–45   4 *musca* / *musea* [1678].

T–46   7 repriev'd / repriev d [1678]. 12 upbraid, / upbraid. [1678]. 73 poverty, / poverty. [1678]. 83 *word,* / *word.* [1678].

T–47   2 Orders, / Orders. [1678]. 86 *Plant,* /*Plant.* [1678].

T–48   8 wilt / will [1678].

T–49   29 past) / past; [1678]. 39 *Da.* / *Da,* [1678]. 106 run, / run. [1678].

Miscellaneous Poems

M–3   1 *canst,* / *canst* [1651].

M–18   2 [Latin] *Aude* / *Audet* [1652]. 1 heav'ns / heavn's [1652].

M–22   Lines 5–6 followed lines 7–8 in [1652] (Martin).

M–59   2 [Latin] *precatus* / *percatus* [1654]. 45 fear, / fear [1654].

M–63   8 justified / justfied [1654].

M–68   16 [Latin] *jugiter / Jupiter* [1654].

M–69   [Title] St. / Saint [catchword 1654]. 5 gay / gry [1654]. 35 live / hie [1654]. 91 *all-fullnesse: / all-fullnesse::* [1654].

SELECTED BIBLIOGRAPHY

SELECTED BIBLIOGRAPHY

EDITIONS

Marilla, E. L. *Secular Poems*. Uppsala and Cambridge, Massachusetts, 1958.

Martin, L. C. *The Works of Henry Vaughan*. Oxford, 1st ed., 1914; 2d ed., 1957.

Martz, Louis L. *The Meditative Poem: An Anthology of Seventeenth-Century Verse*. Anchor Seventeenth-Century Series. New York, 1963. —Selections from *Silex Scintillans*.

REFERENCES

Bennett, Joan. Four Metaphysical Poets. Cambridge, 2d ed. 1953.

Bethell, Samuel L. *The Cultural Revolution of the Seventeenth Century*. London, 1951. —Chapter on the poetry of Vaughan.

Blunden, Edmund. *On the Poems of Henry Vaughan*. London, 1927. —With translations of the principal Latin poems.

Durr, R. A. *On the Mystical Poetry of Henry Vaughan*. Cambridge, Massachusetts, 1962.

Eliot, T. S. "The Silurist," in *The Dial*, LXXXIII (September 1927), 259–63.

Esch, Arno. *Englische religiöse Lyrik des 17. Jahrhunderts: Studien zu Donne, Herbert, Crashaw, Vaughan*. Tübingen, 1955.

Garner, Ross. *Henry Vaughan: Experience and the Tradition*. Chicago, 1959.

Holmes, Elizabeth. *Henry Vaughan and the Hermetic Philosophy*. Oxford, 1932.

Hutchinson, F. E. *Henry Vaughan: A Life and Interpretation*. Oxford, 1947.

Itrat-Husain. *The Mystical Element in the Metaphysical Poets of the Seventeenth Century*. Edinburgh, 1948.

Kermode, Frank. "The Private Imagery of Henry Vaughan." *RES*, n.s. I (1950), 206–25.

Leishman, J. B. *The Metaphysical Poets: Donne, Herbert, Vaughan, Traherne*. Oxford, 1934.

Mahood, M. M. "Vaughan: The Symphony of Nature," in *Poetry and Humanism*. London, 1950.

Marilla, E. L. *A Comprehensive Bibliography of Henry Vaughan*. University of Alabama, 1948. —Lists Vaughan items through 1945.

——— "The Significance of Henry Vaughan's Literary Reputation." *MLQ*, V (1944), 155–62.

——— "The Religious Conversion of Henry Vaughan." *RES*, XXI (1945), 15–22.

——— " 'The Publisher to the Reader' of *Olor Iscanus*." *RES*, XXIV (1948), 36–41.

——— "The Secular and Religious Poetry of Henry Vaughan." *MLQ*, IX (1948), 394–411.

Martin, L. C. "Henry Vaughan and 'Hermes Trismegistus,' " *RES*, XVIII (1942), 301–7.

Martz, Louis L. *The Poetry of Meditation*. New Haven, 1954.

——— "Henry Vaughan: The Man Within." *PMLA*, LXXVIII, 1 (March 1963), 40–49.

Oliver, H. J. "The Mysticism of Henry Vaughan: A Reply." *JEGP*, LIII (1954), 352–60. —Reply to Kermode.

Parker, W. R. "Henry Vaughan and His Publishers." *The Library*, 4th ser., XX (1940), 401–11.

Pettet, E. C. *Of Paradise and Light: A Study of Vaughan's Silex Scintillans*. Cambridge, 1960.

Simmonds, James D. "Henry Vaughan and the Great Chain of Being," in *Studies in English Renaissance Literature*, ed. Waldo F. McNeir (Baton Rouge, 1961).

Vaughan, Thomas. *The Works of Thomas Vaughan,* ed. A. E. Waite. London, 1919.

Walley, Harold R. "The Strange Case of *Olor Iscanus.*" *RES,* XVIII (1942), 27–37.

Walters, Richard H. "Henry Vaughan and the Alchemists." *RES,* XXIII (1947), 107–22.

White, Helen C. *The Metaphysical Poets.* New York, 1936.

INDEX OF FIRST LINES AND TITLES

The entries in the following list are confined to Vaughan's complete original poems, Latin and English, and to his translations whether complete or not. Commendatory poems which appeared in his volumes of verse have not been included. First lines are in *italic type*, titles in SMALL CAPITALS. Initial "The" and "A" of titles have been disregarded in alphabetizing.

BRITISH LITERATURE IN
NORTON PAPERBOUND EDITIONS